OVERLOOKING BACCARAT

GENERAL PERSHING CONFERRING D. S. C.'S

FATHER DUFFY'S STORY

COLONEL DONOVAN IN FIGHTING TRIM AFTER ST. MIHIEL

FATHER DUFFY'S STORY

A TALE OF HUMOR AND HEROISM, OF
LIFE AND DEATH WITH THE FIGHTING
SIXTY-NINTH

BY

FRANCIS P. DUFFY
CHAPLAIN, 165TH INFANTRY

WITH AN HISTORICAL APPENDIX BY
JOYCE KILMER

NEW YORK
GEORGE H. DORAN COMPANY

Printed in the United States of America

TO THE MEMORY OF OUR DEAD

THIS BOOK

IS REVERENTLY DEDICATED

PREFACE

On one occasion, after having had to swallow an exceptionally large dose of complimentary eloquence, I stated that I was going to borrow a title for my book from my favorite philosopher, Mr. Dooley, and call it "Alone in Europe."

The title that has been given it sounds almost as egoistic as that; but there will be found in these pages other names than my own. Indeed, objection may be made from a literary point of view that the book bristles with names. I could not write my story otherwise. I knew these men, and what they did, and my only regret is that I have undoubtedly overlooked some, especially amongst replacements, whose names and deeds should be mentioned. Battles are not fought by commanding officers alone, not even by chaplains unaided; and the men who do the fighting usually get little personal credit for their valor.

My chronicle claims no merit save that of being true. The only critics I had in mind while writing it were those who fought in France. If they say that the pictures are true, I am content. The diary style has been deliberately chosen because it permits the introduction of incidents, and also lends itself to the telling of a plain unvarnished tale.

Every Regiment in a combat division has a similar story, if any one of its members has the knowledge and patience to tell it. "The Irish 69th" had naturally its own special flavor of race with the buoyant spirits, the military *élan*, and the religious ardor that mark the race. No picture of the regiment would be complete that did not give a generous place to this phase of its life.

Happily, the Irish spirit has always managed to combine generous tolerance with its fervors. As a result, there are no more enthusiastic adherents of the Irish 69th than those of its members who did not share in the blood or the creed of the majority.

As for myself, I liked them all. I am a very Irish, very Catholic, very American person if anybody challenges my convictions. But normally, and let alone, I am just plain human. My appreciation of patriotism, or courage, or any other attractive human trait, is not limited in any degree by racial or religious or sectional prejudice. That was the spirit of our Army; may it always be the spirit of our Republic.

Joyce Kilmer was to have written this book. I took over the task after his death in battle. The manuscript he left had been hurriedly written, at intervals in a busy soldier existence, which interested him far more than literary work. I have taken the liberty of adding his work, incomplete though it is, to my own; because I feel that Kilmer would be glad at having his name associated with the story of the Regiment which had his absolute devotion; and because I cannot resist the temptation of associating with my own the name of one of the noblest specimens of humanity that has existed in our times.

I wish to thank Major Meaney, Major Bootz, Captain Allen, Lieutenants Harold Allen and Thomas C. P. Martin, Sergeant Major O'Connell and the Company Clerks for data for this book; Sergeant William Halligan, Privates John F. McLoughlin and Arthur Shea, Mr. Paul Shea, and Father John B. Kelly for assistance in preparing the manuscript for publication; and Sergeants T. C. Ranscht and R. L. Clarke for the maps that appear in this volume.

CONTENTS

ILLUSTRATIONS

FATHER DUFFY'S STORY

FATHER DUFFY'S STORY

CHAPTER I

PREPARATIONS AT HOME

RECTORY, CHURCH OF OUR SAVIOUR, BRONX

June, 1917

WAR with Germany was declared on April 6th, 1917. Immediately the National Guard Regiments, knowing that they would be the first to be called from civilian occupations, began campaigning for recruits. Ours was conducted with little noise or speech making. An Irish Regiment has its troubles in time of peace, but when the call to arms was sounding we knew that if they let us we could easily offer them an Irish Brigade for the service. We were more occupied with quality than with numbers. The one bit of publicity we indulged in was to send round our machine-gun trucks through the city streets with the placard, "Don't join the 69th unless you want to be among the first to go to France." That was the only kind of men we wanted— not impressionable youth who would volunteer under the stimulus of a brass band or a flood of patriotic oratory. The old-timers were told to bring in friends who had the right stuff in them. The Catholic Clergy were asked to send in good men from the Parish athletic clubs.

The response was immediate. Every night the big reception rooms were packed with men taking the physical tests. The medical staff had to be increased at once to meet the situation and officers and enlisted men were impressed into the service for taking the minor tests. These tests were rigid. Nobody was taken who fell below the standard in age, height, weight, sight or chest measurement—or who had liquor aboard or who had not a clean skin. Many of those who were turned down for underweight or imperfect feet were readily accepted in other Regiments which had more difficulty in getting men. And when we received contingents from those regiments later on I often had to listen to the humorous reproach, "Well, I got in in spite of the lot of you."

Amongst the sturdiest and brightest of our recruits were two young men who had recently been Jesuit Novices. I amused one Jesuit friend and, I am afraid, shocked another by saying that they were exercising a traditional religious privilege of seeking a higher state of perfection by quitting the Jesuits and joining the 69th.

We came back from Texas less than a thousand strong. Of these we could count on 500 for a new war, which left us 1,500 to go to meet the number then fixed for an Infantry Regiment—2,002. We were not long in reaching that number. Lieutenant Colonel Reed telegraphed the War Department for permission, pending the proposed increase of a Regiment to 3,600, to establish a waiting list, but the application was refused. In the latter days we were turning away 300 a week, sending them to other Regiments.

Our 2,000 men were a picked lot. They came mainly from Irish County Societies and from Catholic Athletic Clubs. A number of these latter Irish bore distinctly German, French, Italian or Polish names. They were Irish by adoption, Irish by association or Irish by conviction. The 69th never attempted to set up any religious test. It was an institution offered to the Nation by a people grateful for liberty, and it always welcomed and made part of it any American citizen who desired to serve in it. But, naturally, men of Irish birth or blood were attracted by the traditions of the 69th, and many Catholics wanted to be with a regiment where they could be sure of being able to attend to their religious duties. About 5 percent of the 2,000 were Irish neither by race nor racial creed.

69TH REGIMENT ARMORY

July 20th, 1917

Frank Ward O'Malley of the New York *Sun* has written up in his inimitable style a little scene from life in an Irish regiment. The newcomers are not yet accustomed to the special church regulations relieving soldiers of the obligation of Friday abstinence. Last Friday the men came back from a hard morning's drill to find on the table a generous meal of ham and cabbage. The old-timers from the Border pitched into this, to the scandal of many of the newer men who refused to eat it, thus leaving all the more for the graceless veterans. After dinner a number of them came to me to ask if it were true that it was all right. I said it was, because there was a dispensation for soldiers. "Dispensation," said a Jewish boy, "what good is a dispensation for Friday to me. I can't eat ham any day of the week. Say, Father, that waiter guy, with one turn of his wrist, bust two religions."

POLO GROUNDS

July 25th, 1917

A great day for Ireland. Everybody aboard and up the river to 152nd Street and then to the Polo Grounds. Baseball Game as benefit for the 69th, between Giants and Cincinnatis, thanks to the generosity of our good friends, Harry Hempstead, John Whalen, Herbert Vreeland, and John J. McGraw. A fine game—plenty of people, plenty of fun, and best of all, plenty of money for the exchequer, which, after an ancient venerable custom, is going to have an ecclesiastical chancellor. Mr. Daniel M. Brady, the Godfather of the regiment, had procured the signature of President Wilson on a baseball which he auctioned off during the game. I asked him if he had arranged for a purchaser. "I have selected one," he said. "Is he aware that he is going to buy it?" I asked. "He will be informed at the proper time," said Mr. Brady with a smile. "How much is he going to pay for it?" "Well, I don't consider $500.00 too much to pay for the privilege." So after a certain number of bids, real or fictitious, the ball was knocked down at $500.00 to Mr. James Butler, who accepted the verdict smilingly and was allowed the privilege of handing the ball back to me. I am to auction it in Paris for the French Orphans' Fund. So Mr. Brady says, though I wish I had his confidence that we shall ever get to Paris.

ARMORY

August 5th, 1917

Father John Kelly had me meet Joyce Kilmer this evening. Nothing of the long-haired variety about him—a sturdy fellow, manly, humorous, interesting. He was a little shame-faced at first, for he had told Father Kelly that he was going to join up with the 69th and he is now in the 7th. "I went to the Armory twice," he said, "but failed to find the recruiting officer." I told him that if we could not have him in the 69th the next best place was the 7th, but he still wants to return to his first love, so I shall be glad to arrange it. If he left the whole matter up to my decision he would stay home and look after his large family and let men with fewer responsibilities undertake this task, at least until such time as the country would have need of every man. But he is bound to do his share and do it at once, so there is no use taking off the fine edge of his enthusiasm. He is going about this thing in exactly the same spirit that led him to enter the Church. He sees what he considers a plain duty, and he is going ahead to perform it, calm and clear eyed and without the slightest regard to what the consequences may be.

I shall be glad to have him with us personally for the pleasure of his companionship, and also for the sake of the regiment to have a poet and historian who will confer upon us the gift of immortality. I compared him with the old lad that one lot of Greeks sent to another to stir them to victory by his songs; and he wagged a pair of vigorous protesting legs at me to show he was no cripple. So I tried him with a quotation from a poet that no poet could ever resist; and with some reservations about the words "Grey Bard" I managed to drive my compliment home:

> For not to have been dipt in Lethe's lake
> Could make the son of Thetis not to die;
> But that grey bard did him immortal make
> With verses dipt in dews of Castaly.

ARMORY

August 18th, 1917

We are still full of excitement at our selection from among the National Guard Regiments of New York to represent our State in the selected 42nd or Rainbow Division which is to go abroad amongst the very first for active service. It is an undeniable compliment to the condition of the Regiment and we are pleased at that as well as at the prospects of carrying our battle-ringed standards to fly their colors on the fields of France. Our Regimental organization has been accepted intact—it is no composite Regiment that has been selected; it is the 69th New York. Our ranks however are to be swelled to the new total of 3,600 men by the transfer of enlisted men from the five other city Regiments of Infantry. We would have been glad to have done our own recruiting as we could easily have managed; but these are the orders. We shall give a royal Irish welcome to our new companions in arms. They are volunteers like ourselves and fellow townsmen, and after a little feeling out of one another's qualities we shall be a united Regiment.

Already we have received the contingent from our old friends in the 7th—handed over to us with a large gesture of comradeship which that old Regiment knows so well how to make. The departing body of 320 men were escorted by the remaining officers and men, and passed through their guard of honor to our Armory floor. Our 2,000 lined the walls and many perched themselves on the iron beams overhead. They cheered and cheered and cheered till the blare of the bands was unheard in the joyous din—till hearts beat so full and fast that they seemed *too big for the ribs that confined them, till tears of emotion* came, and something mystical was born in every breast— the soul of a Regiment. Heaven be good to the enemy when these cheering lads go forward together into battle.

CAMP MILLS

September 1st, 1917

We are tenting tonight on the Hempstead Plains, where Colonel Duffy and the Old 69th encamped in 1898, when getting ready for service in the Spanish War. It is a huge regiment now—bigger, I think, than the whole Irish Brigade ever was in the Civil War.

We have received our new men transferred from the 12th, 14th, 23rd and 71st N. G. N. Y. Our band played them into Camp with the Regimental Air of "Garry Owen" mingled with the good-fellow strains of "Hail! Hail! the Gang's All Here."

All in all, the newcomers are a fine lot. A couple of our sister organizations have flipped the cards from the bottom of the pack in some instances and worked off on us some of their least desirables. On the other hand, all the Regiments have made up for that by allowing men anxious to come to us to change places with those who prefer to stick where they are. This gives us a large number of the men we want—those that feel their feet on their native heath in the 69th, and those that like its recruiting slogan, "If you don't want to be amongst the first to go to France, don't join the 69th." For the rest, the Company Commanders and Surgeons know "Thirty-five distinct damnations," or almost that many, by which an undesirable can be returned to civilian life to take his chances in the draft. Our recruiting office has been reëstablished at the Armory. We can get all the good men we want.

As he had put the matter in my hands Kilmer did not come over with the men from the 7th, but I had the matter of his transfer arranged after a short delay.

CAMP MILLS

September 26th, 1917

I do not know whether to take it as a mark of general interest in the Old Regiment or as the result of the spontaneous big-heartedness of a kindly and enthusiastic Irish artist—but John McCormack sang for us tonight. Sang in the open air with no stinting of voice or program. Our lads could have listened to him till morning; I never saw such an eager mob. They kept calling for their favorite McCormack songs and he, like the fine big Bouchal that he is, laughed at their sallies and gave them their hearts' desire, until I closed the unique performance by reminding them (and him) that we had a financial interest in his voice because he was to sing for the benefit of our Trustees Fund at no distant date. While I write, the camp is buzzing around me with talk of the great tenor. A voice from the darkness sums it up. "I always knew he was a great singer. We got a lot of his records at home. But the records never learned me that he's such a hell of a fine fellow."

CAMP MILLS

Sunday

I mess with the Headquarters Company, and James Collintine, who has the job of looking after us, always welcomes Sunday morning because it gives a chance for a friendly chat between the two of us. James had been a deepwater sailor for a good many years since he first left his home in the Old Country, but has taken up with the Infantry because it gives more prospects for fighting service in this war. This morning he said, "Father Duffy, did ye iver hear of Father Hearrn of my parish in the County Longford?" "No, Jim, I never did." "Well, he was the grandest man in all Ireland. There was eight hundhred min in Maynooth College where they study to be priests and he could lick ivery dam wan of thim. He was a fine big man, six foot two in his stockin' feet. He used to come down the sthreet with a big stick in his hand, and if anybody gave anny throuble he'd knock you down just as quick as look at you. The whole parish loved him. Wanst there was a fight in the village green between the peelers and the people, and Father Hearrn was sint for to keep the peace and he came down the road bowling over the peelers as if they was nine pins. There niver was a nicer man within the four seas of Ireland."

A soldier of Company K came to my tent one afternoon last week and stood at the entrance fumbling his hat in his hand like an Irish tenant of the old days that had not the rent to pay the landlord. "What's the matter, Tom?" "I took a dhrop too much, and Captain Hurley got very mad about it and brought me up before Major Moynahan. I wouldn't mind if they'd fine me and be through with it, for I know I deserve it. But the Major and the Captain say that they're not going to stand anything like this, and that they won't lave me go to the war. And sure, Father Duffy, if I couldn't go to the war it'd kill me." The smile that came to my lips at this very Irish way of putting it was suppressed when I thought of the number of men born in the country who were worried sick lest the Draft should catch them and send them to the war. I assured Tom that I would use my powers of persuasion with the Captain and the Major to give him his heart's desire, if he would take the pledge. But we shall keep him worried by a suspended sentence until we get him safely away from the temptations of New York.

I have found an old friend in Camp in the person of Mike Donaldson of Company I. Mike was an altar boy of mine in Haverstraw not long after I was ordained. We both left there, I to teach metaphysics and Mike for a career in the prize-ring, in which he became much more widely and favorably known to his fellow citizens than I can ever hope to be. One of his titles to fame is that he was sparring partner to Stanley Ketchell. He has brought me a set of battered boxing gloves which he presented to me with a very moving speech as relics of that departed hero. I do not know exactly what he expects me to do with the relics but I rather feel after his speech of presentation that it would be considered appropriate if I suspend them reverently from the rafter of my chapel like the *ex voto* offerings of ships that one sees in seaport shrines.

I have become a marrying Parson. Love and fighting seem to go together—they are the two staples of romance. I have had a large number of marriages to perform. In most cases the parties enter my church tent from the rear and are quietly married before the simple altar. We have had a few weddings however on the grand scale. Michael Mulhern of the Band had arranged for a quiet wedding with a very sweet little girl named Peggy O'Brien. This afternoon at four o'clock when I was ready to slip over with the young couple and their witnesses to my canvas church I saw the band forming. "What is this formation for, Michael. You don't have to be in it, do you?" "Ah, Father," said Michael, with a blush, "the boys heard somehow what was going to happen and they're going to serenade us." We had to parade over to church behind the band playing a wedding march, with 10,000 soldiers and visitors following curiously in the rear. So Michael and his bride were united in matrimony before a vast throng that cheered them, and showered them with rice that soldiers brought over from the kitchens, many of the lads battling with the groom for the privilege of kissing the bride.

October 15th, 1917

We will soon be off to the war and I have been looking over the Regiment, studying its possibilities.

About the enlisted men I have not a single doubt. If this collection of hand-picked volunteers cannot give a good account of themselves in battle, America should keep out of war. The men will fight no matter who leads them. But fighting and winning are not always the same thing, and the winning depends much on the officers—their military knowledge, ability as instructors and powers of leadership. The Non-coms are a fine lot. The First Sergeants as I run over the list are a remarkable body of good old-time soldiers. Starting with Company A, we have John O'Leary, John O'Neill, William Hatton, Tom Sullivan, William Bailey, Joseph Blake, John Burke, Jerome O'Neill, Patrick McMeniman, Tim Sullivan, Eugene Gannon, John Kenny; with Denis O'Shea, A. McBride, J. Comiskey, and W. W. Lokker, for H. Q. M. G. Supply and Medical. All of these men have been tried out in the eight months of Border service and we are sure of them. Under Colonel Haskell the hard driven Company Commanders had to break their Sergeants in, or break them—life was too strenuous for favoritism. In fact, except for recruits, it is surprisingly Haskell's regiment that is going to the front; Haskell's, that is, with the reservation that his work was done on the basis of Colonel Conley's selection and promotion in the more difficult period of peace service. When we were selected for immediate over-seas service the authorities were free to make what changes they would, and they left the regiment intact except for the transfer of one Major and one Captain. The M. G. Company was vacant by resignation. All other officers remained at their posts, though we have been assigned a large number of newly created Lieutenants to correspond with the new tables of organization for a regiment of three thousand six hundred.

We like our new Colonel, though he was a total stranger to us before the day he came to command us. He is a West

Francis P. Duffy
Chaplain 165th Inf.
69th N.Y.

Pointer, and went into railroading after some years in the army as a Lieutenant; but he has loyally reverted to the army whenever there was a real call to arms. In 1898 if I had achieved my desire to go out as Chaplain of the 1st D. C. I would have had him as one of my Majors. He came into this conflict as organizer and commander of trains, a work for which his experience fitted him. He is a man of middle height with a strong body and an attractive face, healthily ruddy, strongly featured, with a halo of thick grey hair above. He is a man of ideas, of ideas formed by contact with life and business. He is a tireless worker, and demands the same unflinching service from every man under him. He has confidence in his men, especially the tried soldiers, and he has a strong liking for the Regiment and its traditions. The Regiment will do good work under the leadership of Colonel Charles Hine.

Lieutenant Colonel Reed I like better and better every day I am with him. I did not take to him at first and I think he was largely to blame. He kept himself too much aloof. The fault, however, was partly ours. He came to us at a time when we felt suspicious that it was the intention to destroy our character as an Irish organization, and we owed too much to the men who had created the Regiment and made its reputation with their blood to submit tamely to such a scheme as that. Colonel Reed was not used to being where he was not wanted, and his attitude was the result of this decent feeling. When the task of forming a war-strength regiment fell to him he took hold and worked with single-minded vigor, and he then found that everybody was anxious to work with him loyally. He discovered, what I could have told him, that one thing the Sixty-ninth admires is a good soldier. And Reed is a good soldier, keen, active, and aggressive. He learned at once to love the regiment and is as enthusiastic as myself in his regard for it. We spend a great deal of our free time together, for we have much in common.

The senior Major, Timothy J. Moynahan, is the ideal of

the Irish soldier, as he comes down to us in history and in fiction. He inherits from Patrick Sarsfield's cavaliers, from the regiments of Dillon and Burke at Fontenoy, from the Connaught Rangers at Fuentes d'Onoro. A soldier born —trim, erect, handsome, active in his movements, commanding and crisp in his orders. And a soldier bred—he lives for the military game, devotes his life to his work as military instructor in colleges, and to the old 69th. He is ready with a toast or a speech or a neatly phrased compliment, and equally ready to take up the gage of battle, if anyone should throw it down. A vivid interesting character in our drab modern life. He has one fault—a flaring Irish temper when military discipline is violated or high ideals belittled. A fault, yes, but I feel there will be tense moments of life for anybody with Tim Moynahan when the time comes for a death grapple with the Germans. Phil Sheridan would have delighted in him.

Major Stacom is my parishioner and I am his recruit. He acquired his interest in soldiering as a boy at St. Francis Xavier College under the stalwart old soldier, afterwards the hero of Santiago—Captain Drum. He came to the Regiment as a boy out of college, an enlisted man, and the Irish lads, after guying the handsome youngster in his college clothes, learned to love and admire him for his knowledge and ability. When he became Captain of Company B he recruited it by his personal efforts, and on the Border he had one of the best companies in the Regiment. Colonel Haskell picked him from the Company Commanders as the first man to nominate for a Majority. He rules by reason and kindliness, and evokes the best co-operation of all under him—officers or men.

Major William J. Donovan, who commands the first Battalion was transferred to us from the Brigade Staff, but he is no stranger to us. On the Border when he was Captain of Troop I of the 1st Cavalry he was the best known man of his rank in the New York Division. It was almost certain that Donovan would be appointed our Colonel after the efforts to get Colonel Haskell had failed, as he was our next choice, and General O'Ryan knew that there were no politics about it, but a sincere desire to find the best military leader. General O'Ryan esteems Donovan as highly as we do. When we were selected to put the green in the Rainbow all the vacancies were to be filled by transfer, not by promotion. Donovan was a Major on the Staff of our Brigade. Everybody knew that he could get higher rank by staying with the 27th Division but he preferred to join in with us. He would rather fight with the 69th than with any other Regiment, especially now that it is to be the first in the fray, and he would rather be Major than Colonel, for in battles as now conducted it is Majors who command in the actual fighting.

Donovan is a man in the middle thirties, very attractive in face and manner, an athlete who always keeps himself in perfect condition. As a football player at Niagara and Columbia, he gained the sobriquet of "Wild Bill." But that is tribute gained by his prowess rather than his demeanor. He is cool, untiring, strenuous, a man that always uses his head. He is preparing his men for the fatigues of open warfare by all kinds of wearying stunts. They too call him "Wild Bill" with malicious unction, after he has led them over a cross country run for four miles. But they admire him all the same, for he is the freshest man in the crowd when the run is over. He is a lawyer by profession, and a successful one, I am told. I like him for his agreeable disposition, his fine character, his alert and eager intelligence. But I certainly would not want to be in his Battalion.

Major George Lawrence of the Sanitary Detachment is one of the best acquisitions of our Border experience. When Major Maguire had to leave us, we all reached out for Lawrence, who was attached to the 12th, but was doing duty at the hospital there. He is well educated, a product of St. Francis Xavier and Pennsylvania, a competent physician and surgeon, a famous athlete in football and basketball in his day, and an athlete still; and one of the most devoted and most reliable men that God has made for the healing of wounds of mind or body. When I think of what we shall have to go through it makes me feel good to see George Lawrence around.

Captain Walter E. Powers of Headquarters Company is an old soldier though still a young man. He entered the Regular Army out of high school, out of short trousers, I tell him. He was Regimental Sergeant Major of the 7th Cavalry when Haskell was Adjutant of that famous Regiment. And when Haskell became Colonel he pulled Powers out of the Pershing Expedition and made him Adjutant of the 69th; and he was the best Adjutant on the Border. Latterly he has begun to pine for a Company and Colonel Hine gave him the Headquarters Company, the duties of which are so varied and so new that it will take a soldier-lawyer like Powers to organize it. He has the keenest dryest humor of any man I know. If he had not run away to be a soldier he would have made a successful lawyer or journalist.

Captain George McAdie of Company A is a Scotchman. We tell him that is the worst thing we know about him, which is our way of saying that we do not know anything bad about him. Personally I am very fond of our Scottish cousins, because I have known many real Scotchmen and not merely jokes about them. The jokes never give you a suspicion that Scotland idolizes Robert Burns, and produces fighting men as fine as there are in the world. George is my kind of Scot—like a volcano, rugged to outward view, but glowing with fire beneath. A good soldier and a true friend—you like him when you know him a while, and you find something new to like in him the longer you know him. If his health be as strong as his spirit he will do great things in the 69th.

Captain Thomas Reilley of Company B is an imposing being. He stands six feet three or so and fills the eye with seeing any way you look at him. He is also a college athlete, a football player of renown, of Columbia and New York Universities. A lawyer of real power and ability, he has not given himself time yet to reach his full stride in his profession. Since his college days he has been too much in demand for other services for which his endowments and instincts fit him—athlete, soldier, with a short course in political life, characteristically as an independent. He writes well and talks, well—too well, sometimes, for the Irish in him makes him indifferent to the effects of what he has to say. It makes him indifferent to all other sorts of danger too; so with his great physical and mental powers and his capacity for organization he will render invaluable service to the work of the Regiment.

Captain William Kennelly of Company C is also an athlete, with the build of a runner, clean-cut, trim, alert. Brisk is the word that describes him, for the trait is mental as well as physical. He is a Company drill master in the best sense of the word. I have never seen anybody who could get more snap out of a body of men with less nagging, whether it was a parade or a policing detail than Bill Kennelly. I expect to see Company C the smartest Company in the Regiment.

Captain James A. McKenna of Company D is a lawyer— Harvard and Fordham produced him. He is a fellow of great ability, ambitious, energetic and enduring. He will go far in any line he may choose, and as a soldier he will score a high mark. He has fine ideals and fine sentiments which he chooses to conceal under a playfully aggressive or business-like demeanor. But his enthusiasms, patriotic, religious, personal, are the true fundaments of him, and everybody feels it. He lets himself out most in his affection for his men who reciprocate his devotion. Company D under Jim McKenna will play a big part in our annals of war.

Alexander E. Anderson of Company E is a 69th man by heredity. His uncle, Colonel Duffy, commanded the Regiment in 1898. His cousin, Major John Duffy, was in the Regiment when Anderson was old enough to join it—and he joined it as a private just as soon as they would let him. He is a soldier through and through. His family and his business are near to him, but the 69th is first in his thoughts. He has gone through all the stages from private to captain without any family favoritism and today he stands out as the keenest Captain in the Regiment. He went to an Officer's Training School two years ago and graduated with a hundred percent. Sometimes they call him the 100 percent soldier, a title which grates on him exceedingly, for he hates such labels of praise, whether meant or not. Colonel Hine has asked me for the names of three Captains who might be recommended for Majors in emergency. I told him I would name only one, and after that one, half a dozen or more. "Oh," he said, "you mean Anderson. That is what the Battalion Commanders all say."

Captain Michael Kelly is an old soldier, though not an old man. He can wear military medals on dress-suit occasions which puzzle even the experts. A County Clare man by birth, he was drawn by fighting instincts as a youth into the British Army, since there was no Irish Army organized, and fought through the Boer War and Burmese campaigns. In New York he is second in command of the aqueduct police and a Captain of the 69th, succeeding Captain P. J. Maguire, who gave up his beloved Company F with satisfaction only because it fell to his trusted Lieutenant. Captain Kelly is a soldier first, last and all the time. His spear knoweth no brother. He visits infractions of military discipline with sternness and vigor. His Company stands in awe of him, and boasts of him to others. They are well looked after. If I have anything to distribute I have to keep an eye on him and Anderson, the two tyrants amongst Company Commanders. Give them their way and everything would go to Companies E and F, with a humorous growl between the two as to who gets the most of the spoils.

The Irish-American A. C. gave us Captain James Archer,

as it and kindred organizations have given us many of our best soldiers. There are few young fellows around New York who have not heard of Jimmy Archer, and many a one has watched with delight his fleet limbs carrying his graceful figure and shining head around the track to victory. He has the cleanness and fineness of the amateur track athlete—very distinctly a man and a gentleman. He has won his way through every step upward in the Regiment and has fairly won his race to the Captain's bars.

Captain James G. Finn of Company H is a Spanish War veteran, though he looks so young that he has to carry around his service record and the family Bible to prove it. Not that anybody would call Jim a liar. Not after taking one look at him. He is a broad-shouldered, big-chested fellow, one that the eye will pick out of a crowd, even in a congested crowd, for he stands above the heads of ordinary mortals. A football player, of course—Dartmouth College. A big honest manly man and a devoted soldier. Jim Finn thinks that Company H is the best bunch of fighting men that ever shouldered a rifle, and Company H knows that their big Captain is the finest man in the American Army. There are two hundred and fifty of them, and the Captain has thews like the son of Anak, so I don't intend to start anything by contradicting either of them. Anyway, I more than half agree with them.

Captain Richard J. Ryan of Company I is a new comer and, like a boy in a new town, he has his way to make. If I be not "mistook in my jedgments" he will make it. He hails from Watertown, New York, and from the 1st New York Infantry, but that does not complete his military history. He fought in the Boer War, I suspect from the same reason that prompted Kelly—because that was the only war there was, and a man must do the best with the opportunities he has. He is all wrapped up in his Company. He does not seem to care a hang what anybody higher up is thinking about him. He has his job and he wants to see it done right. That is a good sign. A soldier by natural instinct and preference, a Captain devoted to his men—that goes with the 69th. I am for him.

Captain John Patrick Hurley of Company K, is an argument for the continued existence of the Irish as a people. He has everything that everybody loves in the Irish, as found even the reluctant tributes of their hereditary foes. He has a lean, clean handsome face and figure, and a spirit that responds to ideals patriotic, religious, racial, human, as eagerly and naturally as a bird soaring into its native air. He is perfectly willing to die for what he believes in. He would find that much easier than to live in a world of the cheap and commonplace. He always reminds me of the Easter-week patriots of Dublin, Patrick Pearse and Plunkett and MacDonagh. Like myself, and I may say all of us, he is in this war as a volunteer because he feels that it is a war against the tyranny of the-strong, and a fight for the oppressed peoples of the earth. He is an able, practical man withal; an engineer, graduate of Cornell. He rules his company as their military commander, and the tribute of affection and loyalty they pay him is not lessened by the knowledge they have that breaches of discipline will meet with no mercy.

Captain Merle-Smith of Company L came to us on the Border from Squadron A, and the intervening year of intimacy has not changed the judgment I uttered the first time I saw him: "If I had to pick out one man to spend a year with me on a voyage to Central Africa, there is the man I would select." A big fellow—he and Reilly and Finn are our prize specimens—and big, like them, all the way through; and with the astonishing simplicity—in the old theological sense of the word as contrasted with duplicity— that one so often finds in big men. A college athlete (Princeton) and a lawyer, the contests of the campus and the bar have only whetted his appetite for more intense battles. From the time he joined us he has felt that the best opening for real soldier work is in this regiment. He is a 69th man by conviction, and he is as fond of his valiant

Kerrymen in Company L as they are of him. I found no one in the recruiting period more zealous in increasing the numbers of the regiment and maintaining at the same time its characteristic flavor than Captain Van Santvoordt Merle-Smith.

Captain William Doyle commanded Company M when we were called out, but since Captain Powers took the Headquarters Company he has been made Adjutant. It was a good choice. Captain Doyle is a college man (St. Francis Xavier) and an engineer by profession, and has been a National Guardsman for more years than one would guess. His training fits him for his new job. His mind is quick on the trigger, though the speed and accuracy with which it shoots a retort is rendered deceptive by his slightly humorous drawl in delivery. He is not one of the big fellows, but the big fellows think twice before taking him on.

Martin Meaney, Captain of Company M, was a Sergeant of Company G when we were in Texas. I wanted Colonel Haskell to make him a Second Lieutenant, but Martin hadn't left the County Clare soon enough to satisfy the technicality of having his final citizen papers. He could fight for the United States, but he could not be an officer. He came of age as a citizen during the summer and went to Plattsburg, and the people in charge there made him not a Second Lieutenant but a Captain. Colonel Haskell, who is Adjutant at Camp Upton, found the chance to send him back to us as a Captain, and we were very glad to get him. For we know Martin Meaney; and everyone who knows Martin Meaney likes him and trusts him. He is a fine, manly upstanding young Irishman devoted to high ideals, practical and efficient withal. Granted the justice of my cause there is no man in the world I would so much rely on to stick to me to the end as Martin Meaney. It makes us all feel better to have him along with us in our adventure of war.

The vacancy in the Machine Gun Company was filled by the appointment of Captain Kenneth Seibert, an old guardsman of the Iowa National Guard. He has the position of Johnny-come-lately with us yet, but he knows the game and he will be a veteran of ours by the time we get to our first battle. His whole organization is practically new, but he is very keen about it, and is an excellent manager, so we feel that he will soon have it in shape.

Captain John Mangan of the Supply Company is the salt of the earth. I like Jack Mangan so much that I always talk that way about him, and incidentally I waste his time and mine by holding him for a chat whenever we meet. He came to us before we went to the Border. His friends were in another regiment, but all that was nice and Irish about him made him want to be with the 69th. He is a Columbia man and a contractor. Colonel Haskell got his eye on him, when, as a Second Lieutenant, he was put in charge of a detail of offenders who had to do some special work. Under Mangan their work was not mere pottering around. They did things. While we were on the big hike Mangan was left behind with a detail of cripples to build mess shacks. They were built, created is a better word, but we were doomed never to use them, as we got orders during the hike to proceed to another station. I said to Haskell: "Don't forget to compliment Lieutenant Mangan on his work, for he has done wonders, and it looks now to have been all in vain." Haskell answered with assumed grimness: "Lieutenant Mangan will not be Lieutenant Mangan long." He was Captain Mangan, R. S. O. (Regimental Supply Officer) as soon as the formalities could be arranged; and in a short time he was the best supply officer on the Border, as his training as a contractor gave him experience in handling men and materials.

Everybody likes Mangan—half-rebellious prisoners and sodjering details and grasping civilians and grouchy division quartermasters. For "he has a way wid him." At bottom it is humor and justness, with appreciation of the other fellow's difficulties and states of mind. With his fairness and balance, he carries such an atmosphere of geniality and joy of life that everybody begins to feel a new interest in the game and a new willingness to play a decent part in it.

So far as I can see it now, our Captains average higher than our Lieutenants, though time will have to show if I am right. But at present I can point my finger to half a dozen Captains at least who could easily fill the job of Major, without being so certain of finding an equal number of Lieutenants who could make as good Captains as the men they replace. Probably all that this proves is that the Captains have the advantage of experience in their positions, and that their juniors, when equal opportunity is given them, will develop to be just as good. Amongst the Lieutenants the first to my mind is John Prout, a fine young Tipperary man of the stamp of Hurley and Meaney. Others in line are Samuel A. Smith, John Poore and William McKenna, the four Burns brothers (all good, but Jim in my judgment the best), also William Burns, Richard Allen, Clifford, Kelley, Kinney, Joseph MacNamara, Crimmins, Carroll, Andrew Lawrence, John Green, Thomas C. Martin, with Rowley, Grose, Baker, Joseph O'Donohue, James Mangan, O'Brien, Philbin, Cavanaugh, Reune Martin, who came to us while in the Armory. Of the newcomers sent to us here at Camp Mills four of the old regular army men stand out: Lieutenants Michael J. Walsh, Henry A. Bootz, Patrick Dowling and Francis McNamara. Our Medical Department consists of Major Lawrence with Doctors Houghton, Lyttle, Martin, Kilcourse, Levine, Patton, Bamford, Austin Lawrence and Landrigan.

October 25th, 1917

We are the best cared for Regiment that ever went to war. Mr. Daniel M. Brady, who was chairman of the Committee for employment, appointed by Justice Victor J. Dowling of the Friendly Sons of St. Patrick, when we came back from the Border, has reorganized and increased that body and our Board of Trustees now consists of Morgan

J. O'Brien, chairman, Daniel M. Brady, John J. Whalen, Joseph P. Grace, Victor J. Dowling, John D. Ryan, George McDonald, Nicholas F. Brady, John E. O'Keefe, Louis D. Conley, and Bryan Kennelly. They have raised ample funds from private subscriptions and from the generous benefits offered through the kindly generosity of the New York Baseball Club and of Mr. John McCormack. They have given $10,000.00 in cash to the Company and Regimental Funds, and $1,600 for the Chaplain's Fund "for religion and divilment." All sorts of sporting goods, including two complete sets of uniforms of Giants and Cubs, equip us fully for the sort of strenuous life which we most enjoy.

The Women's Auxiliary is also formed, Mrs. Hennings being the President, for looking after the families of soldiers while they are away, and sending gifts abroad.

Some of our wealthy friends in the Board of Trustees have also held dinners to which have been invited the principal officers of Regiment, Brigade, and Division. It has helped us to get acquainted with our chief superiors. I was particularly glad to have the opportunity of getting a more intimate knowledge of General Mann and his Chief of Staff, Colonel Douglas McArthur—a brilliant youthful-looking soldier for whom I had already formed a high esteem and admiration from casual meeting. He has been very helpful in furthering my plans to have a large body of priests from Brooklyn and New York give the men of the whole Division an opportunity of receiving the sacraments before going abroad.

MONTREAL
October 28th, 1917

Orders at last. They came in for the 1st Battalion October 25th. They slipped out quietly by night. I went with them to Montreal, travelling with Companies B and D. The men were in gleeful spirits, glad to have the wait over and to be off on the Long Trail. Edward Connelly and I sat up chatting most of the night. One remark of his struck me. His father was Captain of Company B in the 69th during the Civil War. "Some people say to me, 'With your two boys I don't see how you can afford to go to war.' With my two boys I can't see how I can afford not to go to war."

The two soldiers who appealed to me most aboard the train were Supply Sergeant Billy McLaughlin and Lieutenant Bootz. They stayed up all night to look after our needs, and they showed a combination of efficiency and cheerfulness—a very model of soldierly spirit.

I saw them all onto the *Tunisia* on their way to Liverpool. God speed them.

CHAPTER II

IN TRAINING ABROAD

BREST

November 13th, 1917

We moved out of Camp Mills on the night of October 29th and took trains at the nearby station—off at last for foreign service. Parts of Companies L and M were left to guard the camp. We found at Hoboken that we were to sail on a fine ship—the converted German liner *Amerika* which had been re-christened with the change of the penultimate letter. Our trip was uneventful. The seas were calm, and sailing on the *America* was like taking a trip on the end of a dock—you had to look over the side to realize that she was in motion. No submarines, though we were on constant watch for them. "What are you doing here?" asked one of the ship's officers of big Jim Hillery, who stood watch. "Looking for something Oi don't want to foind," answered Jim with a grin.

We did not know where our journey was to end but finally on November 12th we made port in the beautiful harbor of Brest, where we have been idling all week because we have been the first convoy to put in here, and no preparations have been made to land us and our equipment, and afford transportation to our destination.

November 15th, 1917

This morning I told Colonel Hine that I wanted a day in town to get some necessaries for my church work, and permission was readily granted. I inquired the way to the nearest church, timing my visit to get in around the dinner hour, so as to get an invitation for a meal. As I rang the bell of the rectory, the door opened and a poor woman with two children came out carrying a basket into which the housekeeper had put food. I said to myself: Where charity exists, hospitality ought to flourish. I waited in the customary bare ecclesiastical parlor for the Curé, and at last he came, a stout middle-aged man, walking with a limp. I presented myself, very tall and quite imposing in my long army overcoat, and told him I came in search of altar breads. He immediately proposed to take me to a convent some distance away where my wishes might be satisfied. As I followed him along the cobbled streets I said to myself, "I had thought these Bretons were a kind of Irish, but they lack the noblest of the traditions of the Celtic race, or this old gentleman would have asked me to dinner." It was only later that I found that my tremendous presence had embarrassed him and he had therefore decided to bring me to somebody whom nothing would embarrass. One need not say that this was a woman—the Mother Superior of an institution which was school, orphanage and *pension* in one.

She was of a type not unusual in heads of religious communities—cultivated, balanced, perfectly serene. After supplying my needs she asked gently, "Monsieur has dined?" "No, Monsieur has not dined." "Perhaps Monsieur would accept the humble hospitality of the convent." "Monsieur is a soldier, and soldiers have but one obligation—never to refuse a meal when they can get it." She smiled and brought me to the dining room, where I met the old chaplain and two equally elderly professors from some college, who pumped me about America and myself and Wilson and myself and Roosevelt and myself until the meal was over. Then I sallied forth with my stout Curé who evidently had absorbed, as he sat silent through the meal, all the information I had been giving out, particularly about myself. For he brought me into forty stores and stopped on the street at least a hundred people (and he knew everybody in town) to introduce proudly his prize specimen of an American priest in uniform. The introduction invariably took this form:

"Monsieur is an American." "He is an officer." "Monsieur, though one would not know it, is a priest. He has a large parish in the City of New York. He has been a Professor in the Seminary—of Philosophy, mind you. Monsieur has a parish with three vicaires. He receives from the noble government of the United States a stipend of ten thousand francs a year. That is what this great country gives their Chaplains. He is a Chaplain. He has crosses on his collar. Also on his shoulders. If I were taller I could see them. I saw them when he was sitting down."

And at the end, and always with a little break in his voice as he fumbled with the button of my tunic, "M. L'Aumonier wears the tricolor of our country with the badge of the Sacred Heart, which was pinned there by the great Cardinal of New York." And this was the man that I thought at first to be cold and unfriendly.

I had to break away finally to get back to my ship as evening was beginning to gather. I started for the dock, interested all the way to observe the Celtic types of the passersby and giving them names drawn from my Irish acquaintance, as Tim Murphy or Mrs. O'Shaughnessy. Feeling that I was not making for the dock from which I left, I turned to a knot of boys, introducing myself as a priest and telling them that I wanted to get back to the American transports. They jumped to help me as eagerly as my own altar boys at home would do. One alert black-eyed lad of fourteen took command of the party, the rest of them trailing along and endeavoring to give advice and support. But from the beginning this one youngster was in undoubted command of the situation. I tried once or twice to ask where he was bringing me, but received only a brief "Suivez-moi, Monsieur." Our journey ended in an alley where the calls of my guide brought out two fishermen who needed only red night-caps and knives in their teeth to bring up associations of Stevenson's pirate-mutineers. But they were ready to ferry me over to my ship for a compensation, a compensation which became quite moderate when my Mentor explained their obligation as Catholics and as Frenchmen to a priest and an ally.

I was about to embark in their fishing smack when a French marine came along the dock and said that under no circumstances could a boat cross the harbor after sunset. My fishermen argued; I argued; even my irresistible young guide stated the case; but to no avail. Finally I said to the youngster, "Why waste my time with this creature of a marine. Lead me to the person the most important in Brest, the Mayor, the Governor, the Master of the Port, the Commander of the Fleet. From such a one I shall receive permission." The youth gave me a quick look and I think he would have winked if my face were not so sternly set with the importance I had assumed. He led me off to the office of the Harbormaster. It was closed. I could find no person except the janitor who was sweeping the front steps. I was so put out at the prospect of not getting back from my leave on time that I had to talk to some person, so I told the janitor my worries. He insinuated that something might be arranged. I had traveled in Europe before and had learned how things get themselves arranged. So I produced from my pocket a nice shiny two-franc piece; and in a moment I discovered that I had purchased for thirty-five cents in real money the freedom of the Port of Brest. My janitor descended upon the faithful marine with brandished broom and bellowed objurgations that such a creature should block the way of this eminent American Officer who wished to return to his ship.

I stood in the prow of the smack as we made our way across the dark and rainy harbor and I felt for the first time the touch of romance as one gets it in books. I thought back over the day, and I had the feeling that my adventures had begun, and had begun with a blessing.

NAIVES EN BLOIS

Nov. 27th, 1917

Naives in Blooey we call it, with a strong hoot on the last word. If Thomas Cook and Son ever managed a personally conducted party as we have been handled and then landed it in a place like this, that long established firm would have to close up business forthwith. Guy Empey and all the rest of them had prepared us for the "Hommes 40; Chevaux 8" box-cars, but description never made anybody realize discomforts. Anyway, we went through it and we would have been rather disappointed if they had brought us on our three-day trip across France in American plush-seat coaches (by the way we growled about them when we went to the Border). A year from now if we are alive we shall be listening with an unconcealed grin of superiority to some poor fish of a recruit who gabbles over the hardships he has undergone in the side-door Pullmans.

We are forgetting our recent experiences already in the meanness of these God-forsaken villages. We are in six of them—each the worst in the opinion of the Companies there. Naives will do for a description of Vacon, Broussey, Villeroi, Bovée or Sauvoy. A group of 40 houses along the slopes of a crinkled plain. The farmers all live together in villages, as is the custom in France. And many features of the custom are excellent. They have a church, school, community wash houses with water supply, good roads with a common radiating point and the pleasures of society, such as it is.

The main drawback is that the house on the village street is still a farm house. The dung heap occupies a place of pride outside the front door; and the loftier it stands and the louder it raises its penetrating voice, the more it proclaims the worth and greatness of its possessor. The house is half residence and half stable with a big farm loft overtopping both. The soldiers occupy the loft. I censored a letter yesterday in which one of our lads said: "There are three classes of inhabitants in the houses—first, residents; second, cattle; third, soldiers." Over my head are some boys from Company B who got in ahead of us with the First Battalion, coming by way of England and then via Havre, after a long and tedious trip. They are Arthur Viens, Tom Blackburn and Jim Lannon of my own parish with Gilbert, Gilgar, Weick, and Healey. Their life is typical of the rest. Up in the morning early and over to Sergeant Gilhooley's wayside inn for breakfast. Then cut green wood for fire, or drill along the muddy roads or dig in the muddier hillsides for a target range—this all day with a halt for noon meal. Supper at 4:00 o'clock; and already the sun has dropped out of the gloomy heavens, if indeed it has ever shown itself at all. Then—then nothing. They cannot light lanterns—we have landed right bang up behind the front lines the first jump; we can hear the heavy guns booming north along the St. Mihiel lines; and the aeroplanes might take a notion to bomb the town some night if lights stood out. No fire—dangerous to light even a cigarette in a hay loft. There are a couple of wine shops in town but they are too small to accommodate the men. If they had a large lighted place where they could have the good cheer of wine and chat evenings it would be a blessing. They are not fond enough of "Pinard" to do themselves harm with it and I think the pious inn keepers see that it is well baptized before selling it. Good old Senator Parker of the Y. M. C. A. has been right on the job with tents for the men—of course without any curse of "rum" in them—but the cold weather makes it difficult to render them habitable.

So most of the men spread their blankets in the straw and go to bed at six o'clock—a good habit in the minds of old-fashioned folks. The squad overhead have another good old-fashioned habit. From the stable below I can hear them say their beads in common before settling down to sleep. "Father" Pat Heaney of Company D got them into the way of it on the boat. Good lads!

In comparison with them my fittings are palatial. I have a large square low-ceilinged room with stone floor, and French windows with big wooden shutters to enclose the light. The walls are concealed by the big presses or *Armoires* so dear to the housewives of Lorraine. The one old lady who occupies this house has lived here for all of her 70 years (a German officer occupied the high canopied bed in 1870) and she has never let any single possession she ever had get away from her. They are all in the *Armoires*, old hats, bits of silk, newspapers—everything. She is very pious and very pleased to have M. l'Aumonier, but she wouldn't give me a bit of shelf room or a quarter inch of candle or a handful of *petit bois* to start a fire in the wretched fireplace, without cash down.

"Monsieur is a Curé"
"Yes, Madame."

My landlady has been quizzing me about the Regiment, my parish and myself. She doesn't understand this volunteer business. If we didn't have to come, why are we here? is her matter of fact attitude. She was evidently not satisfied with what she could learn from me herself, so one day she called to her aid a crony of hers, a woman of 50 with a fighting face and straggly hair whom I had dubbed "the sthreeler," because no English word described her so adequately. I had already heard the Sthreeler's opinion of the women in Paris—all of them. It would have done the hussies good to hear what she thought of them. Now she turned her interrogatory sword point at me; no parrying about her methods—just slash and slash again.

"Monsieur has three vicaires." "Yes, Madame."

"Then why has M. l'Aumonier come over here? Why not send one of the Vicaires and stay at home in his parish?"

"But none of the vicaires was aumonier of the Regiment; but myself, M. le Curé.

"Oh, perhaps the Germans destroyed your parish as they did that of our present curé."

"No, the Germans have not got to New York yet so my parish is still safe."

"Ah, then, I have it. No doubt the Government pays you more as aumonier than the church does as curé."

This was said with such an evident desire to justify her good opinion of me as a rational being in spite of apparent foolishness, that I said: "That is precisely the reason"; and we turned with zest to the unfailing topic of the Parisiennes with their jewels and paint and high heels. Not having her courage, I did not venture to ask the sthreeler if she did not really envy them.

They are going in strong for education in the A. E. F. and we have lost temporarily the services of many of our best officers. Lieutenant Colonel Reed has gone off to school and also the three Majors and half the Captains. I hope they are getting something out of their schooling for nobody here is learning anything except how to lead the life of a tramp. The men have no place to drill or to shoot or to manoeuvre. I hear we are moving soon to fresh fields further south—Heaven grant it, for we waste time here.

GRAND

December 23rd, 1917

I think it was Horace who said something to the effect that far-faring men change the skies above them but not the hearts within them. That occurs to me when I see our lads along the streets of this ancient Roman town. It is old, old, old. You have to go down steps to get to the floor of the 700-year-old Gothic nave of the church because the detritus of years has gradually raised the level of the square; and the tower of the church, a huge square donjon with walls seven feet thick slitted for defensive bowmen, is twice as old as the nave. And it has the ruins of an amphitheatre and a well preserved mosaic pavement that date back to the third century, when the Caesars had a big camp here to keep the Gauls in order. I shan't say that the men are not interested in these antiquities. They are an intelligent lot, and unsated by sight-seeing, and they give more attention to what they see than most tourists would. When I worked the history of the place into my Sunday sermon I could see that everybody was wide awake to what I had to say.

But in their hearts they are still in good little old New York. The quips and slang of New York play houses are heard on the streets where Caesar's legionaries chaffed each other in Low Latin. Under the fifteen centuries old tower Phil Brady maintains the worth of Flushing because Major Lawrence hails from there. Paul Haerting and Dryer exchange repartee outside the shrine of St. Libaire, Virgin and Martyr, after their soldiers orisons at his tomb. Charles Dietrich and Jim Gormley interrupt my broodings over the past in the ruins of the amphitheater to ask me news about our parish in the Bronx.

The 2nd and 3rd Battalions are not in such an antique setting, but in two villages along the bare hillsides to the south of us. It is a good walk to get to them; but I have my reward. When I get to the 2nd Battalion, if the men are busy, I drop in on Phil Gargan for a cup of coffee. I am always reminded of my visits to Ireland by the hospitality I encounter—so warm and generous and bustling and overwhelming. I get my coffee, too much of it, and too sweet, and hot beyond human endurance, and food enough offered with it to feed a platoon. And I am warm with a glow that no steaming drink could ever produce of itself. It is the same wherever I go. For instance if my steps lead me to the 3rd Battalion Pat Boland spices his coffee with native wit; or if my taste inclines me to tea I look up Pat Rogan who could dig up a cup of tea in the middle of a polar expedition.

While I am on the question of eating—always an interesting topic to a soldier—let me say a word for French inns. I came to Grand with Regimental Sergeant Major Steinert, ahead of the Regiment in charge of a billetting detail, and thus made the acquaintance of the establishment of Madame Gerard at the Sign of the Golden Boar. I have seen a M. Gerard but, as in all well regulated families, he is a person with no claim to figure in a story. I am in love for the first time, and with Madame Gerard. Capable and human and merry, used to men and their queer irrational unfeminine ways, and quite able to handle them, hundreds at a time. A joke, a reprimand, and ever and always the final argument of a good meal—easy as easy. She reigns in her big kitchen, with its fireplace where the wood is carefully managed but still gives heat enough to put life and savor into the hanging pots and the sizzling turnspits. Odors of Araby the blest! And she serves her meals with the air of a beneficent old Grande Dame of the age when hospitality was a test of greatness. Private or General—it makes no difference to her. The same food and the same price and the same frank motherly humor— and they all respond with feelings that are common to all. I sit before the kitchen fire while she is at work, and talk about the war and religion and our poor soldiers so far from their mothers, and the cost of food and the fun you can get out of life, and when I get back to my cold room I go to bed thinking of how much I have learned, and that I can see at last how France has been able to stand this war for three and a half years.

The Colonel's mess is at the Curé's house. It too is a pleasant place to be, for the Colonel lays aside his official air of severity when he comes to the table, and is his genial, lovable self. The Curé dines with us—a stalwart mountaineer who keeps a young boar in his back yard as a family pet. One would have thought him afraid of nothing. But courage comes by habit; and I found that the Curé had his weak side. His years had not accustomed him to the freaks of a drunken man—a testimonial to his parishioners. We had a cook, an old Irishman, who could give a new flavor to nectar on Olympus; that is, if he didn't drink too much of it first. But he would, trust Paddy for that, even if threatened with Vulcan's fate of being pitched out headfirst for his offense.

One day Tom Heaney and Billy Hearn came running for me. Paddy on the rampage! The aged *bonne* in hysterics. The Curé at his wits' end. Come! I went. I found Paddy red-eyed and excited, and things in a mess. I curtly ordered him into a chair, and sent for Doc. Houghton, our mess officer, to do justice. Meanwhile I studied a map on the wall, with my back turned to the offender, and the following one-sided dialogue ensued—like a telephone scene at a play.

"It's that's making me mad." A pause,

"I don't like you anyway." A pause.

"You're no good of a priest. If I was dying I wouldn't"— (reconsidering)—"I hope to God when I'm dying I won't have to put up with the likes of you." A long pause.

"I've long had me opinion of you. I'll tell it to you if you like."

A pause—with me saying to myself "Now you'll get the truth."

"I'll tell it to you. I've been wanting to do it time and times. . . . You smoke cigarettes with the Officers, that's what you do." A sigh of relief, and the thought "I could have said more than that myself."

Then in bursts Colonel Hine and Paddy was hustled away for punishment. But I know what will happen. We shall eat army food *au naturel* for a week or so; and some noon the meal will be so good that we shall all eat more than is good for men with work still to do, and nobody shall ask a question about it, for everybody will know that Paddy, God bless him! is back on the job once more. Of course I have a special liking for him because when he was in a mood to denounce me he let me off so light.

GRAND

December 25th, 1917

If there is one day in all the year that wanderers from home cannot afford to forget it is Christmas. The Company Commanders have had their Mess Sergeants scouring the countryside for eatables.

It was my business to give them a religious celebration that they would remember for many a year and that they would write about enthusiastically to the folks at home, who would be worrying about the lonesome existence of their boys in France. The French military authorities and the Bishop of the diocese had united in prohibiting Midnight Masses on account of the lights. But General Lenihan, the Mayor, and the Curé decided that we were too far from the front to worry about that, and it was arranged *tout de suite*. I knew that confessions and communions would be literally by the thousands, so with the aid of Joyce Kilmer and Frank Driscoll, ex-Jesuit-novice, I got up a scheme for confessions of simple sins in English and French, and set my French confrères to work; the Curé, a priest-sergeant in charge of a wood cutting detail, a *brancardier,* and another priest who was an officer of the artillery—all on the *qui vive* about the task. Christmas Eve. found us all busy until midnight. I asked one of the men how he liked the idea of going to confession to a priest who cannot speak English. "Fine, Father," he said with a grin, "All he could do was give me a penance, but you'd have given me hell." Luckily the church was vastly larger than the present needs of the town, for everybody, soldiers and civilians, came. General Lenihan and Colonel Hine and the Brigade and the Regimental Staffs occupied seats in the sanctuary which was also crowded with soldiers. The local choir sang the Mass and I preached. Our lads sang the old hymns, "The Snow Lay on the Ground," "The Little Town of Bethlehem," and all, French and Americans, joined in the ancient and hallowed strains of the *Adeste Fideles* until the vaults resounded with *Venite Adoremus Dominum.* It took four priests a long time to give Communion to the throng of pious soldiers and I went to bed at 2:00 A. M. happy with the thought that, exiles though we are, we celebrated the old feast in high and holy fashion.

Christmas afternoon we had general services in the big market shed. The band played the old Christmas airs and everybody joined in, until the square was ringing with our pious songs.

Everybody had a big Christmas dinner. The Quartermaster had sent the substantial basis for it and for extra trimmings the Captains bought up everything the country afforded. They had ample funds to do it, thanks to our Board of Trustees, who had supplied us lavishly with funds. The boxes sent through the Women's Auxiliary have not yet reached us. It is just as well, for we depart tomorrow on a four-day hike over snowy roads and the less we have to carry the better.

LONGEAU

January 1st, 1918

I cannot tell just what hard fates this New Year may have in store for us, but I am sure that no matter how trying they may be they will not make us forget the closing days of 1917. We left our villages in the Vosges the morning after Christmas Day. From the outset it was evident that we were going to be up against a hard task. It snowed on Christmas, and the roads we were to take were mean country roads over the foothills of the Vosges Mountains. New mules were sent to us on Christmas Eve. They were not shod for winter weather, and many of them were absolutely unbroken to harness, the harness provided moreover being French and ill-fitting. To get it on the mules big Jim Hillery had to throw them first on the stable floor.

It was everybody's hike, and everybody's purgatory; but to my mind it was in a special way the epic of the supply company and the detachments left to help them. Nobody ever makes any comment when supplies are on hand on time. In modern city life we get into the way of taking this for granted, as if food were heaven-sent like manna, and we give little thought to the planning and labor it has

taken to provide us.   On a hike the Infantry will get through
—there is never any doubt of that. They may be foot-
sore, hungry, broken-backed, frozen, half dead, but they
will get through.   The problem is to get the mules through;
and it is an impossible one very often without human intelligence and human labor.   On this hike the marching men
carried no reserve rations, an inexcusable oversight.   No
village could feed them even if there was money to pay
for the food; and the men could not eat till the Company
wagons arrived with the rations and field ranges.

The situation for Captain Mangan's braves looked desperate from the start.   A mile out of town the wagons were
all across the road, as the lead teams were not trained to
answer the reins.   The battle was on.   Captain Mangan
with Lieutenant Kinney, a Past Grand Master when it comes
to wagon trains, organized their forces.   They had experienced helpers—Sergeant Ferdinando, a former circus man,
Sergeant Bob Goss and Regimental Supply Sergeant Joe
Flannery, who will be looking for new wars to go to when
he is four score and ten.   It would be impossible to relate
in detail the struggles of the next four days; but that
train got through from day to day only by the fighting
spirit of soldiers who seldom have to fire a rifle.   Again
and again they came to hills where every wagon was stalled.
The best teams had to be unhitched and attached to each
wagon separately until the hill was won.   Over and over
the toil-worn men would have to cover the same ground till
the work was done, and in tough places they had to spend
their failing strength tugging on a rope or pushing a
wheel.   Wagoners sat on their boxes with hands and feet
freezing and never uttered a complaint.   The wagons were
full of food but no man asked for a mite of it—they
were willing to wait till the companies ahead would get their
share.

The old time men who had learned their business on
the Border were naturally the best.   Harry Horgan, ex-
cowboy, could get anything out of mules that mules could

do. Jim Regan, old 1898 man, had his four new mules christened and pulling in answer to their names before a greenhorn could gather up the reins. Larkin and young Heffernan and Barney Lowe and Tim Coffee were always first out and first in, but always found time to come back and take the lines for some novice to get his wagon through a hard place. Al Richford, Ed Menrose, Gene Mortenson, Willie Fagan, Arthur Nulty, Wagoner Joe Seagriff and good old Pat Prendergast did heroic work. "Father" James McMahon made me prouder of my own title. Slender Jimmy Benson got every ounce of power out of his team without ever forgetting he belonged to the Holy Name Society. Sergeant Lacey, Maynooth man and company clerk, proved himself a good man in every Irish sense of the word. Hillery and Tumulty, horseshoers; Charles Henning of the commissary, and Joe Healy, cook, made themselves mule-skinners once more, and worked with energies that never flagged.

Lieutenant Henry Bootz came along at the rear of the Infantry column to pick up stragglers. The tiredest and most dispirited got new strength from his strong heart. "I think I'm going to die," said one broken lad of eighteen. "You can't die without my permission," laughed the big Lieutenant. "And I don't intend to give it. I'll take your pack, but you'll have to hike." And hike he did for seven miles farther that day, and all the way for two days more. The first day Bootz threatened to tie stragglers to the wagons. The remaining days he took all that could move without an ambulance and tied the wagons to them. And they had to pull.

Captain Mangan, the most resourceful of commanders, was working in his own way to relieve the strain. One day he took possession of a passing car and got to the H. Q. of a French Division where the kindly disposed French Officers were easily persuaded to send camions to carry provisions ahead, to be stored for the troops at the terminus of the day's march. Horses were rented from the farmers, or, if they were stiff about it, abruptly commandeered. That wagon train had to get through.

It got through; but sometimes it was midnight or after before it got through; and meanwhile the line companies had their own sufferings and sacrifices. They hiked with full packs on ill-made and snow-covered roads over hilly country. At the end of the march they found themselves in villages (four or five of them to the regiment), billetted in barns, usually without fire, fuel or food. They huddled together for the body warmth, and sought refuge from cold and hunger in sleep. When the wagons came in, their food supplies were fresh meat and fresh vegetables, all frozen through and needing so much time to cook that many of the men refused to rise in the night to eat it. Breakfast was the one real meal; at midday the mess call blew, but there was nothing to eat.

When they got up in the morning their shoes were frozen stiff and they had to burn paper and straw in them before they could get them on. Men hiked with frozen feet, with shoes so broken that their feet were in the snow; many could be seen in wooden sabots or with their feet wrapped in burlap. Hands got so cold and frost-bitten that the rifles almost dropped from their fingers. Soldiers fell in the snow and arose and staggered on and dropped again. The strong helped the weak by encouragement, by sharp biting words when sympathy would only increase weakness, and by the practical help of sharing their burdens. They got through on spirit. The tasks were impossible for mere flesh and blood, but what flesh and blood cannot do, spirit can make them do. It was like a battle. We had losses as in a battle—men who were carried to hospitals because they had kept going long after their normal powers were expended. It was a terrible experience. But one thing we all feel now—we have not the slightest doubt that men who have shown the endurance that these men have shown will give a good account of themselves in any kind of battle they are put into.

LONGEAU

January 10th, 1918

The Regiment is in five villages south of the old Fortress town of Langres in the Haute Marne; Headquarters and Supply in Longeau, 1st Battalion in Percey, 2nd in Cohons, the 3rd in Baissey and the Machine Gun Company in Brennes. They are pleasant prosperous little places (inhabited by *cultivateurs* with a sprinkling of *bourgeois*) the red roofs clustering picturesquely along the lower slopes of the rolling country. None of them is more than an hour's walk from our center at Longeau. The men are mostly in the usual hayloft billets, though some companies have Adrian barracks where they sleep on board floors. Apart from sore feet from that abominable hike, and the suffering from cold due to the difficulty of procuring fuel, we are fairly comfortable.

The officers are living in comparative luxury. I am established with a nice sweet elderly lady. I reach the house through a court that runs back of a saloon—which leaves me open to comments from the ungodly. The house is a model of neatness, as Madame is a childless widow, and after the manner of such, has espoused herself to her home. She is very devout, and glad to have M. l'Aumonier in the house, but I am a sore trial to her, as I have a constant run of callers, all of them wearing muddy hobnailed brogans. She says nothing to me, but I can hear her at all hours of the day lecturing little Mac about doors and windows and sawdust and dirt. I never hear him say anything in reply, except "Oui, Madame," but somehow he seems to understand her voluble French and they get along very well together. I notice that our lads always strike up a quick acquaintance with the motherly French women. They work together, cooking at the fireplaces or washing clothes in the community fountain, keeping up some sort of friendly gossip and laughing all the while, though I never can understand how they manage it, for the villagers never learn any English and the soldiers have not more than forty words of French. After all a language is only a makeshift for expressing ourselves. "Qu'est-ce que c'est"—"Kesky," and pointing supplies the nouns, gestures the verbs, and facial expressions the adjectives.

LONGEAU

January 21st, 1918

Last night the church bells rang at midnight; and waking, I said: "Bombers overhead!" A minute later I heard the cry Fire! Fire! and the bugles raising the same alarm. It was a big stable at the south end of the town—we had gasoline stored in it and some soldier was careless. The street was thronged in an instant with running soldiers and civilians. The village firemen or *pompiers* came running up at a plowman gait—looked the fire over—and went back to put on their proper uniforms. One old lad came all the way from Percey in a gendarme's chapeau. He could not properly try to put out a fire in that headgear, so he went all the way back and arrived at last, puffing but satisfied, in the big *pompier* nickel-plated helmet. Their big pump was pulled up to Longeau, and the hose was laid with the proper amount of ceremony and shouting, and the stream finally put on the blazing shed. The remainder of the population displayed little of the proverbial French excitability. They looked on with the air of men who can enjoy a good spectacle, happy in the thought that the rich American Government would have to pay for it.

The soldiers were happy too at having a chance to fight something. Colonel Barker gave orders in his quiet way, which Captains Anderson and Mangan put into execution. The fountain ran out and bucket lines were formed. I am afraid that some of the contents instead of getting to the fire was dumped on the gaudy uniforms of the funny old *pompiers,* who insisted upon running around giving orders that nobody could understand. This is the second French fire we have witnessed and the general verdict is that our moving picture people have missed the funniest unstudied episode left in the world by not putting a French village fire department on the screen. It was a good show in every way—but incidentally the building was a total loss.

LONGEAU

January 25th, 1918

I walked over to Cohons today and dropped in on Company H. Instead of having to make my visit through the scattered billets that line the entrance to the valley I found what looked like the whole Company along the roadside in vehemently gesticulating groups. I hurried to find what the trouble might be. "What's the matter here," I asked. Val Dowling, the supply Sergeant, picked a uniform out of a pile and held it up. "Look at the damn thing? Excuse me, Father, but you'll say as bad when you look at it. They want us to wear this." He held it out as if it had contagion in it, and I saw it was a British tunic, brass buttons and all. I disappointed my audience—I didn't swear out loud. "Got nice shiny buttons," I said. "What's the matter with it?" What was the matter with it? Did I know it was a British uniform? Frank McGlynn of Manhattan and Bill McGorry of Long Island City were as hot as Bill Fleming or Pat Travers or Chris O'Keefe or William Smythe. "They look a little betther this way," said John Thornton, holding up one with the buttons clipped off. "That's all right," I said, "but don't get yourselves into trouble destroying government property." "Throuble," said Martin Higgins. "What the blazes do they mane by insultin' min fightin' for thim like this. I'd stand hangin' rather than put wan of thim rags on me back."

I went home in a black mood, all the blacker because I did not want to say what I felt before the men; and when I got to mess I found Lawrence, Anderson and Mangan and young McKenna as sore as myself. We all exploded together, and Colonel Barker, at first mildly interested, seemed to get worried. "Well," he said, "at least they wouldn't object if they had to wear English shoes, would they?" "No," I said. "They'd have the satisfaction of stamping on them." The laugh at my poor joke ended the discussion, but I waited after supper to talk with Colonel Barker. I didn't want him worried about us, and he naturally couldn't know; but I felt he could appreciate our attitude from his own very strong anti-German feelings. "Colonel," I said. "We do not want you to feel that you have a regiment of divided loyalty or dubious reliability on your hands. We are all volunteers for this war. If you put our fellows in line alongside a bunch of Tommies, they would only fight the harder to show the English who are the better men, though I would not guarantee that there would not be an occasional row in a rest camp if we were billeted with them. There are soldiers with us who left Ireland to avoid service in the British Army. But as soon as we got into the war, these men, though not yet citizens, volunteered to fight under the Stars and Stripes.

"We have our racial feelings, but these do not affect our loyalty to the United States. You can understand it. There were times during the past two years when if England had not restrained her John Bull tendencies on the sea we might have gotten into a series of difficulties that would have led to a war with her. In that case Germany would have been the Ally. You are a soldier, and you would have fought, suppressing your own dislike for that Ally. But supposing in the course of the war we were short of tin hats and they asked you to put on one of those Boche helmets?"

The Colonel whacked the table, stung to sudden anger at the picture. Then he laughed, "You have a convincing way of putting things, Father. I'll see that they clothe my men hereafter in American uniforms."

And though, as I found later, many of the offensive uniforms had been torn to ribbons by the men, nobody ever made any inquiry about "destruction of government property."

PERCEY

February 2nd, 1918

I usually manage to get to two different towns for my Church services Sunday mornings. General Lenihan always picks me up in his machine and goes with me to my early service, at which he acts as acolyte for the Mass, a duty which he performs with the correctness of a seminarian, enhanced by his fine soldierly face and bearing and his crown of white hair. The men are deeply impressed by it, and there are few letters that go home that do not speak of it. He brought me back from Cohons this morning and dropped me off at Percey, where I had a later Mass. These French villagers are different from our own home folks in that they want long services; they seem to feel that their locality is made little of, if they do not have everything that city churches can boast, and I sometimes think, a few extras that local tradition calls for. It is hard on me, for I am a Low Church kind of Catholic myself; and besides "soldier's orisons" are traditionally short ones. The only consolation I have here in Percey is that the old septuagenarian who leads the service for the people sings in such a way that I can render thanks to Heaven that at last it has been given to my ears to hear raised in that sacred place the one voice I have ever heard that is worse than my own.

I called on Donovan this evening and found him sitting in a big, chilly chamber in the old chateau in front of a fire that refused to burn. He had had a hard day and was still busy with orders for the comfort of men and animals. "Father," he said, "I have just been thinking that what novelists call romance is only what men's memories hold of the past, with all actual realization of the discomforts left out, and only the dangers past and difficulties conquered remaining in imagination. What difference is there between us and the fellow who has landed at the Chateau in Stanley Weyman or Robert Stevenson's interesting stories; who has come in after a hard ride and is giving orders for the baiting of his horse or the feeding of his retinue, as he sits, with his jackboots pulled down, before the unwilling fire and snuffs the candle to get sufficient light to read his orders for the next day's march." I get much comfort from the Major's monologue. It supplies an excellent romantic philosophy with which to face the sordid discomforts which are the most trying part of war.

BAISSEY

February 8th, 1918

Over today and dined at Hurley's mess. Pat Dowling told of a rather mysterious thing that happened to him while he was a Sergeant in the regular army. He was sent from one post to another, a distance of two hundred miles, with a sealed letter which he delivered to the Commanding Officer, who opened it, read it, and said: "Sergeant, you will return to your own post immediately." "I have often wondered," said Pat, "what could have been in that letter." "I can tell you," said Tom Martin, in his quiet way. "Well, what was in it?" "That letter read, 'If you like the looks of this man, keep him.'"

LONGEAU

February 10th, 1918

The Regiment has made huge progress in military matters during the past month. I go over to Cohons and the new French Chauchat automatics are barking merrily at the hill that climbs from the road. At Percey I see our erstwhile baseball artists learning an English overhead bowling delivery for hurling hand grenades at a pit, where they explode noisily and harmlessly. At Baissey Major Moynahan walks me up the steep hill to show me his beautiful system of trenches, though I see no reflection of his enthusiasm in the faces of Jerry Sheehan or Jim Sullivan—they had the hard job of helping to dig them. West of the town against the steep base of the highest hill Lieutenants O'Brien and Cunningham with the 37 mm. or one-pound cannon, and Lieutenants Walsh and Keveny with the Stokes mortars are destroying the fair face of nature. Vociferous young Lieutenants are urging the men to put snap into their bayonet lunges at stuffed mannikins.

I had a little clash of my own with some of these enthusiastic youngsters early in the game. In the British school of the bayonet they teach that the men ought to be made to curse while doing these exercises. I see neither grace nor sense in it. If a man swears in the heat of a battle I don't even say that God will forgive it; I don't believe He would notice it. But this organized blasphemy is an offense. And it is a farce—a bit of Cockney Drill Sergeant blugginess to conceal their lack of better qualities. If they used more brains in their fighting and less blood and guts they would be further on than they are. Our fellows will do more in battle by keeping their heads and using the natural cool courage they have than by working themselves up into a fictitious rage to hide their fears.

Latterly we have had the excellent services of a Battalion of French Infantry to help us in our training. They have been through the whole bloody business and wear that surest proof of prowess, the Fourragère. I asked some of the old timers amongst them how much use they had made of the bayonet. They all said that they had never seen a case when one line of bayonets met another. Sometimes they were used in jumping into a trench, but generally when it came to bayonets one side was running away.

The "Y" is on the job and has some sort of place in each town. With me is Percy Atkins, a good man with only one fault—he is working himself to death in spite of my trying to boss him into taking care of himself.

We have suffered a real pang in the transfer of Colonel Hine to the Railway Service. It gives a foretaste of what we are to be up against in this war. There is evidently to be no regard for feelings or established relations of dependency or intimacy, but just put men in where they will be considered to fit best. I was ready for that after the battles began, but it is starting already. First Reed, now Hine. I shall miss Colonel Hine very much—a courteous gentleman, a thorough soldier, a good friend. He was a railroad man for many years and they say he is needed there. God prosper him always wherever he goes.

His successor was picked by General Pershing from his own staff: Colonel John W. Barker, a West Pointer, who had seen much service and had been on duty in France since the beginning of the war. He is a manly man, strong of face, silent of speech, and courteous of manner. We have learned to like him already—we always like a good soldier. We are also beginning to get some real training, as the weather is more favorable and our officers are getting back from school.

CHAPTER III

THE LUNÉVILLE SECTOR

ARBRE HAUT

March 1st, 1918

THE trenches at last! We have all read descriptions
of them and so had our preconceived notions. The novelty
is that we are in a thick woods. You go out from Lunéville
(where we have been having the unwonted joys of city life
for a week or so) along the flat valley of the Vesouze
to Croixmare, and east to Camp New York, where some
Adrian barracks, floating like Noah's Arks in a sea of mud,
house the battalion in reserve; then up a good military road
through the Forest of Parroy to Arbre Haut, where a
deep dugout forty feet underground shelters the Colonel
and his headquarters. A mile further on, at Rouge Bouquet, one arrives at a Battalion Post of Command dugout
now occupied by Major Donovan, Lieutenants Ames, Irving,
Lacey and Captain Mercier, an energetic, capable and agreeable officer of the French Mission. Duck-board paths
lead in various directions through peaceful looking woods
to a sinuous line of trenches which were, when we arrived
in them, in considerable need of repair. Company D, under
Captain McKenna, had the honor of being first in the lines.
They were followed by Companies B and A, Company C
being in support. Off duty the men live in mean little
dugouts thinly roofed, poorly floored, wet and cold. But
they are happy at being on the front at last, and look on
the discomforts as part of the game. Their only kick is
that it is too quiet. Their main sport is going out on patrols
by night or day to scout through "No Man's Land," to

cut wires, and stir things up generally. With our artillery throwing over shells from the rear and our impatient infantry prodding the enemy, this sector will not be long a quiet one.

CROIXMARE

March 10th, 1918

We have had our first big blow, and we are still reeling under the pain and sorrow of it. Our 1st Battalion left the trenches with few casualties to pay for their ten days of continuous work at trench and wire mending and night patrols. Arthur Trayer and John Lyons of Company D were the first to gain their wound chevrons. On March 5th the 2nd Battalion began to move company by company from Camp New York. I spent the afternoon before with each unit attending to their spiritual needs, and ending the day with a satisfactory feeling of having left nothing undone. I was with Company E on March 6th and will always retain a recollection of certain youngsters who stayed for a little friendly personal chat after confession, like Arthur Hegney, Eddie Kelly, Steve Navin, Arthur Christfully, George Adkins, Phil Finn; while Steve Derrig and Michael Ahearn with Bailey, Halligan and McKiernan were rounding up the bunch to keep me going.

The Company went out in the early morning of March 7th to relieve Company A, and soon had the position taken over. About 4 P. M. the enemy began a terrific shelling with heavy minenwerfers on the position at Rocroi. The big awkward wabbling aerial torpedoes began coming over, each making a tremendous hole where it hit and sending up clouds of earth and showers of stone. Lieutenant Norman, an old Regular Army man, was in charge of the platoon, and after seeing that his guards and outposts were in position, ordered the rest of the men into the dugouts. While he was in the smaller one a torpedo struck it fair and destroyed it, burying the two signal men from Headquarters Company, Arthur Hegney and Edward Kearney. The Lieutenant barely managed to extricate himself from the debris and set himself to look after the rest of his men. He was inspecting the larger dugout alongside when another huge shell came over, buried itself in the very top of the cave and exploded, rending the earth from the supporting beams and filling the whole living space and entrance with rocks and clay, burying the Lieutenant and twenty-four men.

Major Donovan of the 1st Battalion was at the Battalion P. C. with Major Stacom when the bombardment began. As there were six positions to defend and the shelling might mean an attack anywhere along the whole line, the Battalion Commander's duty was to remain at the middle of the web with his reserves at hand to control the whole situation. So Major Donovan requested that as he had no general responsibilities for the situation he might be permitted to go down to Rocroi and see what he could do there. Stacom was unwilling to have anybody else run a risk that he was not permitted to share himself, but he gave his consent.

Major Donovan found the men in line contending with a desperate condition. The trenches were in places levelled by the bombardment and though the enemy were no longer hurling their big torpedoes they kept up a violent artillery attack on the position. The only answer that we could make to this was from the trench mortars which were kept going steadily by Lieutenants Walsh and F. Mc-Namara, Corporal Cudmore, William Murphy, Wisner, Young, Harvey, P. Garvey, Herbert Shannon, F. Garvey, DeNair, Robertson and the one pounders under Lieutenant Cunningham, Sergeants J. J. Ryan and Willermin. One of their guns was blown clean out of its position.

Corporal Helmer with Privates Raymond, McKenzie, Cohen, McCormack, O'Meara and Smeltzer were saved from the dugout and immediately began to work for the rescue of the others, aided by 1st Sergeant Bailey, Sergeants William Kelly and Andrew Callahan, Corporals Bernard Kelly and William Halligan with John Cronin, Thomas

Murray, James Joyce and John Cowie. They knew that many of their comrades were dead already but the voices could still be heard as the yet standing timbers kept the earth from filling the whole grade. The rescuers were aided by Lieutenant Buck and three sergeants of Company A, who had remained until the newly arrived company had learned its way about the sector. These were Sergeants William Moore, Daniel O'Connell and Spencer Rossel. Sergeant Abram Blaustein also hastened up with the pioneer section, Mackay, Taggart, Schwartz, Adair, Heins, Quinn, LaClair, Dunn, Gillman and the rest.

Major Donovan found them working like mad in an entirely exposed position to liberate the men underneath. A real soldier's first thought will always be the holding of his position, so the Major quickly saw to it that the defense was properly organized. Little Eddie Kelly, a seventeen-year-old boy, was one of the coolest men in sight, and he flushed with pleasure when told that he was to have a place of honor and danger on guard. The work of rescue was kept going with desperate energy, although there was but little hope that any more could be saved, as the softened earth kept slipping down, and it was impossible to make a firm passageway. The Engineers were also sent for and worked through the night to get out bodies for burial but with only partial success. Meanwhile the defenders of the trench had to stand a continuous shelling in which little Kelly was killed, Stephen Navin and Stephen Derrig were seriously wounded, and Sergeant Kahn, Corporal Smeltzer and Privates Bowler and Dougherty slightly.

The French military authorities conferred a number of Croix de Guerre, giving a Corps citation to Corporal Helmer for working to save his comrades after having been buried himself, "giving a very fine example of conscience, devotion and courage." Division citations went to Major Donovan, "superior officer who has shown brilliant military qualities notably on the 7th and 8th of March, 1918, by giving during the course of a violent bombardment an exam-

ple of bravery, activity and remarkable presence of mind";
and to Private James Quigley, who "carried two wounded
men to first aid station under a violent bombardment and
worked all night trying to remove his comrades buried
under a destroyed dugout." Regimental citations were
given to Lieutenant John Norman, Lieutenants Oscar Buck
and W. Arthur Cunningham, Sergeant William Bailey and
Carl Kahn of Company E, Sergeants William J. Moore,
Daniel O'Connell and Spencer T. Rossell of Company A,
Sergeants Blaustein and Private Charles Jones of H. Q.
Company.

The bodies of Eddie Kelly and Oscar Ammon of Company F, who was also killed during that night, with those
that could be gotten from the dugout were buried in Croixmare in a plot selected for the purpose near a roadside
Calvary which, from the trees surrounding it, was called
the "Croix de L'Arbre Vert" or "Green Tree Cross." The
others we left where they fell. Over the ruined dugout
we erected a marble tablet with the inscription, "Here on
the field of honor rest"—and their names.

Company E held those broken trenches with their dead
lying there all of that week and Company L during the
week following. Following is a full list of the dead:
Lieutenant John Norman, Corporal Edward Sullivan,
George Adkins, Michael Ahearn, Patrick Britt, Arthur
Christfully, William Drain, William Ellinger, Philip S.
Finn, Michael Galvin, John J. Haspel, Edward J. Kelly,
James B. Kennedy, Peter Laffey, John J. Le Gall, Charles
T. Luginsland, Frank Meagher, William A. Moylan, William H. Sage and Robert Snyder of Company E; Arthur V.
Hegney and Edward J. Kearney of Headquarters Company
and Oscar Ammon of Company F.

ARBRE HAUT

March 12th, 1918

We have given up hope of getting our dead out of Rocroi—it would be a task for the Engineers, and it would probably mean the loss of many more lives to accomplish it. Joyce Kilmer's fine instincts have given us a juster view of the propriety of letting them rest where they fell. So I went out today to read the services of the dead and bless their tomb. Company L is in that position now, and they too have been subjected to a fierce attack in which Lieutenant Booth was wounded. He and Lieutenant Baker and Corporal Lawrence Spencer are in for a Croix de Guerre for courage in action. Today there was a lot of sniping going on, so Sergeant John Donoghue and Sergeant Bill Sheahan wanted to go out to the position with me. They are two of the finest lads that Ireland has given us, full of faith and loyalty, and they had it in mind, I know, to stand each side of me and shield me from harm with their bodies. Val Roesel, Bert Landzert and Martin Coneys also insisted that they would make good acolytes for me. But I selected the littlest one in the crowd, Johnny McSherry; and little Jack trotted along the trench in front of me with his head erect while I had to bend my long back to keep my head out of harm's way. We came on Larry Spencer in an outpost position contemplating his tin hat with a smile of satisfaction. It had a deep dent in it where a bullet had hit it and then deflected—a fine souvenir.

We finished our services at the grave and returned. I lingered a while with Spencer, a youth of remarkable elevation of character—it is a good thing for a Chaplain to have somebody to look up to. Back in the woods I met two new Lieutenants, Bernard Shanley and Edward Sheffler. Shanley is from the Old Sod. Sheffler is a Chicagoan of Polish decent, a most likable youth. I gave them a good start on their careers as warriors by hearing their confessions.

That reminded me that I had some neglected parishioners in Company I, so I went over their set of trenches. Around the P. C. it looks like pictures of the houses of wattles and clay that represent the architecture of Early Britain. Met

Harry Adikes and Ed Battersby and found them easy victims when I talked confession. Where do the Irish get such names? Ask Wilton Wharton what his ancestors were and he will say "Irish"; so will Bob Cousens and Bill Cuffe, Eddie Willett, Jim Peel or Jim Vail. Charlie Cooper is half way to being Irish now, and he will be all Irish if he gets a girl I know. I know how Charlie Garret is Irish,—for he comes from my neighborhood, and if it were the custom to adopt the mother's name in a family he would be Charles Ryan. The same custom would let anybody know without his telling it, as he does with his chest out, that George Van Pelt is Irish too. I saw one swarthy fellow with MIKE KELLEY in black letters on his gas mask, but on asking him I found that he was Irish only by abbreviation, as he was christened Michael Keleshian. Tommy O'Brien made himself my guide and acolyte for my holy errand; and he first took me on a tour amongst the supply sergeants and cooks for he wanted us both well looked after. So when we had gotten Eddie Joyce, Pat Rogan, Michael O'Brien, Tom Loftus and Joe Callahan in proper Christian condition for war or hospitality, we sallied forth around the trenches.

Religion in the trenches has no aid from pealing organ or stained glass windows, but it is a real and vital thing at that. The ancestors of most of us kept their religious life burning brightly as they stole to the proscribed Mass in a secluded glen, or told their beads by a turf fire; and I find that religion thrives today in a trench with the diapason of bursting shells for an organ. I had a word or two for every man and they were glad to get it; and the consolations of the old faith for those that were looking for it. It makes a man feel better about the world and God, and the kind of people he has put into it to know in conditions like these such men as Bill Beyer, Fordham College Man; Pat Carroll, Chauffeur; Tom Brennan, Patrick Collins, whom I am just beginning to know and to like; Bill Dynan, whom I have known and liked for a long time; manly Pat Hackett and athletic Pat Flynn, solid non-coms like Ford, Hennessey, McDermott, Murphy, Denis Hogan, Michael Jordan, Hugh McFadden, not to mention the old Roman 1st Sergeant Patrick McMinaman. It was the vogue at one time to say with an air of contempt that religion is a woman's affair. I would like to have such people come up here—if they dared: and say the same thing to the soldiers of this Company or of this Regiment—if they dared.

The last outpost was an interesting one. It did not exist when I was in these parts with the 2nd Battalion, as our friends on the other side had not yet built it for us. But recently they have sent over one of their G. I. cans (that, dear reader, means galvanized iron can, which are as big as a barrel, and which tells the story of what a minenwerfer torpedo shell looks like when it is coming toward you) and the G. I. Can made a hole like the excavation of a small cottage. In it I found four or five of Company I snugly settled down and very content at being that much closer to the enemy. Here I met for the first time Ed. Shanahan, a fine big fellow who ought to make good with us, and Charlie Stone, whose mother was the last to say good-bye to me as we left Camp Mills. Mess came up while we were there and we did justice to it sitting on clumps of soft earth which had been rolled into round snowballs by the explosion—and chatting about New York.

ST. PATRICK'S DAY IN THE TRENCHES

Sunday, March 17th 1918

What a day this would have been for us if we were back in New York! Up the Avenue to St. Patrick's Cathedral in the morning, and the big organ booming out the old Irish airs and the venerable old Cardinal uttering words of blessing and encouragement. And in the afternoon out on parade with the Irish Societies with the band playing Garry Owen and Let Erin Remember and O'Donnell Aboo, as we pass through the cheering crowds. And how they would shout in this year of Grace 1918 if we could be suddenly transported to New York's Avenue of triumph. But I am glad we are not there. For more than seventy years the old Regiment has marched up the Avenue in Church parade on St. Patrick's Day. But never, thank God, when the country was at war. Other New Yorkers may see the Spring sweeping through the Carolinas or stealing timidly up the cliffs of the Hudson or along the dented shores of Long Island; but there is only one place in the world where the old Irish Regiment has any right to celebrate it, and that is on the battle line.

The 3rd Battalion is in the trenches, so I went up yesterday and spent the night with Major Moynahan, who gave me a true Irish welcome. He and Leslie have made good Irishmen out of Lieutenants Rerat and Jackson and we had a pleasant party.

We had not a Cathedral for our St. Patrick's day Mass but Lieutenant Austin Lawrence had Jim McCormack and George Daly of the Medicos pick out a spot for me among the trees to conceal my bright vestments from observation, and the men who were free slipped up the boyaus from the nearby trenches for the services.

Later in the morning I said Mass back at Camp New York for the 2nd Battalion in a grove of young birch trees on the hill slope, the men being scattered singly over the slope and holding very still when the bugler sounded the alert for an enemy aeroplane over head. I described former St. Patrick days to them and told them they were better here. New York would talk more of them, think more of them than if they were back there. Every man in the town would be saying he wished he were here and every man worth his salt would mean it. The leading men of our country had called us to fight for human liberty and the rights of small nations, and if we rallied to that noble cause we would establish a claim on our own country and on humanity in favor of the dear land from which so many of us had sprung, and which all of us loved.

In the afternoon we had a fine concert under the trees. Sergeants Frye and Tom Donahoe played for Tommy Mc-Cardle's funny songs, and for John Mullin's serious ones. McManus and Quinn played the fife for Irish dances, and Lieutenant Prout, by special request, recited John Locke's poem, "Oh Ireland, I Bid You the Top of the Morning."

In the middle of the concert I read Joyce Kilmer's noble poem, "Rouge Bouquet." The last lines of each verse are written to respond to the notes of "Taps," the bugle call for the end of the day which is also blown ere the last sods are dropped on the graves of the dead. Sergeant Patrick Stokes stood near me with his horn and blew the tender plaintive notes before I read the words; and then from the deep woods where Egan was stationed came a repetition of the notes "like horns from elfland faintly blowing." Before I had finished tears had started in many an eye especially amongst the lads of Company E. I had known it was going to be a sad moment for all, and had directed the band to follow me up with a medley of rollicking Irish airs; just as in military funerals the band leads the march to the grave in solemn cadence and departs playing a lively tune. It is the only spirit for warriors with battles yet to fight. We can pay tribute to our dead but we must not lament for them overmuch.

CROIXMARE

March 18th, 1918

I buried a soldier of the 117th Signal Battalion in Croixmare today with unusual honors. Private Wilkerson had been killed in action and as he was a Catholic Major Garrett had asked me to perform the ceremony. The French were most kind in participating, but that is no new thing. Colonel Dussauge always has his Chasseurs take part with us in funerals, though it is a distraction to me to see them trying to accommodate their short choppy gait ("like soldiers in the Movies" according to Bandsman McGregor) to the air of a Dead March. I said to the Colonel: "There is one thing your men can't do." "What is that?" "Walk to a funeral march." "Thank you for the compliment, Monsieur l'Aumonier." The Curé, too, always came to our funerals. And we had a fine grizzled old Oblate Division Chaplain who has been in all the French wars from Madagascar to Tonquin. The Government tried to put him out of France when the law against Religious was passed, but he refused to go, saying he would live his life in France if he had to live it in jail. I met a number of these religious in the army, most of them returned from exile to offer their lives in defense of their country. If the French Government puts them out after the war is over they will deserve the scorn and enmity of mankind as a rotten set of ingrates.

At the grave we found we had other spectators. I saw General Menoher and General Lenihan with a short spare-built civilian whom I took for a reporter. He had a French gas mask with a long tape, which hung down between his legs like a Highlander's sporran. There were Moving Picture cameras too, which seemed to spell a Presence. I whispered to the old Curé that his picture would be put on the screen in every town in America, at which he was, I could see, somewhat shocked and altogether pleased. After the ceremony a number of the Signal Battalion took advantage of the opportunity to go to confession; and I was standing by the side of a truck performing my pious duties when General Lenihan approached with the slim reporter. They did not intrude, so I missed my chance of making the acquaintance of the energetic Newton W. Baker, Secretary of War of the United States.

LUNÉVILLE

March 21st, 1918

For the past twelve days volunteers from the 1st Battalion have been preparing, under command of Lieutenants Henry

A. Bootz and Raymond H. Newton, for a *coup de main* in connection with the 41st Battalion of Chasseurs. They have been training with the French at Croixmare and I find it interesting to watch them. They go through all sorts of athletic stunts to get into perfect condition, study the ground through maps on the blackboard showing just what each man's position is to be, and then work out the whole thing over a ground which is very much like the Ouvrage Blanc, where the raid will take place.

Last Saturday afternoon, after I had been hearing confessions amongst them, four or five of the Irish lads waited to see me. I went for a walk with them around an old moat and as we stood looking at a stone tablet that commemorated the victory of some Duke of Lorraine over a Duke of Burgundy four hundred years ago, Billy Elwood put the question, "Father, do you think we'll be afraid?" "Not you," I said, "not a bit of it. You may feel rather tight across the chest for the five minutes before you tear into it, but when you get going you'll forget even that, because your blood will be up." "I believe you," he said. "Of course you know none of us are afraid and we are all anxious to have a try at it, but it's our first time in a thing of this sort and the only worry we have is that something might go wrong inside of us and spoil the good name of the Irish."

Before the raid started there was an amusing little interlude. Corporal Bob Foster of Company D had a little Irish flag given to him by Sergeant Evers of the Band, and the lads were determined that that flag would go over the top in the first organized attack made by the regiment. A young officer, not of our Division, who had been sent as an observer, saw the flag stuck at the top of Foster's rifle and felt it his duty to protest against it. After a short parley Bootz demanded, "What are you here for, anyway." "I'm an observer," was the response. "Then climb a tree and observe, and let me run this raid."

Our artillery was busy bombarding the position that was

to be the object of assault and at 7:35 P. M. the men went out through our wires under cover of darkness and took up their position near the *chicanes* (passages) in the enemy wire, which had been reconnoitered the night before. Our artillery laid down a barrage at 7:50 for a space of three minutes upon which the front line advanced and got possession of the German trenches without opposition, as the Germans had evacuated them during the heavy bombardment of the past two days. They were just in time in reaching shelter for the German artillery began to shell their own abandoned line most vigorously. The trouble about this attack was that our own artillery preparation had been too good. The Germans could not help inferring that this point was to be made the object of an assault, so they drew back and waited until the infantry had reached the position. Then they turned on them the full force of artillery and machine gun fire from positions further back, leaving to the assaulters the choice between getting back to their own lines, or attacking an unknown and well defended position in the dark. The French Officer in charge gave the order to retire. During this period Edward Maher of Company B must have been killed because no word of him was ever received. Corporal William Elwood and Joseph Miller of Company C were fatally wounded. Badly wounded were Sergeants John F. Scully, Fred Almendinger and Martin Gill of Company A and Patrick Grogan of Company D. After getting back to the French trenches Bootz and Newton repeatedly led parties back over the shell-swept area to search for Maher, and to see if the Germans had reoccupied their trenches. On this mission Thomas P. Minogue of Company B was killed. Lieutenant Newton carried in one French soldier and Private Plant carried in another. Lieutenant Bootz, with Corporal Joseph Pettit of Company C, helped Sergeant Scully to the lines, and going out again, they found Joe Miller, his right leg amputated by a shell. Miller was a big man but Bootz swung him up on his back and with Pettit assisting, carried him back into the lines.

The following officers and men taking part in this *coup de main* were decorated by the French authorities on March 22nd at Croixmare: Division Citations, First Lieutenant Henry A. Bootz, Second Lieutenant Raymond H. Newton, Private Marlow Plant; Regimental Citations: Company A, Joseph C. Pettit, Frank J. Fisher, Privates George McCarthy, Bernard McOwen, Michael Morley, Sergeant John Scully; Company B, Sergeants Spiros Thomas, Christian Biorndall, Corporal William F. Judge, Privates Frank Brandreth, Vincent J. Eckas, Daniel J. Finnegan; Company C, Sergeant Eugene A. McNiff, Corporal Herman E. Hillig, Privates Bernard Barry, Michael Cooney, James Barry, John J. Brawley, Joseph A. Miller; Company D, Sergeant Thomas M. O'Malley, Corporal Thomas H. Brown, Privates Denis O'Connor, Patrick Grogan, John Cahill, Harry H. DeVoe.

Of the wounded, Elwood died shortly after being brought to the Hospital at Lunéville and Joe Miller succumbed the next day after sufferings borne with a fortitude that begot the admiration of nurses and doctors used to dealing with courageous men. The others are wounded badly enough but they will recover. Almendinger, who describes himself as "half Boche and half County Kilkenny," was going off to the operating ward to have his wounded eye removed when I saw him the second time. "Never mind about that, Fred," I said, "Uncle Sam will look after you." "I'm not thinking about Uncle Sam at all. There's a girl back in New York who doesn't care whether I have one eye or two. so I should worry."

THE GAS ATTACK

March 20th and 21st, 1918

But meanwhile there had been other happenings in the sector which quite overshadowed the 1st Battalion raid.

Company K went into the line in the Rouge Bouquet Sector on March 12th, 1918, relieving Company H. The Company Headquarters were at Chaussailles, and the two platoons in the front line were: on the right, at Changarnier (C. R. 1), one platoon; in the center at C. R. 2 a half platoon; and on the left at Chevert (C. R. 3) a half platoon.

There were no casualties for the first eight days except that John Ring received a bullet in the arm. Our patrols did not come into contact with the Boches (who apparently never left their lines) and except a few minenwerfer and some shelling with 77's the sector was quiet, the weather was fine, and every one spoke of the tour at the front as a picnic.

About 5:30 on the evening of the 20th the Boches suddenly began to bombard the entire company sector, from a line not far from their own trenches to a line several hundred yards in the rear of Company Headquarters, with mustard gas shells and shrapnel, the heaviest bombardment being in the vicinity of C. R. 2, where Sergeant Frank Doughney was in command, of C. R. 3, where Lieutenant Bill Crane was in command, and at the first aid station, where Lieutenant Patten and his group were quartered, together with the fourth platoon under Lieutenant Levi. This bombardment lasted about three hours.

The groups stationed at the outposts were caught on their way in, the two groups under Corporals Caulfield and Joe Farrell being led by Corporal Farrell into an incomplete dugout about 300 yards in front of our lines, the other two going directly in.

The second platoon, under Lieutenant Dowling in Changarnier, were not so heavily shelled and being on higher ground, were not gassed so badly as the others.

In C. R. 2, Harry McCoun was struck by a shell which carried away his left hand. He held up the stump and shouted, "Well, boys, there goes my left wing." Sergeant Jack Ross and Private Ted Van Yorx led him under heavy

fire back to the first aid station, where Doctor Patten
tore off his mask to operate on him (for which he earned
the Croix de Guerre), but McCoun died the next morning.

In C. R. 3, Lieutenant Crane walked from one post to
the other in the midst of the heaviest bombardment in order
to encourage the men. In the midst of this bombardment,
several of the runners, including particularly Privates Ed
Rooney and Ray Staber, distinguished themselves by their
courage and coolness in carrying messages between Company headquarters and the front line.

The men were prompt in putting on their masks as soon
as the presence of gas was recognized, but it was found
impossible to keep them on indefinitely and at the same
time keep up the defense of the sector. Immediately after
the bombardment, the entire company area reeked with the
odor of mustard gas and this condition lasted for several days. It had been raining heavily the night before, and
there was no breeze whatever.

By about midnight some of the men were sick as a result
of the gas, and as the night wore on, one after another they
began to feel its effects on their eyes, to cry, and gradually
to go blind, so that by dawn a considerable number from
the front line had been led all the way back and were sitting
by the Lunéville road, completely blinded, and waiting their
turn at an ambulance, and the third platoon were unable
to furnish enough men to man all their posts and were
compelled to ask for replacements.

Meanwhile, about ten o'clock at night, the first and
fourth platoons had been ordered to leave their reserve
positions and march back to the Lunéville road and down
the cross-road on the other side where they lay down in the
mud and slept till morning. In the morning they filtered
down to replace the casualties in the other two platoons.

About three o'clock in the morning Lieutenant (Doctor)
Martin came down in the midst of the gas to relieve Lieutenant Patten, who had been blinded and taken to the hos-

pital. Lieutenant Martin was himself affected by the gas and went blind on the following morning.

By dawn, the men were going blind one after another, and being ordered to the hospital. Often, by the time they got to the ambulance, the man leading was himself blind and both got into the ambulance together. Not a man lost his head or lay down on the job and not a man left for the hospital until he was stone blind, or ordered to go by an officer, and a number of men were blinded while on post, while others stuck it out for so long that it was finally necessary to carry them on stretchers to the dressing station; and this although all had been instructed that mustard gas was one of the most deadly gases and that it caused blindness which lasted for months and was in many cases permanent.

By ten o'clock in the morning fully two-thirds of the company had been blinded, and about this time Lieutenants Crane, Dowling and Levi, and Captain Hurley one after the other went blind and were led back, followed later by Lieutenant Burns.

Throughout the day the men continued to go blind, until by seven o'clock only about thirty were left, almost all of whom were in the front line, under command of Lieutenant Tom Martin, and they were so few that it was necessary for them to go on post for four hours at a stretch, with two hours off, and some of them, including Tom Hickey, Barney Furey, John McLoughlin, Pat McConnell and Jerry O'Connor were on post for as long as six hours at a time.

At seven o'clock Lieutenant Hunt Warner, with Lieutenant Zipp, appeared with reinforcements, consisting of forty men from Company M. Lieutenant Warner was put in command at Chevert with Sergeant Embrie of Company K, as second in command; Sergeant Von Glahn of Company M, was put in command at C. R. 2, where the gas was at that time especially heavy; and Lieutenant Zipp was put in command at Changarnier, with Corporal Joe Farrell, who knew the sector thoroughly and spent the night going from one post to another, as second in command, Lieutenant Tom Martin at Changarnier being in command of the whole company sector.

That evening about dusk the men in the front line heard an explosion in the rear and looked back in time to see the battalion ammunition dump go up in a blaze of glory, on seeing which all broke into applause and loud cheers. It was thought that the Boches might be so foolish as to think the evening propitious for a raid, and all posts were manned and all were ready to give him a warm reception, but he failed to show up.

At seven next morning the French appeared and the relief was completed by about nine o'clock, when the survivors set out for Lunéville, where they were taken in hand by Lieutenant Arnold, who ordered them all, much against their protest, to a hospital where they were surprised to find that they were casualties, their injuries consisting principally of burns on the body, which had just begun to show up, and which kept most of them in the hospital for at least a month.

On their arrival at the hospital they found there some of the French troops who had relieved them on that morning and who had already become casualties because of the gas which lingered in the area.

The men killed, besides McCoun, were Salvatore Moresca, whose body was found by the French in No Man's Land the day after the Company was relieved, Carl Braun, of Headquarters Company, hit by bullet, with Robert Allen, Walter Bigger, and Lawrence Gavin, who died in the hospital within a day or two as a result of the effect of the gas on their lungs. About four hundred of our men were put out of action in this gas attack including practically all of K Company, many of M, and some from Headquarters, Supply and Medical.

The event had one consoling feature, and that was the superb conduct of the men. They had been told most awful stories of the effect of gas. When they found that their whole position was saturated with it, they felt that their chances to live through it were slender, and that they would surely be blind for a long time. And yet not a single man quit his post until ordered. There was no disorder or panic; the men of Company K were forced to quit their position, but they quit it one by one, and every man was a subject for a hospital long before he left. And the Company M men coming up to take over the position, and seeing the blinded and tortured soldiers going back, had courage in equal measure. Soldiers that will stand up to it as these had done under the terrors and sufferings of that night can be relied on for anything that men can be called on to do.

LUNÉVILLE

March 23rd, 1918

We are quitting this sector and going back to the Langres area to rest up a bit and study out the lessons we have learned. Most of the companies have started already. The Germans are shelling this city today for the first time in over three years. It is an interesting experience to be in a shelled city, and, so far as I can see the results, not a particularly dangerous one.

ST. BOINGT

Palm Sunday, 1918

This has been an ideal Spring day. I said Mass in the village church for the "4th Battalion" (Headquarters, Machine Gun, Sanitary and Supply Companies). Later in the morning Major Lawrence and I dropped in to the High Mass. I was interested in the palms. When I was a lad we used cedar, before the days when ships from the Spanish Main brought their cargoes of broad palmetto leaves, which we carry in our hands on Palm Sunday and wear in our hats through Holy Week. Here they use anything fresh,.

young and growing, that the country and the season afford. The people pluck small branches from the trees on their way to Mass, the preference being for willow shoots with their shiny yellow green bark and furry buds. There is a fine old-world countryside flavor to this custom of plucking these offerings to the Lord from one's own trees or along familiar lanes, that we never get from our boughten palms.

This I felt especially when I saw what they were doing with them. When the procession began, everybody arose and followed the crossbearer out of the church portals into the mellow spring morning. Around the church they went, their ranks now swelled by a crowd of our own soldiers. Our route lay through the graves of the village dead. At each grave a lone figure or a small group would detach themselves and kneel in prayer while they stuck their fresh young twigs in the soil around it. We too found a place for our offerings and prayers when we came to a recently made mound with a Croix de Guerre and bronze palm embossed upon its stone—a French soldier, "Mort pour la Patrie." We borrowed pussy willows from the people and pulled branches of green box, and covered that grave with them while we made our soldier's orisons for the man that was sleeping there, and for our own fine lads that we had left behind in the dugout at Rocroi and under the Green Tree Cross at Croixmare.

After Mass I started off across the fields to visit the 2nd Battalion at Essey la Côte. A wonderful spring day—fresh and sweet and clear. From the hill one could see the dull red tiles of twenty villages clustering along the slopes of the rolling landscape. Faint sounds of distant church bells came to my ears; and nearer, clearer notes from overhead such as I had never heard before. Skylarks! It was the final touch to make it a perfect morning.

I dropped down to the road which led to the nestling village, and met a band of children romping out. Here too was spring. They gathered round me, not at all shy, for they were bubbling with excitement and anxious to talk. The American soldiers—they were so big—and so young—and so nice—and so devout (they filled the church at three Masses)—and so rich (they gave money like nobody had ever seen before, and the Commandant had put a twenty franc note on the collection plate). "Good Old Bill Stacom," I mused, "we are both far away from our little parish in the Bronx, but he has not forgotten my teachings on the first duty of the laity."

I dined with Captain Jim Finn and his happy family of bright young Lieutenants—Sherman Platt and Becker and Otto and Flynn, clean cut active youngsters who enjoy their work and are delighted at serving with the old Regiment. I spent the afternoon amongst the men. They too were enjoying the day lazily, cleaning up equipment in chatty groups or propped against sunny walls, or wandering through the fields. They have heard of the big German Drive in the north and they know that we have been halted and are to be sent in somewhere. They are somewhat disappointed at not getting back to Longeau and Baissey and Cohons and Percey once more, but if there is anything big happening they don't want to miss it. That's what we are here for.

Billy Kaas offered to be my guide to the hilltop, from which the whole countryside can be seen for miles around. The spot is interesting for other reasons. It marks the high water level of the German invasion of Lorraine in 1914, and now it marks the furthest backward step we are to make on this journey. I feel prophetic twitchings that it will be a long long time before we are allowed to pitch our tents in that part of France over there which has not known invasion by the enemy. The news from the North is grave, and our side will need every soldier it has if the Germans are to be held off. And that is a job that will take a lot of doing. Well, as the men say, "that's what we are here for."

ST. REMY AUX BOIS

March 27th, 1918

Dropped over in the morning to call on the First Battalion. I found them in the field, where Donovan had had them lined up for a cross country run. I prudently kept out of his way until he was off with his wild youngsters, and then I looked up George McAdie, who had a stay-at-home duty. Reilley and Kennelly and McKenna were cavorting cross country with the rest. Good enough for them —athletics is a big part of their lives. But George and I are philosophers. So while Donovan led his gang across brooks and barbwire fences and over hills and through woods, George and I sat discussing the most interesting beings in the world; soldier men—their loyalty, courage, humor, their fits of laziness and sulkiness. He pointed out to me a dark Celt who had been discontented with the mean drudgery of a soldier's life and was hard to manage. Different methods had been tried to jack him up. All failed until the Captain gave him a chance to go over in the Lunéville raid. At last he found something the lad was eager about. He went through the training with cheerfulness, distinguished himself under fire for his cool alacrity, and is now playing the game like a veteran.

Finally the harriers got back, the Major the freshest man amongst them. "Oh, Father," he said, "why didn't you get here earlier? You missed a fine time." "My Guardian Angel was taking good care of me, William," I said, "and saw to it that I got here late."

In the afternoon the band came over and we had a band concert in the church square and afterwards a vaudeville show given by the men. The Major was asked to say something and he smilingly passed the buck to me. I got square by telling the story of a Major who had been shot at by a German sniper while visiting one of his companies in the trenches. He made a big fuss about it with the Captain, who in turn bawled out an old sergeant for allowing such things to happen. The sergeant went himself to settle the Heinie that was raising all the trouble. Finally he got sight of his man, took careful aim and fired. As he saw his shot reach home, he muttered, "Take that, confound you, for missing the Major."

BACCARAT

Easter Sunday Night

Yesterday we were at Xaffévillers, Magnières and St. Pierremont. For my Easter celebration I picked Magnières, as the whole 2nd Battalion was there and two companies of the 1st in St. Pierremont, only ten minutes away. For confessions I set up shop in the street at the crossways, and I had a busy day of it. There was always a long file waiting, but when nobody has much to tell the task is soon sped.

I stayed with Stacom. It is always a pleasure to be with Stacom and his officers. He has a way of kindly mastery that begets affectionate loyalty. A man likes Stacom even when he is getting a call down from him. At supper with Doc Houghton, Joe O'Donohue, Arthur Martin, McDermott, Fechheimer, Landrigan, Ewing Philbin, Billy Burns Guggenheim, and Joe McNamara. A man might search the list of all his acquaintances and not find a set of men so congenial and happily disposed.

I looked up the Curé, an alert slender youngish man with a keen intelligent face, a soldier just back that day *en permission* to keep the old feast with his own people. The Germans had held him as a hostage in 1914 and had thrice threatened to shoot him, though he had looked after their wounded. If thoroughness was their motto they would have been wiser to do it, I reflected as I talked with him; for he was a man that would count wherever he went, and he certainly had no use for Germans. "Too big a man for this place. We won't be able to keep him long," said Stacom's landlady, a pleasant thoughtful woman, whose son of seventeen was just back for the holidays from some college where he is beginning his studies for the priesthood.

The village church was a ruin. Both sides had used it to fight from and both sides had helped to wreck it. The roof was gone and most of the side walls. The central tower over the entrance still stood, though the wooden beams above had burned, and the two big bells had dropped clean through onto the floor. The Curé used a meeting-room in the town hall for his services, but that would not do for my congregation. The church faced a long paved square, so I decided to set up my altar in the entrance and have the men hear Mass in the square. The church steps served excellently for Communion. It is one of the things I wish I had a picture of—my first Easter service in France; the old ruined church for a background, the simple altar in the doorway, and in front that sea of devout young faces paying their homage to the Risen Savior. My text lay around me—the desecrated temple, the soldier priest by my side, the uniforms we wore, the hope of triumph over evil that the Feast inspired, the motive that brought us here to put an end to this terrible business of destruction, and make peace prevail in the world. Here more than a thousand soldiers were present, and the great majority crowded forward at Communion time to receive the Bread of Life.

I hiked it into Baccarat with the Battalion. At a point on the road the separated elements of the Regiment met and swung in behind each other. Colonel Barker stopped his horse on a bank above the road and watched his men go by, with feelings of pride in their fine appearance and the knowledge of how cheerfully they had given up their prospects of a rest and were going back into the lines again. With his usual kind courtesy, he wanted to have me ride, but for once I preferred to hike, as I was having a good time.

Arriving in Baccarat I ran into Captain Jack Mangan,—always a joyous encounter. We found a hotel and something to eat; met there Major Wheeler, Ordnance Officer of Division, a Southerner of the finest type. I tried to start a row between him and Mangan. I always like to hear these supply people fight—they battle with each other with such genial vigor. When they began to swap compliments I left them, to look up the Y. M. C. A. to see if there were religious services in town that I could announce to my Protestant fellows.

CHAPTER IV

THE BACCARAT SECTOR

BACCARAT

March, 1918

To speak in guide-book fashion, Baccarat is a town of 15,000 people situated in the wide, flat valley of the Meurthe River. It possesses a well-known glass factory and a rather elegant parish church, whose elegance is just now slightly marred by two clean shell-shots, one through its square tower and the other through the octagonal spire. The most extensive ruins, dating from the German capture of the town in 1914, are those of the blocks on both sides of the street between the church and the river. They were caused, not by shell fire, but by deliberate arson, for some actions of the townspeople, real or fancied. A few broken walls are standing with all the chimneys still intact, sticking up amongst them like totem poles. Charlie Brooks, making believe that the ruins were caused by shell fire, said to me "In case of bombardment, I know the safest place to get. Sit right up on top of a chimney and let them shoot away."

West of the river the hill rises steeply and is crowned by the picturesque old walled village of Deneuvre, dating certainly from the early Middle Ages, and, local antiquarians say, from Roman times. Here are established our regimental headquarters, with the four special companies, and the whole of the third battalion, or what is left of it, as Company K consists of Lieutenant Howard Arnold, Sergeant Embree, Company Clerk Michael Costello and two privates, who were absent on other duties when the Company was gassed; and Company M is reduced to half its strength. The first battalion is very comfortably situated in the Haxo Barracks at the north end of Baccarat, the 2nd Battalion being at present at Neufmaisons, ten kilometers out toward the front lines. The regiment was selected as division reserve on account of the depleted strength of our 3rd Battalion.

BACCARAT

April 2, 1918

At last we have located the gassed members of our 3rd Battalion in the hospitals at Vittel and Contrexéville; and today, as Lieutenant Knowles had the kindly thought of bringing their pay to them, Donovan, Mangan and myself took advantage of the opportunity to go and see them. The hospitals were formerly hotels in these summer resorts and serve excellently for their present purpose. Many of the men are still in bed, lying with wet cloths over their poor eyes, and many of them have been terribly burned about the body, especially those whose duties called upon them to make exertions which used perspiration. Among these is John McGuire of the Supply Company and many of the sanitary detachment, such as Sergeant Lokker, Ed. McSherry, James Butler, Michael Corbett and John J. Tierney, who have been recommended for the Croix de Guerre for courage and devotion in saving the wounded. Sergeant Russell, with Corporals Beall and Brochon of the Headquarters Company are also suffering for their zeal in maintaining liaison.

But it is Company K that had to bear the brunt of it. Of the officers, Lieutenant Crane is in the most critical condition, and it was a touching thing as I went through the ward to hear every single man in his platoon forget his own pain to inquire about the Lieutenant. Some of the men are still in very bad shape, Richard O'Gorman, George Sicklick, Val Prang, Sergeant Gleason, Bernard Leavy, Francis Meade, James Mullin and also Mortimer Lynch,

Christopher Byrne, Daniel Dooley, Gerard Buckley, Harold Benham, Harold Broe, Kilner McLaughlin, and Buglers Nya and Rice. The cooks did not escape—Pat Boland, William Mulcahy, Moriarty, Thomas O'Donnell and Michael O'Rourke, who, by the way, is one of those Czecho-Slovaks who has chosen to fight under a martial name. The Wisconsins also have been hard hit, and two of their men here, Corporal John Sullivan and Leo Moquin, are painfully burned on account of their exertions in carrying others. I have turned the names of these two in with a recommendation for citation, with those of Staber, Farrell, Ross, Van Yorx, Montross, Beall, Brochon, McCabe and the medicos mentioned. Sergeant Leo Bonnard, in liaison with the French, has received his cross on their recommendation. Lieutenant Tom Martin and Dr. Patton also received the same decoration.

Apart from Lieutenant Crane, none of the officers is in serious condition, though more than half of the officers in the battalion are in the hospital, including Major Moynahan, Captains Hurley, Merle-Smith, and Meaney, Lieutenants Leslie, Stevens, and Rerat, with nearly all the lieutenants of Company K and M, and also Major Lawrence with Lieutenants Patton and Arthur Martin of the Sanitary Detachment, who deser high praise for their handling of a difficult situation.

The Company M men were not so badly gassed, with the exception of Sergeant Emerson. A good many of them were walking about with eyes only slightly inflamed. I was immediately surrounded by Eustace, Flanigan, Jack Manson, Harry Messmer, Bill Lanigan, Mark White, Jock Cameron and a lot of others, all clamoring for news about the regiment. I made myself a candidate for being canonized as a saint by working at least a hundred first class miracles when I announced that we had come with the pay. The news was received with a shout, "Gimme me pants, I'm all better now."

There was one thing that disturbed us. We found most

of our injured in these two towns, but there was still a considerable number whose pay we had that we could not find, and nobody was able to tell where they had been sent.

BACCARAT

April 7th, 1918

The reports which have arrived of the death in hospital of Robert Allen, Walter Bigger and Lawrence Gavin of Company K gave us our first information concerning the whereabouts of soldiers whom we could not discover in our trip to the hospital. They died at the new Army Hospital at Bazoilles near Neufchateau. As Tom Johnson of the New York *Sun* was visiting us, he offered to take me back with him in his car to see them. They are in long, one-story hospital barracks and most of them are almost recovered although Amos Dow and Herbert Kelly are still very sick boys. With the assistance of the two First Sergeants of K and M, Tim Sullivan and James McGarvey, who are also patients, I paid them all off.

I also gave them a bit of news which was more gratefully received than the pay, and that is saying a great deal. One of the hospital authorities told me that a special order had arrived that men of the 165th who would be fit for duty by a certain date should be returned direct to the regiment without going through a casual camp. He told me also that the order was entirely an exceptional one, adding laughingly that he would be glad to get rid of them. He said they were the liveliest and most interesting lot of patients he ever had to deal with, but they made themselves infernal pests by agitating all the time to get back to their confounded old regiment. Howard Gregory came up with a side car to take me back and I had another chance to see our men in the other two hospitals and was glad to find that they are all on the road to recovery.

REHERREY

April 25th, 1918

On April 23rd, and a miserable day of rain and mud it was, we relieved the Ohios in the positions on the left of our Division Sector. Looking east from Baccarat one sees only a steep hill which forms the valley of the Meurthe and blocks the view in the direction of the combat line; but a road from the north of the town leads through an opening in the hills to undulating country with small villages dotting the landscape every two or three miles. One of these is Reherrey, which is to be our regimental P. C. during our stay in this section. The next village to the east, called Migneville, shelters our support battalion, the P. C. of the advance battalion being at Montigny, still farther on.

The trenches are more varied and more interesting than those in the Forest of Parroy. Those on the left of our sector run along the front edge of the Bois Bouleaux, which gives its occupants the shelter of trees, but leaves them in a position to see an approaching enemy. The trenches to the right run over open ground and finally straight across the eastern tip of the town of Ancervillers, utilizing the cellars, broken walls, etc. Machine gun nests have been established in some of the cellars which dominate the open spaces, the guns being raised to be able to fire at ground level through carefully concealed concrete openings. The 1st battalion is in line, the 3rd in support, while the 2nd is in "Camp Mud," a group of barracks to the rear of us in surroundings which provoke its title. Poor fellows, they would much rather be in a battle.

REHERREY

April 28th, 1918

Went over Saturday to St. Pol where Companies L and M are in support positions and passed the night with Merle-Smith and his Lieutenants, Carroll, Baker, Givens and

Knowles. The village church is pretty badly wrecked, parts of the walls and most of the roof being tumbled down in crumbled ruins. One shell went through just in front of the altar, but the roof above the altar is fairly well intact. I had doubts as to whether I could use it for services, but Cornelius Fitzpatrick and Frank Eustace offered to have it cleaned up and put in shape for me by next morning. When I arrived to say Mass I was delighted at the transformation they had effected. The half ruined reredos of the altar was a mass of bloom with big branches of blossoms which they had cut from the fruit trees in the garden. It is one of the pictures of the war that I shall long carry in my mind.

One of the men told me that Joyce Kilmer had been out here on his duties as Sergeant of the Intelligence Section to map out the ground with a view to its defence if attacked. As his party was leaving the ruined walls he said, "I never like to leave a church without saying a prayer," and they all knelt down among the broken fragments under the empty vault and said a silent prayer—a beautiful thought of a true poet and man of God.

REHERREY

May 5th, 1918

Headquarters, both American and French, have been very anxious for somebody to take prisoners, and we were all very much pleased this morning to hear that a patrol from Company D had gone out and bagged four of them. Out across No Man's Land from Ancervillers there is, or used to be, a few houses which went by the name of Hameau d'Ancervillers. There was some reason to believe that a German outpost might be found there; so at midnight last night a patrol of two officers and twenty-four men, mainly from Company D, went on a little hunting expedition. They crossed No Man's Land to the old German trenches, which they found to be battered flat.

Lieutenant Edmond J. Connelly remained with a few

men in No Man's Land to guard against surprise, and Lieutenant Henry K. Cassidy took the rest of them, including Sergeant John J. O'Leary of Company A, Sergeant Thomas O'Malley of Company D and Sergeant John T. Kerrigan of the Intelligence Section to examine the ruins of the hamlet. Part of the wall of one house was left standing. O'Leary led three men to one side of it, and O'Malley three others to the other side, while Lieutenant Cassidy approached it from the front. They were challenged by a German sentry and the two Sergeants with their followers rushed at once to close quarters and found themselves engaged with six Germans, two of whom were killed, and one wounded, the survivors dashing headlong into a dugout.

Lieutenant Cassidy, pistol in hand, ran to the opening of the dugout and called on them to surrender. If any one of them had any fight left in him we would have had to mourn the loss of a brave young officer, but they surrendered at discretion, and our whole party, with no casualties, started back as fast as they could, carrying the wounded prisoner and dragging the others with them. It was an excellent job, done with neatness and dispatch. Valuable papers were found on the wounded man and other information was obtained at Division by questioning. The only thing to spoil it was that two of our men, Corporal Joseph Brown and Charles Knowlton got lost in the dark coming in, and have not yet reported.*

REHERREY

May 9th, 1918

War is a time of sudden changes and violent wrenches of the heart strings; and we are getting a taste of it even before we enter into the period of battles. We are to lose Colonel Barker. Back in Washington they are looking for

* These men became confused and wandered into the German lines where they were made prisoners. Information concerning their fate came to us through the Red Cross about two months later, and both rejoined the regiment after the Armistice.

men who know the war game as it is played over here, and, as Colonel Barker has been observing it, or engaged in it, since the war began, they have ordered him back to report for duty at the War Department.

Our regrets at his going are lessened by two considerations. The first is that we feel he will get his stars by reason of the change and it will make us glad for him and proud for ourselves to see one of our Colonels made a General. The other is the news that his successor is to be Frank R. McCoy, of General Headquarters. He was not a Colonel on the General Staff when we crossed his path first, but Captain McCoy of the 3rd Cavalry, stationed at Mission, Texas. I did not meet him down there, but heard a whole lot about him—all good—from Colonel Haskell, and from Colonel Gordon Johnston of the 12th New York, who had been a captain with McCoy in the 3rd Cavalry. About the time we got to Mission he was made Chief of Staff to General Parker at Brownsville. Later I read of his going to Mexico as military attaché with our new Ambassador, Mr. Fletcher, and then that General Pershing had reached out after him there to bring him over here with the A. E. F. In the more remote past he has been Aide de Camp to General Woods, Military Aide at the White House under President Roosevelt, and on special duty for the government on various semi-diplomatic missions. If this list of employments had any tendency to make me wonder how much of a soldier he was, it would have vanished quickly after one look at his left breast which is adorned with five service bars. They say in the army that McCoy has done all kinds of duty that an officer can be called upon to do, but has never missed a fight—a good omen for the "Fighting Sixty-Ninth."

He is a man of good height, of spare athletic figure, with a lean strongly formed face, nose Roman and dominating, brows capacious, eyes and mouth that can be humorous, quizzical or stern, as I learned by watching him, in the first five minutes. He has dignity of bearing, charm of manner and an alert and wide-ranging intelligence that embraces men, books, art, nature. If he only thinks as well of us as we are going to think of him I prophesy that he will have this regiment in the hollow of his hand to do what he likes with it. Everything helps. *"McCoy,* is it? Well, he has a good name anyway," said one of the "boys from home."

Colonel McCoy came to us in the lines, the P. C. being at Reherrey. The *popotte* (mess) occupied two low-ceiled rooms in a three-room cottage. We sat close together on benches at a long plank table, but it was a jolly company. To give the new Colonel a taste of his Regiment I told him a monologue by one of our men *that I had overheard the* evening before. There are a couple of benches right in front of my billet, in the narrow space between the dung-heap and the window, and there is always a lot of soldiers around there in their free time. They know I am inside the open window, but pay no attention to my presence—a real compliment.

There was a military discussion on among the bunch from Company C. They got talking about the German policy of evacuating the front line trenches when we send over a concentrated barrage preparatory to a raid, and then letting fly at us with their machine guns as we return empty-handed. Somebody said he thought it was a good thing. This irritated my friend Barney Barry, solid Irishman, good soldier, and I may add, a saintly-living man. "But Oi don't loike it," he said, "Oi don't loike it at all. It looks *too* much loike rethreatin',—I think they betther lave us be. Take the foive uv us here—me and Jim Barry and Pat Moran and Moike Cooney, and you Unger—you're a Dootchman, but you're a good man—the foive of us in a thrench with our roifles and what we'd have on us to shoot, and a couple uv exthra bandoliers, and a bunch of thim *guinny foot-balls* (hand grenades) and a bit of wire up in front; and if the young officers u'd only keep their heads, and not be sayin' 'Do this; and don't do that'; gettin' themselves excoited, and whot's worse, gettin' us excoited, but just lave us be, I give ye me wurrd that be the toime mornin' u'd come, and ye'd come to be buryin' thim, ye'd think ye had your old job back diggin' the subway." .

The Colonel was delighted with this sample of the spirit of his Irish regiment. And I determined to let him see the whole works at once. He might as well get the full flavor of the Regiment first as last. We had a concert going on in the next room. Tom O'Kelly sang in his fine full rich baritone the "Low Back Car" and that haunting Scottish melody of "Loch Lomond."

"Give us a rebel song, Tom," I called. "What's that, sir—Father, I mean." McCoy twinkled delightedly. "A rebel song," I repeated. "Alright, Father, what shall I sing." "Oh, you know a dozen of them. 'The West's Awake,' 'O'Donnel Aboo' or 'A Nation Once Again.'" Tom responded readily with "O'Donnel Aboo," and as its defiant strains ended in a burst of applause he broke into the blood stirring old rebel ballad, "The Wearing of the Green." Colonel McCoy's face was beaming. He evidently likes things to have their proper atmosphere. I can see the old Irish 69th is just what he expected it to be, and what he wanted it to be. I see there is no worry in his mind about how these singers of rebel songs will do their part in this war.

I had a long talk with him today about the Regiment, and I find him anxious to keep up its spirit and traditions. They are as dear to him for their romantic flavor and their military value as those of the Household Guards or the Black Watch are to the Englishman or the Scot.

REHERREY

May 12th, 1918

Majors Moynahan and Stacom are being transferred to other duties, much to everybody's regret. It looks like a break up of the old Regiment. It would be, I fear, if anybody but McCoy were Colonel. But he has a slate for pro-

motion already; a 69th slate, and he will put it through if
anybody can—Anderson and James McKenna for Majors,
Prout and Bootz and W. McKenna for Captains. It will
save the spirit of the regiment if he can carry this through.
If the vacancies are filled by replacement we shall not know
ourselves in a short time. I feel all the more grateful to
our new Colonel because he had a share in planning the
replacement idea; and besides, I know that there are plenty
of officers at General Headquarters, friends of his, who
are anxious to get to the front and to have the 69th on their
service records. It would be an embarrassment to any other
man to go to G. H. Q. and ask them to change the scheme
of filling vacancies by replacement instead of by promotion. But I know just what will happen, when they say
"Why, you helped to make this plan." He will smile be-
nignly, triumphantly and say "That just proves my point.
Now that I am in command of a regiment I find by first
hand knowledge that the original plan does not work out
well."

DENEUVRE

May 15th, 1918

Our allotted three weeks in line being up, we returned
to our original stations, the only change being that the 2nd
Battalion comes to Deneuvre, while the 3rd has to go to
Camp Mud. I am billetted with the Curé, a devout and
amiable priest—who was carried off as a hostage by the
Germans in their retreat of 1914 and held by them for over
a year. He likes to have Americans around, and we fill
his house. Captain Anderson, Lieutenants Walsh, Howe,
Allen and Parker are domiciled with me. Joe Bruell and
Austin McSweeney have their wireless in a room in the
house, and draw down all sorts of interesting messages
from the other Sergeants. Sergeants McCarthy, Esler and
Russell are next door neighbors, and better neighbors no
man could choose. I can go down to the dooryard if time
hangs on my hands and hear remarks on men and things,

made more piquant by New York slang or Irish brogue.

It is a delight to go to our mess with McCoy's stimulating wit 'and Lieutenant Colonel Mitchell's homely philosophy and Mangan's lively comments, and the various aspects of war and life opened up by all sorts of interesting people—Bishops, diplomats, soldiers and correspondents who drift in from afar, drawn by the magnetism of our Colonel. The food may not always be to the taste of an epicure but "we eat our Irish potatoes flavored with Attic salt," as Father Prout says.

But my chiefest joy in life is to have Joyce Kilmer around. In the army it matters little whether a man was a poet or a grave digger—he is going to be judged by what he is as a soldier. And Joyce is rated high by everybody from the K. P. to the Colonel because he is a genuine fellow. He is very much a soldier—a Sergeant now, and prouder of his triple chevron as member of the 69th than he would be of a Colonel's eagles in any other outfit. If they do not let us commission officers within the Regiment he will come out of the war as Sergeant Joyce Kilmer—a fine title, I think, for any man, for it smacks of the battlefield with no confounded taint of society about it. His life with us is a very full and a very happy one. At first I selfishly took him to help in my own duties regarding statistics. He was glad to help, but he regretted leaving a line company, and especially parting from a lot of friends he had made among the Irish "boys from home," whose simplicity amused him and whose earnest faith aroused his enthusiasm.

Over here he got restless at being on the Adjutant's force, and when Lieutenant Elmer began his lectures on the work and opportunities of the Intelligence Section—scouting, and all the rest of it—Joyce pleaded with me to get him away from a desk and out in the line. Now he is happy all the day long. He has worked himself into various midnight patrols, and Captain Anderson has told me to advise him that he lacks caution in taking care of himself, but as Kilmer has told me the same thing about Anderson, I feel helpless about them both.

I know Kilmer well. He has evidently made up his mind to play the game without flinching, without any admixture of fear. On our last day in Lunéville, when the town was being shelled, I called to him to stand in a doorway where there was a little less danger and he answered with a story about Tom Lacey and a French Major, the moral of which was that a soldier is expendable and officers not; and the outcome of which was that I went forth and walloped him till he came in, though still chuckling. He has been for some time out on an observation post in a beautiful spot which overlooks the German lines, with Watson, Kerrigan, Beck, Mott, Levinson, Titterton—all great admirers of his. Whenever he gets a day off he is in to see me and we break all the rules chatting till midnight and beyond. Books and fighting and anecdotes and good fellows and things to eat and religion; all the good old natural human interests are common to us, with a flavor of literature, of what human-minded people have said in the past to give them breadth and bottom.

Kilmer or I, or both of us, may see an end to life in this war, but neither of us will be able to say that life has not been good to us.

DENEUVRE

May 17th, 1918

Just over to the Regimental Supply Office to see Mangan. I am always looking for reasons to spend a while with Captain Jack. He has a great outfit. I watched his trained youngsters, Lacey, Kennedy, Burke, Nulty and the two delightful Drennan boys at their business of taking care of the Regiment, which they have learned to do so efficiently. I wonder if they will find in civil life jobs to suit the talents they display here. The Regimental Supply Sergeants, Joe Flannery and Eddie Scanlon, could run anything. First Sergeant Comiskey is back with us, and so is Harry Mal-

lon, mule-skinner and funmaker. Everybody was glad to
see Harry once more. Walter Lloyd's gentle voice booming from a nearby stable let me know that the Company
kitchen was near, so I wandered in that direction for a cup
of coffee from Healy and McAviney—always the height of
hospitality for everybody there. Stopped a row between
Frankie Meade and Carburetor Donnelly—Frankie is the
proud guardian of the Regimental ratter and the other boy-
soldier passed a remark about it that no man would let be
said about his dog. I held up Charlie Feick for a canteen,
and before I left Henry and Klauberg and Beverly had
dug me up an O. D. suit, underwear, socks, shoe-laces and
a web belt. Had a good day.

BACCARAT

May 21st, 1918

The new regulations provide for a senior chaplain in each
Division. I felt that General Menoher would appoint me
for the job as I am senior in service, and I had a notion
that my friend Colonel MacArthur would suggest my name.
It has been a worry to me as I do not intend to leave the
regiment for anything else on earth and I am afraid I may
have to go through the war hanging around Division Headquarters. So I asked Colonel McCoy if he would back me
in my refusal to accept the office if I had to quit the regiment, to which I received a hearty affirmative.

I received news of the outcome from McCoy a few days
later. Colonel MacArthur had told him I was to be senior
chaplain, but he was in entire accord with my wish to remain with a fighting unit. Our Chief of Staff chafes at his
own task of directing instead of fighting, and he has pushed
himself into raids and forays in which, some older heads
think, he had no business to be. His admirers say that his
personal boldness has a very valuable result in helping to
give confidence to the men. Colonel McCoy and Major
Donovan are strong on this point. Donovan says it would

be a blamèd good thing for the army if some General got himself shot in the front line. General Menoher and General Lenihan approve in secret of these madnesses; but all five of them are wild Celts, whose opinion no sane man like myself would uphold.

At any rate, Colonel McCoy was so satisfied with the result of the outcome in my case that he went further and said, "Now, if my chaplain is to be senior chaplain of the Division it is not right that he should remain a First Lieutenant. He ought to be a Major at least." McCoy told me with twinkling eyes, "MacArthur said, 'Now, McCoy, if I were you I would not bring up the question of the rank of Father Duffy, for I had serious thoughts of making him Colonel of the 165th instead of you.' You are a dangerous man, Father Duffy," continued the genial McCoy, "and I warn you, you won't last long around here."

DENEUVRE

May 25th, 1918

Being made Senior Chaplain of the Division I judged that my first, if not my sole duty, was to give a dinner to the brethren. We had a meeting in the morning in a large room under the Curé's hospitable roof, and everyone was there. Chaplains Halliday, Robb, Harrington, Smith and McCallum I had known since our first days in Camp Mills, and we had worked together ever since as if we belonged to one religious family. Those who were added to our body since we came to France impress us all as being first class men. Three of them I call the "Young Highbrows": Chaplains N. B. Nash of the 150th F. A., who was a Professor in the Episcopal Theological Seminary at Cambridge, Charles L. O'Donnell, the poet priest of Notre Dame University, who is attached to the 117th Engineers, and Eugene Kenedy, who has been a professor in various Jesuit Colleges and who is now working with the 150th Machine Gun Battalion, after a month of breaking in with our regiment.

Chaplain Ralph M. Tibbals, a Baptist Clergyman from the Southwest, and Chaplain William Drennan, a priest from Massachusetts, were new men to most of us, but made a decidedly favorable impression.

We discussed a number of matters of common interest and every single topic was decided by unanimous vote. The clergy discover in circumstances like these that their fundamental interests are absolutely in common. I do not mean to say that there is any tendency to give up their own special creeds; in fact, they all make an effort to supply the special religious needs of men of various denominations in their own regiments by getting the other chaplains to have occasional services or by announcing such services to the men. I told Bishop Brent that the way the Clergy of different churches got along together in peace and harmony in this Division would be a scandal to pious minds.

I think it would be a good thing if representatives of various churches would have a meeting every year at the seashore in bathing suits, where nobody could tell whether the man he was talking to was a Benedictine Abbot, a Methodist Sunday-School Superintendent or a Mormon Elder. They would all find out how many things of interest they have in common, and, without any disloyalty to their own church, would get together to put them over.

At this meeting there was one thing that I wanted for myself. Some day we shall have three Chaplains for each Infantry regiment, but the time is long in coming, and I am anxious to get someone to hold religious services for my Protestant fellows. I have asked the Division Secretary of the Y. M. C. A. to supply me with one of his Secretaries who is a clergyman, to be attached permanently to the regiment; promising that he would be treated as well as I myself. I have been after this for a long while but the Division Secretary has not too many men, and he is tied down in the placing of them by the canteen situation which makes it necessary to leave the same man in one place as long as possible. Chaplains Nash and Halliday, who are very close to me in all my counsels, are going with me to Chaumont to back me up in a request to the G. H. Q. Chaplains—Bishop Brent, Chaplain Moody and Father Doherty, to have them ask the chief officials of the Y. M. C. A. to assign one of their Protestant clergyman permanently to *my regiment.*

I had left the matter of dinner in the capable hands of the Regimental Supply Sergeant, Joe Flannery, so everybody went home satisfied.

During my stay at Deneuvre I have seen a good deal of Bishop Brent, formerly Episcopal Bishop in the Philippines and now Senior of the G. H. Q. Chaplains. He knew Colonel McCoy in the Philippines, and like everybody who ever knew him, is glad to have a chance to visit him. The Bishop and I have become good friends, the only drawback being that he talks too often about getting me with him at G. H. Q., while my battle cry is that of every member of the regiment, "I want to stick with my own outfit." He is anxious to have some first-hand experience of work in the trenches and he has paid us the compliment of saying that if he can get away he will attach himself to the 165th. I hope he can come for I know that everybody will be as attached to him as I am myself, and he on his part will have some interesting experiences.

May 26th, 1918

I have just been talking with Donovan, Anderson, Mangan and others of the old timers and we all remarked on what a hold Lieutenant Colonel Mitchell had gotten on us during his short stay amongst us. He was assigned to us as a replacement and drifted in so unassumingly that we scarcely knew he had arrived until he was with us a week. But as he has gone about from place to place doing all kinds of jobs,—inspections, courtmartials, and the like, we have grown to know him better, and to like him more the more we know him. He is efficient without bustle, authoritative without bluster, never unreasonable and full of quaint native humor. His father was a Chaplain in the Army which is perhaps one of the reasons why the son and I are already like old chums.

BACCARAT

May 30th, 1918

The uniforms we wear as well as the losses we have already sustained make us appreciate the significance of Memorial Day. General Menoher left the arrangements for a proper celebration of the day to the Chaplains. So I called a meeting at which all were present. It was an easy matter to select speakers from our various commands to address meetings of soldiers in every village in which elements of the Division were quartered. The regimental bands of the Infantry and Artillery Regiments were to be sent by trucks from one station to another, so that all of our soldiers should have the benefit of their services.

The main celebration was to be at Baccarat where our Division Headquarters were, and the burden of arranging for it fell on the 165th, now in reserve. The dead of our Division, mainly men of the 84th Brigade, which has been in this Sector since the beginning of March, are buried in a Military Cemetery; and our first duty was to pay them solemn honors. Polychrom of Company A made wreaths from the flowers lavishly offered by the people of Deneuvre. Everybody of all ranks who could be spared was present at the ceremony, together with large number of the civilian population. Children of the town were selected to place the wreaths upon the graves of our dead, and the last resting place of our French companions was not neglected.

After the ceremony Captain Handy came to me with an invitation from General Menoher to ride back with him. General Menoher is a man who begets loyalty and confidence. Americans are better acquainted with the business type of man than the military type, and I think I can best characterize him by saying that if he were out of uniform he would impress one as a successful business man—one of the kind that can carry responsibility, give orders affecting large affairs with calmness and certainty, and still find time to be human. He is entirely devoid of posing, of vanity, or of jealousy. His only desire is to see results. Consequently his subordinates are doing magnificent team-work, and the excellent condition of the Division is due to this factor as well as his direct care of us. We are exceedingly fortunate in having such a man to rule over us.

Colonel McCoy saw to it that the grave of every one of our dead was properly honored on this day—in Southampton, in Langres, in Ancervillers and here in Baccarat. During the afternoon he and I went to Croixmare; so likewise did General Menoher with Colonel MacArthur and General Lenihan with Major Conway. We found that the Curé and his parishioners, as also the French soldiers, had kept the graves there in beautiful condition—a tribute to our dead which warms our heart to the people of France.

LETTER TO A CURATE

June 10th, 1918

In spite of all you tell me I have lost, I have a stray assortment of arms and legs left, ungainly, I admit, but still serviceable, whether for reaching for the bread at messtime or for pushing me around my broad parish. I hear that I am dead—wounded—gone crazy. I hate to contradict so many good people, but I must say that I know I am alive, and that I never felt better in my life. As for the third count, perhaps I had better leave it to others to testify, but I'm no worse than I always was. I may be considered a bit off for coming over here, but that's a decent kind of craziness, and one I am glad to see becoming quite popular.

I wish that my case could serve as a warning to good folks at home who are distracted by all sorts of rumors about their lads here. If anything happens to any one of us, the folks will hear of it from Washington within a hundred hours. If it says "Slightly Wounded," they may take it as good news. For let me tell you, if I was worrying continually about the fate of some dear one over here, and got word he was "Slightly Wounded," I would sigh a sigh of relief that the beloved was out of harm's way and having a good time for a while.

I don't mind rumors in the army. They are part of the game. With eating and growling, they constitute our chief forms of recreation. Fact is, I am made the father of most of them in this regiment. When some lad starts his tongue going, and everybody tells him just what kind of a liar he is, he says that Father Duffy said so, and Father Duffy got it straight from Secretary Baker or General Pershing, or, who knows?—by revelation. It is a great compliment to me, but a left-handed one to my teaching.

At home, though, rumors don't just interest—they hurt. I know how much they hurt, for my pile of "agony letters" keeps mounting up with every mail. And I can't answer them all at length, as I would wish—not if I want to do anything else.

First-class mail is the bane of my life as Chaplain. Like everyone else, I don't mind reading it, but I know what it means when it comes to answering it. Gosh! how I hate that. I like to keep on the go. I have to keep on the go to get anything done, with the regiment scattered in five different villages, miles apart, and outside work to do in the other outfits for men that want the sacraments, and hospitals to visit. And to have to stick a whole day at a table to soothe sorrows that don't exist, or oughtn't to—whew!

The letters I am most ready to answer are from those who have gotten real bad news from Washington. God be good to them. I'd do anything for them. And the ones I am glad to get—if I don't have to answer them myself—are those that put me onto something I can do for the men —see that Jimmy keeps the pledge, or that Tom goes to Church, or find what's the matter with Eddie who lost his stripes, or break bad news to Michael, or see that Jack doesn't fall in love with any of those French hussies, but comes back to the girl that adores him. These all help, and I get round to them in time—and make the victim write a letter, to which I put my name as censor—a proof of my efforts.

But the biggest bulk of my mail consists of inquiries why no mail has arrived from Patrick for three weeks—and is he dead—or why Jerry's allotment had not been made. When I interview Patrick, he informs me disgustedly that he has written home every twenty minutes. And I know that before any letter of mine can get there, the Sullivans will have received a bunch of mail that will make them the gossips and the envy and the pride of the parish till they begin to get worried and write to me again.

As for the allotments, the nearest I come—don't ask me how near—to falling into the sole vice of our army of using strong language is when I get a letter from some poor mother or wife about their non-payment. Our men have been extraordinarily decent about helping out the folks at home. But it has been new forms to make out, or the demand for a change of the name of Mrs. Michael J. Farrell to Mrs. Mary Farrell—and all the time decent folks going short at home, and the best men we've got fretting in the trenches. That's the way these fountain-pen soldiers are helping to win the war. How have they kept it so secret? Even men like those that make up our Board of Trustees have written me that our men are slack about making allotments. And the poor fellows in most cases have stripped themselves to ten dollars a month, and are scudding along on bare poles half way between paydays—I know all about that, and the Trustees, all good men and true, will hold back *their* language when I report that I had to use their money for lads that had left themselves destitute for their folks, while their folks were being left destitute by those people in Washington.

You ask me to tell you about my work here. Well, in the main it is what I did at home, though under different

circumstances. The old Sixty-Ninth is a parish—an itiner-
ant parish. Probably a sixth of the "parishioners" do not
look to me for dogmatic instruction, but you know how
much that counts for in my ordinary relations with them.
Remember the afternoon last Spring, when Father Prunty
went into the play-hall to get helpers from my gang for his
patriotic gardening and found afterward that his five volunteers consisted of two Protestants, two Jews and Andy
O'Hare.

I have this class of parishioners very much on my conscience. I can't get the other chaplains to help except on
the few occasions when regiments, or parts of them occupy
the same place. Every chaplain has five times what he can
do to supply Sunday services for his own scattered command.

At any rate, I can assure you that the different elements
in the old regiment have fused properly. By the way, I
cannot remember anything that delighted me more than
when I heard Sergeant Abe Blaustein was to get the Croix
de Guerre—he was recommended for it by Major Donovan
and Major Stacom (the pride of our parish) and Lieutenant
Cavanaugh. He is a good man, Abe, and the 69th appreciates a good man when it sees him. John O'Keefe's poem
made a hit with all of us.

That reminds me of something at my expense. Captain
John Prout approached me with a genial grin to tell me
that at our Christmas Mass he had seen a Jew boy present, and later on he asked him "What were you doing at
Mass?" "Oh, Captain," he said, "you know I'd go to Hell
with you." Prout said to me, "The compliment to myself
is very obvious, Father,—I hope that you will be able to
find in it one for yourself too."

.But I started to tell you about my work. I have a congregation of the old faith, approximately three thousand
souls. They are generally scattered through five or six
French villages, when *en repos,* and more scattered still
through trenches and abandoned towns when in line.

To begin with the form of pastoral activity you are no doubt most interested in, for you will be getting a parish one of these days—I take up no collections. 'Tis a sad confession to make, and I expect to be put out of the Pastor's Union when I get back for breach of rules. But the lads are not left entirely without proper training. The old French curés (God bless them, they are a fine lot of old gentlemen) take up the collection. A tremendously important-looking old beadle in a Napoleonic cocked hat and with a long staff goes before, with a money-or-your-life air about him, and in the rear comes the apologetic mannered curé, or perhaps a little girl, carrying a little dish that is a stimulus to stinginess, which is timidly pushed forward a few inches in the direction of the man on the outside seat. If the man is an American he grabs the dish and sticks it under the nose of his neighbor, with a gruff whisper, "Cough up." They cough up all right—if it isn't too far from payday. Even at that they are good for more of the Cigar Store coupons and the copper washers that pass for money here than are the local worshippers. The curés proclaim us the most generous people in the world—and so we are—which makes it unanimous. They listen with open mouths to my tales of financial returns in city parishes at home and wish secretly that they had started life where things are run like that—until I tell them of the debts we have to carry, and they are content once more that their lot has been cast in the quiet, old-time villages of Lorraine.

But to do them justice, they are most impressed by the way our men practice their religion. Two companies of our regiment jam a village church—aisles, sanctuary, sacristy, porch. A battalion shows its good will by filling the churchyard, the windows being ornamented by rough martial visages which don't look exactly like those of the placid looking saints in the stained glass above—but I feel that the saints were once flesh-and-blood people themselves, and that they have an indulgent, perhaps even an admiring eye, on the good lads that are worshipping God as best they can.

There is no doubt anyway about the opinion of the good priests who are carrying on the work of the dead and gone saints. They are full of enthusiasm about our fellows. What attracts them most is their absolute indifference to what people are thinking of them as they follow their religious practices. These men of yours, they tell me, are not making a show of religion; they are not offending others; they touch their hats to a church, or make the sign of the Cross, or go to Mass just because they want to, with the same coolness that a man might show in taking coffee without milk or expressing a preference for a job in life. They run bases with scapulars flying, and it don't occur to them that they have scapulars on, any more than they would be conscious of having a button of their best girl or President Wilson pinned to their shirts—they may have all three.

Come to think of it, it is a tribute not only to our religious spirit, but to the American spirit as a whole. The other fellows don't think of it either—no more than I do that one of our Chaplains who is closest to me in every thought and plan wears a Masonic ring. We never advert to it except when some French people comment on our traveling together—and then it is a source of fun.

I often drop in on soldiers of other outfits around their kitchens or in the trenches, or during a halt on the road, and hear confessions. Occasionally Catholic soldiers in country regiments, with the small-town spirit of being loth to doing anything unusual while people are looking at them, hold back. Then my plan is to enlist the cooperation of the Protestant fellows, who are always glad to pick them out for me and put them in my clutches. They have a lot of sport about it, dragging them up to me as if they were prisoners; but it is a question of serious religion as soon as their confession begins, the main purpose of the preliminaries being simply to overcome a country boy's embarrassment. It proves, too, that the average American likes to see a man practice his religion, whatever it may be.

With my own men there is never any difficulty of that

kind. I never hear confessions in a church, but always in the public square of a village, with the bustle of army life and traffic going on around us. There is always a line of fifty or sixty soldiers, continuously renewed throughout the afternoon, until I have heard perhaps as many as five hundred confessions in the battalion. The operation always arouses the curiosity of the French people. They see the line of soldiers with man after man stepping forward, doffing his cap with his left hand, and making a rapid sign of the cross with his right, and standing for a brief period within the compass of my right arm, and then stepping forward and standing in the square in meditative posture while he says his penance. "What are those soldiers doing?" I can see them whispering. "They are making the Sign of the Cross. Mon Dieu! they are confessing themselves." Non-Catholics also frequently fall into line, not of course to make their confession, but to get a private word of religious comfort and to share in the happiness they see in the faces of the others.

Officers who are not Catholics are always anxious to provide opportunities for their men to go to confession; not only through anxiety to help them practice their religion, but also for its distinct military value. Captain Merle-Smith told me that when I was hearing confessions before we took over our first trenches he heard different of his men saying to his first sergeant, Eugene Gannon, "You can put my name down for any kind of a job out there. I'm all cleaned up and I don't give a damn what happens now."

That is the only spirit to have going into battle—to be without any worries for body or soul. If battles are to be won, men have to be killed; and they must be ready, even willing, to be killed for the cause and the country they are fighting for. While we were still in Lunéville the regiment attended Mass in a body and I said to them, "Much as I love you all, I would rather that you and I myself, that all of us should sleep our last sleep under the soil of France than that the historic colors of this Old Regiment, the banner of our republic, should be soiled by irresolution or disgraced by panic."

The religion of the Irish has characteristics of its own—they make the Sign of the Cross with the right hand, while holding the left ready to give a jab to anybody who needs it for his own or the general good. I cannot say that it is an ideally perfect type of Christianity; but considering the sort of world we have to live in yet, it as near as we can come at present to perfection for the generality of men. It was into the mouth of an Irish soldier that Kipling put the motto, "Help a woman, and hit a man; and you won't go far wrong either way."

BACCARAT

May, 1918

The Knights of Columbus have secured a splendid place in Baccarat. The Curé had a large hall with extra rooms and a nice yard outside, for the young men of the Parish; and this he was glad to hand over to the K. of C. for the use of American soldiers. Early in the game Mr. Walter Kernan had tried to get in touch with me but had failed as we were moving around too much. However, he had sent me a check for 5,000 francs with instructions to use it for the men. I had no need of money, as our Board of Trustees were willing to supply whatever I should ask, and there were very few things that could be purchased on the scale demanded by a regiment of 3,600 men. We have now received the services of Messrs. Bundschuh, May and Mr. Kernan's brother, Joseph, with a French-American priest whom I assigned to look after the Catholics in two of the artillery regiments.

We opened the building with solemn pomp and ceremony in the presence of representatives of Division Headquarters, M. Michaud, the Mayor of the City, Colonel McCoy and many of the Chaplains and a large throng of officers and men. With this commodious building in addition to the quarters of the "Y" the matter of recreation for men in town will be well looked after.

CHASSEURS

June 10th, 1918

Our Division has taken over a new sector from the French just to the right of our line bordering on the sector occupied by the Iowas and it is at present occupied by Major Donovan with Companies A and B of his battalion. It has a picturesque name, "The Hunter's Meeting Place—Rendezvouz des Chasseurs," and is even more picturesque than its name. There is a high hog-back of land jutting out towards the German line between deep thickly-wooded valleys. When this was a quiet sector the French soldiers in their idle time put a great deal of labor on it to make it comfortable and attractive, and when I came out here a few days ago I could easily have believed it if told there was no such a thing as war, and that this whole place had been designed as a rustic semi-military playground for the younger elements on some gentleman's country estate. The officers' dugouts are against the side of the steeply sloping hill so that only the inner portion is really under ground, windows and doors on one side opening on terraces which have flower beds, strawberry plots, and devices made of whitewashed stones.

We dine *al fresco* under the trees. An electric light plant is installed and I spent last night on the Major's bunk indulging an old habit of reading late. Donovan, like McCoy, always has some books with him no matter where he goes; and I got hold of a French translation of "Cæsar's Commentaries," with notes by Napoleon Bonaparte.

I enjoy being with Donovan. He is so many-sided in his interests, and so alert-minded in every direction, and such a gracious attractive fellow besides, that there is never a dull moment with him. His two lieutenants, Ames and Weller, are of similar type; and as both are utterly devoted to him, it is a happy family. Ames takes me aside periodically to tell me in his boyish, earnest way that I am the only man who can boss the Major into taking care of himself, and that I must tell him that he is doing entirely too much work and taking too great risks, and must mend his evil ways. I always deliver the message, though it never does any good. Just now I am not anxious for Donovan to spare himself, for I know that he has been sent here because, in spite of its sylvan attractiveness, this place is a post of danger, so situated that the enemy could cut it off from reinforcements, and bag our two companies unless the strictest precautions are kept up.

Major Allen Potts, a genial and gallant Virginian, who is now in charge of the military police, has obtained permission to bring up one company of his M. P.'s to help our fellows hold the line. It is a good idea. The M. P. have a mean job as they have to arrest other soldiers for breach of regulations; and they are exposed to resentful retorts of the kind, "Where's your coat?" "Where you'll never go to look for it—out in No Man's Land." Nobody can talk that way to Major Potts's outfit.

There was a gas attack last night on the French sector called Chapellotte on the edge of the bluff to our immediate right, and Donovan and I went over this morning to see the extent of the damage. As we climbed the steep hill to reach the French positions we met Matthew Rice of Company A, who was in liaison with the French; and he told us in the coolest way in the world a story of a sudden gas attack in the middle of the night, which put out of action nearly two hundred men, leaving himself and four or five Frenchmen the only surviving defenders of the hill. If the same thing were to happen at Chasseurs the Germans could easily follow it up and capture the whole outfit; and I can see the reason for Major Donovan's ceaseless precautions.

BACCARAT

June 15th, 1918

My principal occupation these days is visiting the hospitals, of which there are three in Baccarat. The Spanish

Influenza has hit the Division and a large number of the men are sick. The fever itself is not a terrible scourge, but when pneumonia follows it, it is of a particularly virulent type. Our deaths, however, have been few: John F. Donahoe of Company F, Richard J. Hartigan of Company I, Fred Griswold of Machine Gun Company and Patrick A. Hearn of Company D, whose death had a particular pathos by reason of the sorrow of his twin brother who is in the same Company. All in all, we have been a singularly healthy regiment, whatever be the reason—some doctors think it is because we are a city regiment. We have been almost absolutely free from the "Children's Diseases" such as mumps, measles, scarlet fever, diphtheria, etc., which have played havoc with the efficiency strength of almost every other regiment in the Division. Occasionally replacements introduce some of those diseases, but they have never made any headway. Since we left home our full total of deaths in a Regiment of thirty-six hundred men has been, outside of battle cases, just fourteen. John L. Branigan, of Company B, died in an English hospital. In the Langres area we lost Charles C. Irons, Company G; Edward O'Brien, Company M, and James Reed, Company E, by illness, and Sydney Cowley, Company G, by accidental shooting. Accidents were also the causes of the deaths of Corporal Winthrop Rodewald, Company H, Donald Monroe, Company F, and Daniel J. Scanlon of Company G, who also left a brother in the Company to mourn his loss. Louis King and Joseph P. Morris of Company I and George W. Scallon of Company A died of meningitis.

In this sector we have had just three battle losses. When Company G was in line, a direct hit of a German shell killed two of our old-timers, Patrick Farrell and Timothy Donnellan, and wounded Peter Bohan. Recently at Chasseurs, Corporal Arthur Baker, a resolute soldier, was killed while leading a daylight patrol in No Man's Land. Sergeant Denis Downing of Company G was killed by one of our own sentries who mistook him for a German.

June 16th, 1918

Donovan's men have been recalled from Chasseurs. The 42nd Division has finished its preliminary education and is to start off for some more active front two days from now. We are to be relieved by the 77th Division, New York City's contribution to the National Army. Today while returning from a funeral I met two M. P.'s from that Division who were members of the Police Force at home. Met also two old pupils of mine, Father James Halligan and Lieutenant Arthur McKeogh.

June 19th, 1918

Yesterday was New York "Old Home Day" on the roads of Lorraine. We marched out from Baccarat on our hunt for new trouble, and met on the way the 77th Division, all National Army troops from New York City. It was a wonderful encounter. As the two columns passed each other on the road in the bright moonlight there were songs of New York, friendly greetings and badinage, sometimes good humored, sometimes with a sting in it. "We're going up to finish the job that you fellows couldn't do." "Look out for the Heinies or you'll all be eating sauerkraut in a prison camp before the month is out." "The Germans will find out what American soldiers are like when we get a crack at them." "What are you givin' us," shouted Mike Donaldson; "we was over here killin' Dutchmen before they pulled your names out of the hat." "Well, thank God," came the response, "we didn't have to get drunk to join the army."

More often it would be somebody going along the lines shouting "Anybody there from Greenwich Village?" or "Any of you guys from Tremont?" And no matter what part of New York City was chosen the answer was almost sure to be "Yes." Sometimes a chap went the whole line calling for some one man: "Is John Kelly there?" the answer from our side being invariably, "Which of them do you want?" One young fellow in the 77th kept calling for his brother who was with us. Finally he found him and the two lads ran at each other burdened with their heavy packs, grabbed each other awkwardly and just punched each other and swore for lack of other words until officers ordered them into ranks, and they parted perhaps not to meet again. At intervals both columns would break into song, the favorites being on the order of

"East side, West side,
All around the town,
The tots sang ring-a-rosie
London Bridge is falling down.
Boys and girls together,
Me and Mamie O'Rourke,
We tripped the light fantastic
On the sidewalks of New York.

The last notes I heard as the tail of the dusty column swung around a bend in the road, were "Herald Square, anywhere, New York Town, take me there." Good lads, God bless them, I hope their wish comes true.

MORIVILLE

June 22nd, 1918

Our first day's march brought us to Moyemont, our second a short hike to Moriville, where we are waiting to entrain at Chatel sur Moselle. I am billetted with the Curé and have sent Father McDonald, an old pupil of mine who has just been sent to me, to the 2nd Battalion. He is not well enough to stand what we will have to go through, so I have sent a telegram to Bishop Brent asking to have him kept for a time at some duty where he can regain his health.

Now I have to turn my attention to the Curé, who is also an invalid. He is living here in this big, bleak stone house, with an old housekeeper who is deaf, and the biggest, ugliest looking brute of a dog I have ever seen. He is run down and dispirited. We Americans don't like that atmosphere so I started in to chirk him up. First I called in Dr. Lyttle, who pronounced the verdict that there was no reason why with rest and change and a new outlook on life he could not last for ten years.

Today is Sunday and I told the lads in church that I wanted a collection to give a poor old priest a holiday.; and they responded nobly. For a second Mass I went down to McKenna's town and found a new device, a green shamrock on a white back-ground, over the door of his battalion headquarters. His is to be known as the Shamrock battalion of the regiment. After Mass and another collection I took breakfast with him. I had brought with me some money that Captain Mangan owed him. While I was at breakfast Mangan came in himself, and in his presence I handed the money over to McKenna. "If I didn't have you around, Father, to threaten Mangan with hell-fire, I'd never get a cent of it." "If you weren't such a piker you wouldn't keep a cent of it, now you've got it. You'd give it to Father Duffy for his poor old Curé." "All right, I'll give it, and double it if you cover it." That meant forty dollars apiece for my nice old gentlemen. But McKenna was not satisfied. "Come on, Cassidy, come across," and the Lieutenant with a smile on his handsome face came across with more than any Lieutenant can afford. McKenna shouted to the others, "Come all the rest of you heretics; you haven't given a cent to a church since you left home," and with a whole lot of fun about it, everybody gave generously. I could not help thinking what a lesson in American broadmindedness the whole scene presented. But the immediate point was that I was able to do handsomely for my old Curé. I went back to him, and from the different collections I poured into his hat in copper pennies, bits of silver, dirty little shin-plasters and ten franc notes, the sum of two thousand francs. He was speechless. The old housekeeper wept; even the dog barked its loudest.

"I'm giving you this with one condition," I said. "Namely, that you spend it all at once." "But ma foi! how can one spend two thousand francs in a short while. I never had so much money before in all my life." "Of course you can't spent it in this burg. I want you to go away to Vittel, to Nancy, to Paris, anywhere, and give yourself a good time for once in your life." "But the Bishop would never permit it. He has few priests left and cannot supply the parishes with them." "Well, he will have to do it if you're dead, and you'll be dead soon if you hang around here. Stay in bed next Sunday and have your parishioners send in complaints to the Bishop. Do that again the Sunday after, and by that time the Bishop will have to send somebody. Then you go off and spend that 2,000 francs on a summer holiday, and don't come back until you have spent the last cent of it."

The old gentlemen gave a dazed assent to my entire scheme; but I am leaving here with little expectation that he will carry it all through. He may get a holiday from the Bishop, and he may spend a little of the money on it, but even if he lives for ten years I am willing to bet he will have some of our 2,000 francs left when he dies. In some ways it is a great handicap to be French.

BREUVERY

June 27th, 1918

On June 23rd we boarded the now familiar troop trains at Chatel sur Moselle, and before we were off them we had zig-zagged our way more than half the distance to Paris, going up as far as Nancy, down to Neufchateau, northwest again by Bar-le-Duc, finally detraining on June 24th, at Coolus, south of Chalons-sur-Marne. We are now in five villages along the River Coole. We have left Lorraine at last and are in the province of Champagne. It is a different kind of country. The land is more level and less heavily wooded; the houses are built of a white, chalky stone with gray tiles instead of red; and with outbuildings in the rear of them—with the result (for which heaven be praised) that the dung heaps are off the streets. The inhabitants strike us as being livelier and less worried, whether from natural temperament or distance from the battle line, I do not know. The weather is beautiful and it is the joy of life to walk along the shaded roads that border the sleepy Coole and drop in on a pleasant company at mess time to share in their liveliness and good cheer. To-day it was a trip to St. Quentin with the Machine Gun Company. Johnnie Webb and Barnett picked me up on the road and formed my escort, leading me straight to the kitchen, where Sergeant Ketchum and Mike Clyne were making ready for the return of the hungry gunners. Lieutenant De Lacour wanted me to go to Captain Seibert's mess but I preferred by lunch on the grass with Milton Cohen, John Kenny, Ledwith, McKelvey, Murphy, Chester Taylor and Pat Shea. This is the kind of a war I like.

CHAPTER V

THE CHAMPAGNE DEFENSIVE

VADENAY FARM, CAMP DE CHALONS

July 2nd, 1918

I LIKE this spot, but it was a terrible place to get to.
We got hurry-up orders to leave our pleasant villages on
the Coole on June 26th. It was payday and some of the
fellows had hiked it into Chalons and back to find something to spend their money on. But it was "pack your
kits and trek" for everybody.

It was a beautiful soft June night. No moon, but the
French highway rolled out before us dull white in the
gloom, as if its dust were mingled with phosphorus. The
men trudged along behind—joking and singing—it was the
beginning of the march. After a couple of hours we entered Chalons, a dream city by night. Not a light was
visible, but the chalk stone buildings showed dimly on
either hand, and the old Cathedral, with the ravages of
the French Revolution obscured by darkness, was more
beautiful than in the day. But before we left that town
behind, all the poetry had departed from it. It seemed to
take hours and hours of hard hiking on uneven pavements
before the wearying men found their feet on country roads
once more. Nobody knew how far the column had to go,
and every spire that marked a village was hailed with hope,
and, I fear, cursed when the hope was unrealized. They
had a weary night ahead before they reached their destina-
tions. The headquarters found itself with Division Headquarters in the Ferme de Vadenay, which is not a farm at
all, but some long low barracks on the Camp de Chalons.

119

The nearest approach to a farmer I saw there was a French soldier, who carefully nursed a few cabbages to feed his rabbits. He was a Breton fisherman, who had gone to the war, and the war had touched his wits. As a younger man he had fished in the North Sea and was the only person I ever found who could confirm the existence of Captain George MacAdie's native town of Wyck. It was a great triumph for George, for my geographical skepticism had aroused a doubt as to whether he had ever been born at all.

The Chalons plains set all of us old Border veterans going again. The first comment was "Just like Texas." A broad expanse of flat brookless country with patches of scrimpy trees that surely must be mesquite. But I delight in it. There is a blue sky over it all, and the long reaches for the eye to travel are as fascinating and as restful as the ocean. In Texas the attraction is in the skies. Half of it is beautiful. The half you see by gazing at the horizon and letting the eye travel up and back till it meets the horizon again. But here the flat earth has beauties of its own. It is God's flower garden. The whole ground is covered with wild flowers—marguerites and bluets by millions and big clumps of violets as gorgeous as a sanctuary of Monsignori, and poppies, poppies everywhere. Colonel McCoy gave me a copy of Alan's Seegar's poems with one marked Champagne, 1915. Two lines of it are running through my head all day.

> The mat of many colored flowers
> That decks the sunny chalk fields of Champagne.

Champagne. The word is a familiar one with other associations. We had thought that the bottles grew on trees and that the thirsty traveler had but to detach the wire that held them. And behold it is a land as dry as Nebraska. There are no such vivifying trees, nor lowly vines, nor even abundant water. A vastly over-advertised country in the opinion of the present collection of tourists.

BOIS DE LA LYRE

July 7th, 1918

Bois de la Lyre—Harp Woods since the 69th got here. We have arrived in two stages. We were to celebrate the 4th of July in proper fashion with games and feasting. But there was not much with which to hold high revelry, and the games were practically spoiled by an order to move. Anyway, our minds are on other things. I came on Terry O'Connor, sitting with his shirt open on account of the heat, busily cleaning his rifle. "Man dear," I said, "Where is your patriotism? Every man home has a flag in his button-hole. I'm ashamed of you." "I've got me roifle" (patting it) "an' me Scafflers" (pointing to the brown string showing on his bared neck) ; "what more does a pathriot need?"

We moved by night, as usual, but not far, to the École Normale de Tir. The Normal School sounded big and fine. One expected a square two-story red brick building with white sandstone trimmings—but we found a collection of half underground iron covered dugouts, and all overground rough little board shacks. We would be happy there now for we find that this poetically named spot is some degrees less attractive. It looks as if somebody had put it up in a hurry because the cattle were out in bad weather. The Officers are in the sheds, the men out in what they call the Bois—which are probably thick enough for conceal-ment from an inquisitive aeroplane. But that is all we need while this blessed weather holds. Sunny France had ceased to be the joke it was.

And then, something seems to be doing at last. We who are in the know have been hearing tales of plans afoot—an attack on the Chateau Thierry salient at Chatil-lon-sur-Marne seemed to be the plan when we first reached these parts. The indications are now that the Germans are due for another inning and we are to meet them here. Anderson has gone up with the 2nd Battalion to hold the trenches with the French. Donovan and McKenna are in support. There is a big dugout in a knoll ahead of us—

they call it a hill, just as in Atlantic City any place four
feet above tide water is called a height—and we are to move
there when action begins. I am sitting on top of it—have
been here all this sunny afternoon reading a book the
Colonel gave me, Gabriel Hanotaux on France under
Henri Quatre—and I certainly do not like the idea of
spending my young life in a dugout P. C. during action. I
am going to tell Colonel McCoy that my spiritual duties
demand that I visit Anderson's Battalion. He says that
he wants his Officers to enjoy this war—the only war most
of them can hope to have. And I hate dugouts anyway.

To get from Harp Woods to Chapel Woods you go
north for about four miles through Jonchèry to St. Hilaire
le Grand—a bit of a village which to borrow from Vol-
taire's remark about the Holy Roman Empire does not look
particularly saintly nor hilarious nor grand. The Ohios
are on the right of it, and our Company E just to the
west with patches of blue Frenchmen dotted all around.
Follow the Ancient Roman Way for a kilometer or two
and you get to a patch of woods with tops of mounds
showing through them as if large sized moles had been
working there. It is marked on the map as Sub-sector
Taupinière in the Auberive sector. But we carry our
names with us, and these bits of the soil of France are to
be called while we inhabit them P. C. Anderson, P. C.
Kelly, P. C. Prout and P. C. Finny; P.C., meaning "Post of
Command."

I have spent the week with Anderson. He has his P. C. in
an elephant hut—a little hole about five feet underground
with a semi-circular roof of corrugated iron piled over with
sand bags and earth,—enough to turn the splinters of a shell.
I passed a couple of days with Captain Charles Baker of
Company E, who is over to the right, along the Suippes.
Charles is all energy and business, as usual. And Lieutenant
Andy Ellett came in one night quite peevish because the
French had countermanded the orders for a patrol. Andy
likes the scent of danger. At P. C. Baker I saw Jim Murray,

whom I once started out for the priesthood. I spent a pleasant day wandering about on my lawful occasions among the men in the different positions, one of which I found very popular, as just there the Suippes had actually enough water for a man to take a decent bath in. At the proper time I did not fail to discover the Company Kitchen, located on the river bank in a charming spot. While doing justice to a good meal I discussed Mt. Vernon politics with Carmody and Vahey.

The battalion is under French command. Colonel Arnoux of the 116th Infantry has us in immediate charge with General Gouraud in high command. Arnoux is an elderly patient kindly man with a lot of seasoned young veterans for officers and for Chaplain a big jolly Breton, whom the men adore. The regiment is not much higher in strength than our one battalion. Like all the regiments over here it has been worn down by constant fighting and the difficulty of finding replacements. During the week they got something to show for the good work they have been doing the past three years—the much desired Fourragère, a bunch of knotted cords worn hanging from the left shoulder. Our fellows call them "pull-throughs," after the knotted cords they pull through their rifles when cleaning them. It was a very interesting ceremony. Our officers were invited to it and those of our enlisted men who wore the French Croix de Guerre. General Gouraud, a remarkable military figure with an added touch of distinction from his empty hanging sleeve and stiff leg—decorated the regimental colors while the officers invested the men with the coveted mark of distinction. The General reviewed his American Allies, each of the officers being introduced by Major Anderson. It was a formal affair until he came to our bunch of husky soldiers who wore no silver or gold insignia on their shoulders but carried on their breasts the red and green ribbon of the Croix de Guerre. Then you can see why every man in his army swears by him. No cannon fodder here, but interesting human beings. I

liked him for it, and felt very proud of the men we had
to show him—Corporals Hagan and Finnegan of Company
F, Sergeants Coffey, Murray and Shalley of Company G,
and Sergeants Jerome O'Neill and Gunther and Corporal
Furey of Company H.*   I was saying to myself, "General,
you're an old soldier but you never saw better men."

It was a good thing for all of us to have met the General—a man that any soldier would be proud to fight under, but we were mighty careful not to tell him that a
phrase from a famous order of his was a by-word amongst
the American Officers under him.   He had issued an address couched along the lines of the Napoleonic tradition
in vigorous staccato phrases, preparing the hearts of his
soldiers for resistance unto death.   The translator had
turned his last hopeful phrase, which promised them it
would be a great day when the assault was broken, into
English as "It will be a beautiful day."   Many of the high-
ups, both French and American, seem to think that the idea
of a general assault along these lines in a direction away
from Paris is a mare's nest of Gouraud's, but the debate
always winds up with the unanimous chant, "Oh, it will be
a beautiful day."   At present we are not in the front line
trenches, but in what are called the intermediate ones.
The General's idea is to hold the front line with a few
French troops who will make themselves as safe as possible
against the vigorous shelling expected and withdraw behind
our lines when the German Infantry make their attack.
Then our fellows are to have the task of keeping goal.   It's
going to bring the battle right down to our doors, as the
battalion and company headquarters are only one or two
city blocks from where the hand to hand fighting will have
to take place.

I spend most of my time amongst the men and am very
much interested in finding out how their minds react at
the prospects of their first big battle.   The other German

* These distinctions were won by men of the 2nd Battalion in a
coup de main led by Lieutenants Ogle and Becker (also decorated) in
the Baccarat Sector.

drives against the British and the French have been so overwhelmingly successful that I was afraid the soldiers might think that whenever the Germans get started they were just naturally bound to walk over everything. I am delighted to find that these bits of recent history have not affected our fellows in the slightest. Jim Fitzpatrick of E Company expressed the feeling of everybody when he said: "Why would I be afraid ov thim? They're just Dootch-men, a'int they? and I never in me loife seen any four Dootchmin that I couldn't lick." I have often read statements by reporters about men being anxious to get into a battle. I never believed it. But I find now at first hand that here at least are a lot of men who are anxious to see Heinie start something. I tell them that I am desirous of getting into our first mix-up right here. This Division has started out hunting trouble and if we don't find it here they will keep us sloshing all over France until we run into it somewhere.

They will have need of all their courage, for if this general attack is made it's going to be a tremendous one. The opinion of the French General staff seems to be that this line will not be able to hold. At any rate they have been making preparations with that contingency in view. The whole plain behind us is organized for defense with our other two battalions in rough trenches and the Engineers in reserve. I hear they are bringing up also a Polish Legion to take part in the support. They have Seventy-fives in position for direct fire on German tanks, and machine guns stuck everywhere with beautiful fields of fire across the sloping plain. Everything is so charmingly arranged, that I have a feeling that some of the people behind us have a sneaking hope that the Germans will sweep across the first lines so that they can be met by the pleasant little reception which is being prepared for them further back. However, I think that our friends back there are going to be disappointed unless the Germans can spare a Division or two to smother this battalion. Their orders are "Fight it out where you are," which is Anderson's translation of Gouraud's phrase, "No man shall look back; no man shall retreat a step."

Gouraud means it; and Anderson means it. I take great pleasure in observing him these days. A young fellow yet, just 29, and fresh from civil life—but a born soldier, with the carefulness of a soldier in making plans and in looking after his men, and the hardness of a soldier in ruling and using men, and a streak of sentiment carefully concealed which is a part of the soldier's make-up. He has some Scotch in him by his name—a good thing for the Irish if it doesn't make them Scotch-Irish—but the military tradition in his bringing-up is on the Duffy side. It is interesting to me to see the elements of school training showing in a man's character and views. In his views of life, discipline and self-sacrifice, Anderson is a Christian Brothers' boy. I sometimes feel that old Brother Michael had more to do with the making of Major Anderson as I know him, than his own parents had. One result of his education had been what most people nowadays would consider a detriment— his devotion to duty is so sincere that it has produced the effect of despising publicity; this he carries to an extreme. Well, he may or may not win fame in this war, but one thing I know, that the soldiers of his Company or of his Battalion who alternately cursed and admired him during the period of training are delighted to have him over them in a fight and will unanimously rank him as one of the greatest soldiers this regiment has ever produced.

Last night he and I made the rounds of all the trenches. General Gouraud had picked it as a probable night for the big attack, so we started around to get the men in right spirits for it. The Major's method was characteristic. As the bright moonlight revealed the men in their little groups of two or threes, the Major would ask, "What are your orders here?" The answer always came, quick as a flash, though in varying words, "To fight it out where we are, sir." "To let nothing make me leave my post, sir," and one, in a rich Munster brogue, "To stay here until we're all dead, sir." "Then, will you do it?" "Yes, sir." Soldiers are not allowed to make speeches, but there's the most wonderful eloquence in all the world in the way a good man carries his shoulders and looks at you out of his eyes. We knew they would stick. I had my own few words to say to each of them, whether they were of the old faith or the new or no faith at all. We were two satisfied men coming back for we knew that the old regiment would give a good account of itself if the assault were made. The night passed uneventfully and this morning I was happy to have another Sunday for my own work. A French priest, a soldier in uniform (a *brancardier*), said Mass for Company F in the picturesque little soldier's chapel that gives the woods its name, and gave General Absolution and Communion, while I did the same in successive Masses for Company G and Company H, and the Wisconsin fellows.

I have served notice on Anderson that unless he produced some kind of a war in the next twenty-four hours I shall have to quit him. I had not been back to the Regimental P. C. for nearly a week, so on Friday I told Joe Hennessey that I wanted him to come up with a side car and bring me down. The side car arrived yesterday morning but with young Wadsworth running it. He had gotten impatient hanging around back there with prospects of a fight up front and he secured the privilege of coming up for me so as to get nearer for a while at least to the front line. It was a great pleasure to be at mess with Colonels McCoy and Mitchell once more—a mutual one evidently, for they both said that I had been too long away and would have to come back. I begged off until after Sunday.

Starting back on foot I ran into Major Donovan, who as usual walked me off my feet. I had to visit every foot of his position on both sides of the Jonchery road and I was glad when Major Grayson Murphy came along in a staff car and offered me a lift any place I wanted to go. Donovan and I are both fond of Major Murphy, so I told him I would go anywhere in the world with him so long as he delivered me from D.

On our way back to P. C. Anderson the Corps Officer who was with him gave his opinion that judging by past performances the Germans should be able to advance at least one kilometer in the massed attack that was threatened. I didn't say anything but it gave me a shivery feeling, especially when I measured out a kilometer on one of Anderson's maps and wondered just what would have happened to poor me by the time the gray mass of Germans would reach the point that the gentleman from the Staff had conceded them in his off-hand way. I needed the trip around the trenches for my own reassurance and I stretched myself out last night for a sleep with the comfortable feeling that the decision in this matter was in the hands of an aggregation of Irish stalwarts who care little for past performances or Staff theories.

We are going to celebrate tonight. Lieutenant Rerat is to bring over a few of the French Officers and the admirable John Pleune is off scouring the countryside and the French canteens for something to celebrate with.

July 14th, 1918 11:00 p. m.

We are here in Kelly's iron shack. Lieutenant Tom Young, a thorough soldier and a good friend of mine, and old boy Finnerty and Harry McLean are waiting for the bombardment. Everything that can be done for the men has been done. There remains the simplest task in the world, though often the hardest—waiting.

Our little Hands Across the Seas dinner was a jolly affair. Anderson had Kelly and myself for guests with his own staff; Keveny, Fechheimer and McDermott (Buck Philbin—God bless him for a fine youth—was just ordered back to the States and we miss him) ; and Lieutenant Rerat brought along two good fellows like himself—a

French-Irish Frenchman named DeCourcy (his ancestors left France, on their mission to teach the English manners and become good Irishmen themselves, somewhere around 1066, and one of their descendants came back to France with the Wild Geese after the Broken Treaty of Limerick) and a plump merry doctor whose name escapes me. The viands were excellent—considering. And Dan Mellett had done his noble best. Anyway, we made it a feast of song, that is, the others did. John Fechheimer (whom Heaven has sent us for our delight) has a complete repertoire, ancient (dating back more than 10 years) and modern—College Songs, Irish Songs, Scotch Songs, Negro Songs, music hall ditties, sentimental ballads and modern patriotic stuff—Upidee and Mother Machree; Annie Laurie and Old Black Joe; After the Ball and The Yanks are Coming. De Courcy received tremendous applause for

> , The prettiest girl I ever saw
> Was suckin-a cidah sroo a sraw.

When Rerat had explained the verbal niceties of the diction, all joined with enthusiasm in the classic verse

Oh the Infantry, the Infantry with the dirt behind their ears,
The Infantry, the Infantry that laps up all the beers,
The Cavalry, the Artillery and the blooming Engineers,
They couldn't lick the Infantry in a hundred thousand years.

We compelled the Major out of loyalty to his native heath to give us Down in the Heart of the Gas House District.

Just then the Adjutant of Colonel Arnoux stepped in to give us the news that the attack was certain and midnight the hour. So we toasted France and America and departed for a final inspection of positions. Everybody is as well fixed as he can be made and I have picked this as the handiest central place to await developments.

July 15th, 1918

It was 12:04 midnight by my watch when it began. No crescendo business about it. Just one sudden crash like an avalanche; but an avalanche that was to keep crashing for five hours. The whole sky seemed to be torn apart with sound—the roaring B-o-o-o-m-p of the discharge and the gradual menacing W-h-e-e-E-E-Z of traveling projectiles and the nerve racking W-h-a-n-g-g of bursts. Not that we could tell them apart. They were all mingled in one deafening combination of screech and roar, and they all seemed to be bursting just outside. Some one of us shouted, "They're off"; and then nobody said a word. I stood it about 20 minutes and then curiosity got the better of me and I went out. I put my back against the door of the hut and looked up cautiously to see how high the protecting sand bags stood over my head, and then I took a good look around. I saw first the sky to the south and found that our own guns were causing a comfortable share of the infernal racket. The whole southern sky was punctuated with quick bursts of light, at times looking as if the central fires had burst through in a ten-mile fissure. Then when my ear became adjusted to the new conditions I discovered that most of the W-h-e-e-z-z were traveling over and beyond, some to greet the invaders, some to fall on our own rear lines and back as far as Chalons. I crawled around the corner of the shack and looked towards the enemy. Little comfort there. I have been far enough north to see the Aurora Borealis dancing white and red from horizon to zenith; but never so bright, so lively, so awe-inspiring, as the lights from that German Artillery.

I stepped inside and made my report to Lieutenant Young, who was busy writing. He called for a liaison man. Harry McLean—just a boy—stepped out of the gloom into the candle light. He looked pale and uneasy—no one of us was comfortable—but he saluted, took the message, made a rapid Sign of the Cross, and slipped out into the roaring night. A liaison man has always a mean job, and generally a thankless one. He has neither the comparative protection of a dug-out or fox-hole under shelling, nor the glory of actual fight. Our lads—they are usually smart youngsters—were out in all this devilment the whole night and I am glad to say with few casualties. Every last man of them deserves a Croix de Guerre.

I wanted to see Anderson. He was only 40 yards away by a short cut over ground. I took the short cut—we were not allowed to use it by day—and had the uncomfortable feeling that even in the dark I was under enemy observation. It was the meanest 40 yards I had ever done since as a lad of 12 I hurried up the lane to my father's door pursued by an ever-nearing ghost that had my shoulder in its clutches as I grasped the latch. But I went in now as then, whistling. Anderson and Rerat were there. They had a word of comfort to tell; that General Gouraud had planned to meet artillery with artillery and that our fire was bursting on the enemy forces massed to attack us in the morning. Just then a nearer crash resounded. The major spun in his chair and fell; Rerat clasped his knee and cried, "Oh, Father, the Major is killed." The Major picked himself up sheepishly as if he had committed an indiscretion; Rerat rubbed a little blood off his knee apologetically as if he had appeared with dirt upon his face at drill; and I expressed jealousy of him that he had gotten a right to an easy wound stripe.

Just then a gas-masked figure opened the door and announced that there were two wounded men outside. That came under my business and it was a relief to find something to do. I followed the messenger—it was Kenneth Morford—one of two good lads the Morford family gave to the service. Around the corner I came on Jim Kane badly hurt in the legs. Kenneth and I lifted him and carried him with difficulty through the narrow winding trench to the First Aid Station where we left him with the capable Johnny Walker and went back for the second man. It was Schmedlein—his folks were parishioners of mine— and he had it bad. I was puffing by now and blaming myself that I had not followed Major Donovan's rules for keeping in condition. As I bent to the task I heard Phil

McArdle's voice, "Aisy now, Father. Just give me a holt of him. Slither him up on my back. This is no work for the likes of you." I obeyed the voice of the master and slithered him up on Phil's back with nothing to do but help Jim Bevan ease the wounded limb on our way to the dressing station.

Corporal Jelley of H—a fine soldier—and Private Hunt of E—he had a cablegram in his pocket announcing the birth of his first born—had been killed by the shell that struck in front of our dugout, and my friend Vin Coryell wounded. We found later that some men of Company H who had been sent to the French for an engineering detail, had been killed—Corporal Dunnigan, whom I married at Camp Mills; Patrick Lynn, Edward P. Lynch, Albert Bowler, Russell W. Mitchel, Patrick Morrissey, James Summers, Charles W. O'Day and Walter M. Reilley. Company G had also suffered losses during the bombardment: Paul Marchman, Theodore Sweet, Harold Cokeley, Patrick Grimes, Patrick Farley, killed; with Corporal Harvey J. Murphy and Charles J. Reilley fatally wounded.

Around P. C. Anderson there was plently of shelling but no further casualties until morning broke. At 4:30 the firing died down after a last furious burst over our immediate positions. The French soldiers in front began to trickle back down the *boyaus* to the defensive positions. Our men crawled out of their burrows, eager to catch the first sight of the enemy. A few wise old French soldiers stood by to restrain them from firing too soon, for in the half lights it is hard for an unaccustomed eye to discern the difference between the Poilu's Faded-coat-of-blue and the field gray of the Germans. Nearly an hour passed before one of them suddenly pointed, shouting, "Boche, Boche!" The enemy were appearing around the corners of the approach trenches. Rifle and machine gun fire crackled all along the front. The Germans, finding that this was the real line of resistance, went at their job of breaking it in their usual thorough fashion. Their light machine guns sprayed the top of every trench. Minenwerfer shells and rifle grenades dropped everywhere, many of them being directed with devilish accuracy on our machine gun positions. Many of ours were wounded. Sergeant Tom O'Rourke of F Company was the first man killed and then one of the Wisconsins.

That day the Badgers showed the fighting qualities of their totem. Several of their guns were put out of action at the outset of the fight, and practically all of them one by one before the battle was over. In each case Captain Graef, Lieutenant Arens and the other officers, together with the surviving gunners, set themselves calmly to work repairing the machines. Corporal Elmer J. Reider fought his gun alone when the rest of the crew was put out of action, and when his gun met the same fate he went back through a heavy barrage and brought up a fresh one. Privates William Brockman and Walter Melchior also distinguished themselves amongst the brave, the former at the cost of his life. There were many others like Melchior, who, when their gun was made useless, snatched rifles and grenades of the fallen Infantrymen and jumped into the fight. As specialists, they were too valuable to be used up this way and an order had to be issued to restrain them. Sergeant Ned Boone, who knows a good soldier when he sees one, said to me: "Father, after this I will stand at attention and salute whenever I hear the word Wisconsin."

Our own Stokes Mortar men fought with equal energy and enthusiasm under Lieutenant Frank McNamara and Sergeants Jaeger and Fitzsimmons with Corporals John Moore, Gerald Harvey and Herbert Clark. They did not take time to set the gun up on its base plates. Fitzsimmons and Fred Young supported the barrel in their hands, while the others shoved in the vicious projectiles. The gun soon became hot and before the stress of action was over these heroic non-coms were very badly burned.

During this interchange of fusillades the Germans were

seen climbing out of the approach trenches and taking their positions for an assault on the whole line.

They swept down on our trenches in masses seeking to overcome opposition by numbers and make a break somewhere in the thinly held line. Grenades were their principal weapons—rifle grenades from those in the rear, while the front line threw over a continuous shower of stick grenades, or "potato-mashers." An exultant cry went up from our men as they saw the foe within reach of them. Many jumped on top of the trench in their eagerness to get a shot at them or to hurl an answering grenade. The assault broke at the edge of the trench where it was met by cold steel. It was man to man then and the German found who was the better man. The assaulting mass wavered, broke and fled. No one knew how it might be elsewhere, but here at least the German Great Offensive had lost its habit of victory. They were unconvinced themselves, and hastened to try again, this time in thinner lines. Again they were repulsed, though some of them, using filtering tactics, got up into places where their presence was dangerous. One of their machine gun crews had established themselves well forward with their light gun, where it was troublesome to the defenders, and an enemy group was forming to assault under its protection. Mechanic Timothy Keane came along just then in his peaceful occupation as ammunition carrier, which he was performing with a natural grouch. Seeing the opportunity, he constituted himself the reserve of the half dozen men who held the position. He found a gun and grenades and leaped joyously into the fray; and when the attacking party was broken up he called, "Now for the gun, min," and swarmed over the parapet. The others followed. The surviving Germans were put out of action and the gun carried off in triumph.

Again and again the Germans attacked, five times in all, but each time to be met with dauntless resistance. By 2:00 in the afternoon the forces of the attacking Division was spent and they had to desist until fresh Infantry could be brought up.

All this while and through nearly three days of the battle the enemy used another power which proved in the outcome to be more annoying than directly dangerous. We had often read of superiority in the air when our side had it. We were now to learn the reverse of the fine picture. The German planes for two days had complete mastery. They circled over our heads in the trenches, front and rear. They chased automobiles and wagons down the road. You could not go along a trench without some evil bird spitting machine gun bullets at you. I doubt if they ever hit anybody. It must be hard to shoot from an aeroplane. After the first day they ceased to be terrifying—in war one quickly learns the theory of chances—but the experience was always irritating, as if some malicious small boy was insulting one. And they must certainly have taken note of everything we did. Well, it was no comfort to them.

When the Infantry assault was over the shelling began again. They put minenwerfer in the abandoned French trenches and threw over terrific projectiles into ours. They dropped a half dozen shells on Captain Prout's P. C. and utterly ruined that humble abode. Prout, with recollections of his native Tipperary, said, "Yes, Father, I got evicted, but I never paid a penny of rent to any landlord."

In spite of these events the issue of the day's battle was not in doubt after 10:00 o'clock that morning. There had been anxious moments before, especially when many machine guns were put out of action and the call for further fire from our artillery met with a feeble response. I dropped in on Anderson. True to his motto, "Fight it out where you are," he was putting the last touches to his preparations for having his clerks, runners and cooks make the last defense if necessary.

"Do you want some grenades, Padre?" was his question.

"No, Allie," I said, "every man to his trade. I stick to mine."

"Well here, then: this is my battalion flag," stroking the silk of the colors. "If things break bad in the battle you will see that it don't fall into the hands of the enemy. Burn it up if it is the last thing you find time to do before you go."

"All right, I shall look out for your flag. That is a commission that suits my trade."

And I received what was to be his last bequest—if things went bad. I said no more, but in my ears was humming "Down in the heart of the Gas House District in Old New York."

They breed good men there. Over in Anderson's old Company E, now in the able hands of Captain Baker, there were a lot of Anawanda braves who met the attack with the same fiery zest as their comrades on the left, as I shall tell in its place. I was not long with Anderson when in sweeps Kelly as brisk and jaunty as if he were on his way to the Fair at Kilrush in his native County Clare on a fine Saturday morning.

"How are things going, Mike?" said the Major.

"No trouble at all," said the Captain. "We've got them beat."

But there was still trouble ahead. All afternoon the trench mortar shells and whiz-bangs kept bursting in the whole sector, making the work of litter bearers and liaison men very difficult. Also the task of burying the dead, which Mr. Jewett of the Y's athletic department volunteered to superintend for me with the sturdy assistance of Corporal Michael Conroy of Company H.

Company H was in support—the most thankless and difficult sort of a job for any unit, whether Company, Regiment or Division. It is called upon for detachments which must go up under shell fire, and go in where the battle is hottest, and in unfamiliar surroundings. The unit generally gets little public credit for its share in the fight though military men know that it is a compliment to be held in support. It means that the Chief Commander has confidence that the smaller fractions into which it may have to be split are under well trained and competent leaders. However, nobody likes the job. Certainly big courageous Captain Jim Finn did not like it. He wanted to lead his own company in the fight and the H men would rather fight under their great hearted Captain than under any other leader in the world. That pleasure was denied them, but the Company surely did honor to the training and the spirit their Captain put into them. I saw a platoon going up the *boyau* with Lieutenant Wheeler, all of them flushed with the joy of action. "Over the top with Fighting Joe," called John O'Connor, from the words of Tom Donohue's song. Their services were needed often on the 15th to support the gallant defenses of Companies F and G.

On the morning of the 16th there was another furious assault. A whole German Battalion attacked one of the defense positions and for a time the situation looked serious. Lieutenant Young of F was killed while organizing the resistance. Lieutenants Wheeler and Anderson of H and Sears of F took all kinds of chances in meeting the situation and were carried off wounded. Some parties of Germans managed to get up into the trench. Joe Daly, while carrying ammunition, almost ran into a German. The latter was the more excited of the two, and before he could recover his wits, Daly had snatched a rifle which was leaning against the trench, whirled it over his head like a shillelah, and down on the German's skull. Then he ran into the middle of the fight.

Sergeant Bernard J. Finnerty and Corporal Thomas Fitzgerald of H saw a group of Germans who had ensconced themselves in an angle of the approach trench whence they were doing terrible damage with their potato mashers. Michael Tracy, a crack shot, who had done great work that day with his rifle, made a target of himself trying to find a better spot to shoot from, and got wounded.

But they had to be dislodged. So Finnerty and Fitzgerald rushed down the trench, hurled over hand grenades into the party, and destroyed it—but at the cost of their own heroic selves. John F. O'Connor, Mechanic of Company O, jumped on the parapet to get a position to bomb out a machine gun crew which were sheltered in a hollow. He drove them into the open where our own machine guns settled them.

The places of the wounded Lieutenants of H Company. were taken by Sergeants Eugene Sweeney and Jerome and William O'Neill (two of "The three O'Neills of Company H"; the third, Daniel, being First Sergeant, was with Captain Finn). In Company F Sergeants Timothy McCrohan and Thomas Erb with Corporals James Brennan and John Finnegan led the fighting under Captain Kelly and Lieutenants Marsh and Smith. Bernard Finnegan and Matt Wynne refused to quit when badly wounded. William Cassidy, Company Clerk, who could not content himself with that work while the fight was on, and Corporal Michael Leonard, an elderly man who had volunteered when men with a better right to do so were satisfied to wave the flag—these too won great renown. They and the others routed the enemy out of the trenches, following them over the top and up the *boyaus*. Cassidy and Leonard were killed, and my old time friend, Sergeant Joe O'Rourke of H, and many another good man. Sergeant William O'Neill was wounded, but kept on fighting, till death claimed him in the heat of the fray. His brother, Jerome, still battled valiantly and he was always worth a hundred men.*

Eugene Sweeney was twice wounded and refused to retire till the enemy was chased utterly from the field. When

* The three O'Neills and Bernard Finnerty as also Sergeant Spillane of Machine Gun Company came from the town of Bantry. "Rebel Cork" added new leaves to its laurel wreath of valor in this battle on the plains of Champagne.

his wounds were dressed he insisted on returning to the lines.

Corporal John Finnegan had been wounded in the leg the day before. He tied a bandage around the wound and stayed where he was. He was with Lieutenant Young when that leader was killed and ran to avenge him. A shell burst near him and he was hurled in the air, falling senseless and deaf. I saw him in the First Aid Station, a little way back, where he had been carried. The lads there had ripped up his breeches to re-bandage his earlier wound. He was just coming to. They told me he was shell shocked. "Shell shocked, nothing," I said. "A shell could kill John Finnegan, but it could not break his nerves." Just then he got sight of me. "There's nawthin' the matther with me, Father, exceptin' that I'm deaf. They got the Lootenant and I haven't squared it with thim yet. I'm goin' back." I told him he must stay where he was at least till I returned from the Battalion Dressing Station, which was 500 yards down the old Roman Road.

Going out I saw Marquardt, Hess and Kleinberg carrying a litter. I offered to help and found it was Dallas Springer, a dear friend of mine since Border days, now badly wounded. We got him with difficulty down the shelled road to the Battalion Dressing Station where I found the Surgeons, Doctors Martin, Cooper and Landrigan working away oblivious of the shells falling around. Landrigan had been out most of the night of the big bombardment arranging for the evacuation of the wounded. I put Dallas down beside Michael Leonard, a Wisconsin lad named Pierre, and Harold Frear, a slim, plucky lad whom we had rejected at the Armory for underweight when he applied for enlistment just a year ago, but who had pestered us all till we let him by. I was told that Lester Snyder of our Sanitary Detachment had been brought in nearly dead, a martyr to his duty, having gone out to bandage the wounded under heavy fire. It was a consolation to me to recall the devout faces of all five of them as I gave them Communion a day or two before.

Between looking after these and others who kept coming in it was a good while before I got back to the First Aid Station in the trenches and John Finnegan was gone. They had kept him for some time by telling him he was to wait for me. But after a rush of business they found John sitting up with a shoe lace in his hand. "Give me a knife," he said, "I want to make holes to sew up my pants." Johnny Walker had mine but he wouldn't lend it. "Lie down and be still." "All right," said Finnegan, "I have the tools God gave me." He bent his head over the ripped up breeches and with his teeth tore a few holes at intervals in the hanging flaps. He carefully laced them up with the shoe-string, humming the while "The Low Back Car." Then he got up. "Where's me gun?" "You are to wait for Father Duffy. He wants to see you." "Father Duffy done all for me I need, and he'd be the last man to keep a well man out of a fight. I'm feeling fine and I want me gun. I'm going back." He spied a stray rifle and seized it. "Keep out of me way, now, I don't want to fight with the Irish excipt for fun. This is business." So wounded, bruised, half deaf, John Finnegan returned to battle. Immortal poems have been written of lesser men.

The attacks on the position of Company G were not so bitter and persistent as Company F had to sustain. The G men felt rather hurt about it, but their genial Captain smilingly tells them that it was because the enemy know they could never get a ball through where G Company soldiers kept the goal. On the 15th the enemy certainly got a taste of their quality. A strong attack pushed in at a thinly held spot and were making off with a machine gun. Lieutenant Ogle mustered his platoon, sped over the top and down upon the enemy with grenades and cold steel. A short sharp fight ensued. The gun was carried back with shouts of laughter and in a few moments was barking with vicious triumph. Sergeant Martin Murphy, Corporals John Farrell, Michael Hogan and Thomas Ferguson —*four soldiers of the jolly, rollicking Irish type,* were Ogle's mainstays in this dashing fight. Lieutenant Boag was wounded, but his platoon was ably handled by Sergeant John McNamara.

When Prout's dugout was smashed to pieces by shell fire, Sergeant Martin Shalley, who is the very type and pattern of the Irish soldier, took charge of the rescue work and *dug out the buried men in time to save their lives.* Another shell destroyed the kitchen of Cook William Leaver. Thus relieved from his peaceful occupation he got himself a gun and belt and ran out into the fight garbed in his blue overalls. Michael Foody, tiring of being made the cockshot of aeroplanes which were flying low over the trenches, determined to try reprisals, and leaning back against the trench, began to discharge his automatic rifle in the direction of one that was particularly annoying to him. It was a long chance, but before he had emptied his feeder he had the joy of seeing the plane wabbling out of control and finally making a bad landing back of the German lines.

Corporal John G. Moore *lived up to the best traditions* of his gallant Company. He had been wounded but refused to go back. Later his post was suddenly occupied by half a dozen Germans. They called upon him to surrender, but Moore does not know that word in German or in any other language. He says he took it to mean a command to fire, so he started to put hand grenades over the plate *and the two Germans that were left made quick tracks for* the exit gate. Moore's delivery is hard to handle. Alfred Taylor also proved his mettle by sticking to his post when wounded and insisting furthermore on joining a raiding party the same day.

Raiding parties were G Company's stock in trade. Lieutenants Ogle and Stout revel in them. They were out at night *looking for the trouble that did not come their way* often enough by day. One of these patrols fell upon what they called a bargain sale and "purchased" new German

boots and underwear for the whole Company. John Ryan
got left behind in one of these raids and had to lie for two
days in a shell hole with Germans all around him. He
finally got back with valuable information concerning movements of the enemy.

Further to the east and separated from the other companies by a battalion of the 10th Chasseurs was Company E
under Captain Charles D. Baker. During the bombardment only one man, Michael Higgins, was killed. The attacks of the enemy on the next two days were of the filtering kind, and were easily repulsed, George McKeon being
the only man slain.

By the 18th they began to grow weary of these trivial
actions and Captain Baker ordered two platoons to go
a raiding. The first platoon, under Lieutenant Andrew L.
Ellett and Acting-Sergeants Malloy and McCreedy, went up
the *boyau* on the left. They had not gone a quarter of a
mile when they saw Germans in a trench. Douglas Mac-
Kenzie, in liaison with the French, reported them as gathering for an attack. The Lieutenant climbed out of the trench
to get a better view, and Matt Cronin got out behind him
with his automatic rifle to start things going. Some of
the enemy were in plain view and Cronin's weapon began
pumping merrily. The enemy responded and he received
a wound. The fight was on. It was a grenade battle. Our
men rose to it with the same zest they had shown when
they fought their boyish neighborhood fights, street against
street, in Tompkins Park or Stuyvesant Square. But this
was to the death. Both Sergeant Malloy and Archie Skeats
took that death in their hands when they caught up German
grenades out of the ditch and hurled them back at the
enemy. Lieutenant Ellett's men were far from their base
of supplies. Three times they fell back along the *boyau*
as their ammunition ran out; and three times with fresh
grenades they advanced to meet the foe. The Lieutenant
was wounded, but a hole or two in him never mattered to
Andy Ellett. He withdrew his men only when he felt he

GENERAL LENIHAN, LIEUTENANT GROSE, COLONEL MITCHELL, FATHER
DUFFY, MR. GEORGE BOOTHBY OF THE "Y," AND JUDGE EGEMAN,
OF THE K. OF C.

had done all that was necessary. Then he handed over his charge to Sergeant Frank Johnston, a warrior every inch, who had joined up with Anderson's old company for the war because he knew Anderson of yore. He had fought with him many a time in the Epiphany Parish School.

The other platoon was commanded by Lieutenant Tarr with William Maloney and Michael Lynch as Sergeants. Dick O'Connor, who always went to battle with song, was the minstrel of the party, his war song being "Where do we go from here, boys?" John Dowling, Cowie, Joyce, Gavan and McAleer went ahead to scout the ground. They passed through some underbrush. Suddenly they flushed two Germans. Dowling fired and shouted, "Whirroo me buckos, here's our mate." His cry was answered by Maloney, a mild-mannered Celt, who knows everything about fighting, except how to talk of it afterwards. Lieutenant Tarr gave the order and led his whole platoon over the top across the level ground and up to the trench where the Germans held the line. It was grenades again and hand to hand fighting on top of it. A party of the Germans fled to the left. They heard the battle of Ellett's platoon from there and they turned with upthrown hands and the cry "Kamerad." Dowling helped the first one out of the trench by the ear. "Aisy now, lad, and come along with me. The Captain is sitting forninst the blotter to take your pedigree." Back went most of the platoon with the prisoners, their mission accomplished. Eleven prisoners had been taken and fifty Germans left dead upon the field. But the never satisfied Maloney elected himself to cover the retreat with Hall, Breen and Hummell; and with such a leader they kept battling as if they were making a Grand Offensive until they were ordered to withdraw.

I have been to the Third Platoon of Company E and everybody talked about that patrol at once. Everybody except Maloney. But everybody else was talking about Maloney. I looked around to see what Maloney would have to tell. And I found no Maloney. Maloney had fled, sick of hearing about Maloney.

This was practically our last shot in the battle. The German attack had evidently come to a complete stand-still. They even lost their command of the air on the afternoon of the 17th, when a fleet of British aeroplanes had come along and driven them to cover. On our part we were preparing to become the aggressors. The 3rd Battalion was being brought forward to relieve the 2nd, and to take command of both came our good old Lieutenant Colonel, jaunty and humorous as always in a fight and without a worry except as to whether he and I had enough smokes to last. All care vanished when my orderly, Little Mac, sneaked up from where I had left him in the rear, bringing two cartons of cigarettes.

Today we received definite word of what had happened meanwhile in the support Battalions. During the bombardment, young Wadsworth was killed at Headquarters, and I lost other good friends in Company B—Sergeant Harry Kiernan, as good a man as he looked, and that is a great compliment; Arthur Viens, one of my own parish lads, and Joseph Newman, and Archie Cahill, mortally wounded. Louis Cignoni of Company C and Sam Forman of the Machine Gun Company were also killed. Sergeant Charles Lanzner of Company A was killed while doing brave work as a volunteer carrying a message to Company B under the fearful cannonading. The Polish Battalion also had met with a savage reception that night.

The French gave news that the enemy was held in every part of the long front, with the exception of a portion of the line around Chateau Thierry and running up the northeast side of the salient. The old Rainbow had not a single dent in it. I got our fellows stirred up by telling them that they had gone and spoiled one of the loveliest plans that had ever been prepared by a General Staff. "What do you mean, spoil their plans? All we spoiled were Germans!" "That's just the trouble. The men who planned this battle did not really expect you to stick, and they were all ready to give the Germans a terrible beating after they had walked through you and gotten out into the open space. The trouble was that you fellows did not know enough to run away, and the Generals finally had to say, 'We shall have to scrap our beautiful plans and fight this battle out where those fool soldiers insist on having it fought.' "

Around midnight we were told that we would be relieved by morning. Why? No one knew. Where were we going? No one knew. The French were to take our place. They were slow in coming. We wanted to be away before sunrise or the enemy would have a fine chance to shell our men as they made their way over the plains. I waited the night there in Kelly's shack, impatient for the relief to come ere dawn. Finally the Poilus, their blue uniform almost invisible by dark, began to appear. I started off with Mr. Jewett down the road to St. Hilaire. We picked up Bill Neacy with a Headquarters detachment, and found a back road down to Jonchery. I watched for the dawn and German planes, filled with anxiety for our withdrawing columns. But dawn came and no shelling, and shortly afterwards I fell into the kindly hands of Major Donovan, and soon good old John Kayes and Arthur Connelly had a beefsteak on the fire for us. The 2nd Battalion came drifting in in small parties, and reported everybody safe. Then I saw Pat Kinney and knew that the Colonel was somewhere about. He had come out to look after his men. I certainly was glad to see him, and I got the reception of a long lost brother. He bundled me into his car, and in a short time had me wrapped in his blankets and taking a long deferred sleep in his cot at Bois de la Lyre.

VADENAY

July 21st, 1918

We packed up our belongings in the Bois de la Lyre on July 20th and went to this town of Vadenay. Colonel

McCoy had a ceremony that afternoon which shows one reason why we are so devoted to him. I had written up the recommendations for citations furnished by Company Commanders during the recent battle; and the Colonel, fearing they might not go through, embodied them in a regimental citation and read them to the assembled soldiers. It was fine and stimulating; the 2nd Battalion is as proud as if it had won the war and the others are emulous to equal its fame.

I went back to my billet and found a visitor who announced himself as Father James M. Hanley of the Diocese of Cleveland. I remembered the name. I received a letter some two months ago, a fresh breezy letter, full of the unrestrained impatience of a young priest who had come over to take part in the war and had landed in an engineer outfit not far from a base port. He appealed to me as an old-timer to tell him how to beat this mean game. I answered and told him what to say to Bishop Brent, and Bishop Brent, nothing loth, had sent him to me for the 42nd Division. The more I talked with the new Chaplain the more 69th he looked to me; so I said to him: "I am going to keep you with me. Father McDonald is in ill-health and has orders for a new assignment. We shall have a big battle in a week or two and we shall need two men because there is a good chance of one of us being bumped off. Major Anderson's battalion will very probably be in reserve so you report to Major McKenna and tag along with him. I shall tie up with Major Donovan."

The next day was Sunday. It was the first day the whole regiment was in one place since we left Camp Mills. There was a beautiful church in the town and I announced four masses with general absolution and communion without fasting. In all my life I never saw so many men at communion in one day. The altar rail was too narrow to accommodate them, so we lined them up on their knees the length of the aisle, and two priests were kept busy passing up and down giving communion. The non-Catholics we took in groups near their companies and had brief exhortation and silent prayer.

I never use the motive of fear in talking to soldiers about religion because it does not suit with their condition, and anyway I can get more substantial results without it. But the government and the army believes in preparedness for death, as is shown by their ambulances and hospitals and pensions. I believe in spiritual preparedness; so too, do the men. I am happy to think that my own charges are well prepared. May the grace of God be about them, for I feel we are in for a big fight.

One thing sure, they are not afraid of it. Coming in to Vadenay I saw Amos Dow, a stripling youth of Company K, just back from the hospital after four months of absence—he was terribly gassed last March and his condition then had me much worried. He was still looking none too well.

"What brought you back," I asked. "You are not fit for this kind of work yet."

"Well, they did offer me other jobs, but I wanted to be with my own outfit, and I wanted to get a Dutchman after what they did to me, and I was sick of hearing the Marines talk about how good they are. I want to get into a first class battle with this Division like you've been through while I was coming up, and when I meet those birds from the Marines, I'll have something to say to them."

"You're a blood-thirsty youth. But far be it from me to stop you. It's your trade. But you can't carry a pack, so I'll fix it up to make it easy for you."

"Joe," I called to Sergeant Flannery, "I want you to get Captain Mangan and Lieutenant Kinney to adopt this savage child in the Supply Company for a week or two. See that he gets up where he can smell powder, but without too much hiking, and then give him his belt and rifle and let him go to it."

"I had better get a lariat and a picket pin and tie him up," growled Joe.

He was right. By morning the lad was gone off with Company K. He was afraid I would spoil his chance for a battle.

The survivors of our 2nd Battalion are camped in a wooded island in the stream and I spent the afternoon with them. The weather was delightful and they were enjoying a lounging, lazy, gossipy day, which is the one compensation for being in the Infantry—the artillery have fewer killed, but their work never lets up. I went amongst them to pick up incidents for my narrative. One of the first things I found was that the recent battle had given them increased confidence and respect for their officers. A Company F man said to me: "I'll take back anything I ever said about Captain Mike. At Baccarat he had me fined two-thirds of three months pay for taking a drink too much and I said that if I had the job of rigging him up for a night patrol, I'd like to tie bells around him and put a lantern on his head."

My first visit was to Company H, which had been the greatest sufferer. In addition to the names I have already cited, one of the most frequent on all men's lips was that of Dudley Winthrop. Dudley is a fine youth and one of my best friends. I tell him that he has a name like a movie actor, but he says he can bring around two cousins of his named Connelly from Company G to prove that he belongs to the Fighting Race. I hope he gets the Croix de Guerre he has been put in for, for he certainly deserves it. Patrick J. Dwyer, William Gordon and Daniel Marshall are also cited by their fellows for sticking it out while wounded, with Thomas McDermott, who was tagged for the hospital and refused to go. High praise also for Martin Higgins (a born fighter) and Andrew Murray, Dan McCarthy, Sergeant Val. Dowling, William Smythe, Sammy Kleinberg, whom I saw going around all week cheerfully carrying the wounded with the clothes burned off his back by a misdirected flare; Tom Heaney, Robert Cooper, Michael Kearns, James O'Brien, John Thornton, John A. Fredericks, Donald Gillespie, John F. Lynch, Joseph Mattiello, with cooks Pat Fahey and Gorman, Timothy Walsh, Peter Breslin, John J. Walker, Charles Rogan, Michael Higgins, Dennis Kerrigan, James Guckian, John J. McCormack, James Todd, John Kelly, Frank Garvin, Lawrence Farrell, Bill Fleming, Charles Klika, William McNamee, James Merrigan, John Maher, Harold Avery, Patrick Connors, John P. Furey, Frank Condit, Robert McGuiness, John Higgins, James Keane, Patrick Travers, Thomas Slevin, John Ryan, John and James French, Bruno Guenther, Daniel Dayton, Frank Doran, Charles Ziegler. The men who were on the digging detail that had such heavy losses in the bombardment praise the coolness and solicitude for their safety of Lieutenants Becker and Otto.

Company G talked most about their Captain, the serenest pleasantest, and most assuring person in the world in time of trial and danger. Also Lieutenants Ogle and Stout, Norris and Joseph Boag, who was wounded in the fray. I myself had seen Carl Kemp of the same Company on duty at Battalion Headquarters standing through the bombardment on the top of the parapet on his duties as lookout. Sergeant Jim Coffey, wounded and still fighting; and, in the same class, Ralph Holmes and John Flanigan; James Christy, working his automatic from the top of the trench; Dennis Roe, always a good soldier in a fight; Sylvester Taylor and Joseph Holland, liaison men; Sergeants Jim Murray, Edward McNamara, Thomas T. Williamson and Frank Bull, Mess Sergeant Hugh Lee; James Henderson, Thomas Gallagher, William McManus, Michael Hogan, William Carroll, Morris Lemkin, Dennis O'Connor, John McNamara, John Conroy, Frank McNiff, Joseph P. Alnwick, Patrick Burke, Patrick Duffy, David Fitzgibbons, Angelo Dambrosio, James Keavey, Nicholas Martone, Lawrence Redmond, James Ryan and John Ryan, the Hans brothers; Thomas Slevin, Herbert Slade, James Walsh, Allen, Henry Curry and John Fay as Company liaison; Arthur Ayres, George Murray, Herman and Lyons as litterbearers; Louis Mugno, Maurice Dwyer, Patrick Keane, Charles McKenna, James Elliott, mechanics; Michael Hogan, Patrick Burke, young O'Keefe, Robert Monahan, Frank Garland; and, to end with a good old Irish name, Mack Rosensweig. I know he'll be with us if we ever get a chance to go over and free Ireland, and he'll be a good man to take along.

In Company F it was all praise for Captain Mike and praise and regrets for Lieutenant Young. I did not need to have them tell me anything about their liaison group, as I saw them at work—from the Corporal in charge, John H. Cooke, who, though wounded, stuck at his job, to Harry P. Ross, John J. Carey, Leon Duane, John Gill, William Grimson, Harry McLean. Sergeant Major Michael J. Bowler did good work looking after the wounded. Tom Kenney carried in Lieutenant Anderson and I saw James Bevan do good service in the same line; also Marquardt, Goble, Gray and Harry Rubin. First Sergeant Joseph Blake was a cool leader, as also Charles Denon, Leo McLaughlin, and Tim McCrohan. Of those who were wounded and stuck, the name of Sergeant Eugene Cunningham was mentioned, as also John Butler, Edward Callan, John Catterson, Albert Curtis and James Brennan. Pat Frawley (one of the best soldiers the regiment ever had), was wounded and stuck, was knocked senseless and still stuck. Others who distinguished themselves in hand to hand fighting were Patrick McGinley, Peter Sarosy, Thomas McManus, Malcolm Joy, always lively in a fight; and on the Roll of Honor the popular vote placed Sergeant Phil Gargan, whose kitchen was ruined ("wounded at Lunéville, killed in Champagne," said Phil); James P. McGuinn, Oscar Youngberg, William Gracely, Hugh Haggerty, Lewis Edwards, Michael Gettings, Joseph McCarthy, John J. Tyson, James Moran, Edward Moore, James Kelly, Cornelius Behan, Ned Boone, James Branigan, Tom Cahill, James Coogan, Joseph Coxe, Morris Fine, Dick Leahy, Nat Rouse, and, to end once more with a good Irish name, "Pat" Levine.

Company E added to my extended list the names of James A. Donohue, Walter Dowling, Ray Dineen, and most of all, Fred Gluck, who rendered heroic service as litter bearer. At Headquarters the Colonel himself spoke enthusiastically about the good work of young Joe Hennessy, who was on the road at all times on his motorcycle, oblivious of danger even after being wounded. I found that Company M was carrying Corporal Dan Flynn as A. W. O. L. on its records. Dan had gone up to the Second Battalion on paper work and finding that a fight was on he got himself a rifle and stayed there till it was over.

We are all well satisfied with the spirit of every man in the regiment during the last fight. I had but one recommendation to make to Colonel McCoy. The Company litter bearers are left to the selection of the Captains. Now the Captains are chiefly interested in front line work and they refuse to spare a good rifleman for any other task. But the litter bearers have a task which is most trying on morale and physique, and it will not be easier if it comes to open warfare, where they will have to stand up when the fighting men lie in shell holes. The litter bearers acquitted themselves well in this fight, but I feel strongly that nothing is too good for the wounded. I want the Colonel to insist that one man in every four be a picked man who will go and keep the others going on their work of human salvage until every man drops in his tracks. I would select in every four men one of our solid Irish, of the kind that with death all around, hears nothing but the grace of God purring in his heart.

CHAMIGNY SUR MARNE

July 24th, 1918

Sur Marne—there is magic in that. I have always wanted to see the Old Regiment add the name of that river, so full of martial associations, to the history-telling silver furls on its colors. We are not in battle yet. Nothing could be more peaceful than the scenes in which we live, if one shuts one's eyes to uniforms and weapons. The broad, silvery Marne forms a loop around the little village and the commodious modern chateau (owned, by the way, by an American), in which we live. We revel in our new found luxury. Following a motto of this land, "We take our good where we find it." I got a variation of that as I came into the lordly halls and stood staring around me. Sergeant Major Dan O'Connell gave a signal like an Orchestra Leader to the Adjutant's Office Force and McDermott, O'Brien, Jimmy Canny, White, Monahan, Farrell, Whitty, with Dedecker and Dietz joining in, sang deliberately for my benefit, "There's nothing too good for the I-i-i-rish." A sentiment which meets with my hearty approval.

A diary is a sort of magic carpet; it is here, and then it is there. Three days ago we hiked it from Vadenay to the nearby station of St. Hilaire-au-Temple where we entrained for parts to us unknown. Our 2nd Battalion and the Wisconsins, which formed one of the sections, had the mean end of a one-sided battle while waiting at the station. The German bombing planes came over and started dropping their "Devil's eggs." C-r-r-unch! C-r-r-unch! C-r-r-unch! the face of the earth was punctured with deep holes that sent up rocks and smoke like a volcano in eruption; the freight shed was sent in flying flinders, but the train was untouched. Animals were killed, but no men.

"We don't know where we're going but we're on our way" might be taken as the traveling song of soldiers. We dropped down to Chalons, crossed the river, going first in a south-easterly direction to St. Dizier, then southwest to Troyes, and rolling through France the whole night long we came in the morning as near Paris as Noisy-le-Sec, from which, with glasses, we could see the Eiffel Tower. Judg-

ing from our experience with the elusive furlough, that is
as near to Paris as most of us will ever get.

We were impressed with the new enthusiasm for American soldiers among the French people; every station, every
village, every farm window was hung with colors, some
attempt at the Stars and Stripes being common. And stout
burghers, lovely maidens, saucy gamins, and old roadmenders had a cheer and a wave of the hand for "les braves
Americains, si jeunes, si forts, si gentils," as the troop
train passed by.

"Looks as if they knew about the big battle we were in,"
said Lawrence Reilly.

"Not a bit of it," said the grizzled Sergeant Harvey. "I
have seen the Paris papers and nobody but ourselves knows
that the Americans were in the Champagne fight. These
people think we are fresh from the rear, and they are giving
us a good reception on account of the American Divisions
that hammered the Jerries three or four days after we
helped to stand them up. Isn't that so, Father?"

"I think you're right, Sergeant. For the time being what
you fellows did is lost in the shuffle."

"Who were these other guys?" asked Mike Molese.

"They say it was the 1st and 2nd Divisions up near
Soissons and the 26th and 3rd around Chateau Thierry."

"How is it these fellows manage to get all the press-agent stuff and never a thing in the paper about the 42nd?"
asked Tommy Murphy.

"Well, those other fellows say that it is the Rainbows
that get all the advertising."

"Well, if I ever get home," said Bobby Harrison, "I'll
tell the world that none of those birds, regulars, marines
or Yankees, have anything on the Rainbow."

"Oh, what's the difference?" said the philosophical John
Mahon, "as long as it is American soldiers that are getting
the credit."

"Do you subscribe to those sentiments, Kenneth?" I
asked John's side partner, Hayes.

"I certainly do, Father."

"Then I make it unanimous. This meeting will now adjourn with all present rising to sing the 'Star Spangled Banner.'"

CHATEAU MOUCHETON, EPIEDS

July 26th, 1918

Somebody is always taking the joy out of life. We had but three days in our pleasant villages on the Marne when they routed us out and lined us up on a hot, broad highway, where we waited for the French camions which were to take us towards the field of battle. Finally they arrived—a long fleet of light hooded trucks, each driven by a little sun-burned, almond-eyed, square-cheeked Chink—Annamese or Tonquinese, to be more accurate. We sailed in these four-wheeled convoys past what is left of the village of Vaux (the completest job of destruction we had yet seen, the work of our American artillery) through Chateau Thierry, which had only been pecked at in comparison, and northwest to the town of Epieds.

Here we witnessed one of those melodramas of war, for the sight of which most civilians at home would sell, I am sure, one year of their lives. There were four of our observation balloons in the air. Four or five German attacking planes were circling above them intent on their destruction; and a few doughty French flyers were manœuvering to resist them. The convoy paused on the road to watch the result of the combat. In fact, all the roads converging there were brown with canvas hoods and khaki uniforms. Both the stage and the accommodations for spectators were perfect. The spectators arranged themselves along the roadside; the scene was set in the clear sky overhead. Suddenly one of the Germans darted high in the air over the balloon on the extreme left. Anti-aircraft guns barked viciously, and the ether broke out in white and black patches around him, but he managed to place himself where they could not fire at him easily, as he had the balloon in the line of fire from the strongest battery. Then he turned and swooped down on the balloon, swift as a hawk at its prey. He swerved upwards as he passed it and all four Germans soared rapidly upwards and away. We saw something drop suddenly from the balloon, which rapidly developed into a parachute with two observers clinging to it. A thin wisp of smoke which we could detect from the balloon then burst into flames, and the blazing material began to drop towards the parachute. But the automobile to which the silk observation tower was attached began to move, and the fiery mass missed the parachute on the way down. We were glad that the observers had escaped, but we felt that in this first round of our new battle we had to concede first blood to the enemy.

We hiked from Epieds—a pleasant walk—to this fine chateau, the main building of which is occupied by French Staff Officers of a Corps d'Armée. Our headquarters is in a large outbuilding, the men being in the nearby woods. I have been circulating around amongst our 1st Battalion and also the Ohios on my own particular concerns. Took supper with Company D. Buck is away, as Major Donovan has taken his four company commanders on a reconnoitering expedition, since his battalion is to be first in. Had supper with Lieutenants Connelly, Daly and Burke. Daly is a fine, intelligent active youth, graduate of Holy Cross and of the Old Irish 9th Mass. Burke got his training in the regular army. He is a soldier of the silent determined kind, and a very efficient officer, with no blamed nonsense about him. The other three of us, of a more normal racial type, cannot see any sense in being too sensible. Connelly winked at me and began to "draw" Burke by expressing envy of the lucky birds who had gotten orders to go back to the States. Daly played up strongly, and Burke's face showed ever-increasing exasperation and disgust. Finally he blurted: "Father, why don't you shut these slackers up? We're here to see this thing through, and such talk is bad for morale." When I laughed as loud as the rest he grinned and said:

"Oh, I know that if they gave you fellows New York City with Boston to boot, neither of you would go back." A true statement, as I know. I paid for my supper by hearing their confessions.

Later

The reconnoitering party came in for a severe shelling, and Buck has gone back wounded and Hutchinson gassed. Donovan is back here, also gassed, but ready to go in again if they want his battalion, though his orders to relieve the French have been countermanded. While I am writing, a polite French Staff Officer came in with the word that the original orders should stand. Donovan buckled his harness on anew and went out to lead his battalion forward once more. I posted myself in the gateway of the Chateau and gave absolution to each Company as it passed. Then I hastened out on the main road, and made similar announcements to the Ohios, as that regiment moved up to the front. There is every evidence that we are in for a battle, big and bloody.

COURPOIL

July 27th, 1918

We spent last night in this shell-torn town, and this evening we take up the pursuit of the withdrawing Germans. Donovan's battalion is out getting touch with them and McKenna is starting up too. The 84th Brigade has already relieved the 26th American Division and a Brigade of the 28th and have been in a hard battle with the enemy at Croix Rouge Farm. It took all their undoubted courage to sweep over the machine gun nests, and they succeeded in doing it at the price of a battalion. The roads coming down are filled with ambulances and trucks carrying the wounded and dripping blood. We are relieving the 167th French Division, but nothing seems definitely settled, and messengers are coming and going with orders and counter orders. I have greater admiration than ever for McCoy these days. He moves in war as in his native element, expending his energies without lost motion or useless friction.

Tonight we go to the Chateau de Fère. If the Germans decide to make a stand at the Ourcq we shall be in action by tomorrow.

CHAPTER VI

THE BATTLE OF THE OURCQ

CROIX ROUGE FARM was the last stand of the Germans south of the Ourcq but it was expected that they would make some sort of resistance on the slopes and in the woods north of this river.

To get to the battlefield from the south one can go on a broad highway running straight north for five miles through the thickly wooded Foret de Fere. Near the northern point of the woods is an old square French Ferme—the Ferme de l'Esperance, and a more pretentious modern dwelling, the Château de Fôret. A little further north one comes to the contiguous villages of La Folie and Villers sur Fere. On the map they look like a thin curved caterpillar, with the church and the buildings around its square representing the head. Beyond the square a short curved street known to us as "Dead Man's Curve" or "Hell's Corner" leads to the cemetery on the left, with an orchard on the right. From the wall of the orchard or cemetery one can see the whole battlefield of our Division on the Ourcq. A mile and a half to the left across the narrow river is Fere en Tardenois blazing, smoking and crackling all the week under the fire of artillery, first of the French, then of the Germans. About the same distance to the right and also north of the river, lies the village of Sergy where the Iowas were to have their battle. To get the Ourcq straight across the line of vision one faces to the northeast. The eye traverses a downward slope with a few clumps of trees for about eight hundred yards. The river, which would be called a creek in our country, has a small bridge to the left

158

and another a little to the right as we are looking, near the Green Mill or Moulin Vert. Straight ahead beyond the river is a valley, and up the valley a thousand yards north of the river is a house and outbuildings with connecting walls all of stone, forming a large interior court yard. It is Meurcy Farm. A brook three or four feet wide runs down the valley towards us. Its marshy ground is thickly wooded near the Ourcq with patches of underbrush. And about two hundred yards west of the Farm is a thick square patch of wood, the Bois Colas. North of the Farm is a smaller woods, the Bois Brulé.

The whole terrain naturally slopes towards the Ourcq. But tactically the slopes that were of most importance in our battle were those that bound the brook and its valley. Facing the Farm from the bottom of the valley one sees to the left a gradual hill rising northwestwards till it reaches the village of Seringes et Nesles, which lies like an inbent fish-hook, curving around Bois Colas and Meurcy Farm half a mile away. To the east of the brook the rise goes up from the angle of the brook valley and the river valley in two distinct slopes, the first, fairly sharp, the second gradual. Six hundred yards or so north of these crests is a thick, green wall across the northern view. It is the Forest of Nesles. The difficulty of attacking up this little valley towards the Farm lay in the fact that it made a sort of trough, both sides of which could be easily defended by machine guns with a fine field of direct fire, and also by flanking fire from the opposite slope as well as from Meurcy Farm and Bois Colas which lay in the northern angle of the valley. And when the attackers got to the top of the eastern crest there were five hundred yards of level ground to traverse in face of whatever defences might be on the edge of the Forest.

With plenty of artillery to crack the hardest nuts, and with regiments moving forward fairly well in line so that the advance of each would protect the flanks of its neighbors, the problem would not have been a terrific one.

But nobody knew for certain whether the enemy would make more than a rear guard action at the Ourcq. His general line still constituted a salient and his ultimate line was sure to be the Vesle or the Aisne. It takes time to get Artillery up and in place. And the Germans might slip away scot free on account of our too great caution in following him. Miles to right and left allied troops, mainly French, were hammering at both sides of the salient. It was the duty of those who followed the retreating enemy to see that his retirement with guns and other property should not be too easy a task.

In our progress to the slopes above the Ourcq there was little resistance in the path of our brigade. The night of the 27th, General Lenihan established brigade headquarters at the Château de Foret. The Ohios were in the forest in brigade support, as the first plan was to send in one regiment. Our second battalion was in regimental reserve and was held by Anderson in the woods to the left of the road, his principal officers being Lieutenant Keveny, Adjutant, and in command of the four companies, E, F, G, H, Captains Baker, Kelly, Prout and Finn. Colonel McCoy had established his post of command near the church at the northern end of Villers sur Fere. With him was the Headquarters Company under Captain Michael Walsh, and nearest to him was the third battalion under Major McKenna, with Lieutenant Cassidy, Adjutant, and Companies I, K, L, M, commanded by Captains Ryan, Hurley, Merle-Smith and Meaney.

Major Donovan with the first battalion, Lieutenant Ames, Adjutant, and the Companies A, B, C, D, commanded by Lieutenant Baldwin, Captain Reilly, Captain Bootz and Lieutenant Connelly with our Machine Gun Company under Captain Seibert, had gone forward on the night of the 26th and relieved the French west of Beuvardes. On the afternoon of the 27th they had passed east through the Foret de Fere and had come out on the crest over the river between Villers and Sergy, the lines being widely extended to keep in touch with the Iowas on the right. Here we witnessed the first operation of cavalry in our battles. A small squadron of French cavalry came out of the woods and proceeded down the road south of the river in the direction of Sergy with the intention of drawing the enemy fire. It was a beautiful sight to see the animated group of horses and men tearing down the road, but a spectacle that did not last long, as very shortly they drew a powerful enemy fire and after some losses cantered back to the woods with their main object accomplished. Our Infantry was thus drawn into the battle but with little opportunity to accomplish much as the enemy were relying principally on heavy shell fire. Of ours, Company C suffered the greatest losses, as Corporal Morschhauser, William V. Murtha and John F. Ingram were killed and Sergeant John F. Vermaelen with Frank Dunn, William Ryan and Harry Fix mortally wounded. Major Donovan drew his battalion back behind the reverse slope of a hill where it was protected from observation by trees, and there ordered them to dig in for the night.

He had detached Company D, under Lieutenant Connelly, to find and maintain liaison with the French on the left. The Lieutenant got in touch with our own 3rd Battalion which was already coming up on that side. Lieutenant Burke of D Company, with Eugene Brady, kept on to find the French to the westward, but just as he started out he received a dangerous and painful wound in the leg. He stopped only long enough to have it tied up and then, in spite of protest, he insisted on carrying out his task. He tramped over fields and through woods for four hours that night before his work was complete and there was no danger of the derangement of plans, and then permitted them to carry him back to the hospital. His wound was so severe that it took months and months to heal, but Burke is the kind of soldier who will carry out any task he is given to do, if he has to finish it crawling.

In the early hours of Sunday, July 28th, the disposition of

the regiment was as follows. Colonel McCoy with his Headquarters Company, Major McKenna's Battalion with Company D of the 1st Battalion, and a Company of the Wisconsin Machine Gunners were in the town of Villers sur Fere and in the orchards east of it. Major Donovan with Companies A, B and C, and our Machine Gun Company were further east in the direction of Sergy. Our 2nd Battalion was two miles behind and to the west, the Ohios being still further west on the same line. A battalion of the Alabamas had come up behind Major Donovan to take the ground he had occupied between Villers sur Fere and Sergy. In front of Sergy the Iowas were already set. West of Villers sur Fere the ground was held by the French, their main effort being concentrated on the capture of Fere en Tardenois. It was reported through the night that they already had that town, but they did not cross the river until well on into the next morning.

Under normal battle conditions Colonel McCoy would not have been justified in having his Post of Command right up with the advance elements of his regiment as they went into battle. But he was a bold as well as a careful commander, and he felt that he could best handle the situation by being where he could see just what was going on.

For two days the situation had been changing from hour to hour. First it was planned to have Major Donovan relieve the forward elements of the French Infantry on Friday night. Then on Friday morning came a corps order for the 42nd Division to attack on Saturday morning. It was then arranged between General Menoher and the French Division Commander to have two battalions of ours, Donovan's and McKenna's, relieve the French that night. As we have seen, the order to attack was recalled and the relieving battalions were sent back. But the two division commanders decided that the relief should be effected and that these two battalions should take the front line with Anderson in support and the 166th in reserve. On Saturday came word that the enemy had withdrawn with the French Division to our left in pursuit. The 166th were to relieve them when the situation settled.

On Saturday morning came General Order 51. "Pursuant to orders from the Sixth (French) Army, 42nd Division will attack at H. hour, under cover of darkness, night of July 27-28." The four infantry regiments were to attack abreast, a battalion of each being in line. "The attack will be in the nature of a surprise, and consequently troops in the attack will not fire during the assault, but will confine themselves to the use of the bayonet."

At 1:00 P. M. Saturday, July 27th, the order was given to execute the relief and await further instructions. Our advance elements were already on the way and the 1st Battalion of the Ohios came up in the rear of the 10th French Chasseurs to make reconnoissance with the purpose of relieving them.

An hour after midnight General Lenihan received a message from Colonel MacArthur containing an order from our 1st Army Corps, that the attack be made before daylight and without artillery preparation, reliance being placed chiefly on the bayonet to drive the enemy from his position. Cavalry were to be in reserve to follow up. General Lenihan ordered all of our three Battalions to take part in the attack.

Colonel McCoy was sent for and the order was given him. Major McKenna expressed his opinion of the order in a manly, soldierly way. Captain Hurley of Company K had felt out the enemy resistance during the night and had found machine gun nests just across the river, the enemy artillery also being very active. The assumption of a retreating enemy against whom infantry bayonets and charging cavalry could be effective was not justified by what the front line could detect. It was a case for artillery preparation and careful advance. Colonel McCoy was already of the same opinion, which he expressed with proper vigor. They were three good soldiers, Lenihan, McCoy and McKenna, and they all felt the same way about it. But it was a Corps Order, an Army order, in fact, commanding a general advance. Whatever might be the cost, it could not be that this regiment should not do its share to keep the advancing line in even contact with the enemy. So when the hour arrived the Colonel gave the order to advance, which order was communicated by Major McKenna, to Hurley, Ryan and Merle-Smith, Meaney being in reserve. Orders were also sent to Colonel Donovan on the right to move his battalion to the west, taking advantage of the woods, and then to cross the river. Lieutenant Colonel Mitchell brought orders in person to Anderson to bring his battalion forward and cross the Ourcq on the left of McKenna, which would bring him to the slope on the west of the little brook leading towards Bois Colas.

Meanwhile General Lenihan at 3:20 A. M. had received word from General Brown of the 84th Brigade that he could not be sure of having his regiments in line in time for the assault. As a matter of fact, the Iowas, under Colonel Tinley, were already abreast of Donovan; and the assault battalion of the Alabamas, under Lieutenant Colonel Baer, was rapidly coming up behind. About 5:00 A. M. General Lenihan received word that the French were not in Fere en Tardenois. He decided that it was too hazardous to push the attack and word was sent at 5:15 o'clock to Colonel McCoy to suspend his advance temporarily pending the advance of neighboring organizations.

But the old regiment had a motto to live up to, "Never disobeyed an order, never lost a flag." McKenna had given his orders to his Captains who all knew just what it meant —and the men under them knew it. Many of them, most of them, as it turned out, would be dead or wounded up that pleasant little valley and along its eastern slopes before the sun rode at mid-heavens. But no man was daunted by the thought.

The first wave was to be Company K, already so cruelly tried by the gas attack at Lunéville. Their leader was Captain John Patrick Hurley, whose slender form and handsome ascetic face seemed to mark the poet or the student rather than the soldier. But he was a keen soldier, one whose blood pumped full and even when death was flying round. Company K was willing to die for him or with him anywhere. At his command they moved forward in advance formation with intervals all perfect at a walk, a trot, a run, down to the Ourcq. It was a sight to remember while life would last, as perfect as a peace manœuvre but with death all around. In that short advance Sergeant Frank Doughney and Corporal Raymond Staber, the heroic son of Mount Loretto, found their way to heaven; and a number of good men were wounded. But they swept on over the Green Mill bridge and across its dam and through the waters of the river with Captain Hurley and Lieutenant Pat Dowling in the lead, and did not stop till they had gained a footing under the bank of the road beyond the river.

Right on their heels came Company I under the Boer War Veteran, Captain Richard J. Ryan, in the same perfect formation. They, too, swept across the Ourcq (Eddie Joyce being the one man killed), and took up their place with Company K under the bank. The two Captains reformed their men and were looking over the situation. Their objective was Meurcy Farm. But that lay in the valley and was impossible to take until at least one of the slopes was cleared to its summit; as a direct advance would expose them to fierce enfilading fire. Even where they were, one group of enemy machine guns could fire direct on their flank; so Captain Ryan sent one of his best men, Sergeant E. Shanahan, with Hugh McFadden, Pat McKeon, Hettrick, Hartnett and others to put it out of action. A forlorn hope, he felt, but they did it without losses, as Shanahan was a born leader.

The line was scarcely straightened out when the men were given the word to advance. The left of Company K moved out on the lower slopes along the little valley towards Meurcy Farm; the right of K and all of I at an angle straight up the bare, smooth slope towards the machine gun nests that were spitting fire from that direction. That kind of action suited Pat Dowling. He jumped to his feet and called to his platoon to follow, when a machine gun bullet gave him a mortal wound. Sergeant Embree and John J. Conefry fell by his side. A heart-broken soldier lifted the Lieutenant. "Did they get that machine gun on the right?" "Yes, sir." Then, "Thank God!" and a dauntless leader of men was no more.

The line swept on. The slope to the right ran through a wheat field and then with a gentle rise to the summit. In the lower portion there was a group of machine guns manned by good men. But they had to deal with better men. The line swung around the guns in a semi-circle, the men crawling on their bellies like Indians now. The rifles were crackling all around, their sharp bursts of fire drowning at times the incessant pop, pop, pop of the machine guns. Many of the German gunners were killed and the others found it nigh impossible to lift their heads from their holes to work the pieces. Not one of them offered to surrender. Most of them died at their posts. A few sought safety in flight and some of these managed to slip back up the hill to safety. We met some of these men long afterwards. They spoke of the sweep of the Battalion across the Ourcq and said they thought Americans were crazy.

Meanwhile big gallant Merle-Smith with Company L had crossed the river and had fallen into line on the hill to the right of Company I. Major McKenna, anxious to extend his flanks as far as possible, had thrown in Company D, half of it on the right of L, well into territory that belonged to the neighboring regiment, and half to the left rear of K, up the valley towards the farm.

The men who had the farm for their objective fared the best. At that moment it was not very strongly held and the shoulder of the hill protected them from fire from its summit. Sergeants Meade and Crotty, with a platoon of Company K, followed by Lieutenant Cook, with two platoons of D, worked their way up the valley. There was a sharp fight under the stone walls of the old building and gallant Bob Foster there found the death that was sure to be his in battle. Carl Nyquist of L was also killed. Finally, rifles were thrust through the windows and the last of the Germans retreated across the courtyard and out the other side. While searching for food (soldiers always go into battle after a long fast), Corporal John Gribbon found one lone German hiding in the cellar and sent him to the rear. Other soldiers ran into the orchard like school boys and picked green apples to satisfy their hunger. Sergeant Crotty was sent to establish a line of sharp-shooters to keep down the fire from the edge of Bois Colas, and Sergeant Dick O'Neill held the Farm with his platoon of Company D, until the Germans, learning from their own fugitives that it had been evacuated by their men, shelled the defenders out into the open.

The main attack had harder going. Near the crest of the hill was a new line of German guns much stronger than the first and with a magnificent field of fire that swept almost every part of the slope. Now that their own men at the base were out of the way, the German Artillery, too, had more freedom to act, and shells began to drop along the slope, carrying destruction. The whine of bullets was incessant and the quick spurts of dust spoke of imminent death. But still the line kept crawling forward, each man keeping his resolution to the sticking point with no exhilaration of a head-long charge nor even a friendly touch of shoulder. In attacks such as this each man must crawl forward in isolation, keeping his interval from his neighbors lest destruction should reach too many at one time. It is the finest test of courage.

The machine guns were the worst—and not alone those in front. The main attack was up the slope on the east of the brook valley. Across the narrow valley along the edge of the Bois Colas until Anderson's men cleaned them out; and outside Seringes, the Germans had other guns which kept up a galling flanking fire on our third battalion. And from their right on their unprotected flank more guns were at work. Before the hill was half won many were wounded or killed. Company K, on the left, exposed to the fire across the valley, was the first to suffer heavily. Lieutenant Gerald Stott was badly hit—mortally, as the event proved.

Father Hanley, whose disposition did not permit him to remain at the dressing station, had gone over the river with Captain Hurley and he rushed forward to save the wounded Lieutenant, followed by Sergeant Peter Crotty with Ted Van Yorx and George Meyer. The dust began spurting around them and Father Hanley went down with a bullet in the knee. Despite his command to the men that they should not risk themselves, the three brave lads carried him in, and also Lieutenant Stott.

Lieutenant Arnold made a desperate attempt to get in behind the machine guns on the crest by following a drain on the lower slope. He had gotten well forward when he was mortally hit. Sergeant John Ross went ahead to get him, but was struck dead by the side of his Lieutenant, as were James Daley of K, and John Hession of L.

Of the five Kellys of Company K, two, John and Francis, both daring youths, were killed. Howard was badly wounded in the leg, Herbert was not yet back from the gassing at Lunéville. Young Jimmy, a lad of seventeen, alone remained, and battled as if he felt he had to do the fighting for the whole clan. Of the five Sullivans, Jim was the only one hit and he refused to quit the field. The same is true of Sergeant D'Acosta and Victor Van Yorx and Mike Bannon and also Herbert McKenna of the Mount Loretto boys of Company K. The other lads of his school showed their training that day. Besides Raymond Staber, George Duffy, Joe Gully and Tom Fleming paid the big price for their patriotism. So too, did another much beloved lad in the Company, James Scott; and Cox, Grey, Patrick Ristraino, Patrick Caulfield, Hugh Quinn, Will Ring, and Patrick Cunningham (the last three in front of

Meurcy Farm), with Lewis Shockler, James Daly, Sylvia and Dale, Sharp and Ramsey, who received their death wounds on the slopes of the hill. This was a heart-breaking day for Captain Hurley, who loved his boys, but he kept on cheerful to outward view with his two remaining Lieutenants, Metcalf and Williams, and non-coms like Meade, Farrell, Crotty, Bernard McElroy, John Gibbons and others already named. But soon Lieutenant Metcalf was sent back wounded and Williams was the only Lieutenant left.

At the extreme right of our line was Company L with the remnants of two platoons of Company D under Lieutenants Connelly and Daly. Captain Merle-Smith was hit early in the day, a bullet piercing his arm as he raised it to signal his men forward. He had a first aid bandage wrapped round it and then forgot about it, as there was too much to do. Lieutenant Wellborne also was hit and refused to quit the field. In his platoon Sergeant George Kerr, a great favorite in the company, was fatally wounded. He was picked up by Sergeant Will Murphy (I always wanted to make a priest out of Will, but he was none the worse soldier for that), and carried down the hill; but George died before the bottom was reached and Murphy himself was badly wounded.

In the 2nd Platoon Lieutenant Watkins was killed in the very front line. Near him fell Sergeant Tom O'Donovan and Bert Landzert, good friends of mine since Border days. Lieutenant Spencer was also wounded doing courageous liaison work, as well as Lieutenants Leslie and Booth and Knowles, who had battalion duties and were there to help in co-ordination. The 4th Platoon was led into action by my loyal friend, Sergeant John Donoghue—like Tom O'Donovan, a Killarney man, and both fine specimens of the Irish soldier. He was hit very badly in the early part of the fray, but remained there for hours spurring on his men. His place as leader was taken by Sergeant Ray Convey, a deep, sincere, religious youth whom the whole Company admired. He was a gallant leader, till death and glory claimed him. The same quick route to heaven was taken by Corporal Neil Fitzpatrick, wounded the night before but still in the fray, and Dave O'Brien, a quiet saint and a model soldier. Owen McNally also, and the two Coneys boys, George Heinbock, John J. Booth, and two youths dear to all for their nobility of character, Lawrence Spencer and Bernard Sheeran. With Lieutenant Watkins and Sergeant O'Donovan and Convey on the hilltop lay Mat Moran and Mario Miranda, Earl Weill, Roland Phillips, Herbert Stowbridge, M. Simpson, John Hayden, Harold Yockers, Elmer Shaner and Preston Carrick, Dan Reardon, Alexander Jornest (Russian) and James Santori (Italian), all making the same sacrifice for the land of their birth or adoption.

Arthur Turner, Walter McCarty, E. J. Morrissey, Raymond Murphy were killed in town. William J. Ormond, James Cook, James Watson, Herbert Ray and Leroy McNeill died of wounds.

Johnnie McSherry, the irrepressible youngster, and Maurice Hart, the staid veteran, were both carried from the field. Sergeant Arthur McKenny was wounded and carried into Meurcy Farm, where he was afterward made prisoner by the enemy. Of the two McLaughlin brothers, Dan was wounded unto death, while doing great work, and Harry, less severely. Two other brothers of the same name, Longford men, Bernard and Thomas McLaughlin, battled through it all and came out unscathed. The three McCabes fought like Maccabees. Sergeants Bezold, Thomas Kiernan and Bernard Woods were wounded, but Sergeant William Malinka, Tom Dunn and Leo Mullin came through.

On the left of L and in the middle of the line, Company I held the field and suffered even greater losses; but they too kept working steadily forward and no man went back whose duty it was to stay. Lieutenant H. H. Smith was killed on the last slope, urging his men forward. Sergeant Frank McMorrow and William Lyle, Paddy Flynn, and Hugh McFadden kept the platoon going. Lieutenant Cortlandt Johnson, like Captain Ryan, kept moving all along the line unmindful of danger, until he was badly wounded. His platoon was in good hands. Sergeant Charles Connolly took command and kept them advancing till death called him from the fray. Across his body fell Tommy Brennan, his closest friend—"In death not divided." Sergeant Billy McLaughlin, a thorough soldier, took command but five minutes later he, too, was killed as he led the advance shouting, "Let's go and get 'em, men!" Otto Ernst and John O'Rourke were killed at the very top of the hill, but Lenihan and Vail, Adikes and Lynch, still held the survivors together until they, too, were wounded. John J. Maddock, a veteran of the Regular Army, was badly hit while trying to save Corporal Beckwith.

Here, too, fell Lieutenant Beach, killed by shrapnel while shooting an automatic. Along side him lay in a row like harvest sheaves, Matt O'Brien, William Corbett, Roger Minogue, Patrick McCarthy, Patrick McKeon, Floyd Baker, Louis Bloodgood and James Powell. Sergeant Charlie Cooper escaped severely wounded and Dan Mullin led what was left of the platoon.

It was at the top of the hill that the Captain was wounded, a bullet going through his left side. Before he fell he had looked the situation over. The forward lines were now able to see clearly the whole field. In front the terrain stretched over perfectly level ground for five hundred yards to the edge of the forest of Nesles where one could detect the prepared emplacements and regularly wired positions. It was useless to advance in that direction; not a man could ever cross that stretch alive. To the right a company of the Alabamas had come up, but they, too, had been swept to pieces by the German fire and no more managed to reach the top. To the left, across the valley, our second battalion had begun to work its way up the opposite slope towards Seringes. Their fire could be detected as they wormed their way forward.

Looking back down the hill the sight was discouraging. The ground was littered with the bodies of the brave, and the slopes of the Ourcq were dotted with the wounded, helping one another to the dressing station across the river in Villers sur Fere.

Half the battalion was out of action. Of five Lieutenants, Hurley had lost three killed, and one wounded. Merle-Smith was wounded and also three of his four officers, the fourth being killed. Eugene Gannon, a brave and competent soldier, was now his second in command. Ryan, badly wounded, was the only officer left in I, though he had well placed confidence in his first sergeant, Patrick McMiniman, a rock-ribbed old-timer, and Sergeants Shanahan and Patrick Collins.

All three commanders decided that the position on the top of the hill was untenable. When they had swept over the last emplacements of the German guns on the hill they not only found that their own further advance was impossible; they had also left the German artillery free to act, and the shelling began with terrific vigor. So the main body drew back a little below the crest, leaving automatic gunners and sharp-shooters to keep the Germans from venturing forward from the woods. Our own machine guns, the Wisconsin lads manning them, had followed the advance, the gunners fighting with desperate courage. The ammunition was carried up by their men and ours at a fearful cost. Five feet or so a man might run with it and then go down. Without a moment's hesitation, some other soldier would grab it and run forward to go down in his turn. But the guns had to be fed and still another would take the same dreadful chance. Death was forgotten. Every man thought only of winning the fight. Finally the guns were put out of action by shell fire at the top of the hill and there they stood uselessly, their gunners lying dead around them.

Death was busy on that hill that morning. It claimed Johnnie Bradley, the baby of the Company, for whom life was still an unexplored field; and Ben Gunnell of the Northwest Mounted Police, who had tried most earthly things and found them wanting. Pat Stanley, who had left his kitchen to fight, found a noble end to his fighting. Arthur Matthews, mortally wounded, spent what remained to him of breath, calling words of encouragement to his companions. Two men worked side by side,—one was taken and the other left. Frank Mulligan and Frank Van Bramer worked an automatic. Van Bramer was called. John O'Hara went the long road and Jim O'Connor stuck it out untouched. Frankie Connolly took the automatic from McCarthy's dead hands and kept it going all morning. Eddie Martin and Will Corbett, liaison men, were shot down, and Charlie Garrett wounded. The voices of Thomas Curry and Henry Lynch and Arthur Thompson were hushed forever. Frank Courtney, Will Flynn, Earl Rhodes, Thomas Boyle, Carl Moler, John McCabe, Harold Van Buskirk, Louis Ehrhardt, Fred Muesse, Darcy Newman, Melvin Spitz, kept up the fight of that bare hillside with no thought of retreat until their heroic souls were sped. Charles Ford and Spencer Ely, Albert Schering and Thomas Shannon were carried from the field and died of their wounds.

Captain Hurley, in command of the battalion on the hill, had gone down to confer with the Colonel. Captains Ryan and Merle-Smith were both wounded. The latter kept cheerfully moving around amongst his men, while Ryan had to lie in a depression and try to keep up the spirits of his followers by calling to them. When his voice failed him, Paddy Flynn, a clean-cut young Irish athlete, came and lay along side him and coached the team like a captain on the base lines. As he raised his head to call he was hit on the cheek, but he kept on urging resistance until he was finally wounded severely. Paddy Hackett's voice was also heard throughout the fight urging the old gallants to stick, until he, too, found his place among the heroes of the regiment that are gone.

And still the remnants of the battalion held their ground,

though that ground was being plowed by shells. They had the hill; and if a general forward movement was on, as they had been told, it was their place to hold that hill till the other organizations could come up, even though the last man amongst them should remain there for his long sleep. Captain Meaney had sent up reinforcements to piece out the thinned line. A platoon under Lieutenant Ahearn arrived, but reinforcements only added to the slaughter. What was needed was artillery fire and strong supporting movements on the flanks. Lieutenant Ahearn was wounded and two of his best Sergeants, Patrick Clark and Patrick Hayes. Sergeant William Francis was killed, also Corporals Patrick Cooke and George Hoblitzell, one of two fine brothers; and Patrick Byrne, Hubert Hill, James Scanlan, John Tobin and John Donahue fought their last fight. Mat Mahoney, Frank Cullum, John Powers and Bill Conville, with many others, were badly wounded.

Lieutenant Connelly had tried to remove Captain Ryan from the field. But the Captain threatened to shoot anybody who would attempt to take him away from his men. Finally, about noon, Captain Merle-Smith came to him with information that the order had come to withdraw through the 1st Battalion, which already occupied the lower slopes of the hill.

That task remained to carry in the wounded. Company M gave great help, but every man who could walk lent a hand to this task of friendship. Corporal Dynan, who had already done more than his share of the fighting, got wounded finally while helping others off the field.

Lieutenant Williams remained out to hold the advance position with a platoon of Company K, including Sergeants Joe Farrell and Peter Crotty, Corporals George Meyer, Patrick Ryan, John Naughton and John McLaughlin.

The survivors were a sorry remnant of the splendid battalion that had so gallantly swept across the Ourcq that morning. But they had carried out a soldier's task.

Their's not to reason why,
Their's but to do and die,

Disputes may arise about the orders that sent them in
but they will not affect the place in the martial annals of
their race and country which was made on that day of tragic
glory by the Shamrock Battalion of the old Irish regiment. Laurels grow from the graves of the dead. Laurels,
too, encircle the brows of every man who fought that day
on Hill 152.

Still further news of tragedy waited for them. Their
gallant Major was dead. Major McKenna had tried to
recall his Company when the word came to countermand
the attack order. But his wild Irish had rushed to the attack
with too much eagerness for that, and the situation was
beyond mending in this way. They could not retreat under
the fire of the machine guns on the hill which could mow
them down as they recrossed the river with nothing gained
from their sacrifice. They had to go ahead and put these
guns out of action. When he had seen how things were
going, the Major started back along the Ourcq to consult
with Colonel McCoy. A shell came over knocking the
Major down and wounding his Adjutant, Lieutenant Cassidy. When the Lieutenant, with Sergeant Major Joyce and
George Strenk, ran to pick him up, they found him dead,
though without a wound upon his body. They bore him in
sorrowing, as every man in the regiment sorrowed when the
news went round, at the loss of a brave and beloved leader
whose talents fitted him for a high destiny if life were
spared him, but to whom had fallen the highest destiny
of all, and one which he had always expected would be his—
that of dying for his country.

His Company, Commanders had been informed of his
death not long after it happened, and Captain Hurley had
taken general direction of the fight when Ryan was
wounded. Hurley came back to report on the situation to
Colonel McCoy, and while talking to him was badly

wounded by shell fire. The Colonel had already made up his mind on the matter and Major Donovan, with the 1st Battalion, was crossing the river to effect a relief.

But meanwhile another battle, scarcely less fierce, had been going on on the western slopes of the brook. On Saturday afternoon Major Anderson, with the 2nd Battalion, had received orders to proceed from Courpoil, north through Beuvardes, and maintain close liaison with the 3rd, which was to go to the river and get contact with the enemy. Anderson marched his men up to a place north of the forest of Fere at the southwestern extremity of Villers sur Fere. Scouts were sent out to examine the ground toward the river, while the Major and his four Captains went to the town to interview the French Commander, who told them that it would be impossible to cross the Ourcq without artillery preparation, owing to the strong position held by the enemy. They obtained information about the dispositions and plans of the 3rd battalion and then returned to their commands.

About half past three in the morning Lieutenant Colonel Mitchell came with the information that the attack was to be made at 5:45 and that they were not to remain in support, but to advance to the attack at the left of the 3rd Battalion. Anderson aroused his men and formed them in the field north of the forest with Companies E and F in the front line, E being on the right, and G and H behind them. They advanced in approach formation through the fields until they reached the southern slope of the crest just south of the river, where orders were received for the battalions to halt.

This advance was made under heavy shell fire and at serious cost. Early in the advance Charles B. Wethered and William Hurst were killed by the same shell, which also wounded Haggerty, Dearborn and Strang; and nearer to the river Company H suffered a tremendous loss by the severe wounding of Captain James G. Finn, whose leg was so badly gashed that he had to be carried from the field. The place where the battalion was to cross was to the west of the little brook. To their left was Fere en Tardenois, which was being systematically attacked by the French troops. Our people had time to admire the method in which these seasoned warriors went about their business. They had dug in during the night so that they could place their fire against three sides of the town, but they evidently had no intention of going over the river until the fire of the machine guns had been fairly well blanked. Some of their men were engaged in drawing fire from the German nests, while others were sniping at them from their shelters.

Our men got the advantage of the French thoroughness when, as they came over the crest, they were liberally spattered with bullets from two or three detached houses on the left just outside Fere en Tardenois. Our one pounders were directed at them; but the French gave those hornet's nests their *coup de grace* when they pulled up one of their 75's which they had handy, right into the front line and sent a few shells straight as rifle bullets into the houses. Captain Kelly sent my old friend, John Finnegan, with a patrol to see if any of the enemy were left in the houses. John came back with the report that there were no Germans there but dead ones.

The battalion rushed down and across the Ourcq without a casualty. There was one German gun which commanded the little bridge and which could have caused great losses, but the gunners were daunted by the resolute advance of our men, as they knew that no matter how many they might kill, they could not themselves escape, so they threw up their hands and surrendered.

Companies E and F rushed over the little bridge and through the river and up the slope of the hill towards Seringes and Bois Colas. Here Captain Charles Baker of Company E was badly wounded in the neck and shoulder, one of his best Sergeants, Michael Lynch, was killed, and the bold Steve Derrig got a mortal wound. (Long afterwards we learned with deep and universal regret that Captain Baker died of his wounds.)

Company F on the left had the place of danger, as their route lay straight up the hill and over the flats, to skirt the village of Seringes, the village itself being allotted to the Ohios when they could take their place in the line. Since they had been unavoidably detained and the French were still working in their business-like fashion at the task of getting Fere en Tardenois ready for capture, Kelly's left flank was bound to be in the air with the prospects of worse to come if he got far enough forward to have it pass the village, which was giving trouble enough while in front.

He sent messengers to Company E on his right to see whether Bois Colas was rid of the enemy, for if it were strongly held, his men would be simply fighting down a lane into a trap. Jim Quigley of Company E had been in there already and Jim came around to report that the woods was not held by the Germans. Later Captain Prout sent a party into the wood and Lieutenant Conners, commanding E Company, took possession of it up to its northern edge. Kelly's men had meanwhile been going forward in spite of Artillery and Machine Gun fire, until they found a spot from which they could effectively retaliate. This was a cutting in the roadway between Fere en Tardenois and the north edge of Bois Colas. The shelter it gave was not very great, but Lieutenant Frank Marsh had his automatic and rifle men lined up in the ditch, happy to get a shot at the foe that had been sending death amongst them. In the advance they had lost Frank Connaughton, Charles Fox and Michael Campbell, and later on Charles Caplinger, Harry Jennings and John J. McGloin. While holding the road other good men were killed. Matt Wynne, who was known to the whole regiment; Frank Divine, Lawrence Brennan, Alfred O'Neill, Sergeant Thomas Erb and Eugene Doty were mortally wounded, and also Harry Mansfield and Charles Melsa.

Kelly with his headquarters group, 1st Sergeant Joseph

Blake, Sergeant John P. Mahon, Corporals Long and Finnegan, Harris and McLean and also Lieutenant Ogle had his post at the crest of the hill where he could watch the fortunes of his forward detachment. Finding them hard pressed he got two automatics from the Ohios, who had now crossed the river and were forming under the bank, and sent Long and Finnegan for reinforcements from his own Battalion. Colonel Anderson ordered them sent, and detachments from all three Companies proceeded through Bois Colas and started working forward to support the right flank of the F Company men. In this operation Company E lost Thomas Cullen, Philip Ford, Edward Fuld, Frank O'Meara, Louis Hazelton, Louis Cohen, John Costello, Michael Breen, Emmett Bingham, Corporal Gus Winter (hit carrying Cullen in), and Corporal John Cronin, the saint of the Company (who had gone as a volunteer), and whose body lay when I came to bury him the nearest to the enemy of any soldier of ours. Not far from Cronin's body lay four men of Company H, John T. McCarthy, Patrick Reynolds, George Smith and Thomas Hayes. G Company lost John Conroy, Floyd Graham, and Edmund Reardon. Patrick Scanlan, whose brother Dan I had buried at Baccarat, was wounded this day, but stuck to his Company to meet his death the day following, as did James Higgins of the same Company. Of the two guides from Company F, Long was wounded and the heroic John Finnegan fought his last fight.

It was evident to anybody that a further advance without careful artillery preparation was impossible. Like the 3rd Battalion on the other hill across this valley, they had reached the level approach to the strong defenses in the village and along the southern edge of the forest. It was an artillery job. And any infantry commander who would send his men across that open space would deserve a court martial. The difficulty for both battalions arose from the alacrity with which they had obeyed the orders from above which sent them across the Ourcq on a bayonet charge against a fleeing foe. They had followed the orders, and overcoming the first resistance of the enemy, they found themselves opposed to the main line of defense with practically nobody else, French or American, on their side of the river. Their flanks unsupported, to go forward would be to hand the Germans a couple of geese to pluck, and as there were no means of communication with the distant artillery except runners, that arm of the service could not act without grave danger of shooting up its own side.

The Ohios meanwhile had pushed their way up to have their share in the battle. But since they had been considered as a support regiment, they naturally thought they were coming to relieve the New Yorkers, and officers and men announced that supposed fact to the groups of our men. Anderson stormed around when he heard of it and Kelly and Prout were disgusted, but they finally accepted the situation of falling back into a support position when orders came to make it final. After their struggles in the battle less than two weeks before the second battalion deserved a comparative rest from the toil of fighting. They withdrew to the northern edge of the Ourcq, where they supported the advance of the 1st Battalion the next day. Later the same day they formed a connecting link with the Alabamas on our right. The losses of the battalion in the remaining days of the fight were few in comparison. John McGeary of G was killed while saving the wounded of Company H. Sergeant James P. Robinson and Thomas Bugler were killed by shell fire and also Arthur Baia of Company E. On July 30th, while providing for the needs of men in line, two Sergeants of Company F, Charles Denon and Charles D. Echeverria, were killed, and Lieutenant Smith and Thomas Kelleher of the same company seriously wounded. While engaged in a similar task the First Sergeant of Company H, Daniel O'Neill, whose brother, William, had been killed in Champagne, was mortally wounded, leaving only one of that famous trio still alive.

It was between nine and ten in the morning that Major

Donovan's battalion had reached the river, and not long after midday the relief of the 3rd Battalion was practically complete. Major Donovan brought into line with him three Companies, A, B and C. Company D, which had been on the hill since early morning, was told that it could retire with the 3rd Battalion. It had suffered losses, though not

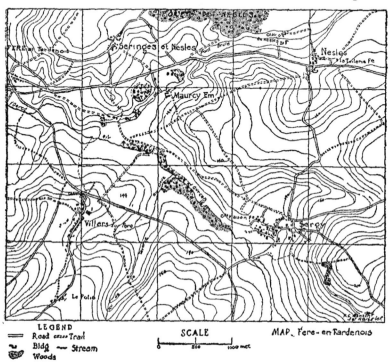

THE BATTLE FIELD OF THE OURCQ

so severe as the other companies. The platoons on the left of the line had occupied Meurcy Farm with Company K. On the right the headquarters group and one platoon under Lieutenants Connelly and Daly had performed a very neat job of infilitration. There was a group of German machine guns in a clump of trees some distance beyond the right flank of our battalion, which was exceedingly annoying. So Connelly took his detachment far to the right, shielded by the bank of the river road, and led them up a gully into the rear of the Germans, driving them out by rifle fire and hand grenades. Two of his men, James Hayes and Harry Silver, an automatic rifle team, occupied a lone outpost which was attacked by the enemy. Silver was mortally hit, but kept on working his rifle till it dropped from his hands. Hayes grasped it and kept up the fight till he was wounded and taken prisoner.

In spite of their hard day, Company D wished to remain in the fight with their own battalion. Connelly and Daly represented this to the Major, who was very glad to keep them.

Major Donovan did not try to retain occupation of all the hill, since the results of the gallant work of the preceding battalion were preserved if the German machine guns could be prevented from re-establishing their posts on it. So he placed automatic riflemen and sharp-shooters in the wheatfield, and drew up the main body of his troops under the lea of the high inner bank of the river road, the one under which McKenna's Battalion had formed for their attack. The Alabamas were under the same bank further to the right, while Anderson's men held the river bank and the wooded swampy ground across the valley to the left, keeping in touch with the Ohios, who were also along the river.

The afternoon and night passed without any special infantry action. When the strength of the enemy resistance became manifest, the artillery were put to work. Both regiments of our divisional light artillery were given to the 83rd Infantry Brigade: The 151st (Minnesota) behind us and the 149th (Illinois) behind the Ohios. Further back our heavies, the 150th (Indiana) and Corps Artillery were sending their huge missiles over our heads at the enemy's position. The edges of the forest of Nesles and the roads behind were heavily shelled. This led the enemy to a great deal of counter-battery work, and the infantry had it easier. But their shelters were exposed at all times to machine gun fire and it was dangerous for a man to lift up his head. Companies B and C successively held the hill slope and had many casualties. Captain Reilley was wounded, but kept right on till the whole battle was over. Tommy Mooney was hit four times and came off the hill joking with his friends, who had so often said that he was too thin for a German to hit him. B Company lost good men in James Phillips, William Doyle, Michael Tierney, Joseph Chambers, John A. Lane and Thomas Kelley. That night, too, Barney Barry, soldier and saint, pulled the latchstrings of the gate of Paradise. From C Company also Mat Carberry and Richard Dieringer, Joe Augustine and John O'Connor, good lads all and true, received their mortal wounds and John J. Campbell and John F. Autry, litter bearers of Company A, were killed while performing their work of mercy.

By morning the plans were made for a new alignment for attack. The 165th Infantry was to sweep the valley along both sides of the brook, with Bois Colas on the left of it, and Meurcy Farm on the right, as their immediate objectives. The second battalion was to be in close support. Further left, the Ohios were to advance on the right of the French and occupy the Village of Seringes et Nesles. The movement of the 84th Brigade was co-ordinated with the advance of the 83rd.

This called for a shifting of Donovan's battalion to the left, to face up the valley. The movement was carried out in the early morning of Monday, July 29th, with few losses, but one of them a costly one. Lieutenant Daly, thinking as usual of the safety of his men, and paying little attention to himself, was killed. Well, as Lieutenant Burke had said of him two days before, there was no place else he would rather be. His sacrifice was made with a generous heart.

The Battalion was lined up in the following order. Right of the brook, Company A, with Lieutenant Baldwin in the lead, and Company B in support, under Captain Reilley, their mission being to debouch from the scattered trees which concealed them, and advance up the gentle slope

forward and right to Meurcy Farm. On the left, Company
C, under Captain Bootz, had the van, with Company D,
under Lieutenant Connelly, in support. Their work was to
push on to the left of the brook and clean up Bois Colas,
a thickly wooded clump of trees about as big as three
city blocks, which lay two hundred yards west of the
farm.

Company A had only one officer with them in the attack
as Lieutenant D'Aguerro, with Sergeants Duff and Schmidt,
had charge of a platoon whose duty it was to carry ammunition. Lieutenant Baldwin, an earnest, courageous
man, was in command, with Sergeant Thomas J. Sweeney
as First Sergeant. They advanced at eight o'clock in the
morning and were immediately made to feel that they
were in for a hard time. There were German machine guns
now in Meurcy Farm and on both sides of it. The shelling,
too, was vigorous, as all their motions could be seen and
reported. Sergeants Fred Garretson and Don Matthews
led a detachment with great prudence and dexterity, capturing one of the machine gun nests and seven prisoners.
The direct attack against the farm, however, was not to be
successful that day. Sergeant Scully, who had been badly
wounded in the Lunéville raid, was wounded again early in
the fight. Acting Sergeant Willie Mehl, whose father used
to bring him to our encampment as a lad, was also hit;
and many another good man was put out of action forever.
Corporal Petersilze was killed and Corporal Michael O'Sullivan, a big, bright, good-natured giant, whom I had held in
my arms as a baby, and another of the Campbells of Company A, Louis, this time, slender Harry Kane and sturdy
Dan O'Connell, Stephen Curtin, who did good work
with his automatic; James Ronan, Leroy Hanover,
Joseph P. Myers, James Robinson, John Gray, John
Williams, Clyde Evans, John Boneslawski, William Barton,
John Gilluly, John Rice, William Thompson, W. V. Kelley,
John Fisher, Dennis Donovan, Fred Floar, William Mallin,
were killed on the field. Fred Finger was killed going back

with the wounded. Tom Fleming and Charles Mack died in the dressing station, and Anthony Michaels, Albert Poole, James Tiffany, Patrick Carlisle and Edward Blanchard died of wounds in the hospital.

Lieutenant Baldwin was in the van waving his pistol, when a machine gun bullet struck him in the chest. His last words were: "Sergeant (to Sweeney), carry out the orders!" His spirit animated the brave men who followed. Moreover, they had still a fine leader in Tom Sweeney, and they kept pushing ahead, some of them meeting their fate under the very walls of the farm. It was all that they could do. One officer and twenty-five men of the diminished company were killed that morning. Multiply the deaths by six to get the total casualties and one can see that few indeed were left. Sergeant Sweeney ordered his men to dig in and wait. They were still full of spirit and vigor. Major Donovan tells of the impression made on him by a New York High School boy who carried his messages under fire with a cigarette nonchalantly drooping from his lip, coming and going as if he were an A. D. T. messenger on Broadway. It was Harold Henderson. Ed. Chamberlain, whom I had always admired, also did credit to the good opinion of his friends. He was hit across the stomach and as he rose to go back, holding the ripped edges together to keep his bowels from falling out, he said to Sweeney: "Have you any messages for the rear?"

It was some hours after Lieutenant Baldwin's death that Lieutenant Henry Kelley arrived with Major Donovan's orders to assume command. "Hec" Kelley, a young lawyer who enlisted as a private in B Company when we went to the Border, was never one to take good care of himself in a fight. He lasted just half an hour and was carried back with a bad wound which robbed us of his hearty, courageous presence for the rest of the war. Sweeney and the rest stuck it out till morning. Corporal John F. Dennelly, who had left his country newspaper in Long Island to join the 69th, spent the night with an outpost which was busy discouraging the nocturnal efforts of the Germans to erect barbed wire defenses in front of the farm.

In the morning the remnants of Company A withdrew a slight distance down the valley to merge with Company B. This Company, too, had had its losses. One platoon, under Lieutenant Wheatley, was in line with Company A, and the rest of them were close behind. Lieutenant Wheatley met the usual fate of officers in this battle by being wounded. Timothy McCarthy, Denis Bagley and Albert Lambert were killed and Phil Schron died at the dressing-station. It was a pleasant surprise to everybody in the Company that their gigantic captain, Tom Reilley, was not hit again, as he walked around using a rifle for a crutch and exposing his massive frame to the enemy. But he escaped with no further wounds.

Company A failed to get the farm that day, but their dogged persistence helped to make the task of Company C an easier one. This Company was led by Captain Bootz with Lieutenants Irving, Allen, Betty, Stone and Friedlander. They advanced with their right near to the brook and their left on the slope of the hill towards Seringes. A machine gun on the south edge of Bois Colas hampered them, but they got up one of our guns with Lieutenant Davis and Sergeant John O'Leary and soon put it out of action. When they got to the woods they beat their way through them cautiously, expecting every moment to find resistance, but they met only one frightened German who was glad when they made him prisoner. From the other side they could see a disconcerted enemy dotting the slopes in front of the forest of Nesles. The riflemen immediately got busy and when Lieutenants Davis and Bell came up with the machine guns, commanded by Captain Seibert, the field-gray uniforms disappeared under their fire.

The first platoon, under Lieutenant Allen, had harder going. Its task was to cover the left flank as the line advanced, which brought the men along the top of the hill, where they suffered severely. Sergeant Crittenden was killed and Louis Torrey, a pious lad, Charles Geary also, and Carlton Ellis and R. J. Schwartz. Sergeant Dan Garvey and Frank Daley, John J. Murphy, Patrick Cronin and one of the Gordon brothers were fatally wounded and carried off the field. Harry McAllister was badly wounded. Big, impulsive Mike Cooney carried him down through a rain of fire to the bottom and then went back through it to get his rifle. James Allen lay out on the hill moaning. Harry Horgan started up to get him but was killed before reaching him. Thomas O'Connor crept up cautiously and coolly. He was stooping to pick him up when a bullet struck him and he fell on the body of his comrade. Nothing daunted, Michael Ruane and William McCarthy made their way up that hill of death and carried down their wounded comrade. Both Allen and McAllister afterwards died of their wounds.

The biggest price paid for the capture of Bois Colas was when the courageous soldier and trusted leader, Captain Henry Bootz, was put out of action by a bullet which passed through his chest from side to side. He had a wound which would have killed an ordinary man, but he merely grinned, took his pipe which he used in action to signal to his men and threw it to Lieutenant Betty, saying: "Here, son, I won't need this for a while." He started back, followed by his faithful orderly, Michael Sypoula, better known as "Zip," who had gotten a wound himself and was happy that he had a reason for sticking to his beloved Captain. First Sergeant Gene Halpin and Maguire assisted Captain Bootz to the rear. Lieutenant Friedlander had also received a dangerous face wound and had been carried off the field by Austin McSweeney of the Headquarters Company.

Major Donovan, never happy unless in the middle of things, had gone up the bed of the brook so as to keep ahead of the advance of C on the left and A on the right. Lieutenant Ames, his Adjutant, was with him, led by devotion as well as duty, for the Major was his ideal leader. They lay half in the brook, resting on the bank, when a sniper's bullet from the farm yard whizzed past Donovan's ear and struck Ames in the head, liberating for larger purposes a singularly attractive and chivalrous soul.

Lieutenant Connelly tells of coming up with Sergeant Tom O'Malley and Corporal Gribbon to receive orders from the Major about taking over the line from Company C. He did not know just where to find him until he met Bootz going down the brook bed with his faithful attendants. Following up the stream he found Donovan still in the water with Ames's body by his side. The Major also had received a bullet wound in the hand. Nearby, Pete Gillespie, whose machine gun was out of order, was absorbed in the game of getting the sniper who had killed the Lieutenant. All stopped to watch him and his rifle. Pete settled down, intent on a dead horse near the farm. Suddenly he saw something had moved behind it. He cuddled his rifle, waited and fired. They could see the sniper behind the horse half rise, then drop. The beloved Lieutenant was avenged.

The day's work had improved the situation immensely. Control of Bois Colas gave a better command of the terrain northwards to the edge of the forest, although Bois Brulé, a narrow strip of woods which lay between, was still alive with machine guns. Meurcy Farm was not yet occupied, but its capacity for being troublesome was reduced by its being outflanked by our left. Anderson's battalion held the lower slopes of the hill that had been taken by the third battalion the first day, and kept the Germans from reoccupying it permanently. Anderson was in touch with the 84th Brigade which was on the same line with himself. The Iowas and part of the Alabamas had taken the town of Sergy. It was a tough nut to crack, and took all the dash of the Southerners and the stubborn persistence of the Westerners to conquer and hold it. The elements of the regiment on our immediate right delayed their advance until the whole brigade was in a position to move forward.

The other regiment in our Brigade made a fine advance on our left. The 2nd Battalion passed through the first, and after our regiment had taken Bois Colas, the Ohios could be seen pushing up to the road running from Fere en Tardenois to Meurcy Farm. To co-operate with them Major Donovan sent Lieutenant Betty with what was left of Company C (sixty-five men) to move with their flank, Company D holding Bois Colas with forty-two men. The Ohios kept advancing and by nightfall had captured the southern half of Seringes et Nesles. The upper portion which curved over to the top of our valley was not occupied until the German retreat had begun.

The situation was set for a further advance. Headquarters at regiment, brigade, and division were busy preparing for it and the Artillery were ready to co-operate. They had been shelling Bois Brulé just in front of us, and the upper edge of Seringes et Nesles and the edge of the forest all day. Telephone lines had been stretched to the front by the 117th Signal Battalion and our own signal section of Headquarters Company.

These were exceedingly busy days at Colonel McCoy's P. C., for at last there was a spot that one could dignify with the title of Post of Command. The first day of the battle there had been three or four posts in succession. On Saturday evening Colonel McCoy was in the Chateau de Fere, but when he got orders for his regiment to make the attack he went forward with them himself to join McKenna near the river. When the battalion went over he set up his headquarters right there in a shallow trench on the exposed river slope. It seemed no place for a commanding officer on whom so much had to depend, but he made up his mind that it was his place to be where he could view the battle himself, as there was no speedy way for him to get information, and the immediate decision concerning the actions and fate of his men would rest largely on his own judgment. These were his reasons; but there is always a good deal of the element of personality back of anybody's reasons. And Frank R. McCoy, soldier of five campaigns, would naturally see the force of reasons which brought him as close as possible to the firing line. The Germans began to argue the point in their usual violent way, but the Colonel remained unconvinced.

Lieutenant Rerat was wounded slightly in that hole, and many men hurt around it. Finally Captain Hurley was badly wounded while reporting to his Chief, and the Staff united with the Germans in arguing that it was not the best place to do regimental business. So Colonel McCoy brought them back a ways to a sunken road that ran across the town. Here the shelling pursued them and Lieutenant B. B. Kane, a fine, manly fellow, received a mortal wound from a shell that exploded a few feet from where he was standing in a group around the Colonel.

Meanwhile the reliable Captain Michael J. Walsh had been scouring the town for a suitable place, and had found one in the cellar of a house still nearer the lines, but accessible to messengers from the orchards on the east, thus obviating the trip through Dead Man's Curve.

On the morning of the 29th Colonel McCoy with Lieutenant Colonel Mitchell went up to look over the whole situation and consult with Donovan and Anderson. The decks were now cleared for a battle. The telephone was in to the front line, to the Brigade Post of Command, and to the Artillery. There was a chance for a commanding officer to be of real service to the Battalion Commanders. With the telephone to the front and rear at his elbow, he had the strings in his hands, and he certainly kept pulling those strings day and night. A message would come in from an O. P. (Observation Post) where Captain Elmer and Corporal Bob Lee were on the watch: "Shells needed on machine gun nests at crest of hill 195.45-274.05 to 196.1-274.5." Or one from Donovan: "Important to shell Bois Brulé, where forty machine gun emplacements are reported." And Lieutenant Weaver, a smart youngster from the 151st Field Artillery, would be put on the job in a second. Or it might be a message of the Colonel to General Lenihan in response to a call from Donovan: "Cut out fire on neck of woods south of Bois Brulé. It is endangering our Infantry in Bois Colas." Night and day that telephone was working, receiving news from the front, effecting co-operation with neighboring regiments or sending back requests for barrages, counter-battery work, food supplies, ammunition, ambulances, air service. Soldiers in the line never fully realize how much their lives, and victory, which is more to them than their lives, depend on the alertness and intelligence of those in command.

It was an interesting group at the regimental P. C., McCoy with his spare soldierly figure and his keen soldierly face, radiant with the joy of action and the prospects of victory, always a stimulus to those who might be downhearted. For the first day, as operations officer, he had George McAdie, patient, painstaking and enduring, until the order came, less endurable to him than an enemy bullet, that he should proceed forthwith for duty at a home station. A hard sentence for a born soldier in the middle of a battle. And succeeding him Merle-Smith, just come out of the carnage, with an untidy bandage around his wounded arm, but with his mind set only on his job. Alert youngsters, Lieutenants Rerat, Seidelman, Jim Mangan, Heinel (afterwards wounded) and Preston, with Captain Jack Mangan drifting in occasionally to see if his supplies were coming up satisfactorily.

And next to the Colonel was one big personality dominating all; the rugged personality of Captain Michael J. Walsh, old soldier and solid man. He was disgusted with his part in the conflict. "I came out here to be a soldier and I am nothing but a damn room orderly," he growled. But who fed the hungry fighting men? Captain Michael Walsh. Who scoured the yards of houses for utensils to send up the food to them? Captain Michael Walsh. Who saw that the ammunition was delivered on time to the front line. Once more, Captain Walsh. And the Colonel, when there was a task of real importance to perform, never delegated it to the bright young men; he always said: "Captain Walsh will attend to that."

The principal task for July 30th was assigned to the 84th Brigade. They were to try to get forward and even up the line on our right. The Ohios were to hold fast, but Donovan requested to take advantage of the forward movement on the right to improve our position with reference to Bois Brulé. Company C was still in line west of Bois Colas maintaining our connection with the Ohios. Company D was at the upper edge of this woods with the machine gunners under Captain Seibert, Lieutenants Doris, Davis and Bell. Companies B and A were dug in around the approaches to the farm. Food came up on the night of the 29th for the first time. The men were all hungry, as their reserve rations had been consumed long before. Lieutenant Springer had been sent to take command of Company A, succeeding Lieutenant D'Aguerro, who had been wounded in his turn. He and his First Sergeant, Tom Sweeney, were sitting on the edge of a hole preparing to enjoy a can of corn when one bullet got both of them. They were helped back to the dressing station and Sergeant Higginson took command. The affair had its compensations. Higginson and young Henderson got the corn.

Major Donovan's Post of Command was a hole at the southern edge of Bois Colas. Lieutenant Ames' body had been brought in during the night and buried nearby. Ames' place as battalion adjutant was filled by Sergeant Joyce Kilmer, whose position as Sergeant of the Intelligence Section would naturally have entitled him to a place nearer regimental headquarters. But he had preferred to be with a battalion in the field and had chosen Donovan's. The Major placed great reliance on his coolness and intelligence and kept him by his side. That suited Joyce, for to be at Major Donovan's side in a battle is to be in the center of activity and in the post of danger. To be in a battle, a battle for a cause that had his full devotion, with the regi-

ment he loved, under a leader he admired, that was living at
the top of his being. On the morning of the 30th Major
Donovan went forward through the woods to look over the
position. Kilmer followed, unbidden. He lay at the north
edge of the woods looking out towards the enemy. The
Major went ahead, but Kilmer did not follow. Donovan
returned and found him dead. A bullet had pierced his
brain. His body was carried in and buried by the side of
Ames. God rest his dear and gallant soul.

At 3:30 that afternoon the 84th Brigade had made progress, though it was slow and difficult going. The artillery
was doing good work but all their efforts could not keep
down the fire of the German Machine Gunners. The gratifying surprise of the day was when two escadrilles of
friendly planes came over. Our companies in the line had
not been pushed very hard. They repelled a couple of
counter attacks on their position, and the machine gunners were on the alert to fire whenever our artillery work on
Bois Brulé started the Germans running.

Donovan was to move forward when the progress of
the 84th Brigade brought them abreast of him. But regiments, brigades, and it was said, divisions, sloped away to
the right like steps of stairs, and each was hanging back for
the others to come up. So Major Donovan insisted on
making a try for Bois Brulé without waiting for any
help except what our Brigade would give. Colonel Hough
was perfectly willing to back him up. So Lieutenant Connelly with Company D moved out to the attack.

It was the pitiful remnant of a company, one officer and
forty-two men instead of the six officers and two hundred
and fifty men who formerly swung along like an old time
battalion in the parades on the Hempstead Plains. But
the few who were left were inured to danger by patrols
and raids and battles, and they were ready for anything.
The ground in front was rough and hummocky for two
hundred yards, and then a double row of trees led up to the
Bois Brulé. At the right it sloped off to the brook where

it ran past Meurcy Farm. Sergeant Dick O'Neill was to cover the ground in front with fifteen men, including Masterson, Peterson, Bedient, Gugliere, McGee, McAree, Stoddard, Lord, and Edward Moran.

Lieutenant Cook led a smaller number of picked men to work to the right and up the bed of the brook, cooperating with Companies A and B working around the farm. In his command were John Gribbon, his red head an oriflamme of war; Colton Bingham, the fighting nephew of the gentle Bishop of Buffalo, John Curtin, a tall young Irishman who afterwards became regimental standard bearer, Tommy Blake, later Lieutenant Blake, and the steadiest of riflemen, Pat McDonough. Lieutenant Connelly came in the rear of his skirmish line where he could control their movements. With him were his First Sergeants Edward Geaney, Sergeant Hubert Murray, Corporal John F. Moran and others. Tom O'Malley had already been wounded.

Some distance out there was a deep, irregular sand pit. O'Neill, carefully rounding the corner of it, suddenly saw right under his eyes a body of about 25 Germans. He uttered a shout of warning and jumped into the midst of them with his pistol cracking. He had shot down three Germans before they realized what was happening, and produced great confusion amongst them. Some rushed to the other side of the pit while others began firing at O'Neill, who kept firing after he was hit, and when finally carried back to the dressing station had seven bullets in him. The Germans who had run across the sand pit found themselves face to face with Lieutenant Connelly and his little group. What followed was as sudden, as confused in plan, and as resolute in spirit as the action around the log house in Stevenson's Treasure Island. The Company D men came running from all sides to take part in the fighting. On our side Connelly was hit; also Geaney, Gribbon and McDonough. And James J. Gugliere, Paul McGee, Louis Peterson and Rollie Bedient were killed. This all happened in an instant. The Germans paid a fearful price for it. Those that were left scrambled out of the pit to flee in the direction of their own forces. There they saw the advance elements of O'Neill's section running back toward them, and they turned toward Bois Colas at a headlong gait. The cry went up that a counter attack was coming. Colonel Hough saw it and telephoned to our headquarters. Anderson heard back in the woods and stormed up from the support with reinforcements. Our machine-guns were turned on the advancing Germans; and the advent of a few bedraggled prisoners in dirty field gray uniforms let the rear line see that the counter-attack was a myth. The whole business was over in a few minutes.

But the Germans in Bois Brulé were again at work sweeping the ground with their bullets and it was under fierce fire that John Burke, Joe Lynch, McAuliffe, Bingham and Blake carried in Lieutenant Connelly and the other wounded. Sergeant Murray took command and kept the survivors going forward until they had outposts established in the approaches to Bois Brulé.

Besides those already mentioned, Company D lost, killed in these three days, Corporal Frank Fall, Privates George Johnson, Terance McAree, John McCormick, Michael Romanuk, Harvey J. Venneman, Robert Luff, Frank J. Lackner, Attilio Manfredi, Edward G. Coxe, John Dolan and the senior of the two Michael J. Sheas, who died of his wounds.

July 31st was a day of comparative quiet. The longer the struggle lasted the more it was borne in upon the Lords of High Decision that the ousting of the enemy from their position was a matter for artillery. It was the first time we had the opportunity to observe with reluctant admiration the German development of the use of the machine gun in defensive warfare. To send infantry in under the intense fire of their numerous guns was like feeding paper to a flame. Our artillery, however, was good,—none better in the whole war, we confidently assert, and we waited with assurance for them to reduce the resistance. If our air service were sufficiently developed to give them good photo-

graphs of positions, and to register their fire, we felt sure
that the Infantry would soon be in a position to make short
work of enemy opposition.

That day we had our first experience of another auxilliary
arm. The day before there landed at the regimental P. C.
a section of our 30th Engineers, our Gas and Flame regiment. With them there was an Australian officer with a
name that would qualify him for the 69th, and a young
lieutenant who, we discovered after he was killed, was a son
of the famous baseball manager, Ned Hanlan of Baltimore.
They came out with their men on the 31st and threw over
thermite and smoke bombs on Bois Brulé and Meurcy Farm.
Under their protection Company D occupied the woods.

Company A, under Lieutenant Stone, finally took possession of the Farm. The first attempt failed. A patrol
led by Corporal Sidney Clark started up but four men were
hit in the first three minutes, Michaels dying of his wounds.
Another attempt was made in the evening and the farm
was occupied by a patrol under Corporals John Dennelly
and Van Arsdale.

It was evident that the enemy's resistance was weaken-
ing and that it would be a matter of a very short period
before he would retreat to his next line of defence. On
August 1st the 3rd Battalion relieved the 1st in line. Company M had had serious losses after being drawn out from
the line on July 28th, as the battalion had been bombed
in its reserve position at the sunken road, and the Company
had suffered other losses in a ration detail which was caught
out under a heavy fire. Of its officers, Lieutenant Hunt
Warner was badly wounded; Lieutenant Collier was
wounded but stuck to his post. Edward Brennan, Hugh
Kaiser, Alfred Schneider and Johnnie Madden were killed
and Sergeant Nicholson wounded. Captain Meaney and
Lieutenants McIntyre and Bunnell escaped uninjured. Lieutenant McIntyre was blown into the Ourcq by the concussion of a shell, but he stuck to his task till he finished it.

Company K also suffered further disaster while in reserve, and Sergeants Peter Crotty and Bernard McElroy, who had done prodigious deeds in action, received mortal wounds; and also William Bergen, who did more work as a stretcher bearer than any other man I have ever seen in a battle. Louis Gilbert and Everett Seymour of Company L were killed in the same bombardment and Sam Klosenberg fatally wounded.

In fact, the town of Villers sur Fere was throughout the action a part of the battlefield. Its church square at the northern end was not more than a thousand yards from the place of actual conflict. The front line forces were at times too near each other to allow artillery fire from either side, as each side had to avoid the danger of shelling its own infantry—an event which is always most disastrous to the morale of troops. But the approaches to Villers sur Fere lay under the eyes of the enemy, and they could see a constant stream of liaison men, litter bearers, hobbling wounded, and food and ammunition carriers going in by the entrance to its one street. They knew it to be the center of our web so they very wisely concentrated most of their fire upon it and especially on the square which opened out after the short narrow northern entrance of Dead Man's Curve. Even before dawn they had been raking its streets as a natural mode of approach of an oncoming enemy, killing and wounding a large number of men. Indeed nearly one-third of those who lost their lives in this action received their death wounds from shell fire in and around Villers sur Fere.

Early in the morning of July 28th, Lieutenant Joseph J. Kilcourse, Medical Officer attached to the Third Battalion, had opened his aid post in the schoolhouse facing on the square, and the development of the battle soon made it the regimental dressing station. The schoolhouse quickly filled up with wounded. A constant stream of limping men, of men with bandages around their heads or with arms carried in rough slings, of men borne on rude litters, were coming into town along the narrow entrance. No ambulances had gotten through and there were no directions as to where a *triage* could be found. The courtyard in front of the hospital was filled with "walking cases," discussing the battle with that cheerfulness which is always characteristic of soldiers who are not fatally wounded. A menacing whiz came through the air and a shell fell amongst them, followed by two others, one of which struck the wall and spattered the litter cases with plaster and broken bricks. The survivors in the yard scattered in all directions but nine of them lay quivering or motionless. Lieutenant Kilcourse ran out sobbing and swearing and working like mad to save his patients from further harm. Those who could walk were started down the road towards the Château de Foret in the hope of being picked up by an ambulance or truck. Inside the hospital nobody was seriously hurt, but the men of the Sanitary Detachment labored energetically to get them into places of comparative safety. These were Sergeant 1st Class William Helgers, James Mason, James McCormack, Ferraro, Planeta, Larsen and Daly.

Before long, Lieutenants Lyttle, Martin, Mitchell and Lawrence had arrived, and the wounded received all the attention they could be given with the facilities at hand. But the worst cases lay there till the next morning before they could be evacuated. They bore their sufferings with cheerful fortitude, their thoughts being for others. Father Hanley was sore because he had been put out so soon. Sergeant John Donahue's thoughts were with his beloved Company L; Tommy Delaney, an innocent lovable boy, talked of his mother and what a good son to her he had planned to be if he had lived, and Tom Mansfield, with his leg shattered, was full of Irish pride that he had been given a chance to be in a big battle with the "Ould Rigiment."

Headquarters Company was located in town in the shattered houses and stables but most of its sections had to take a frequent part in field operations. The signal section, under Lieutenant James Mangan, labored at great risk in putting down the wires for connection with the front line

on the night of July 28th. Sergeant Beall, Corporal Bro-
chen and Privates J. McCabe, Kirwin and Olson kept the
lines intact, while the remainder of the platoon did great
service as ammunition bearers. The intelligence section
under Captain Elmer had an observation post 100 yards
northwest of Villers sur Fere which did excellent work in
reporting machine gun nests and the direction of fire of
enemy artillery. Dick Larned acted as Chief of Scouts with
the Third Battalion and Joyce Kilmer and Levinson with
the First Battalion. In the headquarters section little Corporal Malone was on the job day and night with his runners. Edward Mulligan of this section was killed.

Coming to what we might call the Infantry Artillery, the
Stokes mortar platoon rendered excellent service throughout the battle. Two sections of this platoon under Sergeants Jaeger and Fitzsimmons took up the advance with
the Infantry on July 27th. Early Sunday morning, July
28th, an infantry patrol drew fire from enemy machine guns
located on the banks of the Ourcq river. Major McKenna
called for one trench mortar, and a gun crew in charge of
Sergeant Fitzsimmons and Corporal Harvey reported and
shelled the enemy position in front of the Ourcq. At three
in the morning Colonel McCoy ordered a barrage to be
fired by the four guns on a machine gun nest. This was
done and then the men waited for the advance of the Infantry at 4:30. When the first wave started to cross the
Ourcq a barrage was laid down until the troops had crossed
the river and were ascending the height beyond it. The
men then followed the advance as far as the river when
they were ordered back to their position of reserve in the
village. It was during this advance that John Perry, a fine
youth, received the wound which later caused his death.

On July 29th, one section under Lieutenant Frank Mc-
Namara and Sergeant Cudmore, entered the lines to support the first battalion. This section fired an effective barrage when the enemy attempted a counter-attack. During
this action Private Malcolm Robertson was killed by an

enemy shell and Sergeant Cudmore and F. Garvey were wounded. On August 1st at two in the afternoon one gun was set up in front of the woods facing Meurcy Farm. Despite the fact that enemy aeroplanes constantly harassed them, machine gun nests in and about Meurcy Farm were shelled with good results. After two hours work the men were driven to cover by enemy machine guns, Corporal Clark and Private Casey receiving severe wounds. The platoon was relieved on August 2nd and lent their aid to the burying of the dead.

The 37 mm. guns, commonly known as the one-pounders did excellent work, the small platoon paying a heavy price in losses. On July 28th, three members of the crew were killed with one shell in the village square as they were advancing with their gun—Cornelius Grauer, Joseph Becker, Frank Guida—Grauer, a youngster of seventeen, being a particular favorite with everybody that knew him. On July 30th the platoon took part in the attack on Meurcy Farm. During the operations the crew were caught in a box barrage by the enemy artillery and serious wounds were sustained by Sergeant Willemin, who was in command, and Privates Monohan, B. J. McLaughlin, John Seifried and John Kelly. Although the crew was almost entirely wiped out, the gun was kept in action by Corporal Charlie Lester and Private Berry. Another gun crew under command of Lieutenant Joseph O'Donohue was kept going all morning and did great execution. Of this crew John C. McLaughlin was killed while firing his gun.

The members of the Company whose duties detained them in the village worked for the interest of the whole regiment in positions almost equally exposed with those in the front line. Captain Walsh, a soldier of many campaigns, knew what the men in line needed was not encouragement (he took it for granted that every man had courage) nor sympathy (his own feeling was one of envy of them), but ammunition and food. His own company kitchen worked night and day to feed everybody who came into town on any business. Mess Sergeant Louis Goldstein and Cooks John Wilker and Leo Maher, moved by his example, set up their kitchen under an arch just off the square and fed 800 men a day while the engagement lasted.

That square was an interesting sight throughout the battle. Men drifted in, singly or in twos or in parties, fresh from scenes of death. Liaison men, ammunition details, litter bearers carrying stretchers dripping blood. They were fresh from the field where bullets were flying. They had been forced to drop on their faces as they crossed the valley under fire. They had scurried around Dead Man's Curve and they were still only about 1,000 yards from the fighting, with shells still screaming in the air above their heads and enemy planes forcing them to scuttle out of sight, but they were not breathless or anxious or excited. They borrowed the "makings," or got a cup of coffee from John Wilker and stole a few minutes to gossip about the fight or to relate something that struck them as interesting. A year ago if one lone maniac had been lying in Central Park taking pot shots at passers-by going along Fifth Avenue they would have run down a side street calling for the Police, would have gotten home excited and out of breath, and would have stood outside of the church the next Sunday after ten o'clock Mass to tell all their friends what an adventure they had had.

It was magnificent, but it was not war. Especially with the aeroplanes overhead. Those German aeroplanes—they circled over our troops in line, over our men in the rear. Colonel McCoy sent word to inquire about the aeroplanes that were promised us. General Lenihan wanted to know. General Menoher sent orders; entreated. But the only ones we could see had the black Maltese cross—the same old story.

There was but one thing to do if we would prevent a recurrence of the catastrophe which had already occurred at the hospital in that same square. And that was to prevent the men from gathering there. The kitchen was moved to a less exposed spot. This was done to draw the men away from the square and not from any sense of timidity on the part of its operatives. On the contrary they had made a bold attempt to get that kitchen up to the front line. On the night of July 29th the bowld Jim Collintine had hitched his trusty mules to the beloved goulash wagon and driven it right up to the Ourcq. When they found they could not cross, the Mess Sergeant and cooks unloaded its contents for the men in line. Mooney of Company A tried the same thing, and, when the river stopped him, sent the food up on litters.

One of the officers whose duties kept him near the hospital appointed himself as Police Officer in addition to his other duties, to keep the men under cover. On the second day of the fight he saw a tousled looking soldier without hat or rifle coming from a barn.

"What outfit do you belong to?"

"I belong to the 165th Infantry, sir."

"What are you doing here?"

"I came in last night with an ammunition detail and we got scattered under shell fire and I crawled into the barn."

"Yes, you slept there all night and let the other fellows do your work. You must be a new man. But I see you have a service stripe."

"Well, I am new in the regiment and I don't belong in this game. I was in the S. O. S. and they sent me up here as a replacement after I got into the hospital."

"Where is your rifle."

"I lost it and it ain't no good to me anyway cause I don't know anything about it, and I can't see good anyway."

The situation was too much for the officer and, like everyone else in emergency, his mind turned to Captain Walsh.

"Go down that road about forty yards and you will see a farm yard with soldiers in it and ask for Captain Walsh. Tell him I sent you and tell him the story you gave me."

The hatless soldier obeyed very willingly because the street led towards the rear. An hour later Captain Mike breezed into the square and came over to the officer with the demand,

"Who was that bird you sent me?"

"What did you do with him, Mike?"

"What did I do with him. I salvaged him a nice new rifle, strapped two bandoliers around him, led him gently out into the street, faced him north and said, 'Keep right on going in that direction until you see a Dutchman and when you see him shoot him for me.' And I gave him a good start with my boot and by the way he made his getaway I'll bet he's going yet."

The Commander of our Sanitary Detachment was Captain Wm. B. Hudson, who had been assigned to us from the 117th Sanitary Train when Major Lawrence was called to Division Headquarters. On July 28th, Captain Hudson had taken his post at the Château de Foret, General Lenihan's Headquarters, most of which the General had given over for the accommodation of the wounded who had managed to get back that far. Here, too, the wounded men met with fresh disaster. A German aeroplane dropped bombs in the courtyard and killed seven men, including Sergeant Brogan of Company B, one of the best men we had.

On the next day Captain Hudson started to look for a better place for the wounded in Villers sur Fere, accompanied by the ever-faithful Jewett, the "Y" athletic instructor. He was standing in the door of the place he had selected when an enemy gas shell came over and a fragment of it hit him full in the chest, killing him instantly.

We buried him sadly by the cemetery wall where already too many of our men were lying in their last long sleep.

In the town also we buried many who were killed by shell fire as they advanced to go into action during the night of the 27th-28th. In this our Machine gunners were the greatest sufferers; almost a whole platoon was wiped out. A shell landed in the midst of them, creating havoc. The uninjured rushed boldly to succor their comrades, when another shell and still another, fell in the same spot, scattering death afresh. Sergeant Phil Brooks here gave up his life and Ray Nulty, J. R. Keller, H. Van Diezelski, Frank Carlin, G. Foster and C. G. Sahlquist.

Accompanying Lieutenant Connelly on his mission of the morning of the 28th was the Second Platoon of our Machine Gun Company under Lieutenant Carter, who was wounded during the action.* The Platoon was kept together by Sergeants Bruhn and Kerrigan, and Doherty, and afterwards went through the whole battle with our First Battalion.

While the first battalion was lying under the hill during the afternoon of the 28th they were very much harrassed by enemy planes which came across flying low and shooting from their machine guns at the men on the hill and under the bank. Here Harry Martenson was killed and Hugh Heaney badly wounded and carried back by Sergeant Devine. Sergeant Frank Gardella thought it was time to try reprisals, so he set up his machine gun as an anti-aircraft weapon and began blazing away at fourteen planes which were above his head and flying low. He got a line on two planes which were flying one above the other, and by a lucky shot hit the pilot of the upper plane which crashed into the lower one and both came tumbling to earth not far from the river, their crews being killed.

When Company C was advancing towards Bois Colas they met opposition from enemy light machine guns some of which were operating from the tree tops. Lieutenant Bell's platoon, Sergeants Stephens and Gardella, Corporals J. McBride, Paul Fay and Williams were given the task of dislodging them. They carried up their heavy guns on their backs, and without taking time to set them up, they made use of them as if they were automatic rifles, with great effect, killing or capturing the enemy.

*Wounded here were Harris, Fleckner, Lang, McDonald and later during the battle Sergeant Kerrigan, Hal Sang, Jack Corrigan, Bart Cox, William Patterson, James O'Connor, Maurice O'Keefe, H. McCallum, Frank S. Erard, Bob Holmes, J. J. Spillane and Tom Doherty.

From the time that Company C took possession of Bois Colas the Machine Gunners kept their pieces busy from their positions on the north edge of the woods, keeping down German fire from Seringes and around Meurcy Farm. Of their twelve guns, five were put out of action. In the later encounters Lieutenants Davis and Bell were wounded and Jack O'Leary, a famous fighting man, received a wound which afterwards caused his death.

In the front line, on August 1st, there was a comparative lull in the activity. Our artillery was still going strong, but the Germans held command of the air and used it to the full. They flew down to the rear of us and hovered over the tree-tops of the woods where our artillery was emplaced, dropping bombs on them and shooting at them from levels so low that the artillery men answered with fire from their pistols.

It was the sudden leap of the cat at the dog's nose before she turns to flee. At four A. M., August 2nd, our patrols reported no resistance. Word was sent to the Ohios, but they found the enemy still in their path. However, under orders from General Menoher, the whole Division started forward and found that the main body of the enemy had gone. Our Infantry hastened on through the Foret de Nesles, keeping in touch with neighboring regiments left and right. Finally they encountered resistance near Moreuil en Dole, north of the forest. The 4th Division was coming up to relieve us but Colonel MacArthur wanted a last effort made by his Division. He called on one regiment, then on another, for a further advance. Their commanders said truthfully that the men were utterly fatigued and unable to go forward another step. "It's up to you, Mc-Coy," said the Chief of Staff. Our Colonel called Captain Martin Meaney, now in command of what was left of the third battalion. "Captain Meaney, a battalion is wanted to go ahead and gain contact with the enemy; you may report on the condition of your men." "My men are few and they are tired, sir, but they are willing to go anywhere they are ordered, and they will consider an order to advance as a compliment," was the manly response. As the brave and gallant few swung jauntily to their position at the head of the Division, Colonel MacArthur ejaculated, "By God, McCoy, it takes the Irish when you want a hard thing done." The battalion located the enemy and took up the fight with them, but already the 4th Division was coming up and the orders for relief were issued.

In that bloody week the Rainbow Division had met the 4th Prussian Guard Division, commanded by the Kaiser's son, Prince Eitel Friedrich, the 201st German and 10th Landwehr and the 6th Bavarian Division, had driven them back 18 kilometers to the last ridge south of the Vesle at a cost in killed and wounded of 184 officers and 5,459 men.

Back came our decimated battalions along the way they had already traveled. They marched in wearied silence until they came to the slopes around Meurcy Farm. Then from end to end of the line came the sound of dry, suppressed sobs. They were marching among the bodies of their unburied dead. In the stress of battle there had been but little time to think of them—all minds had been turned on victory. But the men who lay there were dearer to them than kindred, dearer than life; and these strong warriors paid their bashful involuntary tribute to the ties of love and long regret that bind brave men to the memory of their departed comrades.

CHAPTER VII

AFTER THE BATTLE

FORET DE FERE

August, 1918

THIS is a dirty, dank, unwholesome spot and the daily rains make it daily more intolerable. But they are keeping us here in reserve till some division—they say our old townies of the 77th—has time to come up. The forest has been occupied by the Germans and its sanitary conditions are no credit to their boasted .efficiency. Sixty per cent of our men are sick with diarrhœa and everybody is crawling with cooties. The men are sleeping in shelter tents or in holes in the ground in the woods and they are a sorry looking lot.

A number of them have been busy with me in the heartbreaking task of burying the dead, which is hard for everybody, but particularly I think, for myself, because I knew these men so well and loved them as if they were my younger brothers. It has been the saddest day in my life. Well, it is the last act of love I can do for them and for the folks at home. God comfort them in their sorrow. I must not think of the tragedy of it too much; the main thing is to keep up the spirits of the living, for battles must still be fought and the awful price paid if the war is to be won. Many of us who have come through this will be dead after the next battle; and if the war lasts another year or so there will be few, very few left of the infantry in our First Hundred Thousand. It is a soldier's fate and we must be ready for it.

In this one battle nearly half our strength is gone. We have lost fifty-nine officers and thirteen hundred men and of these thirteen officers and about two hundred men have been killed outright. Many of our wounded have been badly hurt and we shall have other details to grieve over.* But in spite of losses and sorrow and sickness I find the men surprisingly cheerful and willing to carry on. They have what soldiers most wish for, Victory. And they know now that the men who opposed their path and had to give way to their persistance were the famous Prussian Guards, of the very flower of the German Military Machine. The old 69th had again lived up to its reputation of the past; there were no German troops, no troops in the world that could withstand its stubborn bravery.

I went amongst the survivors to gather items for my chronicle of the war. I may say here as I rewrite these chapters that I have had to obtain many of the incidents months afterwards from men that have been wounded, for many of those who could best tell the story were then lying suffering from agonizing wounds on hospital cots, and still burning with the courage and devotion of their race for the day when they could once more return to the post of danger with their beloved regiment. These are the real heroes of the war. It is easy under the stress of emotional enthusiasm to volunteer for service, but the true test of a man comes when, after he has faced the danger of sudden death and

* Final figures.

	Killed	Wounded	Missing
Officers	14	45	0
Enlisted Men	224	1,135	153
Total Losses	238	1,180	153
Grand Total			1,571

Practically all of those marked "missing" were wounded men of whom no record was sent back to us from the hospitals.

In the Lunéville Sector our battle losses had been 1 officer and 29 enlisted men killed; 19 officers and 408 enlisted men wounded.

In the Baccarat Sector, 3 men killed and 8 wounded.

In Champagne 1 officer and 43 men killed; 7 officers and 245 men wounded. Our missing on all three of these fronts was 9 men.

Between March 1st and August 1st the Regiment lost 315 killed, 1,867 wounded, 162 missing, making a grand total of 2,344.

has passed through days of racking pain, he once more insists, in spite of offers of easier service from kindly officers, on taking his place again in the battle line with his old comrades. And now that the war is over, there is nothing that stirs my blood like the petty arrogance of some officials in hospitals and casual camps who rebuke the requests of men (many of whom have been wounded and gone back into line and got wounded again) to rejoin their former outfits. My malison on their tribe.

I shall present first the lists of names mentioned for good work (a soldier's meed) and afterwards incidents of more general interest. Company A gives credit to three snipers for working out to the front ahead of them and making the Fritzies keep their heads down during the attack on July 29th: Corporal Charles Hallberg, Edwin Stubbs, and John McDonald. They also spoke highly of their Sergeants or Acting Sergeants on whom leadership devolved during the fight: Joseph Higginson, Joseph Pettit, John R. Scully, Hugh McFadden, Harry Blaustein, Will Mehl, Don Matthews, Michael Walsh, Frederick Garretson, Sidney Clark, and John Dennelly. With Dennelly in the occupation of Meurcy Farm were John Sheehy, Maurice Cotter, Pilger, Newton, Thorn, Iverson and Frechales. Besides Henderson, those who distinguished themselves by liaison work were Corporal Lester Hanley, Joseph M. McKinney, Michael Polychrom, Louis Tiffany, John Gannon and Edwin Dean. Litter Bearers: Matt Kane, Howard Hamm and in a volunteer capacity Cook Edward Mooney, Albert Cooper, August Trussi. Others mentioned with high praise are Patrick Thynne, Patrick J. Doolin, Fred Stenson, John J. Morrissey, James Partridge, Paul Smith, John Barrett, Richard Campion, Louis Cornibert, Brady and Buckley.

If Company B ever loses its big Captain they have already a candidate of their own to succeed him in his senior lieutenant, John J. Clifford, a cool and capable officer, as all his men say. The greatest loss the Company has suffered is from the death of the First Sergeant, John O'Neill, a remarkable old soldier with regular army experience, who was frightfully wounded by shell fire while getting up supplies, and died in hospital. Al Dunn, a game youth, was hit by the same shell, but refused to allow anybody to touch him until O'Neill was looked after. Among other good men who received wounds were John Mooney, William Judge, Al Whalen, Harry Guenther, Dan Finnegan, Thomas Fitzpatrick, Vincent Farrell, Francis X. Goodwin, and William O'Sullivan. The platoon under Lieutenant Wheatley that joined the attack with Company A, had for its non-coms Edward Kelly, Langan, Cullinan, Travis, Patrick Kelly, Foster, Tinker, McClymont and Mearns. Lieutenant Clifford had high praise for Sergeant Thomas, who had gone out on the night of July 28th to repulse a counter-attack of the Germans and, of those in the detachment, Connie Reuss, Corporal Michael Tierney, a Clare man, who was killed; and also amongst the killed Charles Chambers, a patriotic volunteer who leaves a wife to mourn him in the city of Dublin. James Dwyer, Joseph McCarthy, Joseph Maher and John A. Lane were also badly wounded. As John A. Lane was lying out in a very exposed position his namesake, John B. Lane, a lad of eighteen, and the pride of the Company as a clever little boxer, declared that he was going out to carry the other in. He did so without scath, but was killed three days later in front of Meurcy Farm. Private Frank McGovern received praise for a similar action on the 29th; also Harold Kyte, Thomas Walsh, John O'Connor, James Lannon, James Austin and John Matthews, litter bearers. John Mahoney especially distinguished himself in this line, carrying the wounded to the rear and then lugging up food for the surviving fighters. Good liaison work was done by Charles Weick, James Murray, James Brennan, Ed. Powers, Jim Brundage, Arthur LaSalle, and John Kane, a youngster of seventeen. Thomas Herlihy and Charles Kavanagh were also commended.

Inquiry at Company C gave me the name of John Teevan,

who on the 31st left cover to save a wounded comrade and
was himself wounded while doing it; Sergeant Herman Hillig, always a good man, who led the advance patrol on the
29th; Corporal Frank Drivdahl, who took charge of a half
platoon when his seniors were wounded and led it into
handgrips with the enemy. All of the non-coms distinguished themselves. First Sergeant Gene Halpin, always a
steady leader; Tom O'Hagan, the *beau idéal* of an Irish
soldier; Sergeants Joe Hennessey, John Knight, John McAuliffe, Peter Keller, Frank Colyer, Corporals Frank Duffy,
James Barry, Charles Quinn, Edward Gordon, Edward
Brown, and amongst those wounded Arthur Totten, Arthur Slicklen, Peter Gammel, the Peisel brothers, and Denis
Cahill, sturdiest of old-timers. This Company claims that
it has the most heroic and devoted lot of litter bearers that
ever deliberately took their lives in their hands. By the
stories I hear it is hard to choose between them. They are
Thomas P. McPherson, Edmond McCarthy, James and Joseph Burns (twins in birth and twins in courage) and Edward F. Brown. They were always at the front, day and
night, and they should all have the Distinguished Service
Cross. Liaison men mentioned are Clarence Smith and
Vivian Commons. Others that received praise were Frederick Craven, Corporal Childress, who came over on the
torpedoed *Tuscania* and joined us at Baccarat; Corporal
Pat Moran, Thomas Leddy, James Heaney; and Mess Sergeant Grace with cooks Duffy and Wilson, who won the
eternal gratitude of the Company by carrying food to them
in line.

William Hisle was one of the first names I got from
Company D, a man who did extraordinarily fine work as
a litter bearer. John J. Kolodgy also, and Edward Coxe
(wounded at the same task and sticking on the job until
killed) are in the same class. Liaison men: Louis Murphy, William P. White, John Conway, John Dale, Frank
DeMuth; while others mentioned are Mess Sergeant Edward McIntee, Pat Crowley, "the wild Irishman," Pat Gro-

gan (wounded again), John L. Burke, Peter Carberry, Charles Edgerton, Richard Dwyer (who said "Tend to me last" when wounded), Thomas Keyes, Sergeant Denis Murphy, badly wounded; Denis O'Connor, Charles Lynch, Everett Smith, John Cahill, Andrew O'Rourke, Peter O'Sullivan, Martin Hurst, Arthur Comer, John L. Thompson, John Cox, Joseph P. Tracy and Patrick Finn (both '98 men) and Fred Urban, a new man and a great shot with the rifle, with Chief Powless and Tony Zaliski.

Company E told me of Michael Breen, who received his death wound, covering the advance of his Company by the use of smoke grenades; William Foley and James Fitzpatrick, going out under fire to rescue two companions; George M. Failing, who did noble work as a litter bearer; John Costello, Thomas Cullen (both killed), with Bechtold and William Goldenburg, four privates who saved their Company by putting a machine gun out of action. Sergeant Augustus T. Morgan, also Sergeant Frank Johnston and Corporal John Cronin did heroic work.

Company F, Bernard Corcoran got a bullet across both his eyeballs which will render him blind for life. John Fitzgibbon, Michael Douglas, Frank Dunn, Charles Dougherty, William Garry, Leo Hanifin, Owen Carney, George D. Lannon, Frank Kelly, Gottfried Kern, Edward Chabot, James McCormack, John McAuliffe, Daniel McGrath, Peter McGuiness, William McQuade, John P. Mahon, Herbert Doyle, Peter Malloy, shot through the lung, William Mulligan, Charles O'Leary and William Moran, Sergeant Pat Wynne, John Smith, Peter Rogers, Frank Sweeney and William Walsh are on the honor roll.

Company G had the greatest praise for Edmund Reardon and Charles McGeary, who did remarkable work saving others until finally death came to themselves. Others mentioned with praise are Corporal Edward Fitzgerald and Sergeant Edward McNamara, who had to be ordered out of the line when wounded. Also Corporal David Fitzgibbons, Thomas Meade, Michael Shea, Michael O'Brien, Patrick

Donohue, Frank Cahill, Thomas Bohan, First Sergeant John Meaney, Corporal Frank Garland, Thomas McGowan, James Brennan, Sergeant James Coffey; Robert Monohan and Patrick McNamara, liaison men; and Maurice Dwyer, mechanic, who always dropped his tools and picked up a rifle when a battle was on.

Company H thinks that it is about time that Sergeant Dudley Winthrop got a citation. His latest feat was to go wandering out in the open where everybody that went had been hit, searching out his wounded comrades. Martin Higgins has also been recommended for citation for the same kind of heroic activity. Patrick Reynolds went out alone and, by expert sniping at close range, put out of action a machine gun that was holding up the advance. Later on, he was killed. Sergeant John J. Walker kept his platoon going when his seniors were wounded. Callahan, Dunseith, Ernst, Conway, Bealin, McDonald, O'Brien, McKenna, Sweeney, White, Frieburger, Crose and Bushey are also recommended for excellent work.

I have already gone through the list of Company I, so I shall just add an additional list of non-coms who were wounded: Sergeants Harold J. Murphy and William Lyle, Corporals Wilton Wharton, Charles Beckwith, L. Vessell, James Brady, William Burke, William Crossin, Patrick Farrell, Alfred Georgi, Hugh Kelly, Michael Learnahan, John Maddock, H. R. Morton, Patrick O'Brien, Francis O'Neill, Edward Powers, William Reutlinger, and James Sullivan.

The men from Company I whose names were selected at the time for a Regimental Citation were First Sergeant Patrick McMeniman, who was really in command of the Company during most of the trying time on the hill; Dexter, Dynan, Howard, Coen, Farley, Coppinger, Battersby, and Lesser as stretcher bearers; Cook Michael J. O'Brien, who carried food to the front line no matter how dangerous it was, and carried wounded on the return trip; and Thomas A. Boyle, who seeing an abandoned automatic rifle ran forward under vicious fire, loaded it and started it working against the enemy; and finally, William B. Lyons, prominent as liaison man and stretcher bearer.

Company K recommends Nicholas E. Grant, a liaison man, along with its heroic Captain, Sergeant Joe Farrell, Victor Van Yorx, John Doyle, stretcher bearer, and the self-sacrificing William Bergen, Francis I. Kelly, also a martyr to loyalty, as he was killed while rendering first aid to Lieutenant Stott. Burr Finkle and John J. McLaughlin are recommended for a display of extraordinary heroism.

In Company L the valiant Captain and Lieutenant Spencer have been recommended for the D. S. C. For rescue work, Thomas Deignan, Joseph Coogan, John Ahern, Joseph Grace, Charles Oakes, William Hughes, Michael Fallon (twice wounded) and James Santori, the latter being killed while placing a wounded man on a stretcher. Lieutenant Wellbourne, with the Sergeants already mentioned, and also Corporals Edward McDonough, Harry McDermott, Eugene McCue, and Wild Bill Ryan distinguished themselves by their work in the line. So, too, did James Judge, Thomas Boyle, Eddie Bloom, Arthur Campbell, John Burke, Will Coleman, John Murphy, Matt Devlin, Hugh Fagan, Fred Meyers, Leslie Quackenbush, John Mulvey, Peter O'Connor, Maurice Powers, Val Roesel, John B. McHugh, Sam Ross, Peter Deary, James Streffler, Harry Baldwin, expert sniper, and Eddie Morrissey, liaison man.

Captain Meaney of Company M gave the highest recommendation to Lieutenant Collier and also to Corporals Thomas J. Courtney and Patrick Ames, both of them soldiers of remarkable coolness and resolution. The men of this Company were kept busy throughout the week as food and ammunition carriers and stretcher bearers. Amongst those who distinguished themselves in these tasks were Corporals James Duffy and Jack Manson, with Edward Mendes, Daniel Leahy, William Lynch, John Feeley, Thomas Ferrier, William O'Neill, Frank Sisco, James Shanahan, Edward Flanagan, Patrick Bryne, Frank Cullum, James Igo,

James A. Watts, the Rodriguez brothers and Herbert Dunlay.

Captain Walsh of Headquarters Company recommended Sergeant Arthur Jaeger, Sergeant John J. Ryan, Corporal Charles Leister of the one-pounders, with Corporal Leslie Reynolds and Privates Robert Callaghan, Clarence Cumpston, Maurice Small, Charles Goecking, Spencer Sully, John C. McLaughlin and William Hearn (who also did heroic work rescuing the wounded), Corporal A. A. Brochon and Privates James P. McCabe and Arthur Olsen and Kirwin of the Signal Platoon. In the Stokes Mortars Sergeant Thomas Fitzsimmons, Jeremiah J. Casey, Thomas J. Kelly and Malcolm Robertson, Thomas J. Taylor, Herbert Clarke with Moore, Wisner, Hayes, Nugent, Robb, Levins, Orr, Shannon, Dugdale, and my old friend, John Mahon, who always has some special reason why he should be selected as a member of every gun crew sent to the front line; George Utermehle, Stable Sergeant; Jerome Goldstein, Mess Sergeant; with Cooks John A. Wilker, Maher McAvoy and Wagoner James Collintine; and Jim Turner, wounded while doing courageous work as a liaison man.

The Machine Gun Company cites their runners, John L. B. Sullivan, William Murphy, Hantschke, Charles Smith, and James Ledwith. Also Lieutenant Billings, who had the dangerous task of keeping up the supply of ammunition, which he accomplished with the aid of two excellent noncoms, Sid Ryan and Joe McCourt (one of the most efficient men in the whole regiment). Every man in the company sang the praises of Bill Sheppard, Paul Fay and Pete Gillespie; also of Leon Baily and Frank Gardella, who spent their leisure moments carrying in Company C's wounded.

The Supply Company wagoners Peter J. Seagriff, Albert Richford, A. Brown, Philip Smith and Thomas J. Ferris, won praise for difficult and dangerous tasks courageously performed by night and day.

The Sanitary Detachment, in addition to those mentioned, gave me Milledge Whitlock, Louis Bidwell, John

McKeough, John P. Murphy, Patrick Fawcett, Thomas V. Boland, Walter Clark and Sergeant Arthur Furman. Whitlock, Wright and Walker were at an advance aid-post under the river bank all week long.

The most striking incident I heard described took place in Company D as they were waiting in the street of Villers sur Fere about three o'clock in the morning of the 28th. The Germans were raking the streets with high explosives and shrapnel, and men were falling, hit by the flying pieces. The most trying moment in battle is going into action under shell fire, especially at night. The shells come wh-e-e-e--zing over. One goes Whannng! up the road—another in a field to the right! Then one falls on a house and the tiles, plaster, fragments of stone are scattered over the men who are lying in the lee of it. Then another comes, more menacing in its approaching whistle. Men run, drop on the ground, stand petrified. And it lands in the midst of them. There are cries, ceasing suddenly as if cut off with a knife, curses, sobs of "Oh, God!" "They got me!" "For God's sake, pick me up, Jim." The survivors rush back, ripping open their First Aid packages, the non-coms bawling orders, everybody working in a frenzy to save the wounded. And then perhaps another shell landing in the same place will send them all away from the troubles of this awful world.

Company D was going through all this, and for the time being, without officers. Buck was gassed the day before; Connelly and Daly had gone off to execute their difficult operation to the right, First Sergeant Geaney being with them; Burke was away on his mission of danger and glory. The remaining Lieutenant had been called to receive orders. Two corporals, Patrick MacDonough and John Gribbon, had been working hard, giving first aid to the wounded, and they began to worry about the possible effect of the shelling on the men. So they went up the line to look for some person in higher authority.

They found no officer but they did find Sergeant Tom

O'Malley sitting against a stone wall, sucking philosophically at his pipe, as if the wall were the side of a stone fence in his native Connemara. Now the sight of Tom O'Malley breeds confidence in the heart of every soldier in Company D.

"Where's the officers, Tom?"

"Oi don't know where th' hell they are," says Tom, between puffs of his pipe, and in the slow, soft speech of the West Coast Irish, "If ye were in camp and ye didn't want to see thim, ye'd be thrippin' over thim. But now whin ye want t' know what ye got to do in a foight ye can't find wan of thim."

"Well, Tom, we'll elect you Captain and you take charge of the men until some of the officers get back, or they may be getting out of hand."

"No, lads, Oi don't fancy meself in a Sam Brown belt. Dick O'Neill here is a noice young fellah, so we'll elect Dick Captain, and O'll make ye fellahs do what he tells ye." So Sergeant O'Neill, a youth of twenty-one, took charge of the situation, got the men together in small groups under their non-coms, and in places of comparative safety, and had them all ready when Lieutenant Cook came back from the conference to issue their orders to cross the Ourcq.

It is something that we call typically American that a number of men under a stress and in an emergency like this, should get together, choose their own leaders and obey them implicitly for the common good. These four men are Americans of the type we are proudest of. Yet it is worth noting that three out of the four were born in an island whose inhabitants, we are often told, are unfit for self-government. As for Dick O'Neill, he is one hundred per cent American, but it would take a braver man than I can claim to be to tell Dick O'Neill that he is not Irish, too.

One of the members of D Company who was wounded in this spot was Matt Sullivan, an old-timer, and a kindly pleasant man who always took an interest in the younger lads, so that he was known as "Pop." His two special protégés were Barney Friedman and George Johnson. When he was hit he was ordered to the rear, but he said, "I'll not stir out o' this till I see if the children are safe, God bless them." He hobbled around in the gray dawn until he found the boys and then started for the rear.

Company I had a number of little battle pictures to give me besides those I have already written. One was of Barney Farley, who was busy all morning dressing wounds, and after he had stopped the flow of blood, before picking up his man, he would roll a cigarette, stick it in the wounded man's mouth with a cheery "Here, take a pull out of this, avic. It'll do ye good."

Mike Lenihan, wounded while on the hill and told to go back, said, "No, I've waited so long to get at them I won't lave this hill." Another shot got him, and he was carried off.

Tom Shannon, being carried in, got off his stretcher and wanted to give his place to another man who, he said, was worse wounded than himself. An officer ordered him back on the stretcher and he was carried in, and since then I have heard he has died of his wounds.

William Cleary, wounded in the shoulder, refused to leave without orders, so they led him to where Captain Ryan was lying in a shell hole, himself wounded. The Captain looked up at him. "You've got a bad wound. No use around here. You're young—got good color in your face—live long. Got good legs yet—run like hell."

The Captain saw a German near the top of the hill who was using an automatic, and he wanted to try a shot at him, so he borrowed Pat Flynn's rifle, fired and missed, the pain of the recoil disconcerting his aim. He tried again; then he said: "I'm going to pull the last bit of Irish in me together and get that fellow." With the last shot in the clip he got him.

Two men from Company L had a laugh about Fortgang, who, one of them said, is the champion moocher of the Company, and can always get something to eat no matter how short the rations are. They were lying out on that shot-swept hill on the morning of the 28th when Fortgang produced from somewhere a can of solidified alcohol and three strips of bacon. He calmly proceeded to start his little fire, and fried his bacon, which he shared with the men on each side of him; and thus fortified, picked up his rifle once more and began to blaze away at the Germans.

While the topic is food I may add that the whole company is devoted to Mess Sergeant McDonald and Cook Connelly, whose kitchen was hit but who swore they would "stick to it while there's a spoke left in it." Hugh Fagan was one of the men who had to be driven off the hill after being badly wounded.

I saw several men who were hit through the helmet, the bullet entering in front and going out at the back without inflicting a wound. One of them was Edward McDonough, who seemed to consider it a great joke, though another man who had the same thing happen to him, a man whom I did not know, was walking in wide circles, unable to pursue a steady course unless he had a wall or a fence to guide on.

Captain Hurley of Company K got four or five wounds at once in leg, arm and back, but refused to allow himself to be carried, saying impatiently, "Now, don't be bothering with me. I'd like to see myself on a litter while there's men much worse off than myself still lying on the ground."

I was in the dressing station one evening when a sturdy young lieutenant walked in with one hand almost blown away. He announced himself to be Lieutenant Wolf of the 150th Machine Gun Battalion, and settled down on the table for his operation with more coolness than most people display when getting their photograph taken. He had just one thing on his mind, and that did not concern himself. He had come in with an ammunition detail, which was ready to start back when a shell got him just outside the hospital door. That detail had to go back. He was much relieved, one would say perfectly contented, when I assured him that I would convey his orders to the sergeant in charge.

Through such men battles are won, and nations made famous for bravery.

On one of the days of the battle I was coming up the street of Villers sur Fere with Jack Percy when an enemy gun began to land shells just across the narrow street from us. We dropped alongside a wall when the shriek of the first one told us it was coming across the home plate, and as we lay there I saw a ration wagon coming down the road with George Utermehle, Sergeant of mounted section, H. Q. Company, on the box. George had no whip and was urging his team by throwing cherries at their heads. I shouted at him, "This is a bad corner just now, they're shelling it." "Oh, this old team of mine can beat out any shell," said George, as he hit the ear of his off animal with a cherry; and he went tearing by in time to miss the next, and, I was happy to find out, the last one that came over.

I overheard a conversation in the woods which gave me a good story on Major Donovan. The majority of his battalion have always looked on him as the greatest man in the world. But a certain number were resentful and complaining on account of the hard physical drilling he has continually given them to keep them in condition for just the sort of thing they had to go through last week. As a result of watching him through six days of battle—his coolness, cheerfulness, resourcefulness—there is now no limit to their admiration for him. What I overheard was the partial conversion of the last dissenter. He still had a grouch about what he had been put through during the past year, and three other fellows were pounding him with arguments to prove Donovan's greatness. Finally he said grudgingly, "Well, I'll say this: Wild Bill is a son of a ——, but he's a game one." When I told it to Donovan, he laughed and said, "Well, Father, when I'm gone write that as my epitaph."

I shall always think that the finest compliment paid to Major Donovan was the devotion of John Patrick Kayes, an Irishman, very tall, very thin, somewhat stoop-shoul-

dered, not at all young, and a servant of the rich in civil
life. The Irish in him had made him a volunteer. He was
put in charge of the Battalion H. Q. mess, and I used to tell
Donovan that I came to visit him, not on account of his own
attractions, but because of what John Kayes had to offer
me. He refused to remain behind in action. He wanted
to be where the Major was, though he knew that anybody
who kept near Donovan stood an excellent chance of being killed. On July 31st he went forward with him on his
restless rounds, which led them out of the shelter of Bois
Colas into the open country. A German machine gun began firing at them and Kayes was struck in the ankle. He
fell forward into the path of the bullets and as different
portions of his long body neared the ground he was hit
successively in the thigh, arm and face. He still had
strength enough to protest that the Major should not risk
himself by carrying him in. He died in hospital weeks
later, his last thoughts being that Major Donovan would be
neglected with him gone. The terms "hero" and "butler"
are not generally associated in fiction, but they met in the
person of John Patrick Kayes.

Major Lawrence tells me that he met Captain P. P. Raf-
ferty, a doctor in our Divisional Sanitary Train, who told
him,

"We had an original character from your outfit through
here last week—a Lieutenant Connelly. He was lying on
a cot and in a good deal of pain, I knew, when I was surprised to hear him laugh a hearty laugh. I thought he was
going out of his head and I went over to him and said,
'What's happened to you that's funny, Lieutenant?"

" 'Oh,' he said, 'I was just thinking about something.'

" 'Let me in on it,' I said. 'There is not much to amuse
a man happening around here.'

" 'Well,' said he, 'it's just an incident of battle. I was
in command of a Company that had just about forty men
left, and Major Donovan gave me orders to send some of
them one way and some another and take the rest and cap-

ture a woods and Meurcy Farm. Just after I started I got into a mix-up and was put out of action and my first thought was 'Thank God! Now I don't have to take that damn farm.' "

One of my own prayers of Thanksgiving is "Praise be! Major Lawrence is back." When I told him so he thanked me for the compliment, but I said, "George, don't take it as coming from me. It is only for my own peace of mind. Since the day you left I have been pestered by everybody, officers and men, who have the right to wear your red cross armlet, with the plaintive petition, 'Father Duffy, can't you do something to get out Major back?' "

We joke Rerat about the size of the French rivers. I told him that one of our soldiers lay badly wounded near the river, and I offered him a pull at my canteen. Raising himself on one elbow and throwing out his arm in a Sir Philip Sydney fashion, he exclaimed, "Give it to the Ourcq, it needs it more than I do."

The Germans nearly had a grim joke on me during the action. We picked up our dead in the town, and I had the Pioneers dig me a long trench on the south side of the cemetery wall, which screened them from observation while their own trench would give protection. I said "This spot is the safest place in France." We finished our sad task and went away. A few hours later I passed that way again and found that the wall against which I was sitting was smashed to the ground; a tree eight inches in diameter which had shaded me was blown in two, and two other missiles had exploded five feet from the line of graves. Evidently a German aviator, seeing the freshly turned earth, thought that it was a gun emplacement and dropped three of his nasty eggs. I smiled grimly as my words came back, "The safest place in France."

Going through the woods I heard John McMorrow discussing a date with Monzert of Headquarters Company, and he was saying, "It happened the first day we went over.

I tell you it was. It was on the mornin' that we crossed the
O'Rourke River and captured Murphy's Farm."

Colonel McCoy felt deeply grieved at the news of Quentin Roosevelt's heroic death in an air battle some time before, as he knew him from boyhood, having been military
aide at the White House during part of President Roosevelt's term of office. We knew that Lieutenant Roosevelt
had met his death in this sector, and our Colonel had instituted inquiries to find if any person had discovered his
grave. Word was brought to him that the grave had been
found in the sector to our right, which was occupied by the
32nd Division, and Colonel McCoy determined to have it
suitably marked. I had a cross made and inscribed by
Julius Horvath, and the Colonel with Lieutenant Preston
and myself went by automobile to the place to erect it over
the grave. We found the roughly made cross formed from
pieces of his broken plane that the Germans had set to
mark the place where they buried him. The plot had already been ornamented with a rustic fence by the soldiers
of the 32nd Division. We erected our own little monu-
ment without molesting the one that had been left by the
Germans. It is fitting that enemy and friend alike should
pay tribute to heroism.

The Germans had not retreated ten miles before the advance guard of the French civilian population began coming
in to take possession of their shattered homes. I was coming down today from the battlefield whither I had gone
with Emmet Watson and Bill Fernie to make a map of
the graves when I met the incoming civilians in Villers sur
Fere. Most of them were men who had been sent ahead
by the family to see what was left. But occasionally we
met a stout old peasant woman pulling a small cart behind
her on which rested all her earthly substance, or a hay-cart
drawn by oxen with the family possessions in it and two
or three chubby youngsters with their mother perched on
top. I followed a middle aged farmer and his son into one
of the houses near the church and we made our inspection

together. All the plaster had been knocked off the walls and the glass from the windows, and there was a big hole in the roof, and altogether it looked anything but a home, but after looking it all over the young man said to his father, with a satisfied grunt, "Pas trop demoli" (not too badly banged up). I certainly admired the optimism and courage of people who could take up their lives once more with cheerfulness under such desperate conditions.

The Germans had made their most of the time in which they had possession of this salient. They had harvested a great deal of the grain and anything else that was already ripe and in some places they had ransacked the houses of any goods that were worth while. There were many evidences, though, that they had no idea that they were so soon to be dislodged. At Seringes they had installed an electric light plant, and the French road signs had been supplemented with the large legible German signs. Their sense of security was the cause of their largest losses in material, as they had made of the Forest of Fere a great ammunition dump, and the large shells, gas, shrapnel, high explosives, were left behind by thousands.

I got back to Château Thierry looking for hospitals which might contain our wounded but found none of them, as they had all been transferred to other places, no one knew exactly where. In the burying ground I hit upon the graves of Sergeant John O'Neill of B and Sergeants Peter Crotty and Bernard McElroy of K and Walter Wandless of H. The city already presented a lively appearance with a great deal of traffic, not all of it military, over the bridge of boats which replaced the bridge that had been destroyed during the German drive.

Our men are getting more and more restless in these dirty woods and the first question that anybody asks is, "When do we get relieved." I stepped into the woods on the other side of the road to visit my Alabama friends and one of their fine lads voiced the common mind by asking whether the govament hadn't othah soldiehs than the Fohty-Second

Division. I answered, "Well, if they're using you so much, it is your own fault." "How iŝ it ouah fault?" demanded my friend, and twenty pairs of eyes asked the same question. "It's your fault all right; the trouble with you fellows is that you're too blamed good."

I have become a specialist on what they call the morale of troops and as I go around I find that the morale of the men in this division is still very high. They hav⸗ had a tough week of it and nearly half the infantry are gone while of those remaining more than half are sick. But they know that they have whipped the enemy on his chosen ground and they feel confident that if they only get rested up a little bit they can do it again and do it cheerfully.

The Quartermaster's Department has helped considerably by fitting us all out with new clothes, underwear, shoes, everything we need, and the food supply is steady. And Miss Elsie Janis has done her part, too, as a joy producer by coming up to us in our mud and desolation and giving a Broadway performance for an audience which was more wildly appreciative than ever acclaimed her on the street of a million lights.

The long desired orders for relief finally arrived. We marched out on Sunday morning, August 11th. I had planned with Colonel McCoy to have my Sunday Service a memorial one for the brave lads we were leaving behind. He had me set up my altar in an open field just south of the forest on our line of march to the rear. The men, fully equipped for the march, came down the road, turned into the field, stripped their packs and formed a hollow square around the altar. After Mass I preached on the text, "Greater love than this no man hath than that he lay down his life for his friends." When the service was over the regiment took the road again and began its march, with the band in advance and the regimental wagon train in the rear.

As we passed through Beauvardes General Menoher and officers of his staff were in front of Division Headquarters.

Colonel McCoy passed the order down the ranks, the band struck up the regimental air of "Garry Owen" and the regiment passed in review, heads up and chests out and stepping out with a martial gait as if they were parading at Camp Mills and not returning from a battlefield where half their numbers had been lost.

Two days later they marched through Château Thierry in similar fashion. Colonel McCoy came to mess with a smile of pride on his face telling us he had encountered an old friend, a regular army officer who had said to him, "What is that outfit that passed here a little while ago? It's the finest looking lot of infantry I have seen in France." "That is the 165th Infantry, more widely known to fame as the 69th New York, and I am proud to say that I command it."

I have been playing truant for a few days. I had been suffering with a great sense of fatigue. Nothing particular the matter, but I felt as if I were running on four flat tires and one cylinder. Two of the War Correspondents, Herbert Corey and Lincoln Eyre, came along and insisted on bringing me down to their place in Château Thierry; and General Lenihan brought me in in his car. Corey cooked supper—a regular *cordon bleu* affair—and Lincoln Eyre gave me a hot bath and, like Kipling's soldier, "God, I needed it so." Then they bundled me into Tom Johnson's bed, and as I dropped asleep I thought, and will continue to think, that they are the finest fellows in the world. They were ordered out next morning and I went with them for a couple of days to Bossuet's old episcopal city of Meaux, where I had a fine time gossiping with Major Morgan, Bozeman Bulger and Arthur Delaney of the Censor's Bureau and Ray Callahan, Arthur Ruhl and Herbert Bailey, a delightful young Englishman who writes for the *Daily Mail*.

I rejoined the regiment at Saulchery—somebody says that sounds like a name for a decadent cocktail—and found myself housed in a large and pleasant villa, the garden of which looked out upon vineyards and fields down to the banks of the Marne. It was one of the pleasantest places we had been in in France. The weather was perfect, and the men enjoyed the camping out in their shelter tents, especially since the river was handy for a swim. The whole thing made us feel more like campers than soldiers. And by the time we had gotten well rested up and most of the cooties washed off, we had forgotten the hard days that were past and saw only the bright side of life once more.

We were there from August 12th to 17th, on which latter date we entrained at Château Thierry to go to our new training area. This was down in the Neufchateau district, and to get to it by the railroad we were using we went south until we got to the vicinity of Langres, where we had spent our last two months before going into the trench sector. Regimental headquarters was at Goncourt and the regiment was accommodated in barracks and billets in that and two close lying villages. The towns had been used for some time by American troops and had unusual facilities for bathing, etc. The warm reception given to us by the townspeople was a tribute to the good conduct of the 23rd Infantry which had been billetted there for a considerable period before occupying the front lines.

After a couple of days' rest the men were started on a schedule of training which was laid out for four weeks. Target ranges were prepared by the engineers and everything looked like a long stay. The training was necessary not so much for the old-timers as for the replacements who had been sent in to take the places of the men we had lost. We received five hundred from the 81st Division. We had known cases where our replacements had to go into line without anything like proper training. The night we left Epieds to advance into action at the Ourcq we received new men, some of whom knew very little about a rifle and had never once put on a gas mask; and the Captains took them out by night and drilled them for an hour with the gas masks in order to give the poor fellows some sort of a chance for their lives if exposed to danger of gas.

The second day that I was in Goncourt Colonel McCoy came to see me with Major Lawrence and Major Donovan to lay down the law. They had decided that I was to go to the hospital at Vittel, where Major Donovan's brother was one of the doctors, "for alterations and repairs." General Menoher, with his usual kindness, sent over his car to take me there, and Father George Carpentier was brought over from the Sanitary Train to fill my place. I told him "Your name is French but it has the advantage of being the one French name that is best known and most admired by our bunch of pugilists."

I have had a nice lazy week of it at Vittel, which was a French watering place before the war, the hotels and parks now being given over to American soldiers. I hear a great deal of talk about a coming offensive in which the American Army is to take the leading part. I had gotten an inkling of it before from a French source, with strictest injunctions to secrecy. But here in Vittel I find it discussed by private soldiers on the park benches and by the old lady who sells newspapers. If it is a secret, all the world seems to know it. We have taken every step to make the Germans aware of it except that of putting paid advertisements in the Berlin newspapers. The fact is, these things cannot be kept secret. Here in Vittel they are cleaning out all the hospitals of wounded and that means that a big battle is expected somewhere in this vicinity within a short time. Then up along the line ammunition and supply trains are busy establishing dumps, and the drivers are naturally talking about it in the cafés, so that everybody knows that the Americans are planning something big and the place where it is going to happen.

VITTEL

August 24th, 1918

Major Donovan is over every few days to have his wound attended to and incidentally to see his brother Tim, who is a surgeon with the Buffalo Unit. Today he gave me a piece of news that came as a shock though hardly as a surprise—the orders are out to make Colonel McCoy a Brigadier General and he is to leave us. He has been with us less than four months yet I feel as if I had known him for forty years, and this war is going to be a different sort of thing for me lacking his presence. But the staying thing about life is that institutions go on even though men may pass. My thoughts turned to the regiment.

"Who is likely to be Colonel?" I asked.

"We are all united on Mitchell," said the Major, "and I think General McCoy will be able to arrange it for us."

"I have always thought that General McCoy can do anything he sets out to do. As for Mitchell, with the possible exception of yourself, Major, there is no man I had rather see have it."

"Oh, Hell, Father, I don't want to be Colonel. As Lieutenant Colonel I can get into the fight and that's what I'm here for. We all want Mitchell."

"You are a selfish creature, Bill. Did you ever see anybody more contented in action than the man you want to tie up to a telephone?"

"Well, somebody has to be tied up to the telephone, McCoy didn't like it, nor MacArthur. And then, as you know, they can always find some reason to get away from it and have a little excitement."

VITTEL

August 29th, 1918

The orders have come already to move up to the next battle area. Instead of having a month for rest and training the Division has had but ten days in its new area. Orders came in on the 28th and the regiments moved out on the 29th, our headquarters being at Gendreville. On the next day they moved to Viocourt, the 2nd and 3rd battalions being at Courcelles. Major Lawrence came to see me at the hospital to tell me about the new move and I obtained permission to leave and rejoin my regiment. I shall always have a warm place in my heart for the doctors and nurses of the Buffalo and Westchester County Units.

VIOCOURT

September 1st, 1918

I walked into Division Headquarters at Chatenois today on my business as Senior Chaplain. I sent off a couple of telegrams to the G. H. Q. Chaplains about a Protestant chaplain that I want them to send for the Alabamas' and also stirring them up about a Protestant chaplain that I had been asking them for a long time for my own regiment. Another telegram went to the K. of C. at Paris to send a priest to look after Catholics in the Illinois and Indiana artillery regiments, as the chaplains there are anxious to have one. My final inquiry was about transportation to Toul for Jewish members of the Division in order to have them celebrate their approaching feast. Sergeant Marcus looked up at me and grinned: "Say, Father Duffy, aren't you glad you have no Buddhists to look after?" He added that the adjutant had a surprise in store for me.

He had—two official announcements, one, that the corps commander had made me a major and the other that I had been cited for the D. S. C. Being a Major has no particular thrills to it, except no doubt when I come to sign my pay vouchers; but there is no man living who can truthfully say that it means nothing to him to receive the bronze cross and red, white and blue bar of our Army. To everybody, I think, the greatest satisfaction comes not from what it means to himself but from the gratification it will give his friends. Another feeling uppermost in my mind was one of grateful affection for Colonel McCoy because I knew that it was he who had recommended me both for the rank and the distinction. I wrote to him "The British reward their military heroes with a peerage, a pension, and a tomb in

Westminster Abbey. You have gotten for me the American equivalent for two of them—the distinction and the emoluments—and it only remains for you to fix it up so that I can have a tomb in St. Patrick's Cathedral. All that is necessary to give me a right to that is to make me Archbishop of New York; Cardinal, if you insist. I never knew you to fail in anything you went after so I shall consider this matter as settled."

We remained in Viocourt six days and then began our journey north by night marches. The 4th of September was spent in the Bois de Raidon. On the 5th of September the whole regiment was together at Bulligny. On the 6th, still marching by night, we were at Foug, and September 7th found us at Boucq, where we spent two days.

Here we had the honor of a visit from the Commander in Chief. General Pershing had come on for the ceremony of presenting Distinguished Service Crosses to those who had been cited in our Division, and the ceremony took place in a field to the northeast of our village of Boucq. The recipients from our Regiment were Lieutenant Colonel Donovan, Major Reilley, who quite overshadowed me, Captain Merle-Smith, Lieutenant William Spencer, Lieutenant John J. Williams, Sergeant Frank Gardella, Corporal John McLaughlin, Corporal Martin Higgins, and Burr Finkle. Captain Ryan and others who had been cited were still in the hospital, while others were of those who had perished on the field. A complete list will be given in another place.

CHAPTER VIII

THE ST. MIHIEL OFFENSIVE

THE field orders for the attack on the St. Mihiel salient were received on September 10th, the date not being specified. Our division was to attack as part of the 4th U. S. Army Corps of the 1st U. S. Army; and we were given the honor of being made the point of the arrow which was to pierce through the center of the salient along the base of the triangle that was to be cut off. The 89th Division was on our right and the 1st Division on cur left, with the 3rd in Army reserve.

Our Division was to be formed with both brigades abreast, the 83rd being on the left of the 84th. The relative places of regiments with regard to each other was to be in the same order in which they fought at the Ourcq—from left to right: Ohios, New Yorks, Alabamas and Iowas. Each regiment was to have one battalion in the first line and one in the second, the remaining battalions acting as brigade or division reserves. Battery F, 149th F. A. was to follow up with the infantry of our brigade after their capture of the first position. The brigade had also the co-operation of a battalion of our Engineers for road and bridge work, one platoon of the first gas regiment and two groups of French Schneider Tanks.

On the night of September 10th we moved forward to the vicinity of Mandres, where we relieved elements of the 89th Division which were transferred further to the right. Our headquarters on September 11th were at Hamonville, not far from Seicheprey where the 26th Division had played a savage game of give and take with the Germans when they held the trenches last Spring.

Copies were issued of the very elaborate plans which had been prepared by Army Chiefs of Staff outlining with great definiteness the part that each element of our Army had to play in the work that lay ahead of them.

The men were encamped in a forest of low trees, a most miserable spot. It had been showering and wet all the week and we were living like paleozoic monsters, in a world of muck and slime. The forest roads were all plowed by the wagon wheels and when one stepped off them conditions were no better, for the whole place was really a swamp. I made my rounds during the afternoon and got the men together for what I call a silent prayer meeting. I told them how easy it was to set themselves right with God, suggesting an extra prayer for a serene mind and a stout heart in time of danger; and then they stood around me in a rough semicircle, caps in hand and heads bowed, each man saying his prayers in his own way. I find this simple ceremony much more effective than formal preaching.

When I got back to headquarters I found my own staff very considerably increased. Father Hanley had come back a couple of days before. The rumors of approaching action were all over France, so, sniffing the battle from afar, he got the hospital authorities to let him out and rejoin his regiment for the coming fight. I kept Father Carpentier attached to the regiment for the time being until I could get the Protestant chaplain that I had been petitioning for so long. Father Hanley still had a perceptible limp and was moving around with the aid of a stick so I told him that he would have to look after the hospital center (*Triage*) while the fight was on, a commission that he took with no good grace. To Father Carpentier I gave a roving commission to look after Catholics in the Ohio and Alabama regiments, a task for which his zeal and endurance especially qualified him.

Now I found two more Chaplains on my hands—one from the Knights of Columbus, Father Moran, an Irish Priest, and one assigned to the regiment, Chaplain Merrill

J. Holmes of the M. E. Church. I liked him on sight and we were not long in getting on a basis of cordiality which will make our work together very pleasant. It was too late to send the extra chaplains to other regiments as we were even then getting ready to move forward into line, so I decided to keep them all under my wing. I told the lieutenants of the Headquarters Company that it would not be my fault if they did not all get to Heaven because we had five chaplains along. "Five Chaplains," said Lieutenant Charles Parker. "Great Heavens! there won't be a thing left for any of the rest of us to eat."

The terrain which was to be the object of the attack of our three divisions was completely dominated on the left by the frowning heights of Mont Sec; and if they had been held in force by the enemy artillery it would have exposed our whole army corps to a flanking fire which would soon make progress impossible. It fell to the 1st Division to make their advance along the mountain side.

The ground over which we were to pass was for the most part fairly level up as far as the twin towns of Maizerais and Essey, to the left of which the Rupt de Mad made its way through swamps at the base of the hill which was crowned by these two villages. A number of woods dotted the surface; one of them, the Bois de Remières, stood directly in front of our advance. No Man's Land at this point was seven or eight hundred yards wide; and the German trenches, as we afterwards found, were not in very good condition, though there was plenty of wire standing both here and at other points that were prepared for defence. We were to jump off at the east of Seicheprey, and regimental headquarters and dressing station were established by Colonel Mitchell and Major Lawrence in the Bois de Jury, not far to the rear.

We moved up to our jump-off point on the night of September 11th. The rain was falling in torrents. The roads were like a swamp and the night was so dark that a man could not see the one in front of him. And of course no lights could be lit. The road could not be left free for the foot soldiers, but was crowded with ammunition wagons, combat wagons, signal outfits and all the impedimenta of war. Time and again men had the narrowest escapes from being run down in the dark, and scarcely anybody escaped the misfortune of tripping and falling full length in the mud. It is a miracle of fate or of organization that the units were able to find their positions on such a night, but they all got where they belonged and found the lines neatly taped by Colonel Johnson's excellent body of engineers. The 1st Battalion was in the front line commanded by Lieutenant Colonel Donovan, who was not willing to let his newly conferred rank deprive him of the opportunity of leading his battalion in another fight. The 2nd battalion under Major Anderson was in the second line, and picked men from each of its companies were given the task of following close behind the 1st, as moppers up, i. e., to overcome points of resistance which might be passed over, take charge of prisoners, etc.

The men shivered through the night in the muddy trenches waiting in patient misery for morning and the orders to attack. At 1:00 A. M. September 12th, our artillery opened fire on the enemy. We had expected a night of terrific noise like that which preceded the German offensive on July 15th, but the present one was not nearly so fierce, though it would have seemed a wonderful show if we had not heard the other one. In July the guns on both sides were shooting everything they had without cessation. But, here, there was no enemy counter preparation fire and our own fire was more deliberate.

Dawn broke on a cold, windy day and a cloud darkened sky. Donovan had been moving up and down his line with a happy smile on his face (unless he detected anything out of order) telling the men: "There's nothing to it. It will be a regular walk-over. It will not be as bad as some of the cross-country runs I gave you in your training period." And when H hour arrived at 5:00 A. M., the feeling of the men was one of gladness at the prospect of getting into action.

Their way was prepared by a screen of smoke and a rolling barrage delivered by our artillery. Tanks advanced with our infantry crawling like iron-clad hippopotomi over the wire in front to make a passage-way. Some of them came to grief on account of the rain-softened ground, the edges of a trench giving way under the weight of a tank and standing it on its nose in the bottom. During the two days of advance we were well supplied with aeroplane service and possessed undoubted superiority in the air.

The four-inch Stokes Mortars had been put in position to lay down a smoke barrage and the barrage began to pound the enemy front line at the zero hour. The shells whistled overhead much closer than they had done during the artillery preparation and broke on the enemy trenches kicking up red fire and black clouds where they hit. It was raining slightly, there was a mist, and dawn was not yet breaking when the machine gun barrage which took the men over began to fire. The men began to whisper among themselves "That's our stuff; no it's not, yes it is." All the sounds of battle were heard; the artillery, the small guns, and then, a little too soon, the Stokes Mortars in front of the Alabamas starting their fire-works which illuminated the entire front when the thermite shells exploded.

Then everybody jumped and started forward. The Bois de Remières lay in front of the right flank of our first battalion and as they moved forward, the flank units gave way to the left to pass around instead of through the woods. For a moment they lost direction. The support companies seemed to hesitate at the first belt of wire and began picking their way rather too fastidiously through it. Lieutenant Harold L. Allen was with the headquarters group which consisted of a mélange of runners, pioneers, liaison men, snipers, etc. He tells about Donovan running back from the front line shouting to the men "Get forward, there, what the hell do you think this is, a wake?" These words seemed to inspire Captain Siebert and as the lines moved forward he shouted loud and profane encouragement to the machine gun carriers burdened with boxes of ammunition and struggling forward through the tangle of trenches and broken wire.

Machine gun resistance was met on the enemy's second line. The assault waves deployed and began firing. Automatic teams and snipers crawled forward to advantageous positions. Donovan, with his usual disregard of danger (never thinking of it in fact, but only occupied with getting through), moved back and forth along the line giving directions, and the enemy resistance did not last long, most of their men surrendering. Donovan led his men at heartbreaking speed over the hills, smashing all resistance before them and sending in small groups of prisoners. St. Baussant was taken at the point of the bayonet and the line swept on. On the hill overlooking Maizerais the battalion was halted once more by machine gun fire, and a battery of artillery behind the village less than five hundred yards away. The Germans had evidently decided to make some sort of a stand, taking advantage of the hill and the protection of the Rupt de Mad. But Donovan with about thirty men jumped into the river, made his way across it under fire, and when the Germans saw this determined assault from their flank they threw up their hands and cried "Kamerad."

They attempted further resistance near Essey where they had machine gun pits in front of the village, but the resistance was quickly reduced by the aid of a tank and the village was cleared of the enemy. Donovan kept the battalion in the stone walled gardens on the outskirts of the town. Our own barrage was still pounding the village, for Essey represented the objective of the "First Phase, First Day," and some of our men who wandered into town were hit by flying stone from the walls of houses.

Prisoners began to come in and a prisoner park was established near a big tree on the road leading into the village.

French civilians were still living in this village, having spent the period of bombardment in a big dugout—the first civilians that we had the pleasure of actually liberating. They laughed and wept and kissed everybody in sight and drew on their slender stock of provisions to feed the hungry men. The soldiers began wandering everywhere looking for souvenirs. Corporal Kearin was in charge of the prison park. All the captives were from the regiments of the 10th Division, except a few from an attached Minenwerfer company and an artillery regiment. They were eager for fraternization and chatted and laughed with their captors. The men of the support battalions and from the units on our right and left, attracted by the town, began to straggle over. It resembled a County Fair, the prisoner park being the popular attraction of the day. Americans literally swarmed around the prisoners in idle curiosity while others rummaged through the German billets and headquarters looking for pistols, maps, German post-cards and letters—anything that would do for a souvenir.

However, this did not last long, Donovan had his battalion out and going for the objective which was marked as "Second Phase, First Day," which lay beyond the next town of Pannes; and Anderson, coming in with the bulk of the 2nd Battalion, imposed his rigorous discipline on those whose business it was to be in town. He certainly was not loved for knocking in the head of a barrel of beer which some of the fellows had found (and, by the way, there can be no better proof of the rapidity with which the Germans evacuated the town than the fact that they had left it behind).

Donovan met with further resistance when he arrived before Pannes about one o'clock in the afternoon. He called for artillery and tanks and filtered up his men along the trees on the edge of the road while the Ohios advanced on the left and the Alabamas make a flanking movement against the town from its right. They soon had the opposition broken and by 1:45 P. M. our advanced elements,

AT QUENTIN ROOSEVELT'S GRAVE
THE CENTRAL FIGURE IS COLONEL M'COY

widely extended, were proceeding from Pannes towards
the Bois de Thiaucourt, and at 1:55 the objective "Second
Phase, First Day" was occupied by the 165th Infantry.

The whole day it had been a wild gallop with occasional
breathing spells when the Germans put up some resistance.
From the rising ground around Essey men looked back,
and towards the west and east where the 1st and the 89th
were also moving forward. It was like a moving picture
battle. Tanks were crawling up along the muddy roads and
khaki colored figures could be seen moving about in ones
and twos and fours along the edges of the woods and across
the grassy plains. Toward the rear were passing ever
larger groups of prisoners in their blue gray uniforms,
carrying their personal belongings and in many cases their
own wounded as well as ours on improvised litters. Overhead the shells were still screaming from our heavy artillery with a good deal of answering fire from the German
batteries, which caused most of our losses.

The prisoners were mainly Austrians and Austrian Slavs.
They had not been very keen about the war at any time
and were made less so on finding that they had been left
behind after the bulk of the army had withdrawn. Many
of them had been in the United States, and the first question that one of them asked was "Can I go back now to
Sharon, Pa?" One of them was found seated in a dugout
with a bottle of Schnapps and a glass. He immediately
offered a drink to his captor saying "I don't drink it myself,
but I thought it would be a good thing to offer to an American who would find me."

During the afternoon of the 12th the brigade P. C. was
moved to Essey, regimental P. C. to Pannes. The 1st battalion organized their position just south of the Bois de
Thiaucourt which was held by patrols who took more prisoners; the 2nd battalion about 1,000 yards further back on
the reverse slope of a hill; and the 3rd battalion just outside
the town.

The next day's task was still easier. Donovan's men

jumped off at 6:10 A. M. with Companies B and C in the lead and A and D in support. Their patrols to the front at the time reported no contact with the enemy. Major Reilley with the 3rd Battalion was sent as Division Reserve for the 1st Division but was later ordered back. The 1st Battalion, followed by the 2nd, pushed through the Bois de Thiaucourt and the Bois de Beney capturing a couple of prisoners and meeting with no resistance. At the Sebastopol Farm a woman told them that the Germans were just ahead and retreating. The advance of our men was somewhat delayed by a gun in our supporting artillery which kept firing short and endangering the men, as one of the greatest difficulties in a rapid advance such as was made at St. Mihiel is that of maintaining liaison with the rear. By half past nine they had captured the enemy's supply depot along the railway track, with the neighboring village of St. Benoit and the Chateau St. Benoit. It was a foot race all the way between the four infantry regiments and our fellows claim they won it by a good half hour, but I haven't heard yet what the others have to say. I only know that if I ever have to follow up our infantry again in such an attack I am going to wait for an express train.

One thing that stands out most impressively in the memories of the 165th regarding this action is the devotion and courage of one of our former commanding officers. The dugout where Lieutenant Colonel Donovan established his temporary headquartres on the night of September 11-12th, was very small and very crowded. Every officer commanding a unit of the auxiliary arms crowded into it to avoid the nasty drizzle and darkness outside. The room was full of smoke, some of which managed to get outside as officer after officer came in to report the position of his unit. It was like the headquarters of an army corps. Parker of the one-pound cannons was perched on the upper deck of a bunk flanked by Siebert of the machine guns and a French Lieutenant who had come in to report that the accompanying tanks were ready. Lieutenants Allen and Betty were *trying to carry out Donovan's numerous orders.* Captain Stone of the 149th Field Artillery pushed his way into the crowded room and reported to Donovan that his battery had been detailed to roll forward with the assaulting infantry. There was some conversation between them as to the conditions of the roads near Seicheprey and the possibility of having the battery follow close behind the assault, the number of available rounds of ammunition with the guns and the chance of delay in getting them forward over No Man's Land. The conversation continued for a few minutes and was ended by Donovan saying, "Well, we have not done it before but we'll give it a whirl this time."

Just then Major Lawrence opened the door and called "Colonel, here's an old friend of yours." It was Colonel Hine. Wet and muddy and tired but evidently delighted to be back with the old regiment. Donovan gave him an enthusiastic welcome as did all the rest, although Betty whispered to Allen in a humorous grouch "I'll bet Donovan will want us to get a room and bath for him"—referring to the Colonel's practice of inviting everyone in to dinner or to share quarters no matter where he was or what he might have, and then putting it up to the staff to provide. Everybody naturally thought that Colonel Hine had come to view the battle from the regimental observation post on the hill near the Bois de Jury but later in the night when they moved down to the parallel of departure Colonel Hine was still along, sharing the experiences of the rest of them, stumbling into shell holes and tripping over barbed wire in the darkness. When they went over in the morning he was still there, and with the first wave; and all through that day's fight and the next, he fought along by the side of his old men, who conceived an admiration for him in their loyal souls that nothing will ever efface.

Colonel Hine had obtained leave from his duties in order to satisfy his desire of going through a big battle with his beloved 69th. It was a unique compliment to the regiment itself. The regiment appreciates it as such, but it dwells more on the soldierly ardor and high courage of its first Colonel, who, though he had been transferred to less dangerous duties, found his way back to us and fought as a volunteer private in the regiment he had commanded. Such deeds as this are set forth in the story-books of history as an inspiration to the youth of the land.

In picking up stories of the fight I got one from Lieutenant Allen which I have jotted down as he gave it to me. "We came in front of Essey. Here there was a hill marked on the aeroplane photographs and maps which were issued before the attack as 'Dangerous, go to the right and left.' As we came over the top of this hill and advanced on its forward slope the battalion drew machine gun fire from the enemy guns disposed in pits in front of the village. I was out in front in a shell-hole with two snipers. One of them I sent back to Donovan with a message; the other began firing on the enemy who now began to run back into the village. In an adjoining shell-hole a few feet away, a soldier from our battalion sold a German Luger Pistol to an officer from some other regiment who had wandered from his sector, for thirty-five francs. A French tank caught up to us at this stage of the fight and moved down the hill until it was in front of the shell-hole where I was. I rapped on the side of his turret and called to the pilot, who reversed the turret and while the bullets slapped the side of his tank, opened the window. He was a dapper little Frenchman with the ends of his moustache waxed in points, and was clean and smiling. I gave him a target in front of the town and he fired several round at a mass of retreating Boches hurrying over the next hill. Opening the window again, he smiled and said 'How's that?' then he went lumbering on."

As the first battalion was making its advance during the second day it was held up in front of Sebastopol Farm by our own barrage which had not yet lifted. While waiting there they saw a French peasant woman with a small boy grasping her hand running through the shell fire from

the direction of the farm. When questioned, she was in a
great rage against the Boches and reported that a battalion
of their troops had evacuated St. Benoit during the night.
She also gave the welcome information that there were
supplies of food in the farm and was very grateful to the
Americans for releasing her from four years of captivity.
She was the only woman that we saw actually on the battlefield during the war.

    When our fellows reached St. Benoit they found that
the Germans had started a fire in the Chateau, but it was
quickly extinguished. The church too, had been set on fire
and was beyond saving. When Jim Barry of C. Company
saw it blazing he shouted "Glory be to God, those devils
have burnt the church. Let's see what we can save out of
it." With Tierney and Boyle and others following after
he ran into the burning building and carried out statues
and candelabra which they deposited carefully outside.
Having finished their pious work they began to remember
that they were hungry. Barry took from his musette bag
some German potatoes which he had stored there in place
of grenades that had been used up in action, and said, "Well
we have done what we could, and now we've got a good fire
here, and we might as well use it." They stuck the potatoes
on the ends of their bayonets and roasted them in the em-
bers. Just then another party came along with some bottled
beer that they had salvaged from the German supplies in
Pannes, so they picnicked merrily in the square in front of
the blazing temple.

    It was well for all of us that the Germans had departed
so suddenly that they left supplies behind, because it was
an almost impossible task to get the kitchens and ration
wagons through, on account not only of the poor condition
of the roads but of the congestion of traffic. We never saw
a worse jam in the whole war than on the main road from
Seicheprey to Pannes—tanks, guns and caissons, ammunition wagons, trucks, infantry trains, all trying to get forward along one narrow road, and the whole line held up if

a single vehicle got stuck; mounted men and foot soldiers trailed along the edge of this procession often having to flounder through the swamps of the Rupt de Mad.

The situation became dangerous towards evening of the second day when a large squadron of enemy battle planes swooped down on our own, and after the fiercest contest I have ever seen in the air drove two of ours to earth and regained the mastery. They did not, however, resort to bombing, satisfying themselves with reporting conditions to their own artillery. Our wagon train had a most uncomfortable half hour as it passed along the road between Beney and St. Benoit. Shell after shell came hissing towards them, but luckily the German guns were firing just a trifle short. If the shells had carried another fifty yards the train would have been wiped out; but the drivers sat steady on their boxes and kept the mules going at even pace until they reached their destination.

Pannes had still a number of civilians, about thirty in all, and all of them very old people or children, the able-bodied ones having been carried off by the enemy. Those remaining received their deliverers with open arms, and all the old ladies insisted on kissing Lieutenant Rerat, very handsome and blushing in his neat uniform of *horizon-bleu*. They had been rationed by the Germans during the four years of occupation; none too well, but with enough to keep them fit to work. They gave us all they had, and we had an opportunity to get an idea of what German soldiers got to eat. The bread was an indigestible looking mass on the order of pumpernickel. The coffee was far from being Mocha, but sugar seemed to be more plentiful than in France. The Fall vegetables were not yet ripe but the fields had been sown with potatoes, turnips, kohlrabi, and acres and acres of cabbage. The French authorities gave orders to have all civilians evacuated to the rear whether they wanted it or not; and Lieutenant Rerat and I assembled them with their pitiful little collection of belongings and sent them back in ambulances.

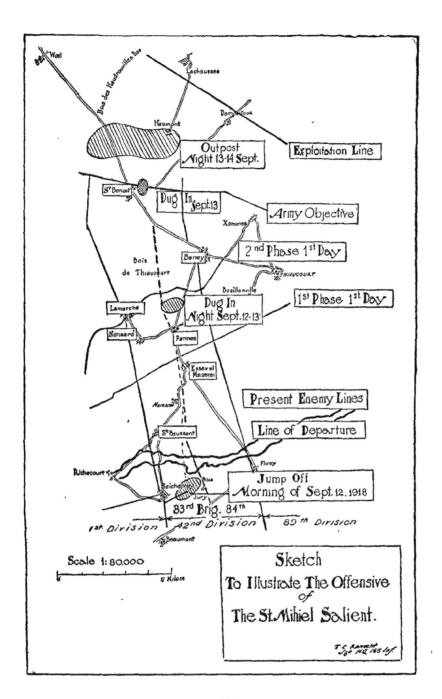

Sketch
To Illustrate The Offensive
of
The St. Mihiel Salient.

245

It was a great place for souvenir hunting—pistols, spurs, German post-cards, musical instruments—all sorts of loot. I saw Bill Schmidt with a long steel Uhlan's lance; while Tom Donohue, true to his instincts, came by with no less than four violins. Most of the men, of a more normal type of soldier, passed up the musical instruments in search for German sausages and beer. There were also vast amounts of military stores and ammunition, as well as the field pieces and machine guns which had been captured in the battle.

Major Lawrence thinks that five or six of his men deserve a citation, for going out voluntarily under the leadership of Sergeant Eichorn and James Mason to rescue a wounded officer in another regiment. The Sanitary Detachment is very happy because they not only have the Major back but also three popular sergeants—Grady, Hayes and Maher who for a time have been attached to the Ohios.

Lieutenant Clifford is enthusiastic about the courage of Sergeant Gilgar of Company B who went ahead with five men against an enemy position, manœuvred his party into a position where he threatened the German rear, and then, by putting on a bold front as if he had a whole company behind him, frightened them into surrender and returned to our line with thirty-two prisoners. Sergeant John Mohr's life was saved by the quickness of John Moran who was just in time in killing a German who was trying to get our veteran Sergeant.

Chaplain Holmes, who had walked into fight his very first day at the front, was anxious to do his full share, and volunteered while we were at Pannes to scour the battlefield in order to bury the dead. Lieutenant Flynn and a detachment from Headquarters Company went with him and carried out this mournful task. At the time we had no way of knowing for certain just how many of ours had fallen on the field. The battlefield was in our hands from the first and anyone who had a spark of life in him was carried quickly to the rear. Later estimates placed the number of our dead, up to the present, as about thirty-five. The highest in rank was Thomas J. Curtin, 1st Sergeant of Company D, who was hit by a rifle bullet advancing at the head of a platoon. In Company A we lost another good Sergeant, William Walsh; and in the same company Corporals Patrick Doolan, Patrick McDermott and John McDonald with Privates Joseph Biskey and William Williams; in Company B, Mechanic Henry Schumacher and Private N. W. Blackman, Douglas Cummings, Humberto Florio, William Poole and Dominic Zollo; in Company C, Privates John Nanarto, Felix Curtis, Manfred Emanuelson, Thomas F. Petty and Augustus Altheide; in Company D, Corporal Philip Greeler, Privates Ferdinand Urban, Ernest E. Martin, Horace Musumeck, William Mitchell, Walter Long, Clarence Gabbert, with Corporal James MacDonald and Daniel Harkins (died of wounds); Company E lost Corporals Michael Rooney and William Bechtold; Company F, James Wynne, Rex Strait, Eugene Rogers, Angelo Kanevas and Jesse Scott; Company G, William Perkins; Company H, James Spiker and Joseph Deese; Company K, Privates Joseph Dearmon, G. C. Kenly and W. H. Leach, Company M; O. O. Dykes and Edward Kiethley, while the Machine Gun Company suffered the loss of John F. MacMillan, Edward Hantschke and Charles Brown. Lieutenant Boag was wounded.

The Chateau St. Benoit is a fine roomy building—a perfect palace of dreams after the outlandish places that had constituted our abodes. But every body in it has an uneasy feeling that it makes a splendid target for enemy artillery. Charles Carman said to me: "Any gunner that couldn't hit this building at night with his eyes shut ought to be sent back to whatever the Heinies call their S. O. S." They have missed it however, and more than a few times; but perhaps that is because they have still hopes of occupying it. Three big 150's came over last night and just missed knocking off the corner of the building where General MacArthur was sleeping. They landed in the stable and killed some of our horses.

We are in for a considerable amount of shelling periodically. A high trajectory shell, like our American rattle-snake, has at least the rudimentary instincts of a gentlemen. It gives fair warning before it strikes, and a man can make an attempt to dodge it; but the Austrian 88's are mean all the way through. It sounds Irish to say that you hear it coming after it explodes, but that is literally true if it falls short of you.

The whole sector has been pinched off by the operation and we are now in touch with the French on our left, the 1st Division being crowded out by the operation, and the 89th Division still occupying the postions to our right. We are faced now in the general direction of Metz, and the Germans occupy the Hindenburg line as their line of defense. Our main business has been to organize our newly acquired positions and to throw out frequent patrols to test out the enemy.

Colonel Donovan established his battalion headquarters in the Forester's House on the road to Haumont which was the nearest village held by the enemy. Here Sergeant Moore of B Company brought him a German prisoner whom he had just captured. On interrogation he said that he was a sentinel of a machine gun cossack post and that in the post there was an officer and eight men including one non-com. All of these he thought would be willing to surrender except the officer and perhaps the N. C. O. Colonel Donovan suggested that a rope be tied to the prisoner and that he be compelled to guide a patrol to the outpost, but the German protested that it was entirely unnecessary, as he was willing to betray his comrades. A patrol was sent out which captured the outpost and killed the officer, who, as predicted, put up the only resistance encountered. Our patrol was delighted at making the capture, but if a chance shot had ended the career of the man who had betrayed his own officer, no one amongst ours would have shed any tears.

Patrols from the 1st and 2nd battalions were sent out frequently both by day and by night until September 17th. Some prisoners were captured, and we had our own losses.

In the first battalion a patrol of Company F came back without Bernard Cafferty and Lawrence Whalen who put for shelter with the rest, under withering German fire, and are probably killed.

I have picked up a couple of stories which relieve a little this sombre side of war. Lieutenant Ogle took out a patrol one dark night and found in his party one soldier without a rifle, for which he rebuked him in a savage whisper. Later on he discovered that it was Father Carpentier who had accompanied the patrol—he says to render spiritual first aid if anyone was wounded. "Yes," I said, "that's what the priest told the bishop: that he went to the horse races so as to be handy if one of the jockeys were thrown."

Allen likes to tell stories on Donovan, for whom he has great admiration. One afternoon he came in from patrol very hungry after being away since early morning, and he dropped into Captain Buck's shack near Hassavant Farm, which was also occupied by Colonel Donovan. "Captain Buck's orderly promised me a roast beef sandwich and left the room to prepare it. I repeat I was very hungry and was anticipating with great pleasure the coming roast beef sandwich. In a few minutes the orderly returned with the food. It was a large sandwich with a luscious rare slice of roast beef protruding from the slices of bread, and with it the orderly brought a cup of coffee which he placed with the sandwich on the table. Precisely at this moment a soldier entered with two prisoners; one a small Roumanian about sixteen years of age, and the other a tall, gaunt, dirty looking soldier, both members of a labor battalion. They had been lost in the retreat and had wandered several days in the woods, until encountering one of our patrols they had surrendered. Donovan grabs the sandwich with one hand and the cup of coffee with the other. The small boy got the sandwich and the old man the cup of coffee. I immediately protested 'Colonel,' I said, 'it is against regulations to feed prisoners before they have been questioned at Divison. You should not feed these men.' 'Allen,' he said, 'you ought to be ashamed of yourself. This poor little boy has been wandering around in the woods for two days with nothing to eat.' 'Besides,' I said, 'that was my sandwich.' 'And you,' he continued, 'a great big healthy man, would take his meal away from him.' "

LA MARCHE

September 26th

On September 17th our regiment was relieved by the Alabamas and the men were encamped altogether in the town of La Marche, which consists of one large *ferme* with a few extra stone buildings and a number of wooden shacks which were constructed by the Germans. In the big farm house we are a happy party. Colonel Mitchell likes to have his officers around him and they share his feelings to the full. We have plenty of provisions, a good many of them German, and Staff and Field Officers are messing together. At table are Colonel Mitchell, Lieutenant Colonel Donovan, Majors Reilley, Anderson, Kelly and Lawrence, Captain Meaney, Adjutant, Captain Merle-Smith, Operations Officer, Lieutenant Rerat, Lieutenant Spencer and myself. If my fancy leads me to the open air I can walk down the road to Pannes where Captain Mangan with Kinney and Frank Smith are working away with their doughty mule-skinners, unless perchance the German shells chase them underground; or across the open field to the woods where our men are leading a lazy though muddy existence.

Various incidents, amusing or tragical as is the way of war, broke the comparative monotony of these ten days. There was a captive observation balloon just outside the village which evidently must have had a good view of the enemy because they were most anxious to get it down. No aeroplane succeeded in setting fire to it, so the Germans got after it with long range guns. One afternoon the fire got so hot that the chauffeur of the truck to which it was attached started down the road to get out of range with the big sausage still floating in the air at the end of its cable, the Germans increasing their range as their target moved. Sergeant Daly, the mess sergeant of the Machine Gun Company, was peacefully crossing the field on a lazy going mule unaware of what it was all about, when a German shell aimed at the aeroplane down the road passed with the speed and noise of a freight train about twenty feet above his head. The mule gave one leap forward, and Daly was not trying to stop him; and two thousand soldiers who had been watching the flight of the balloon burst into a tremendous laugh.

On the night of September 23rd, a large calibre German shell made a direct hit right into a shelter pit in the woods where five of the best men in our machine gun company were lying asleep; Sergeant Frank Gardella, who had won the D. S. C., Sergeant Harry P. Bruhn and Sergeant J. F. Flint, with Privates H. McCallum and William Drake, who was one of three brothers in the company. All five were blown out of the hole by the concussion as high as the lower branches of the trees. Sergeant Flint landed, bruised and stunned, but untouched by the fragments. He gathered himself together and found Gardella killed instantly and the other three terribly wounded. He bound them up, calling for help, which was brought by Lieutenant De Lacour, and the three wounded men were gotten back to the hospital by Major Lawrence and Captain Dudley, but we had little hopes for them, and have since heard that they died of their wounds.

Jim Cassidy, Frankie Maguire and Jimmy Kelly found some German flour which they brought into the Headquarters Kitchen. They are a guileless looking trio and I cannot say to this day how deep a part they played in this affair. They gave the flour to Joe De Nair. Now Joseph Patrick De Nair has knocked around this world for more years than he will acknowledge to anybody—long enough at any rate, to have learned how to turn his hand to anything; and he announced his intention of making pancakes for all hands, especially me. Everybody was set to work under Joe's direction. Fred Miller and Anderson salvaged some molasses. Al Ettinger was hustled off on his motorcycle to Pannes to use my name with Lieutenant Scheffler for some oleo, of which we were short. Pat Sharkey rustled wood; Frank Clason built a fire and John Brickley flattened and polished a tin for Joe's cooking. Bill Hanley and Humphrey were appointed assistant chefs. There was a group around me consisting of Proctor, Holt, Katz and Proudfoot, and Joe came over: "All you ginks have got to work. There are no guests around here except Father Duffy." I told him they had been reading an article in the "Daily Mail" on the Irish question and were asking me about it. That saved them, for Ireland counted more with Joe than even the success of his pancakes.

The bustling preliminaries were finally completed and Joe proceeded to make his batter. He poured it on the tin and waited, turning-spoon in hand until, like St. Lawrence, it should be done on one side. Then with the air of an artist, he turned his first pancake with a flourish. It landed on the pan with a bang like a shell striking an elephant hut. "What the ——," muttered Joe, as he picked up the results of his labor. "Well I'll be ——!" "What's the matter Joe?" I asked, conscious that something was going wrong and that my presence deprived him of the normal outlet for his feelings. "What's the matter. Where's those dummed kids?" "Well, what *is* the matter?" "What's the matter. What's the matter? The stuff they gave me for flour is plaster of Paris. That's what's the matter. Where the —— Oh for Heaven's sake, Father, go inside until I can let myself spill."

BOIS DE MONTFAUCON

October 10th.

On September 27th, we relieved the 84th Brigade in the line, taking over the positions of the Iowas in sub-sector

Marimbois, Major Anderson's battalion being in the forward position. It was the usual business of patrolling until September 30th, when our Division was relieved in the Sector by the 89th, and withdrew to the Bois de la Belle Ozière, a little south of where we were before. Next morning, October 1st, we marched about 10 kilometers to *our embussing point*, where we found a tremendously large fleet of camions driven by the little Chinks whom our fellows now call the undertakers, because they associate them with deaths and burials.

Here I met an old friend, George Boothby of the New York *World,* who had finally succeeded in getting over to the war by entering the publicity department of the Y. M. C. A. The uniform with the red triangle somehow caused a smile when seen on George, but he was the first to grin.

We got started at four o'clock in the afternoon and spent the whole of a freezing night on the journey, most of it lying along the Voie Sacrée or Sacred Way, over which the supplies and reinforcements had been sent which saved Verdun. Our destination was Mondrecourt where we remained until October 4th, when we marched by daylight to Jubécourt. On October 5th we moved north again, an interminable march, with all the infantry in the Division going up on one mean road, to the woods of Montfaucon.

I had it easy myself because Colonel Mitchell with his usual fine way of doing a courtesy, asked me as a favor to get the automobile and some personal baggage through, as he was going mounted. So Brown and Dayton and myself got there by better roads ahead of the rest and found ourselves at the headquarters of the 32nd Division, where Colonel Callan and Father Dunnigan gave me a hospitable welcome. When I heard "32nd Division," my first thought was "Now I can see McCoy again," as he had been made General of the 63rd Brigade, but it was two days before I descried his familiar figure crowned with the French *casque,* a parting gift from the Comte de Chambrun when he left Chaumont. It was a memorable meeting, but all too short, for he had his brigade in line to look after.

The woods of Montfaucon, which lie in the area of the great battles for Verdun, fills exactly a civilian's idea of what No Man's Land should look like. In its day it was a fine forest of thick-girthed trees, but they had been battered by long cannonading until not one of them was as nature had fashioned it. Big branches had been torn off and heavy trees knocked to the ground. The shell-holes lay close together like pock marks on a badly pitted face. It was almost impossible to find a level spot to pitch a small pup tent. Owing to recent rains and the long occupation of the woods by troops, both our own and the enemy's, the place was in a bad state of sanitation. The roads, too, were bad and difficult for all kinds of traffic, particularly motor traffic. There were very few dugouts, all of them small and most of them dirty and wet. Division headquarters established itself in trucks as being better than any existing accommodations. General Lenihan kindly took me in and gave me a share in the dugout occupied by himself and Lieutenant Grose. Together we made a happy week of it in spite of bad conditions.

While here we received word that the Germans had asked for an armistice. The older and wiser heads amongst us felt quite certain that they would not get what they had asked for until they were reduced to a more humble spirit; but we were worried about the effect it might have on the morale of the troops, because it would be particularly hard for soldiers to face another big battle if they had made up their minds that the fighting was over. So Colonels Mitchell and Donovan asked me to go amongst the men, sound them out, and set them right if necessary. It was an easy commission. One of the first men I spoke to was Vincent Mulholland, one of my parish recruits and now 1st Sergeant of Company B. In answer to my first question he replied "Of course I would like to see the war over, but not while the old regiment is back here in army corps reserve. I want to see this war end with the 69th right out in the front line, going strong." Not everybody was as emphatic as that, but I was able to make a very assured report that the old timers at least would go into a battle with the same spirit they had at Champagne or the Ourcq or St. Mihiel.

Jack Mangan has left us to take charge of the organization of the Headquarters Battalion of the new Second Army at Toul. Colonel Haskell, who is assistant Chief of Staff in the 2nd Army, visited us during our journey from Baccarat to Chalons and got a great reception from the old-timers. Even then, he had his eye on Mangan and wanted him to come with him. There is nothing that so much impresses me as a proof of the absolute sense of duty and loyalty of our old officers to this regiment as the attitude which they invariably take concerning invitations to improve their rank and fortunes by going elsewhere. The younger officers have no choice in the matter. We have been sending home as instructors a few of them each month, and have lost a large number of very efficient lieutenants. But those who are free to exercise any choice invariably view the opportunity as a question of conscience and put the matter up to me. Major McKenna (then Captain) did this in the Lunéville area when he had a chance for the office of Judge Advocate. In the same spirit Mangan said he would not quit to join Haskell unless I decided that the Regiment could spare him. My decision was that he could not go until Kinney was made a Captain, as I knew that the latter could fill admirably the extremely important post of R. S. O.

The hardest battle of all has been to keep Donovan with the Regiment, but he has made that fight himself, as there is no place else in the world that would tempt him for a minute. He has dodged orders to send him to Staff College (which would inevitably mean a transfer after he was finished), orders to go on special duties, invitations or suggestions to receive promotion by transfer. General Meno-

her and Colonel MacArthur have been always alert to take
up the battle to retain him with us. He and I tramped the
muddy road tonight while he disburdened himself of a new
worry. The Provost Marshal General wants an assistant
who is at once a good lawyer and a keen soldier, with a
knowledge of French, and he has demanded that Donovan
be sent to him. Colonel Hughes, our new Chief of Staff,
has done his best to block it; but he has been informed by
General Headquarters that the authorities of the 42nd Division have managed to evade the wishes of military authority
in Colonel Donovan's case six times already and that this
order is peremptory. All that General Menoher has been
able to do is to hold him until the next battle is over.
Donovan is disgusted and sore for the first time in my
knowledge of him.

Every now and then there is some desultory shelling in
the woods, but the only sight of warfare that we get is in
the sky. Our balloons must be well placed, because the
German flyers have been very persistent in their attempts to
bring them down, and their efforts are too often successful.
Today, we saw a German aviator perform a feat which was
one of the most daring things that any of us has seen during
the war. The rapid and sustained discharge of anti-aircraft
guns (which have their own unmistakable note) brought
everybody to the edge of the woods. Guided by puffs of
white or black smoke which dotted the sky above us, we
were able to detect a single German plane headed unswerv-
ingly towards us, and not flying very high either. Our own
planes were swooping towards him, but he came right on,
without any change of altitude or direction. He passed
over our line of balloons, and then turned abruptly and
dived towards the one nearest us, throwing his dart and
passing on. The flames did not show at once, and evidently
noticing this, he checked his flight and started back to finish
the job. Just then the flames burst up, and he wheeled in
air to make his escape. Soldiers in combat divisions are
the best sports in the world. There must have been twenty

thousand of them watching this daring exploit of an enemy, and I feel certain there was not a man amongst them who did not murmur "I hope to God the beggar gets away." There were a dozen of our planes after him by this time and before he reached his own lines they forced him to earth, landing in safety.

As I make my rounds amongst the men scattered through the woods, I find many whose names I do not know. In the original regiment I knew practically everyone by his name; but through a variety of causes half of those men are no longer with us and their places have been taken by others, with whom, on account of our constant motion, it has been impossible to get acquainted.

The wearing down of a regiment, even outside of battle, is constant. Brigade and Division Headquarters select those that they want for their own work, bright sergeants are sent off to Army Candidate's School to be trained for officers, and are invariably sent to other divisions. There is a constant trickle of sick men to hospitals, from which many never return to us; and most of all, there are the tremendous losses that a regiment, particularly an infantry regiment, has to pay in battle. Our total losses in action of killed, wounded and missing up to the present are about 2,600 men. Taking all causes into consideration nearly 3,000 of our original men have been dropped, at least temporarily, from our rolls since we came to France. If none of them had returned there would be now only 600 of them left, but as a matter of fact, nearly all of our wounded who have graduated into the "Fit for Service" class have insisted on their right to come back. So about half of our present total of 2,983 men are of the original outfit. It is easy to pick them out by glancing down a company roster, because our serial numbers are all under 100,000 while the new men have numbers running into the millions.

I do not find that the spirit of the regiment as a whole has changed on account of these fresh accessions. A regiment is largely what its officers and non-coms. make it. Practically all of our present officers have been through all the fights with us and have gained their present ranks in battle, and the non-coms are naturally men of the original regiment who have earned their stripes by good soldiering in camp and in the field. These men are the custodians of regimental pride and regimental tradition, and their spirit is communicated to or imposed upon the new-comers.

Most of these newcomers moreover, have proved themselves excellent material. The first few that were sent us in Lunéville were poor foreigners from the coal mining districts who could scarcely speak English, but in Baccarat we got three hundred men from Camp Devens who were a fine lot of fellows, and, now that they have gone through the big fights with us, are not to be distinguished in any way from the original volunteers. We received a lot of first class men also from the Kentucky-Tennessee and the Texas-Oklahoma National Guard organizations, among the latter being a number of Indians. All of these replacements who have gone through battles with us are now absolutely part and parcel of the 165th Infantry and have created bonds of battle friendship with our Irish and New York lads which are closer than any family tie can be.

In any extended campaign it is a very rare soldier who does not get the experience of being in a hospital at least once; although we could not possibly spend as much time in them as rumors that they get at home make our people think we do. I myself have been killed or wounded at least a dozen times. The other day Lester Sullivan, who comes from my parish, looked up from a letter he was reading and said to me "Father Duffy if you had ten thousand dollars insurance for every time you were killed you'd never need to work for the rest of your life."

After battles of course they are being sent back by hundreds and thousands. Jim Healey was telling me a yarn which hits off a type of humor that is characteristic of the American. A hospital train pulled into a French station with its doors and windows and platforms crowded with "walking cases" and stopped on a track alongside a similar train with the same kind of a crowd looking out. "Where are youse guys from?" shouted one of the soldiers. "Fohty-second Division. Whey you all from?" "De rest of de Forty-second Division" came the reply—everybody shouting with laughter at this bit of delicate and tender humor.

Hospitals thus become, like London coffee houses in the 18th century, the clearing houses of news and the creators of public opinion. They are the only place where soldiers meet men who do not belong to their own Division; in fact, soldiers seldom meet anybody outside their own regiment and many a man's friendships do not extend beyond his company. But in hospitals, and more particularly in convalescent and casual camps, where they are able to move around, they come into touch with the whole American Expeditionary Force. Battles are discussed, organizations criticized, reputations of officers made or unmade.

It is in these places also that the sentiment for one's own Division grows strong. Regiments may fight with each other within the Division, but as opposed to other Divisions they present a united front. The regulars and marines in the famous 2nd Division have their own little differences, but they do not show when they come up against men from the 1st, 26th, or 42nd. Our own New Yorks and Alabamas started off with a small family row at Camp Mills which has been utterly forgotten, partly because they have always been fighting side by side on every battle front and have grown to admire each other, but even more, I suspect, because they have formed ties of blood brotherhood back in convalescent camps by getting together to wallop the marines.

Every soldier in a combat division thinks that his own division is doing all the work and getting none of the credit. But then I never met a soldier yet who does not say "It's a funny thing that my platoon always happens to get the dirty details." This much is true—that there is a number of divisions which can be counted on the fingers of one's two hands that have been kept right up against the buzz-saw ever since last June. Of course we are not proper judges of the policies or exigencies of the high command, but everybody who is in touch with men knows that they would be better fitted for their work in the line if they could be taken out for a few weeks rest. The discomforts and anxieties of life at the front are cumulative, and men gradually get fretful and grouchy as well as run down physically. It is surprising to see how quickly they recuperate in a rest area. We ought to be taken out of these woods to some more civilized place where the men can go on leave or hang around billets, writing letters, reading, cleaning equipment and forgetting all about battle and bloodshed, and getting freshened up mentally and physically. As one fellow said to me "I'd like to get somewhere where I could hear a hen cackle and see a kid run across the road. I'd like to be where I could get a change from corn-willie by going off some evening with a few of the fellows and getting some old French lady to cook us up some oofs (*oeufs*) and *pommes frites,* with a bottle of red ink to wash it down."

We knew that there had been going on for three weeks now a battle for the possession of all this Argonne District, in which many American Divisions were taking part, and amongst them our sturdy fellow citizens from New York, the 77th Division, who had succeeded us at Baccarat and in the Château Thierry Sector. We expected that we would be called upon to relieve the 32nd Division which was fighting just in front of us. But today, October 10th, came orders to proceed to the west along the river Aire for the relief of the 1st Division.

CHAPTER IX

THE ARGONNE OFFENSIVE

In the general operation which was shared in by all the Allied armies in France to turn the German retreat into a rout, the most difficult and most important task was assigned to the Americans. The Belgians, British and French could only exercise a frontal pressure on the enemy except for a few local salients which might be created here and there. But if the American army could smash their resistance on the southeast end of the German lines, and particularly if it could break through so as to capture the military trunk line which ran through Sedan to their depot at Metz, large bodies of Germans farther to the west would be brought close to the point of surrender. Naturally, the German Commanders knew this as well as Marshal Foch or General Pershing and they massed their defenses at the point of greatest danger. To the civilian mind, when troops are advancing ten or fifteen kilometers a day and capturing prisoners and guns, they are heroes of tremendous battles. But soldiers know that in the tremendous battles an advance of two or three kilometers is a big gain, to be paid for at a great cost of human life. We had an example of the first kind at Saint Mihiel, which loomed large in the imagination of the folks at home, but which to the soldiers was a walkover. The Argonne was no walkover during the first five weeks.

The nature of the country made it easy to defend, hard to capture. It is a hilly country—and that always means plenty of woods. The hills, moreover, connect themselves up in a general east and west direction and the advance had to be made by conquering a series of heights. When we

261

went into the fight the line-up of Divisions nearest to us were the 77th, on the extreme left, going up through the forest, the 82nd on the other side of the Aire, the 1st, which we relieved, and on our right, the 32nd. Further east were other divisions extending up to the Meuse, while yet other bodies of Americans were working to cross that river and fight their way up its eastern bank.

In the sector on the east side of the Aire, which we now took over, the 35th Division had been first to go in. At great sacrifice it had captured successive villages and ridges, but had finally been repulsed on the last hill before reaching Exermont and had been forced to fall back. Then the old reliables of the 1st Division, who had been our first troops to arrive in France and the first to engage with the enemy at Cantigny, were called upon to do their share. They did it, and more than their share. They captured the ridges up to Exermont and Fleville and Sommerance, swept the Germans off the Cote de Maldah and there established their lines at the price of half the infantry in the Division.

Now it was our turn. If the others had a hard task, ours was certainly no easier, because it was given to us to break the final and long prepared line of German defenses, called the Kriemhilde Stellung.

We marched to our new positions on October 11th, our strength at the time being 53 officers and a little less than 3,000 men. Regimental headquarters were set up at Exermont, the Supply Company being down the road at Apremont. The first day the support and reserve battalions were in a wide gully to the east, called Chaudron Farm. The 3rd battalion effected the relief on the front line, Major Reilley commanding, Lieutenant Heller, Adjutant, Company I under Captain Michael J. Walsh, who had insisted on giving up the Headquarters Company and taking a line Company so that he could take part himself in the fighting; Company K under Lieutenant Guignon; Company L, Captain Given, Company M, Captain Rowley. In support was the 1st Battalion now commanded by Major Kelly, Lieutenant O'Connor, Adjutant, Lieutenant Connelly being Intelligence Officer. The commanders of A, B, C, and D, being Lieutenant W. Hutchinson, Lieutenant Clifford, Captain Bootz and Captain Buck. Second Battalion under Major Anderson, Lieutenant Fechheimer, Adjutant, with E, F, G and H under Captain Conners, Captain Marsh, Captain Stout and Lieutenant Ogle.

As the companies marched up to take their place in line I stood on a rising ground in the bleak and open plain to perform my own duties in their regard, which for many of them would be the last time. The frequently recurring rows of rude crosses which marked the last resting places of many brave lads of the 1st Division were an eloquent sermon on death; so that no words of warning from me were needed and I was able to do my holy business in a matter of fact way which soldiers like better than being preached at. General Lenihan is fond of quoting Private Terence Mulvaney's remark: "What I like about the old church is that she's so remarkable regimental in her fittin's."

In former days men massed together for battle; today they scatter. It is interesting to watch the deliberate disintegration of a Division as it approaches the front line. It breaks into brigades and into regiments for convenience in using the roads. Then the regiments are broken into battalions, usually, according to the stock phrase "echeloned in depth" that is, one on the line, one in support and one in reserve. The battalion breaks up into companies as it gets nearer the front; and the companies, when they reach the point where they are likely to be under shell-fire, separate into platoons with considerable distance between them. In action men advance with generous intervals between.

When they get close to the enemy the advance is made by frequent rushes, about a fourth of the men in a platoon running forward, taking advantage of the ground, while their comrades keep the enemy's heads down by their fire, until all of them can get close. In its last stages the warfare of these small groups is more like the Indian fighting in which the first General of our Republic learned the profession of arms, than anything which the imagination of civilians pictures it. To take machine gun nests—I am not speaking of regularly wired and entrenched positions which it is the business of artillery to reduce before the infantry essays them— it is often a matter of individual courage and strategy. Sometimes the fire of a platoon can reduce the number of the gunners or make the less hardy of them keep their heads down so that the pieces cannot be properly handled; but often the resistance is overcome by a single sharp-shooter firing from the elbow of a tree, or by some daring fellow who works his way across hollows which are barely deep enough to protect him from fire, or up a gully or watercourse, until he is near enough to throw hand grenades. Then it is all over.

Our supply company and band were stationed at the Ferme de l'Esperance on the Aire River. Going north along the river road as far as Fléville one finds a road going to the right through a deep defile which leads to the village of Exermont about a mile and a half away. On the north and on the south the view is bounded by steep hills which have been captured by the 1st Division. To the north a muddy trail winds around the base of hill 247 leading to a wide, rough, partly wooded plain. This was covered with the bodies of the brave soldiers of the 1st Division, more thickly than I have seen anywhere else with the exception of the hill where lay our 3rd Battalion north of the Ourcq. There were many German wooden shelters at the base of the hill to the right, with bodies of dead Germans, many of them killed in hand to hand conflict.

Our 3rd Battalion took over the front line on the Cote de Maldah, a maze of woods and ravines. Companies M and I were on the twin knolls of the Cote, K and L in the woods behind. To their left were the Ohios at Sommerance, while the Alabamas and Iowas held positions similar to our own on hills 263 and 269. Our 2nd Battalion was in a shrubby woods to the rear, and the 1st Battalion was originally held under protection of the hill just ouside of Exermont, in which town were the headquarters of the 165th and 166th and the Regimental Dressing Stations of the 165th and 167th. Our artillery, which had been in support of the 32nd Division, rejoined us on October 13th, making a hard, forced march with animals that had been reduced in strength and numbers by our continuous warfare. Colonel Henry Reilly, a West Point graduate, and a man of great intelligence and force of character, was appointed to direct the operations of the artillery brigade, leaving Lieutenant Colonel Redden to take charge of his own regiment, the 149th Field Artillery. The artillery of the 1st division also remained to assist in the sector.

The German main line of defense—the Kriemhilde Stellung, was about three kilometers in front of our brigade but less than two in front of the 84th Brigade. It was a well prepared and strongly wired position consisting of three lines of wires and trenches. The first rows of wire were breast high and as much as twenty feet wide, all bound together in small squares by iron supports so that it was almost impossible for artillery to destroy it unless the whole ground were beaten flat. Back of this were good trenches about four feet deep with machine gun shelters carefully prepared. Behind this front line at thirty yards intervals they had two other lines with lower wire and shallower trenches. Starting from our left these trenches ran from west to east on our side of two small villages called St. Georges and Landres et St. Georges. From in front of the latter village the wire turned in a southeasterly direction towards us, following the lowest slope of the Cote de Chatillon and embracing LaMusarde Ferme, thence swinging east again to take in the Tuilerie Ferme. The Cote de Chatillon was a high wooded knoll which commanded the terrain to west and south.

The task of the 84th Brigade was to work their way through the Bois de Romagne and capture the two farms and the Cote de Chatillon. Our brigade front was of a different character, and with its own particular kind

of difficulty. The terrain was the most nearly level section
we had seen in this country, and was mostly open, though
with irregular patches of woods. From the Cote de Maldah
it sloped off towards the north to a small brook that ran
in a general east to west direction through ground that
was a bit swampier than the rest; and from there, rising
gradually, up to the German wire. A good road with a
bridge over the brook ran northeast and southwest between
Sommerance and Landres et St. Georges. At the beginning it lay entirely in the Ohio sector but our advance to
the north would bring us astride of it.

Our attack had to be made over open ground with the
purpose of carrying by direct assault wired entrenchments.
It was the warfare of 1916 and 1917 over again, and
everybody knows from the numerous British and French
accounts of such action that it can be accomplished only by
tremendous artillery preparation, and that even then gains
must be made at a great loss of Infantry. But a glance at
the maps, in which blue dotted lines represented the enemy
wire, showed us that we had greater danger to fear than
the resistance which would come from our direct front.
The blue dots ran straight across the right of the Ohio front
and all of ours, and then swung in a southerly direction for
a kilometer or more. They prophesied eloquently to anyone
who had the slightest knowledge of war that our main
danger was to come from our right flank unless that hill
could be taken first. Donovan's desire was to advance until
we would be on a level with the wire to our right, hold that
line with a sufficient number of troops to guard against
counter attack, and throw in our main strength on the left
of the 84th Brigade, they striking from the south and we
from the west until the Cote de Chatillon should be taken.
Continuing the advance from there, we could take Landres
et St. Georges from the east. The orders however were
to attack, head on, with four regiments abreast. The 84th
Brigade was given three hours start to fight their way
through the southernmost German defences. It was cal-

culated that they could get far enough forward during this time so that both brigades could keep advancing in even line.

Preparations for the assault were made difficult by weather conditions. The sun never shone and a large part of the time it rained steadily. It was difficult to observe the enemy lines or their troop movements from balloons, and the advantage of aeroplanes was theirs—not ours. The abominable condition of the roads made it impossible to get sufficient ammunition forward and our artillery was working under a great handicap. Facilities for communication with the front line were poor throughout the whole action. The wire, strung along the wet ground, was all the time getting out of order; horses were few and runners had to make their way back through seas of mud, which also caused untold difficulty in getting forward food and ammunition.

However, everything was planned as well as possible under the conditions. It was arranged to have tanks to help our men get through the wire. The gas and flame Engineers were also to render assistance, and Colonel Johnson sent detachments of his Engineers (for whom I have supplied a motto from an old song: "Aisy wid the Shovel and Handy with the Gun") to go with the Infantry as wire-cutters, and to follow up to repair roads.

During the two days in which these plans were being made the battle activity on both sides was conducted mainly by the artillery. Company G had barely occupied its position in the woods on the evening of October 11th, when it was subjected to a heavy shelling, with the loss of M. Black killed and Sergeant Edward McNamara, Corporal Framan, Kessler, Dan McSherry and William McManus wounded. Young Jim Gordon of Company E was running for a litter to carry off the wounded when a fragment from a gas shell struck him in the chest and killed him instantly. Arthur Brown of Company I was killed on the Cote de Maldah. Early on the morning of the 12th the men of Company C who were lying along the southern bases of the hill not far from a battery of artillery which the enemy were trying to get, had some shells dropped amongst them and H. Harbison, L. Jones and Frank Foley were killed and Gorman and others wounded.

Lieutenant Colonel Donovan was assigned by Colonel Mitchell to have general charge of the situation at the front while he with Captain Merle-Smith as operations officer and Captain Meaney as Adjutant, handled it from the P. C. in Exermont. Lieutenant Lawrence Irving, in charge of the Intelligence Section, was at the observation post.

Our artillery preparations for the assault were begun at 3:30 on the morning of October 14th. Our brigade, in touch with the 82nd Division on our left, jumped off at 8:30 in the same morning. In our regiment Companies I and M were in advance, with K and L in immediate support, a company of the Wisconsin Machine Gunners being with them and our 2nd Battalion supplying details for carrying ammunition, etc. The front wave had not gotten well started before it was evident that the enemy were expecting an attack, and from the beginning our men went forward through steady shell fire which increased as their purpose became more clearly manifested. Two enemy aeroplanes flew along the lines of our Division discharging machine guns and no doubt keeping their own artillery posted on the results of their fire. But, in spite of losses, our men kept going forward, stimulated by the encouragement of Major Reilley and his Company Commanders Walsh, Guignon, Given and Rowley. They had about two miles to go before reaching the enemy's wire.

Captain Rowley with Company M was to the left alongside of the Ohios and Captain Michael Walsh to the right, and at the beginning in touch with the Alabamas, a touch which was soon lost, as the latter regiment came to close grips with the enemy at a point further south than our point of attack, and our companies pushing northward found it difficult to maintain liaison with them. The amount of time assigned to the 84th Brigade to capture Hill 288, the Tuilerie Farm, and the defenses at the base of the Cote de Chatillon was not sufficient for the magnitude of the task that was given them to accomplish. By noon their line had passed Hill 288 and was close to the enemy outposts, but at that time our Brigade was already at their Second Objective. From the outset the most destructive fire we had to undergo came from machine guns firing from this Cote to our right and enfilading our whole line; and the further forward we got the more destructive it became. By 1 o'clock half of the third battalion had been killed or wounded. Colonel Donovan, with Lieutenants Wheatley and Betty, and Major Reilley with Lieutenant Heller and Sergeant Courtney, were all over the field sustaining the spirits of the men.

There is no tougher experience than that of advancing over a considerable distance under fire. The trouble is that the men are being shot down by an enemy whom they cannot see. They reply with their rifles and machine guns, but have only the vaguest hope that they are accomplishing anything more than disconcerting their opponents. When a soldier gets where he can see the foe he develops a sort of hunter's exhilaration. His blood warms up and he actually forgets that the other fellow is shooting at him. Advancing in the open against trenches he has only the sensations of the hunted. Heavy fire begins to rain around them, men are hit, the line drops, each man in whatever shelter he can find. Then the order is given to rise and go forward again; spurts of dust are kicked up, the first three or four men to advance walk into the line of bullets and go down before they have gone ten feet. And the others who have seen them fall must go straight ahead and take that same deadly chance, never knowing when they themselves will stop a German missile. It takes undaunted leadership and tremendous courage to keep going forward under such conditions.

That leadership the men possessed in their battalion commander and those under him. Captain Rowley, a quiet, determined man, kept M. Company moving forward until he was knocked senseless by a tree which was blown down upon him through the explosion of a shell. His place was taken by Lieutenant Collier, who was shortly afterwards also wounded, and Lieutenant Don Elliott found himself in command. Company I was led by Captain Mike Walsh until he received a long tearing wound through the arm. He left his Company under command of Lieutenant Roderick Hutchinson, who led the company until he too was wounded, and started back alone to the Dressing-Station under the slope of the hill, to have his wound bandaged up. On his way back to the line he was hit once more and instantly killed. Nobody knew that he was killed until his body was discovered by Edward Healy, who buried him; and was shortly afterwards killed himself. It was well for his Company that they did not know the misfortune they had sustained because no loss in our whole campaign was more deeply felt than that of this rugged, whole-souled soldier and leader of men. Companies L and K, under Captain Given and Lieutenant Guignon, were also having their troubles, especially Company K under the daring leadership of its youthful commander. In all of the companies there was great loss amongst our old time non-coms as they moved around looking after the men instead of taking shelter with them.

But the outstanding figure in the mind of every officer and man was Lieutenant Colonel William J. Donovan. Donovan is one of the few men I know who really enjoys a battle. He goes into it in exactly the frame of mind that he had as a college man when he marched out on the gridiron before a football game, and his one thought throughout is to push his way through. "Cool" is the word the men use of him and "Cool" is their highest epithet of praise for a man of daring, resolution and indifference to danger. He moved out from the Cote de Maldah at the beginning of the attack with his headquarters group, just behind the supporting companies—his proper place, though he had no intention of remaining there if he could do more efficient work further forward. He had prepared himself for the task he had determined on in a characteristic way. Instead of taking off all signs of rank, as officers are supposed to do to avoid being made a mark for sharpshooters, he had donned a Sam Brown belt with double shoulder straps, so that none of his men could miss knowing who he was; that the enemy also would pick him out was to him a matter of serene indifference. As soon as the advance began to slow up under the heavy losses, he passed to the front line of the leading elements. The motto of the Donovan clan must be "Come on." It was "Come on, fellows, it's better ahead than it is here," or "Come on, we'll have them on the run before long," or with his arm across the shoulder of some poor chap who looked worried, "Come on, old sport, nobody in this Regiment was ever afraid." He would stand out in front of the men lying in shell holes into which he had ordered them, and read his map unconcernedly with the Machine-gun bullets kicking up spurts of dust around his feet; and would turn smilingly, "Come on now, men, they can't hit me and they won't hit you." It was more like a Civil War picture than anything we have seen in this fighting to watch the line of troops rushing forward led by their Commander.

But their task was more than any battalion could perform. The conditions on the right made it impossible to reach the wire in front with strength enough to break through it. The 84th Brigade was doing heroic work, but it was to take two days more of tremendously hard fighting for them before the Cote de Chatillon could be reduced. The nature of the fighting turned their front obliquely in a northeast direction, while our Brigade was advancing due north. Major Norris of the Alabamas filled in the gap between our right and their left during the afternoon, thus insuring against an attack from the Germans which might break through our line. Their brigade captured Hill 288 that day but was held up in front of the Tuilerie Farm. It was not until the evening of the 16th and by continuous and desperate fighting that our gallant brothers of the 84th Brigade pounded their way to the crest of the Cote de Chatil-lon.

In the afternoon, after six hours of battle, Donovan reported that the 3rd Battalion, which had gotten up to the slopes under the German wire, was too badly shot up to be able to push through. He requested an artillery barrage of an hour and a half to keep the Germans distracted while he withdrew the 3rd Battalion carrying their wounded, through the 1st Battalion under Major Kelly, who would take their place. At dusk Kelly made his advance by infiltration, Company C on the left, Company D on the right. The men stole forward, losing heavily but taking advantage of every inequality in the surface of the ground. Towards the right of our position a rough wagon road run up through a draw between two gradual slopes and just before it reached the main road between Sommerance and Landres it passed through a deep cut, in some places eight feet deep, part of which was included in the enemy's wire defenses.

The battalion fought its way right up to the enemy's wire, only to find it an impassable barrier. Our artillery fire had not made a break in it anywhere, as for lack of aeroplanes to register the effects of their work they had been shooting entirely by the map. Groups of our lads dashed up to the wire only to be shot down to the last man. Some ran through a passage made for the roadway, the only possible method of getting through, but this of course was absolutely covered by the German guns, and every man that went through it was shot and, if not killed outright, taken prisoner. Soldiers of ours and of the Engineers with wire-cutting tools lay on their faces working madly to cut through the strands, while riflemen and grenadiers alongside of them tried to beat down the resistance. But they were in a perfect hail of bullets from front and flank, and every last man was killed or wounded. Further back was a concentration of artillery fire, of bursting shells and groans and death, that made the advance of the support platoons a veritable hell.

The attackers finally fell back a short distance to the deep cut in the road. Our second attempt to break through had failed. Major Kelly with Lieutenant Connelly and parts of companies A and C held this place as a vantage point to make a third attempt in the morning. Bootz was in charge on the left of the main road. About one hundred and fifty yards south of the wire the ground sloped, and on this reverse slope Colonel Donovan established his P. C., with Lieutenant Betty as his adjutant, Wheatley having been wounded. With him also were detachments from the Headquarters and Machine Gun Companies under Lieutenant Devine and Sergeants Sheahan, Heins, Leo Mullin, Doherty and Gillespie. During the night, accompanied by Sergeant Major Bernard White, the Colonel himself scouted up to the enemy wire to examine the conditions for the next days' attack. Tanks were promised to roll through the wire, shoot up the machine gun nests and make a passage for the infantry. Morning came but no tanks in sight. Lieutenant Grose and Boberg and Brosnan of Brigade Headquarters were scouring the roads in search of them. It took two hours to get a message back, as the telephone was out. The artillery barrage ran its appointed course and still no tanks. Kelly once more made his attack, under conditions that he soon discovered to be impossible for success. Every man that reached the wire was hit, and losses were heavy in his elements further back.

About half an hour after the advance began a rifle bullet struck Colonel Donovan in the leg, going through the bone and rendering him helpless. He would have ordered anybody else to be evacuated, but he refused to allow himself to be removed. In answer to the protests of his Adjutant he swore he would stay there and see the thing through. So he lay in his shell-hole and continued to direct the battle. It was bound to be a one-sided one until the tanks should come up. Our men in the sunken road were being shelled by trench mortars which dropped their shells into the narrow cutting, spreading disaster. Our elements in the more open ground to the rear were under continuous shell fire as the enemy artillery had the exact ranges.

One of the creepiest feelings in war is that of being boxed in by artillery fire. A shell lands to the right of a group of men; no harm in that—all safe. Then one lands to the left, to front, or rear, and the next is closer in between them. Then everybody knows what is happening. That square is in for a shelling until nothing living inside it will escape except by miracle. This was the experience of many a group that morning, and Colonel Donovan and his headquarters men had to undergo it to the utmost. There always has to be a good deal of motion around a Post of Command, so this slope was made a special target. Shells fell all over it, and men were blown out of their holes by direct hits. Thus perished Patrick Connors of Company H and Color Sergeant William Sheahan, one of the finest and bravest of men. Donovan (and Major Anderson, who had come up and was lying in the same hole with him) escaped without further injury. Messages which had to be carried the short distance between his shell-hole and where Kelly was were sent with difficulty, many runners being killed or wounded. They had no direct connection with the rear. It was a lone fight, but both Donovan and Kelly were of the same mind, not to desist from the attack so long as any chance remained of putting it through.

Finally the tanks appeared coming up the road from Sommerance. Everybody was elated. At last there was a chance to get through that wire and mop up those infernal machine gun nests. But the tanks were under artillery fire, some of which was evidently doing damage to them, and with disappointment and disgust the Infantry saw them pause, turn about and rumble down the road to the rear. About 10:30 Captain Buck, who had been wounded and was on his way to the Dressing Station, brought word to Donovan that a counter-attack was evidently in preparation. Donovan's party urged him to let them carry him back, but he swore at them, and ordered them to bring up more machine guns and the Stokes Mortars, under Lieutenant O'Donohue and Sergeant Fitzsimmons. These were disposed in an advantageous position, which means a dangerous one, and the counter-attack was smothered in its inception.

By 11:00 o'clock Donovan had decided that the 1st Battalion had too many losses to make it possible for them to get through. He told Anderson, who was with him, to return and bring forward his battalion so that Kelly's men and their wounded could pass through.

Kelly, whose fighting blood was up, at first refused to retire, demanding written orders from his chief before he would give up his claim on the post of danger and glory. Donovan gave the orders and then permitted himself to be carried in, leaving the situation in the very capable hands of Major Anderson.

This relief was begun about noon with the aid of a heavy barrage from our artillery, of which nobody in the line knew the exact reason. The reason was that Brigade had ordered another attack which was originally scheduled for 11:15. Merle-Smith had protested that we had only one battalion left and that it was unwise to use up our last effectives. The only result was that the barrage was extended until noon, on Colonel Mitchell's report that .it would be impossible to get the orders forward to the front by 11:15. He sent the order in three different directions, but none of his messages arrived until the barrage which was to cover the attack had passed over and the relief of the 1st battalion had already begun.

The situation was a stalemate. We had made an advance of three kilometers under desperate conditions, but in spite of our losses and sacrifices we had failed to take our final objective. Well, success is not always the reward of courage. There is no military organization, no matter how famous, that has not its record of failures. In this war every regiment and division in the older armies has known times when it was impossible for them to do all that it was hoped they might be able to accomplish, and most especially when they were called upon to capture well defended trench positions.

Indeed, since 1915, no commanders in the older armies would dream of opposing to strongly wired and entrenched positions the naked breasts of their infantry. They take care that the wire, or part of it at least, is knocked down by artillery or laid flat by tanks before they ask unprotected riflemen to try conclusions with its defenders. When the wire is deep, and still intact, and strongly defended, the infantry can do little but hang their heroic bodies on it.

But we shall not dwell on this. The most glorious day in the history of our regiment in the Civil War was Fredericksburg, where the Old 69th in the Irish Brigade failed to capture the impregnable position on Marye's Heights, though their dead with the green sprigs in their caps lay in rows before it. Landres et St. Georges is our Fredericksburg and the Kriemhilde Stellung our Marye's Heights.

Whatever the mature judgment of history may decide about it, the opinion of our Corps Commander, General Summerall, was the one that counted most. He had been in command of the 1st Division when it made its attack in this same area, and was promoted after the battle to the duty of commanding the corps into which we moved. On the evening of the 15th he came to our brigade and made a visit to our P. C. in Exermont to demand why our final objective had not been taken. He was not well handled, Colonel Mitchell is a good soldier, and one of the finest men in the world, but he is entirely too modest to say a strong word in his own defense. Everybody is familiar with the kind of man who, in spite of the merits of his case, makes a poor figure on the witness stand. Donovan, who is an able lawyer and likes the give and take of battle, verbal or otherwise, would have sized up the Corps Commander's mood and would have been planning a new attack with him after the first ten minutes. Captain Merle-Smith stated the facts of the case—the enfilading fire from the Cote de Chatillon, the unbroken wire in our front, the inadequacy of artillery against it on account of lack of air service to register their fire, the failure of the tanks and the extent of our losses. General Summerall was in no mood for argument. He wanted results, no matter how many men were killed, and he went away more dissatisfied than he had come.

As a result, by his orders the Division Commander relieved General Lenihan, Colonel Mitchell and also Captain Merle-Smith and Lieutenant Betty. As a matter of fact, a few days later when the ill humor had cooled down, Merle-Smith was sent back to us in command of a battalion and Betty also returned. When General Lenihan submitted his statement of the actions of his brigade (supplemented by messages and maps) to the Army commander, General Liggett, the latter assured him that he would name him to fill the first vacancy in a combat Brigade on the fighting line. This happened to be in the 77th Division, and two weeks later I met him at St. Juvin, still in line and going strong.

I do not wish to adopt too critical a tone with regard to the action of the Corps Commander. He is the military superior, and his judgment must be accepted even if it is wrong. Moreover, the loss of rank or position by officers weighs nothing with me in comparison with the two big factors: the proper handling of the men under them; and victory. In the heat of action every commanding general has to make rapid decisions. General Summerall came to one of these decisions in our regard, and we must abide by it.

But speaking as an historian, I think that his decision was wrong. It was a question of whether our Colonel was a man to get out of his regiment all that it was capable of. No person who knows him could ever accuse Harry D. Mitchell of losing his nerve in a battle. He liked a fight. He would have been happier out on the line as Lieutenant Colonel than back in his P. C., but he knew that there was nobody who could handle an attack and put courage and dash into it better than Colonel Donovan, and that any body of troops, even less experienced and willing than our own, would fight to the last under such leadership. Colonel Mitchell's spirit was equally resolute and his orders crisp and strong. The whole regiment was devoted to him, and anxious to do their very best under his command. Indeed, amongst the older men, there was never any doubt about our ultimate success. It had taken five days to reduce the German resistance at the Ourcq, but we did it. With more help from artillery and tanks, they said, we can make it yet. The worst blow to our morale that we ever received was inflicted by the order relieving our Colonel.

The days following were anxious and gloomy ones for us, and our spirits were kept up by the unchanged dry humor of the man we were sorry to lose. When he was going, I said, to relieve the tension: "Now you are leaving us just when I had you running fine and I'll have the job of breaking in another new Commanding Officer." "Father," he said, "this continuous change of Commanders would break up any other regiment I ever knew, but this old regiment can keep itself going on, no matter who commands it. It would get along on spirit and unity if it never had a Commanding Officer."

Our new commander was Lieutenant Colonel Charles H. Dravo, who had been Division Machine Gun Officer. A number of us have known him for a considerable time and like him already, all the more because his first action was a report on conditions in the regiment which was aimed at the restoration of Colonel Mitchell to his command.

We had 53 officers going in at the Argonne and of those five were killed and fifteen wounded. Of those killed, after Captain Michael Walsh, the greatest sense of loss was felt at the death of Lieutenant Andrew Ellett of Company E, a soldier of unlimited courage. We did not know until long afterwards that Lieutenant Henry Davis, an officer of the same type, who had been wounded by shell fire on October

12th, died in Hospital. Two young officers who were comparatively newcomers in the Regiment, but who had made many friends, Lieutenants William O'Connor and John P. Orr, were killed on the field.

Headquarters Company lost, beside Color Sergeant Sheahan, Sergeant Edward J. Hussey, with Gustave Cosgrove and Charles Schulmerick and James Gaunthier, died of wounds.

Company A lost Sergeants James P. Duff and Fred. Stenson; Corporals Sidney H. Clark, Bernard McOwen, John Nallin, and Peter Barbee, David Bignell, William Cook, Jeremiah Dineen, Silas Donegan, Raymond Fitzpatrick, Charles Freeman, Frank Gilday, Lester Hess, Oscar Iverson, Edward Kelly, Lafayette Sharp, A. B. Harrell, William Smith, William Bress, Leo Tully, Charles Hallberg and Earl Wilder.

Company B lost Sergeants James Donnelly and John J. Mahoney; Corporal Thomas F. Winters; and Philip Benoit, Joseph Cole, Thomas J. Cronin, David Dempsey, Thomas Doyle, Dewey Houck, Jesse Johnson, Benjamin Robert, Ed Zeiss, Robert Wallack.

Company C lost Sergeant Edward Kearin; Corporals James Farnan, Arthur Potter, Daniel J. Slattery; and Avery Bridges, James Cody, Lloyd Harris, Clinton Hart, Martin Haugse, W. P. Hensel, Harold J. Hogan, Samuel Key, Daniel Medler, James Murnane, J. P. Myers, Charles Nabors, George O'Neill, Anthony Palumbo, William Fountain, J. H. Reneker, Edward Sheridan, Francis Conway and Thomas D. Vegeau.

Company D lost Corporals John J. Haggerty, Harry Adkins, William Boetger, Walter Crisp, Lacy Castor, J. W. McPherson, S. Scardino, W. Schmelick; and C. R. Kerl, William Cundiff, Frank Fall, George Saladucha, R. Robbins, Lawrence P. Mahoney, Peter J. Wollner, James W. Hasting, Fred Smith, John Mc-

Namara, Gordon Wynne, Charles Evers, James Butler, Edward Clement, Frank F. De Muth and Richard Fincke.

Company E lost Corporals William Dougherty, William Bechtold, Matthew Colgan, and George Failing; and Joseph Carroll, Frederick Gluck, Kennedy Hardy, Fred Conway and John Naughton.

Company F lost Arthur Armes, William M. Binkley, Charles Park, Fred Riddles, Joseph Woodlief, Joseph Elzear, Charles Ash.

Company G lost Daniel McSherry, Clarence Leonard, Charles Jacobs, Marvin Black, John Hemmer, Archie Lilles, William McManus.

Company H lost Corporal Clifford Wiltshire, Arthur N. Frank, Roger Folson, Clinton Bushey, J. Moscolo, Patrick Connors and heroic Sergeant John J. Walker.

Company I lost Sergeants Patrick Collins and William Harrison; Corporals Allen Crowe and Charles Stone; and A. G. Brown, Robert Cousens, Harry Gill, Edward F. Healy, Earnest Keith, Albert Mortenson, James Nealon, Gilbert Neely, George A. Peterson, Warren Regan, Thomas Stokey, Earl Thayer, Elcanor Yow, James Brown, Kenneth Trickett.

Company K lost Sergeants John J. Gavaghan and John J. Butler; Corporals Henry D. Hawxhurst and Thomas Madden; and N. Farhout, John P. Quinlan, James C. Wright, Joseph Barzare, John L. Sullivan, Francis Gioio, Daniel Buckley, Leonard Giarusso, Andrew Goeres, Claude Best, George Pennington.

Company L lost Corporal Edward Bloom and Joseph Metcalf, Fred Parr, Homer C. Coin, John H. Jumper, E. Epperly, John P. Ryan.

Company M lost Sergeant Peter Cooney; Corporals Charles T. Elson, Charles J. Brennan and William H. Crunden; and John T. Byrnes, Emmett Davidson,

Frank Manning, H. F. Brumley, Patrick J. O'Neill, Charles Blagg, Joseph McAndrews.

Machine Gun Company lost Harry A. Dearing, Fred Martin, John A. Claire, Thomas McCabe, Thomas Norton, Leonard Hansen and John McKay.

Supply Company lost Giuseppe Mastromarino.

Nobody wants to talk very much about the recent battle. It was a nightmare that one does not care to recall. Individual acts do not stand out in actions of this kind. It is a case of everybody going ahead and taking the punishment. Everybody who stood up under it and kept carrying on deserves the laurel crown. Some men, however, stand out in more striking way than their companions, either through natural coolness and willingness to take added risks or by their acceptance of a position of command that the chances of battle offered them. Prominent amongst these is Sergeant Michael Fitzpatrick of Company L, whose brother Cornelius was killed at the Ourcq, and who took charge of a platoon and kept it going with great spirit after First Sergeant Wittlinger was wounded. The veteran First Sergeant of Company K, Tim Sullivan, was also wounded in this fight, and another of the Sullivans, John L., was killed. Company K also lost a fine character in Sergeant Gavaghan, a stalwart, heroic, innocent-minded young Irishman.

When Colonel Donovan called for the Stokes Mortars to repel the threatened counter-attack on the morning of the 15th, the pieces were set up under the slight protection of the sloping ground, but from this point the gunners could not observe the accuracy of their own fire. So Sergeant Fitzsimmons ran forward to the top of the slope, making himself an easy cockshot for the German gunners while he signalled to his own men his corrections on their aim. He escaped himself by a miracle and had the satisfaction of seeing the shells dropping right amongst the Germans who were gathering for the attack, and doing dreadful execution.

The battalion runners received great praise from everybody, as they had to take untold risks in moving from place to place without shelter. Ammunition carriers also had a dangerous task, those from Company H suffering severe losses. Amongst those killed were Corporal Clifford Wiltshire, a nice quiet boy who was married to Sergeant Winthrop's sister; and Clinton Bushey, who once before was reported dead when out on the digging detail during the bombardment of July 15th. The sergeants we lost were all good men. Hussey was a clean-cut young athlete; Duff and Stenson of Company A were both very dependable men, as were also Sidney Clark, who did great work at the Ourcq, and Bernard McOwen, who had the Croix de Guerre. Donnelly and Mahoney of B had worked their way up from being privates by character and merit; and Tom Winters was also a good man. Eddie Kearin of C was one of the best liked youths in the regiment and James Farnan, a solid Irishman; Dougherty, Colgan, Bechtold and John Naughton of E have figured before and in these annals; also Fred Gluck, heroic litter-bearer. Company I was hard hit in the loss of Patrick Collins and William Harrison. Charlie Stone's mother was the last person I shook hands with before our train left Camp Mills for the transport. Robert Cousens was killed while looking after his brother who had been wounded. Sergeant Peter Cooney of M Company was out with the regiment in '98 and the three corporals, Elson, Brennan, and Crunden, were fine types of soldiers. Harry Dearing, John Claire, John McKay and the others from the Machine Gun Company will be sorely missed by their fellows.

With Colonel Donovan on the slope on October 15th were Sergeants of Headquarters Company and the Machine Gun Company. The Colonel told me later that the shell which blew Sergeant Sheahan heavenward took the legs off another Irish soldier who was with him. This I knew was Patrick Connors. Another Irishman jumped from a neighboring shell-hole, picked up the wounded man and kissed him, saying: "Me poor fellow, me poor fellow." He put tourniquets on the stumps and then, unaided, started down the dangerous slope carrying him to the rear. Gillespie and Doherty tell me that this deed was performed by Corporal John Patrick Furey of Company H, who was in charge of the ammunition carriers for the machine guns. Furey had been wounded already himself, and the sergeants wanted him to go to the rear, but he refused, as so much depended on keeping our machine guns fed. When he was carrying Connors back they shouted to him to get in an ambulance when he got there; but later in the morning Furey reappeared alongside them after his two-mile journey in each direction; and this in spite of the fact that the strain of carrying his burden had reopened another wound that he got at the Ourcq. It was an exhibition of tenderheartedness and sheer courage that honors humanity.

Liaison men have to take untold risks in action of this kind. Of Major Kelly's group in the sunken road nearly all were killed or wounded. Young Eddie Kelly (killed), Cody (killed), White (a hero in every battle), Liebowitz (wounded), and Matty Rice (often mentioned in these annals) worked their way from Kelly to Bootz or from Kelly to Donovan. When they were gone Corporal Thomas O'Kelly offered to deliver messages, but the Major wished to keep him by his side as a valuable man in combat. "Send me, Major," insisted Tom, "I'll carry it through, and if I don't come back, you'll know I'm dead." He got it through alright, though wounded. He wanted to go back with a message, but Colonel Donovan ordered him to go back to the Dressing-Station. Every last man amongst these men deserves a citation for bravery.

In this battle one of the tasks which required the greatest courage was that of getting back the wounded when the retirement from the wire of the first battalion was ordered. Their rescuers had to abandon their pits and advance in full view of the enemy in their work of succor. The men who stood out in accomplishing this dangerous duty were in Company A: First Sergeant Thomas Sweeney and Sergeant John H. Dennelly; In Company C, First Sergeant Thomas P. O'Hagan, Sergeant Joseph Burns and Corporal Archie Reilly. Also Mike Donaldson, of Company I, who volunteered for this service and carried in man after man under heavy fire. Two of the liaison men from A Company, Matthew J. Kane and Martin Gill, as also John Hammond and Fred Craven of Company C, are also highly recommended for the cheerful and efficient manner in which they performed their perilous job.

Company M is very proud of its youngest corporal, little Jimmy Winestock, the mildest looking and most unassuming youth in the regiment. When troops advance under fire, there are always some who get strayed from their command, especially when their platoon leaders have been hit. Jimmy picked up all these stragglers from their companies, formed them into a detachment, issued his commands as if he were a major at least, and led them forward into the thick of action.

Major Lawrence very early in the battle had established his regimental dressing station as near to the front line as an ambulance could possibly go. There was absolutely no protection where he was, and his group which included Chaplain Holmes and the "Y" Athletic Director, Mr. Jewett, were exposed to danger from shells at all times. Father Hanley stuck as usual to his beloved Third Battalion and was out further living in a hole in the side of a hill, with Doctors Kilcourse, Martin, Mitchell, Cowett and our dental officers Bamford and Landrigan, who always rendered good work in battle.

When they were carrying Donovan in I met him at Lawrence's station. He looked up from the stretcher and said to me smilingly, "Father, you're a disappointed man. You expected to have the pleasure of burying me over here." "I certainly did, Bill, and you are a lucky dog to get off with nothing more than you've got." He was in great pain after his five hours lying with that leg in the shell-hole, but it had not affected his high spirits and good humor. He was still of opinion that the regiment could get through the wire, with proper artillery preparation and coordination of infantry forces.

On October 12th I was in Jim Mangan's little dugout at Exermont with his Lieutenants Joe McNamara, McCarthy and Flynn when in walked Dennis O'Shea, formerly our color sergeant, and now a Lieutenant in the 1st Division. Accompanying him was Father Terence King, a Jesuit Chaplain. They had been detailed for the task of burying their regimental dead. It was a joyous meeting, but they had one thing to tell that made me sad. Father Colman O'Flaherty had been killed by shell fire while attending to the wounded. I had never met him, but when we were alongside of the 1st after Saint Mihiel I met a large number of officers and men, all of whom spoke of him with affectionate admiration. An Irishman, well read, brilliant and witty in conversation, independent in the expression of his opinions; sometimes irritatng at first encounter by reason of his sallies, but always sure in the long run to be admired for his robust and attractive personality.

I got this story with no names mentioned and was too discreet to ask for them. A patrol was out for the purpose of getting in touch with the enemy. As they were ascending the reverse slope of the hill a young officer who was with two or three men in advance came running back, stooping low and calling breathlessly to the Lieutenant in command, "The Germans! The Germans! The Germans are there." Nobody thought him afraid but his tone of excitement was certainly bad for morale. There was a sudden halt and a bad moment, but the situation was saved when a New York voice in a gruff whisper was heard, "Well, what the hell does that guy think we are out here looking for?—Voilets?" If eloquence is the power to say things that will produce the desired effect on one's hearers, neither Demosthenes nor Dan O'Connell himself ever made a better speech.

We were very short of officers during the Argonne fight and, since advancing under shell fire necessitates a deliberate scattering of men, a great deal depends upon the efficiency of our non-coms, especially the sergeants. The result of their activity was that an extraordinary number of them were wounded. I came on Sergeants Tom O'Malley and Jim O'Brien of Company D, both wounded severely and bound for the rear. "Tom," I said, "what did you want to get yourself hit for? We're short of officers as it is, and it's only men like you that can put this thing through." "Well, Father," says Tom, smilingly apologetic, "you see it's like this: a sergeant stands an awful fine chance of gettin' hit as things are goin' now. We got a lot of new min that he's got to take care of to see that they don't get kilt; and whin the line moves forward, there's some of thim nades a bit of coaxin'."

I have gathered from my record a list not only of officers, but also of non-coms wounded in this battle, because they deserve to be commemorated as men who have fought throughout the war, men who, if they have not been in every one of our battles, have a wound stripe to show the reason for their absence, and who have gained their stripes of office by good soldiering in camp and in the field.

Colonel William J. Donovan; Captains, Oscar L. Buck, Edmond J. Connelly, John J. Clifford, John F. Rowley; First Lieutenants, James Collier, Paul D. Surber, Roderick J. Hutchinson; Second Lieutenants, Joseph P. Katsch, Charles D. Huesler, Clarence Johnson, Samuel S. Swift, Lester M. Greff, Henry W. Davis (Deceased), Arthur N. Hallquist, John J. Williams.

Company A, Sergeants Purtell, Armstrong, Sweeney; Corporals Gladd, Roberts, Newton, Thynne, Rice, Wylie.

Company B, Sergeants Thornton, Mulholland, Meniccoci, Graham, Gilbert, Whalen, Coyne; Corporals Quigley,

Brady, Geraghty, Van deWerken, Longo, Lofare, Hayes, Healey, Lehman, Neary.

Company C, Sergeants James Burns, Hillig, Hennessey, Knight, McNiff; Corporals, James Kelly, Hannigan, Lynott, Minogue, Munz, O'Kelly, Osberg, Quinn, Stratico, Blythe, Boyle.

Company D, Sergeants Crotty, O'Malley, Moran, Sheahan, McDonough, Tracey, Morton; Corporals Dale, Plant, Dalton Smith, Murray, O'Dowd, Lynch, O'Brien, DeVoe, Terry O'Connor, Bambrick, McAuliffe, Edward B. Smith, Reilly, Harkins, Tuers, Brady, Thompson, O'Connell.

Company E, Corporals Corbett, Maloney, Geary.

Company F, Corporal Patrick Frawley.

Company G, Sergeants McNamara, William Farrell, James Murray; Corporals, Framan, Allen, Christy.

Company H, Sergeant Walker; Corporals, McGorry, Ryan, McGlynn, Doran.

Company I, Sergeants Shanahan, Lyons, Dynan, Mullin, Joseph O'Brien; Corporals, Cousens, Dexter, Gaul, Horgan, Kennedy, Smiser, Welsh, Zarella, Beyer, Lenihan, New, Regan, Conway, Hettrick, Neary.

Company K, Sergeants Timothy Sullivan, Gleason, Hellrigel; Corporals Van Yorx, McKessy, Clinton, Ryan, Ostermeyer, Casey, Gallagher, LeGall, McMahon, Caraher, Wakely, Hoey.

Company L, Sergeants, Southworth, Kiernan, Wittlinger, Fitzpatrick, Mullins, Blood; Corporals Kennedy, Martin, O'Brien, Oakes, McCallum, George McCue, Murphy, John J. Murphy, Hearn.

Company M, Sergeants Major, Clark, May; Corporals Igo, Feely, Begley, Shear, Scott, Donovan, McGovern, Cook, Bailey, Kiernan, Berger, Harry Murray, Knowles.

Headquarters Co., Corporals Dick, Brochon, Albrecht.

Machine Gun Co., Sergeants Stevens, Spillane, Gillespie, Doherty; Corporals Erard, Cohen.

ESPERANCE FARM

October 28th, 1918

Our rear Headquarters are in two buildings on the main road that parallels the river Aire. In one of them is the Supply Company and the band. Solicitude for the welfare of bandsmen is the sole tribute that the army pays to art. In a neighboring building is an Ambulance Company and our Company Clerks, who have been ordered to be left in the rear because records are never properly made out if the Company Clerk becomes a casualty. I often make use of a returning ambulance to come back to Captain Kinney's Hotel for a decent sleep and a good breakfast. Across the road in the field a number of the men have made little dugouts for themselves, as the buildings are overcrowded.

Shell fire does not come back this far except occasionally, but the nights are often made hideous by enemy bombing planes. Aeroplanes carrying machine guns are futile things, but a plane at night dropping bombs is absolutely the most demoralizing thing in war. It is a matter of psychology. The man in front discharging his rifle has the hunter's exhilaration. Even shells can be dodged if not too numerous, and after a man has dropped on his face or jumped into a doorway and has escaped, there is the satisfaction that a hare must have when it eludes the dogs and pants contentedly in its hole. But when one lies at night and hears the deep buzz of a plane overhead, and most especially when the buzz ceases and he knows that the plane is gliding and making ready to drop something, the one feeling that comes is that if that fellow overhead pulls the lever at the right spot, a very very wrong spot, it means sudden and absolute destruction. There is no way of getting away from it. One simply lies and cowers.

Last night we heard the crunching roar six times repeated in the field just across the road. Flannery and I got up and pulled on our shoes to go over and see what happened. Mules had been hit and two of our men slightly wounded. The bombs made holes in the soft earth, ten feet deep and nearly twelve in diameter, and one of them had fallen at the feet of two of our lads and had not exploded. I was particularly anxious about a lot of nice youngsters whom I had picked out after St. Mihiel for the Band—John Kyle, Robert Emmett Mitchell, Howard Casey, Pat Campion, Will Maroney, Will King, George Forms, John Killoran, Denis Glynn, Will Howard,—all lads that had volunteered before they were eighteen. I found them unharmed and rather enjoying the show.

Lieutenant Bernard Byrne, who is not long with us and whose experience in warfare has not been of great duration, was ordered from the Supply Company a couple of days ago to duty with Company G. His first night in line he took out a patrol which he handled admirably and came back with two prisoners. A very good start indeed.

Everybody has slept in his clothes for weeks. It would not be true to say that we never take them off, because that is part of the morning, though not of the evening ritual. Every morning officers and men, refined or roughneck, strip to the waist for the process of "Reading his shirt." Not to put too fine a touch to it, we are all crawling with lice. Holmes has a boy who is at the interesting age of four, and his wife writes to him the usual domestic stories about his bright ways and sayings. "You ask her if that kid can read his shirt. Tell her I said that his old man can do it." Mrs. Holmes sent word back to Father Duffy that while the youthful prodigy had not all the accomplishments of a soldier he could hike with any of us. I did not get the message for weeks afterwards, as my brother Chaplain was very much run down and Major Lawrence and I shipped him off, despite his protests, to the hospital. I do not need to worry about Father Hanley. As long as Ambrose Sutcliff's Goulash Wagon can supply him with an occasional meal, he will keep going any place I put him—though that is not the right way to phrase it, for I always have to keep him pulled back from the places where he thinks he ought to be. I think I will take both my Chaplains home with me to the Bronx as curates. A Catholic church with a Methodist annex would be a novelty. Back in the peaceful days, a Jew friend of mine whom I was showing over my combination church and school said to me, with the quick business sense of his race, "You use this building for Church on Sunday and for school five days in the week. The only day it's idle is Saturday. What you ought to do is to hire a good smart young Rabbi and run a synagogue on the Sabbath. I'll bet you'll make money at it."

The two weeks that elapsed between October 16th and November 1st were the dreariest, draggiest days we spent in the war. The men lay out on the bare hillsides in little pits they had dug for themselves, the bottoms of which were turned into mud by frequent rains. They had one blanket apiece, and were without overcoats, underwear or socks, in the unpleasant climate of a French Autumn. They were dirty, lousy, thirsty, often hungry; and nearly every last man was sick.

Captain Bootz, an old-time regular army man and therefore not sympathetic with imaginary ills, made the following report on Anderson's battalion as early as October 17th. "Checked up strength of battalion shows 405 men for active combat, including liaison detail. Of this number about 35% are suffering various illnesses, especially rheumatism, colds and fevers. The Company commanders state that these men are not receiving medical treatment, which should be given to them without fail or conditions will be worse in the next day or so. Some men are doubled up and should really be in the hospital. I cannot allow these men to leave, as it would set a precedent for many others to follow, and this would deplete our fighting strength so much more. First aid men attached to companies have no medical supplies other than bandages. A lack of proper clothing, such as overcoats, heavy underwear and socks, brings on a great many of these maladies. The majority

of the men have summer underwear, if any, and no overcoat and only one blanket; and this is entirely inadequate
to keep a soldier in fit physical condition for field service
in the climate that is found this time of year in France. I
deem it my duty that this be brought to the attention of
higher authorities so that they may be rightly informed
as to the actual conditions we are living in, and that means
be found to have the defect remedied immediately."

As the days went on, conditions got no better. Hundreds and hundreds of men had to be evacuated as too
weak to be of any military value; and nothing but the need
of man-power kept our doctors from sending half the regiment to the hospital. The only relief from monotony was an
occasional night patrol, or the prospects which were held out
to us of a fresh order to attack. In spite of the bloody nose
we had already received, our men wished for the order to
try again. Patrols and observation posts reported a lessen-
ing of the enemy's strength, and our fellows felt certain that
if the tanks would do their share they could get through.
They had met their first repulse. If they had been in the
war as long as the British or French, they would have
learned to take it philosophically as part of the give and take
of the game. But it was their first one, and they were burning with the desire to get back at the enemy.

On the 21st our brigade relieved the 84th, our 2nd Battalion taking over the front line on the north edge of the
Cote de Chatillon. The next day orders were out for a new
attack in which the 165th were to work around the eastern
end of Landres et Saint George. Everybody was on the
qui vive for a new battle but the thing dragged from day
to day until the 26th, when word came that we were to be
taken out of the line and that the Second Division was to
make the attack. Our men were sorely disappointed and
grieved about it, but the decision was a proper one. With
the artillery support that has been gathering in our rear I
have no doubt that our fellows could have broken through,
but we have become too weak in man power to exploit an

initial victory in a way that should be done to make the most of it. Three weeks in line under such conditions do not fit men for the hardships of a sustained advance. During this period we lost killed, in Company H, William Murray and P. Nicholson; and in Company M, Davidson and Patrick Ames, a soldier who never knew fear.

October 28th, 1918.

I went in to see General Menoher about my concerns as Division Chaplain. After my business was done he said that he had received orders to send me back to the States to make a speaking tour for the Welfare Funds. He kept talking about these orders long enough to get me worried, although as I watched his face closely I thought I could detect a humorous and reassuring twinkle in his pleasant eyes. Finally, after having been kept on the griddle for five minutes, I ventured the question, "May I ask, General, what reply you made to these orders?" Then he laughed in his genial way. "I told them that you had better work to do here than there and that I was not going to let you go." I certainly do like that man.

Our land battles during these days are being conducted mainly at night as fights between patrols, the war in the day time being mainly in the air. On October 16th a German plane which had been separated from its escadrille came wabbling over the heads of Major Lawrence's group and landed in a field alongside them, the occupants being made prisoners. Two days later I had the good luck to witness from the same spot a unique spectacle. There had been an air fight in which ours got the better of it. A German plane was evidently in a bad way. As we watched it we saw a dark object drop from it, and while we held our breath in sympathetic terror for a human being dropping to destruction, a parachute opened above him—the first instance of the kind we have seen in this war. Captain Bootz, who was under him at the time, said that he managed it by climbing out on the tail of his plane and dropping off it from the rear. The great difficulty about using a parachute for aviators has been that the on-moving plane hits the ropes before they can drop clear. Most of the air fights have been the result of the determination of the Germans to get our balloons. They brought down four of them one afternoon, much to our disgust.

There is a stock story about the rookie who is persuaded by his fellows that his tin hat is guaranteed by the government to turn the direct hit of a German 77. When Colonel Dravo and the rest of us start to tell how an inch of planking turned a German 77, we shall be greeted with smiles of incredulity, but the thing actually happened. Dravo has a pleasant little Chalet out on the hill 263, beautifully situated in the forest and affording an excellent place of repose for weary American officers if the Germans who were kind enough to build it would only leave their work alone. But the hill is shelled by day and shelled and bombed by night, in a picky sort of a way. A small portion of the shack is boarded off for a kitchen and in it sleep, or rather slept, for they don't like the place any more, the force of our Headquarters mess: Sergeant Denis Donovan, Jimmy Dayton, Tex Blake, McWalter, and John McLaughlin in superimposed bunks, so that the lads above were only a couple of feet below the roof. A shell hit just above them, the explosion ruining the roof and pitching them all to the floor; but every particle of iron in it spread itself into the air outside of the building. Luckily for them it must have been one of those long-nosed devils that explode on contact and cause much greater destruction than those that plow out the ordinary shell hole. The first time I saw the roads barely scratched where they hit I thought the German powder was becoming inferior. I know better now.

HALLOWE'EN

We are out of the line tonight with the exception of Reilley's 3rd Battalion, which is to lie out there in their

shelter pits under our barrage and whatever the Germans
may send back in reply until the 2nd Division goes through
them tomorrow. Twelve months ago we had scarcely left
our native shores, a wonderful year in the lives of all of us,
and the last one for many a poor fellow now sleeping in the
soil of France. A lot of the officers are crowded together
in Kinney's quarters at the Esperance Farm. The room is
hot and close, as shelter-halves and blankets screen every
nook through which light might pass to give information
of human habitation to a passing bomber. Everybody feels
tired, dirty and discouraged.

I said to them, "You are the glummest bunch of Irish
that I ever saw on a Hallowe'en. Johnnie Fechheimer, you
are the best Harp in this bunch; start them singing. Frank
Smith, warm us up with some coffee, since there's nothing
better to be had." So Pete Savarese soon had the coffee
boiling and the two Ganymedes, Bob Dillon and Charlie
Lowe, ministered to our needs. Pretty soon they were all
singing—Major Anderson, Kinney, Mangan, Fechheimer,
McDermott, Flynn, McCarthy, O'Donohue, Joe McNamara, Smith, John Schwinn, even Flannery, Scanlon, and
myself. Joe McNamara, who is as good a youth as they
make them, and who has done great service during the
past three weeks with his signal men, sang a song that was
just on the verge of being naughty, with his handsome blue
eyes twinkling provokingly at me. Dan Flynn knows all
the old songs that our mothers used to sing, "Ben Bolt,"
"You'll Remember Me," and all that sort of thing. Fechheimer and MacNamara supplied the modern element in the
concert. But no matter what it was, everybody joined in,
including the men in the loft upstairs and in the shelter
tents outside, especially when it came to songs in praise of
Good Little Old New York; and truck drivers and ambulance men and passing officers along the road got first-hand
information that the New York Irish 69th had come
through their three long weeks of fighting and hardship
with their tails still erect.

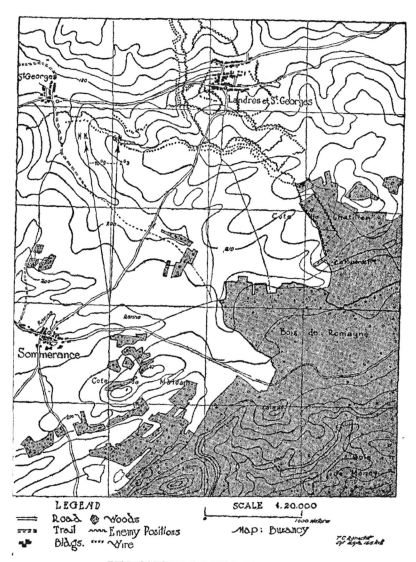

LEGEND
Road   Woods
Trail   Enemy Positions
Bldgs.   Wire

SCALE 1.20.000

Map: Buzancy

THE BATTLE OF THE ARGONNE

We had no doubt of the success of the 2nd Division. Artillery was lined up hub to hub on all the roads around Exermont, Fleville and Sommerance and the machine guns of both divisions were to give them a sustained preparatory barrage. I may add incidentally that the thorough preparations for their attack were the best justification for our failure to reach the last objective. We heard the artillery hammering away through the early morning and it was soon evident that the sturdy infantry and marines of the 2nd Division had carried the battle line well towards the north.

I started up with Sergeant Fitzsimmons on my own sad quest of looking for our dead in the enemy wires. Just ahead of us as we passed through Sommerance a German shell lit on the road right in a party of five German prisoners and four American soldiers. The nine men lay scattered in all directions. We ran up and I found one of ours with both legs blown completely off trying to pull himself up with the aid of a packing case. In spite of his wounds he gave not the slightest evidence of mental shock. While Fitzsimmons ran for an ambulance, he told me his name was Conover, and that he was a Catholic, and said the prayers while I gave him absolution. He had no idea his legs were gone until a soldier lifted him on a stretcher, when I could see in his eyes that he was aware that his body was lifting light. He started to look but I placed my hand on his chest and kept him from seeing. Three men were dead already and it did not seem to me as if any one of them could live. One of the Germans was an officer who cursed his fate that brought him to this death by the fire of his own guns after lasting through four years of war.

When we reached our old battleground I found that one man had gotten there before me on the same errand as myself. It was Father Davitt of Lenox, Mass., who had been detached from the 32nd Division as Corps Chaplain.

On both sides of the Sommerance road as it neared the wire we saw the bodies scattered, still well preserved and recognizable by reason of the cool weather. Right around the wire and in the sunken road that ran into it the Germans had buried them. It was a surprise to find that even now the wire was absolutely unbroken in any place. An occasional shell had landed in it, as was evidenced by the holes made, but the whole fabric was so well bound together that it simply jumped up and then dropped back into place again. The 2nd Division had evidently been wise enough to carry their attack around it as I found just one of their dead and he was lying in the *chicane* or passage made by the highway as it passed through it.

I arranged with Father Davitt to have his detachment of Pioneers look after the sepulchre of our dead in case the Regiment got orders to move on, and returned to make my report to Colonel Dravo.

The 3rd Battalion got back to our place in the rear during the morning, having suffered some losses from shell fire, amongst them being Jimmy Fay, who had part of his foot blown off. Orders to take up the advance were received on November 2nd, our 3rd Battalion being out of the line less than 24 hours.

The first day's route laid down for us showed us that we were going to take over in the region to the west of that in which we had been fighting. In the plans for the attack of the 2nd Division they had moved rapidly towards the NNE., leaving the Germans on their left to wake up and find themselves in a salient between our troops and the northern extension of the Argonne Forest. The 78th Division was engaged in expediting the evacuation of these Germans. Two days' march, neither of them very long, brought us to Brieulles, just north of which we were to relieve the 78th. The only difficulty about the march was for the wagons. Every outfit had lost half of its animals, and those that were left were in miserable condition. The artillery felt this hardest, but it made trouble for the infantry, too, in getting up the supplies and the kitchens. The worn down roads were frightfully crowded with am-

bulances, trucks, kitchens, guns, caissons, ration and combat wagons, headquarters automobiles; and the M. Ps. were
kept swearing till their voices gave out trying to keep traffic conditions tolerable. When we got to Brieulles we found
that the Germans were blowing up bridges and roads in
their retreat. Colonel Dravo, following tradition and his
own generous instincts of being nice to an old fellow like
me, had sent me on with his car; and Brown was carrying me rapidly out of Brieulles towards the front when
Major Doyle, our Brigade Adjutant, stopped me and said
that while it didn't matter much what became of me, cars
were getting scarce and he had decided objections to presenting what was once a perfectly good car to the Germans.
I deduced from this that the enemy were in the next town
and that I had better stay where I was. The regiment was
stopped at Authé, to which place I returned.

The villages which the Germans had left had a number of
civilians, and in accordance with the order of the German
Commander, the Mayors put a white flag on the church
steeple to warn us against shelling them. I have never seen
a happier lot of old people in my life than the French civilians whom we were instrumental in saving after four
years of captivity. At Authé our P. C. was in what had
once been a village inn. The proprietress was old and little and lively and pious. She gave a warm reception to
M. l'Aumonier when she heard that I belonged to the Old
Church, and immediately proceeded to make plans for a
High Mass next Sunday in spite of my telling her that we
would not probably be there more than one night. "I have
been doing most of the preaching to the people around here
the last four years," she said. "M. le Curé is old and quiet
and he hasn't much to say; but me, I talk, talk, talk all the
time. I tell these people that God sent the German Devils
amongst them because of their sins. I preach so much that
they have given me a nickname. Do you know what they
call me? They call me Madame Morale. And I preach to
the Germans, too. I tell them they will all be in Hell if they

do not mend their ways." "What do they say to you?" "Most times they laugh and call me Grossmutter, but some of them swear and get mad. But I preach at them just the same. My sister she does not preach, she just prays."

I went up to see the sister. They must have been both around eighty; and she sat in her chair looking absolutely like Whistler's picture of his mother, except that the hands were not idle in her lap, but fingered unceasingly a worn rosary.

Madame Morale's piety was not limited to preaching. It included hospitality. We have brought along some fresh supplies of food for our Headquarters Mess; and as soldiers from different outfits kept drifting in to the kitchen looking for water and incidentally anything else they could get, the old lady dipped into our scanty stock, saying, "Here, my poor boys, there is much food here"—until nothing was left.

In going into action in this last phase of the Argonne fight Lieutenant Colonel Charles Dravo was in command, with Major Anderson second in command, Captain Merle-Smith (vice Kelly, evacuated with fever) commanding the 1st Battalion, Captain Henry A. Bootz, in charge of Anderson's Battalion, and Major Reilley with the 3rd. We relieved the 78th Division at the village of Artaise-le-Vivier. Here the Germans had left in such a hurry that large stores of flour and vegetables had been left behind. On asking the inhabitants the reason for this extraordinary occurrence we were answered by the word *"Avions."* In this sector we have absolute mastery of the air and we see vast flights of planes spread out like wild ducks in V-shaped fashion advancing over the German lines. I almost sympathize with the poor Boches, for I certainly do not like aerial bombs.

The next three days was a foot-race, each battalion taking its turn in the lead as the others became exhausted They swept from village to village, or rather from hill to hill, carefully closing around the villages, generally meeting with but little resistance, the last of the Germans, invariably a machine gun group, taking their flight fifteen minutes to a half hour before our men could get up. Colonel Dravo was out in the front with his wild Irish, while Anderson had the equally important task of trying to get the kitchens and supplies through. Lieutenants Schwinn, McDermott, Goodell, Henry and Bell and Sergeant Scanlan labored night and day to get the kitchens through, crossing muddy fields and fording small streams because the roads were everywhere destroyed. Lieutenant Seidelman and Corporal Malone were busy putting up signs at every corner to guide the rear elements in the right direction to reach our swiftly moving advance.

I missed Major Lawrence, who is generally very much in evidence when action is on, but I discovered that he had very wisely made up his mind that the main thing was to see that the ambulances found a way to follow up the Infantry. He had plenty of willing doctors under him to look after any wounded men in the field, but it was evident by the rate our Infantry was traveling that wounded men would not be evacuated for several days unless the ambulances got through. When finally they were needed, he had them there, both for the use of our men and those of other outfits which had not been so carefully provided for.

For two days the advance was an interesting race. The 6th Division was coming up the road behind ours, anxious to get a chance to relieve us and get into line before the war would come to an end. Each night they thought that surely by morning they would catch up; but our lads, moving freely across the open country, always kept well in advance of troops that had to move by column; and each day they were still further in the van. Our own Mess Sergeants and Cooks labored night and day to get the food forward, but for two days and more they, too, were left behind in the race. The men in front were not left entirely hungry, as in every village from which they drove the enemy the inhabitants drew out all of their scanty stores and served them with coffee, vegetables and a little bread, with unlimited supplies of bouquets and kisses. In spite of drawbacks it was a nice war.

At 10:30 on the evening of the 6th, there came a most extraordinary order from Corps through Division that it was imperative that Sedan should be captured before the end of the next day; that if troops were resting they should be immediately aroused and sent on their way; and that the city should be taken if the last officer and man should drop in his tracks. Luckily for the men it took some time to get that order forward to the line, as the horses of Jack Percy, Earl Pierce and young Underwood were fatigued by the incessant work, in which their riders shared, of carrying messages night and day. So the kitchens got through and the men were fed before they started out once more.

On November 7th, Bootz with the 2nd Battalion was in the van. On Hill 332 the Germans put up a stronger resistance than they had hitherto shown; and it came at a time when our fire was growing weak on account of the expenditure of ammunition, which there was little means of replacing. Bootz told Captain Stout, who was in command of G Company, that the hill must be taken, and Stout advanced with thirty-eight men of his own company and a detachment from Company H to capture the hill. As they kept crawling in on the Germans the latter began to waver, and the Captain called on his followers to advance upon them with fixed bayonets. With a great cheer our fellows swarmed up the crest and the daunted Germans, after a futile stand, grounded their guns, threw up their hands and surrendered. The men whose names stand high in the Company annals for this deed are, first of all, the dead: John Danker, George Spiegel, Onefrio Triggiano and Raymond Hawkins. Also the gallant captain and Lieutenant Otto; First Sergeant Meagher, Sergeants Martin Murphy, Martin Shalley, Irving Framan, Denis Corcoran, John Brogan and Francis Malloy, the two latter being wounded; James Regan, Thomas Gallagher, Hilbert and Henry, Remington, Youmans and Leavensworth, and, to complete the list, a bold Choctaw Indian with the martial name of Mc-Coy. Sergeant Patrick Travers, of Company H, received high praise from everybody. While the German resistance was still determined, he went alone against a machine gun on the right and captured it single-handed, taking three German officers and four men.

The same day B Company lost Sergeant Ed. Kramer, and Martin Gilfoyle; C Company, Frank Casserly, Michael Golinski, and Joseph Peressine; Company E, Orliff Gilbert, Samuel Kelly and William Lambert; Machine Gun Company, William Gunnell; and the Sanitary Detachment, Michael Cavanaugh.

Meanwhile events were happening which made the order to advance without ceasing seem more extraordinary. Elements of the 1st Division appeared on our flank and rear. They, too, had received orders to the same effect from their Corps Commander, and had advanced to the left across the front of the 77th Division, and were taking possession of our line, which was the one leading straight towards Sedan. They had crept up around Bulson in the morning, only to find General MacArthur and 84th Brigade Headquarters in possession of the village. Elements of the 16th Infantry now came on Bootz's hill and claimed it as theirs. "This is my hill, and my line of advance," said Bootz. "If you say it's yours, show your booty. I have twenty-five prisoners and twelve machine guns; what have you got to show for it?" And Bootz ordered his battalion to advance, leaving to the others to do what they would.

Nobody blamed the 1st Division for this mix-up, because they certainly had orders the same as ours to advance and capture Sedan. The whole thing is a mystery. A staff officer told me that neither of us had any right here, as Sedan lies in the sector of the French Division on our left, and considering what it means to the French, they are certainly the ones who have the best right to capture it.

In this sector we had a visit from Sergeant Alexander

Woollcott, who is well known in New York as a dramatic critic, and who has been assigned by G. H. Q. to the duties of reporter for the *Stars and Stripes*. He is always on hand when there is trouble, and the field of war becomes a pleasant place for me whenever he is there. We have swapped stories and discussed men and books in the weirdest places. He is communicative rather than inquisitive and one never thinks of him as a reporter, but he gets all the information he wants and all the more effectively because there is no appearance of seeking it. He can even make Anderson talk.

During this period Anderson had been forging ahead with his Headquarters group, expecting to find Bootz in Chaumont. He entered that town with a couple of doctors, Lieutenant Rerat, and his liaison men, only to find that they were the first to get there, and the enemy had not yet completely evacuated it. They were under rifle fire as they came along the street, and had a merry little sniper's battle before they got possession. Then Lieutenant McCarthy set up his one-pound cannon on the edge of the village, and soon had the German gunners putting for safety over the hill. So Anderson captured a town for himself, and for once did Colonel Dravo out of the bouquets and kisses. Though, even here, Rerat got the cream of it.

We kept going through that day, the 3rd Battalion relieving the 2nd during the night, and reaching on November 8th, the village of Wadelincourt on the heights of the Meuse, directly overlooking Sedan. A patrol from Company M with orders to go down to the Meuse and scout up to the suburbs of Sedan, got nearest of all American troops to that famous city. Eighteen men started out, of whom most were wounded, but Corporal John McLaughlin, with two men, carried out the mission and reported the results of the reconnaissance. Under shell fire that night Albert Bieber and Carl Maritz of Company I were killed and Lieutenant Behrendts, the Company Commander, and many others were wounded. James P. Smith of Company

M was also killed and Sergeant Lester Lenhart of Company E was mortally wounded.

That night our Division was relieved by the 40th French Division, which from the beginning had the right of way. As a matter of courtesy the French Division Commander invited a company of the 165th and 166th to enter with his troops for the occupation of the suburbs of Sedan. Company D of our regiment was selected for the purpose and Lieutenant Cassidy had them all ready, but through some mix-up of orders they were not called upon to share in the little ceremony.

On November 8th we marched back to Artaise and the next day to Les Petites Armoises; on the 10th, to Vaux-en-Dieulet. The 11th found us at Sivry-les-Buzancy, where we spent two days.

On our way in I got a rumor that the Armistice was signed. I had always believed that the news of victory and peace would fill me with surging feelings of delight. But it was just the contrary; no doubt because the constraint I had put upon my natural feelings during the year were taken off by the announcement. I knew that in New York and in every city at home and throughout the world men were jubilant at the prospects of peace. But I could think of nothing except the fine lads who had come out with us to this war and who are not alive to enjoy the triumph. All day I had a lonely and an aching heart. It would be a lesser thing to have been killed myself than to go back to the mothers of the dead who would never more return. Luckily for me my dear friend Chaplain Nash came over to see me and walked me for hours through the desolate country, encouraging me to express my every feeling until fatigue and the relief of expression brought me back to a more normal mood.

The men had no certainty that the rumors were true, and discounted them. On November 13th we marched to Landres et Saint Georges which we had striven vainly to enter from the other side five weeks before. The village was almost completely demolished and our troops with others of the Division pitched their shelter tents on all the hills surrounding the town. That night official information was given of the Armistice. The men raided the Engineer and Signal Stores for rockets of all descriptions and the whole sky was filled with lights which in war would have demanded the expenditure of at least a million shells. Bonfires were blazing all over the hillside *Finie la Guerre*. The war was over.

My duties, like my feelings, still lay in the past. With men from all the companies I went round the battlefield to pay as far as I could my last duties to the dead, to record and in a rough way to beautify their lonely graves, for I knew that soon we would leave this place that their presence hallows, and never look upon it again.

On the 15th, in accordance with Division orders, a formal muster was held. Our strength was 55 officers and 1,637 men, with 8 officers and 43 men attached, 1,300 short of the number we had brought into the Argonne. Of the survivors, not many more than 600 were men who had left New York with the regiment a little over a year ago. And most of these belonged to the Adjutant's Office, Battalion and Company Headquarters, Kitchens, Band and Supply Company. In the line companies, there are about twenty-five rifle men to each company who are old-timers and nearly all of these have wound stripes earned in earlier engagements. The great bulk of the old regiment is in hospitals, convalescent and casual camps; some of them promoted, some transferred, hundreds of them invalided home, a great many, alas! buried on battlefields or in hospital cemeteries.

CHAPTER X

WITH THE ARMY OF OCCUPATION

On the 16th we took to the road again, happy at the thought that the Rainbow Division had received the honor of being chosen as part of the Army of Occupation. At the end of the first day's march our Headquarters were at Baalon. Crossing the Meuse at Duns sur Meuse I ran into Hogstrom and Mullen of Company C, whom I had thought dead, but who had been captured by the Germans in the wire on the night of October 14th. They had been well used, they said, except for the fact that there was little to eat. We crossed the Belgian frontier on the morning of November 21st at the village of Fagny, which was all decorated up like Old Home Day. The village band—a nondescript outfit—played us into town. The people had made out of dress material American flags, or rather well-meant attempts at them, as five or six stripes and a dozen stars was about as near as they could come to it. After crossing the border we received a new commanding officer in the person of Colonel Charles R. Howland, a regular army man who had a regiment in the 86th Division. When that Division was broken up for replacement purposes, he was assigned to fill the vacancy in ours. About the same time Colonel Henry J. Reilly, who had been ably handling our brigade during the past five weeks, was superseded by General F. M. Caldwell, U. S. A. Colonel Reilly returned to the command of the 149th F. A.

As we crossed Belgium at its southmost tip, we made only a two days' job of it, headquarters being at Ste. Marie on November 21st and at Thiaumont November 22nd. My chief impressions were of a clean, orderly, prosperous country as compared with the ruined parts of France, and a very intelligent curé in whose house I stopped at Ste. Marie. When we passed the borders of the Grand Duchy of Luxembourg at Oberpollen on the 22nd there were no brass bands to greet us. The inhabitants were civil and pleasant but they adopted a correct attitude towards us as foreigners crossing through their territory. Most of the regiment was billetted, and rather well accommodated, at Useldingen, a comfortable town with a fine new parish church. Here we stayed until the 1st of December, till arrangements could be made for our passage into Germany. We are part of the Third Army now, and the Third Army has been organized on a shoestring. It cannot be said to be functioning very well, and the system of supplies and equipment is not in good shape. We have gotten a good deal of equipment—and we never needed it worse than after leaving the Argonne—but there are many old and ill-fitting shoes, which makes hiking a torture for the men.

The principal sight of Useldingen is the ruins of a very extensive medieval castle, standing on an elevation in the middle of the town. I wandered through it with Vandy Ward and Read of H. Q. Co., trying with the aid of the Curé to get an idea of its original plan and the sort of life that was led there by other soldiers a thousand years ago.

Thanksgiving Day came round while we were here and everybody worked to celebrate it in proper fashion. There is a fair supply of food in the country, though one has to pay high prices for it, all the higher because the national currency is in marks and the people demand the old rate of 100 francs for 80 marks. But, like all Americans, we want what we want when we want it, so the canny Luxembourgeois get what they ask for. Our religious services were in thanksgiving for peace. In the church we had a solemn high mass and Te Deum and I preached, Father Hanley singing the Mass. As Chaplain Holmes had not yet returned, I unfrocked myself of my papistical robes and went out to hold general services in the romantic courtyard of the old Schloss, using a breach in the fortifications as a pulpit. My friend Chaplain Halliday of the Ohios came along and added a few words in his earnest, sensible style.

There is great joy in the regiment, for Captain Hurley is back. He looks thin and none too fit, and I know he is with us, not because the hospital authorities thought that he should be, but through his own strong desire and pleading eloquence. We had a visit from Donovan also—on crutches. The Provost Marshal General had him transferred to his department while he was in the hospital, and now he is touring the country in a car, performing his new services. It is not a bad sort of a job at all—with headquarters in Paris, and a chance to tour all over France in a first-class automobile, with the best billets and the best food wherever he goes—but not for Donovan. No one of our enlisted men marooned in a casual camp with a lot of absolute strangers ever uttered with greater longing and pathos the formula, "I want to be back with my old outfit." For Donovan's case I shall omit the pathos. When that young man wants anything very bad he gets it. I expect to see him back on duty with us in a very, very brief time.

My mail is a very full one these days. All of our old-timers back in hospitals and camps are clamoring to return to the regiment, and they think that if I only speak to somebody, a word from me will manage it. I went to Mersch to see my ever kind friend, Colonel Hughes, our Divisional Chief of Staff, to inquire if some general arrangement could not be made for the return of all men in combat divisions who had been evacuated from the line through wounds or sickness. I found that he was doing everything that he possibly could to get our Rainbow fellows back, and he promised to work for an order along the lines I proposed.

The regiment marched on the 1st of December, Headquarters passing the night at Mersch; and on December 2nd to Waldbillig. December 3rd was the day on which we finally accomplished what we had started out to do—make our invasion of Germany. We crossed the border by a bridge over the Sauer river into the village of Bollendorf. Captain John Mangan, who had come to the regiment on business from the 2nd Army, George Boothby of the New York *World* and myself crossed the bridge ahead of the others, very curious to see what reception we would get in the land of the enemy. The first indication of the sort of reception we were to have came from an invitation from an old farmer and his wife whose house stood at the end of the bridge to step inside and have a glass of schnapps; when we prudently declined this, we were offered apples, but not being there as visitors, we felt it proper to say no. The proffered kindnesses were inspired partly no doubt by a desire to propitiate, but nobody could doubt that it was largely the decent impulse of a nice old couple. We rejoined the regiment for the march across.

The column came down along the river, the band in front playing "The Yanks Are Coming" and, as we turned to cross the bridge, the lively regimental tune of "Garry Owen." In front of us, above the German hill, there was a beautiful rainbow. As we marched triumphantly onto German soil, nothing more hostile greeted us than the click of a moving-picture camera. Every soldier in the line was glowing with happiness except myself, perhaps. On occasions like this of glory and excitement my mind has a habit of going back to the lads that are gone.

We marched, with advance and rear guards, as if entering a hostile country, our first stop being at Holsthum. We had hopes that our line of march would take us down the Moselle Valley towards Coblenz, but instead we struck off to the north and northeast, through the rough Eiffel country, along mountain roads that were badly worn down by the traffic of war. Our Headquarters for December 5th, 6th, 7th, 8th and 9th were Blickendorf, Wallerschein, Hillesheim (a romantic spot), Weisbaum and, after a desperate hike, Wershofen.

The greatest surprise of our first week in Germany was the attitude of the people towards us. We had expected to be in for an unpleasant experience, and I have no doubt that some of our fellows had a picture of themselves moving around in German villages with loaded rifle and fixed bayonet ready to repel treacherous attacks. We were received very peacefully, one might almost say, cordially. Farmers in the fields would go out of the way to put us on the right road, children in the villages were as friendly and curious as youngsters at home; the women lent their utensils and often helped soldiers with their cooking, even offering stuff from their small stores when the hungry men arrived far ahead of their kitchens. There were many German soldiers in these towns still wearing the uniform (they would be naked otherwise), and they, too, were interested, curious, almost friendly. Some of them had been against us in battle, and with the spirit of veterans in all times and places, they struck up conversation with our men, fighting the battles over again and swapping lies. I talked with the priests in the different towns—one of them a Chaplain just returned from the Eastern front. Like all the others that we meet, they say that their country had the French and British licked if we had stayed out; to which I make the very obvious retort that they had followed a very foolish policy when they dragged us in.

But it is only occasionally that this note is struck, the attitude of most people being that the war is over and they are glad of it. In fact, a surprising number have wanted to have it over for a considerable time past. No doubt the historical background of life in these countries makes them able to take defeat with more philosophy than we could ever muster up if foreign troops were to occupy our country. As for us, we are here in the rôle of victors, and our soldiers are willing to go half way and accept the attitude that for them also (unless somebody wants to start something) the war is a past issue.

Civilians hold grudges, but soldiers do not; at least the soldiers who do the actual fighting. The civilian mind is fed up on all sorts of stories about atrocities, most of which I believe are fabricated to arouse decent human beings up to the point of approving of this rotten business of war. We fought the Germans two long tricks in the trenches and in five pitched battles and they never did anything to us that we did not try to do to them. And we played the game as fairly as it can be played. We followed their retreat through three sectors, in two of which they had been for years, and we never witnessed at first hand any of the atrocities we read about. A church burned at St. Benoit without any good military reason that I could see; the shelling of the hospital in Villers sur Fere, in which case there was no way for them to know it was a hospital; some valuables piled up for carrying away—that is the whole indictment. But no crucified soldiers, no babies with their hands cut off, no girls outraged in trenches, to provoke our soldiers to rush on to death to rescue them, no poisoned food or wells (except of course through gas shells) no women chained to machine guns, and no prisoners playing treachery.

In the invaded territory of France we found plenty of evidence of harsh military occupation. It was bad at its best, and some local commanders made it more intolerable. The people were taxed without much to show for their money, forced to work for little or no pay, rationed rather slenderly though with enough to sustain strength, had to put up with requisitions of animals, houses and some minor property, such as linen and copper down to bedsheets and the brass knobs off the stoves. They were also dragooned about to various places to do work for their conquerors. I heard plenty of tales in Eastern France and Belgium of terrible experiences and unwarranted executions during the first couple of weeks of the German occupation from witnesses whose word I believe absolutely. After the civilians were thoroughly cowed these atrocities ceased, though many of the lesser hardships of military occupation persevered during the four years.

Most of the French and Belgians told me (though some voiced suspicions to the contrary) that the Germans saw to it strictly that none of their soldiers took the relief goods sent from America. One old lady told me that she had proof that all Germans were robbers; for they give her some patched clothing as coming from America and she knew that nobody in America would send over such stuff as that. It was hard to have to choose between being just and being loyal American. I refuse to state which attitude I took, but I am afraid that the dear old lady still thinks she has an argument to prove that the Boches are robbers.

At any rate, the older griefs of these people are for the soldiers who have come through an intense war experience, echoes of "Old unhappy far-off things, and battles long ago." They judge the German soldier by their own experience and by soldier standards. They do not fear him, they do not hate him, they do not depise him either. They respected him when he put up a good fight or made a clean getaway, and that was most of the time. It was a rare thing to hear a soldier in a combat division talk about "Huns." It was always the "Heinies," the "Jerries," the "Boches" or, simply the "Germans."

The fine spirit on the part of our troops was much better, even for military value, than hatred would have been. I cannot see that deep bitterness could have made them any bolder. It would only have made them less efficient. And the spirit is admirable in itself.

At any rate we were convinced from the beginning that our experiences as part of the army of occupation were not going to be as unpleasant as we expected.

Aside from the attitude of the people the things that strike us most are two. Putting the two into one, it is the number and the fatness of the children. There are few children on the streets in French villages; German villages swarm with youngsters. Our coming is like circus day and they are all out, especially the boys. Boys everywhere! And such sturdy little towheads—chubby is the word for the smaller ones. I do not know about the rest of Germany, but the Rhineland is certainly not starved. Perhaps, as in Belgium, it is the townspeople who do the suffering. These children wear patched clothing, but the clothing covers rounded bodies. We find it easy to purchase meals at rates that are astoundingly reasonable after our experience in other European countries. Germany lacks many things— edible bread, good beer, real coffee, kerosene, rubber, oil, soap and fats; and in the cities, no doubt, meat and milk. The people here say that they eat little meat, their sustenance being largely vegetable and based on the foundation of the potato. It scores another triumph for the potato.

But I would like to know how they fatten the children. With good advertising a man could make a fortune on it at home. German breakfast food for boys, with pictures of chubby young rascals playing around American soldiers. But perhaps Germans are plump by nature or divine decree, and it would not work with lantern-jawed Yanks like ourselves.

During this period Lieutenant Colonel Donovan returned to duty with us by direct orders of General Headquarters, Lieutenant Dravo going back to his duties as Division Machine Gun Officer, thus being still near enough to us to keep up the ties of friendship which he had established in the Regiment. We remained in Wershofen and surrounding villages for five days, during which time the equipment was gone over, animals rested and some attempt made to patch up the shoes of the men, which had been worn to nothing by hiking with heavy packs on rough roads. On December 14th, we marched through the picturesque valley of the Ahr river over a good road to Altenahr, the scenery of which looks as if it had been arranged by some artistic stage manager with an eye to picturesque effect. It is a summer resort country and we had the advantage of good hotels for billets. On December 15th, we marched through Ahrweiler, an old walled town which was to be our Division Headquarters, and Neuenahr, a modern summer resort place with good roads, commodious hotels and attractive shop windows, and thence to the Rhine, where, turning north about two kilometers, we entered the most pleasant and excellent town of Remagen-am-Rhein, which was to be our home for the next three or four months.

Remagen was already in existence in Roman days. It is a charming well-built place of 3,500 inhabitants, with a large parish church and also an Evangelical church and a synagogue. In addition, there is on the hillside a striking pilgrimage church attended by Franciscan Friars and dedicated to St. Apollinaris, with the Stations of the Cross built on the roadway leading up to it. The much advertised bottled waters which flow from a source near Neuenahr get their name from this shrine. Remagen has also a large convent, Annacloster, a hospital and a town hall, in front of which our daily guard mounts are held.

I am afraid, however, that these edifices for religious and municipal uses made less immediate appeal to our fellows than the fact that the town possessed a number of large and commodious hotels, some of them ample for a whole company. We immediately took possession of these as well as of stores, beer-gardens and extra rooms in private houses; the principle being that every soldier of ours should have a bed to sleep in, even if the German adult males had to go without. Donovan and I went on ahead to billet for Headquarters. We called on the Bürgermeister, a kindly, gentlemanly, educated man, who was anxious to do everything to make our stay in town a harmonious one. His assistant, an agreeable young man who had been in America for a couple of years and had every intention of going back, came along with us on our tour. We had our pick of two or three modern villas of grandiose type north of the town on the hillside, the only difficulty about them being that they were a little too far away.

At first two of our battalions were placed in mountain villages to the west, but after a week or so we had everybody accommodated in Remagen. I settled down with my gallant followers, Halligan and McLaughlin, in the house of the Bürgermeister, which faced on the river just north of the parish Church. My German is a very sad affair, but he speaks French and his wife English. They have three nice children, the oldest about twelve. I keep my relations with the parents as official as is possible, when one is dealing with gentlefolks, but if I am expected to avoid fraternizing with the youngsters, they will have to lock me up or shoot me. I had a conference with the Parish Priest, a sturdy personality who has his flock in good control, at my house the other day and we were talking four languages at once —German, French, English and Latin. But I worked out my plans for a Christmas celebration.

Christmas Mass on the Rhine! In 1916, our midnight mass was under the open sky along the Rio Grande; in 1917, in the old medieval church at Grand in the Vosges; and now, thank Heaven, in this year of grace, 1918, we celebrated it peacefully and triumphantly in the country with which we had been at war. Attendance was of course voluntary, but I think the whole regiment marched to the service with the band preceding them playing "Onward Christian Soldiers" and "Adeste Fideles." We took full possession of the Church, though many of the townsfolk came in, and when at the end, our men sang the hymn of Thanksgiving, "Holy God, we praise Thy name" the Germans swelled our chorus in their own language "Grosser Gott wir loben Dich." I preached on the theme "Can the war be ascribed to a failure on the part of Christianity?" I have been often irritated by ideas on this subject coming from leaders of thought who have given little place or opportunity to Christianity in their lives or projects. As Chesterton says: "Christianity has not been tried out and found wanting; Christianity has been tried—a little—and found difficult." Father Hanley sang the Mass, the Guard of Honor with the Colors being from Company K, with Captain Hurley in charge.

For the Company dinners I was able to supply ample funds through the never-ceasing generosity of our Board of Trustees in New York City, and funds also placed at my disposal which were sent by Mrs. Barend Van Gerbig through the Veteran Corps of the 69th New York. But in their purchase of food, the wily mess sergeants found that soap was a better medium of exchange than money.

During January and February the men were kept busy during the day in field training, infantry drill, range practice and athletics. Particular attention was paid to smartness of appearance and punctiliousness in soldierly bearing and courtesy. The weather was mild though often rainy. Coal was not too hard to procure and the billets were kept fairly comfortable. The regiment being all in one town there was a fine soldier atmosphere in the place. The townspeople are a kindly decent sort, but our fellows have enough society in themsleves and there is little fraternization, and none that is a source of any danger—there is more chance of our making them American in ideas than of their making us German.

The Welfare Societies are on the job with good accommodations. In the "Y" we have still Jewett and the ever faithful Pritchard and two or three devoted ladies, one of whom is Miss Dearing, a sister of Harry Dearing who was killed in the Argonne. Jim O'Hara of the K. of C. got the Parish Priest to give up his Jugendheim, a new building with large hall, bowling alleys, all the German Verein sort of thing. There is no lack of places to go or ways to spend an evening. Lieutenant Fechheimer took charge of athletics and we had brigade contests, and also with the Canadians, who were just to the left of the Ohios.

The 3rd Battalion has lost the service of Mr. Kelly of the "Y." When I first knew Mr. Kelly of the "Y" he was

Corporal Kelly of Company I, 69th Regiment, at McAllen, Texas, and was sometimes known, Irish fashon, as "Kelly the Lepper," as he was a famous runner. His eyes were not as good as his legs, so he was turned down for re-enlistment. Being determined to have a part in the war he got the "Y" to send him over as an athletic instructor and finally worked his way up to our regiment and was attached to the 3rd Battalion which includes his own company. The assignment was more to the advantage of the 3rd Battalion than of the Y. M. C. A. for Kelly gave away gratis everything he could wheedle, bully, or steal from the "Y" depot officials. When we reached the Rhine, things were too quiet for Kelly and he started off to visit his native town in Ireland. If I ever hear that somebody has gotten stores from the police barracks to equip the Sein Feiners, I shall know that Kelly the Lepper is on the job.

My own life is an altogether pleasant one. I have for my office a well furnished parlor on the ground floor of the Bürgermeister's house where I spend my mornings with Bill Halligan, mainly at the task of writing letters to soldiers who want to get back and to folks at home who ask news of their dear ones, living or dead. In the afternoons I float lazily around amongst the companies, just chatting and gossiping, and getting in a good deal of my work in my own way, sort of incidentally and on the side; or I drop in at headquarters and bother Captain Dick Allen and Jansen and Ed Farrell of the Personnel Department for correct data for my diary, or Ted Ranscht and Clarke for maps. Or I look in on the juvenile pro-consuls Springer and Allen to smile at the air of easy mastery with which they boss the German civilians into observing American Military Commands. My nights I spend at the building of the "Y" or K. of C. amongst the men, or at home, receiving numerous guests with a world of topics to discuss. It is an agreeable kind of existence, with no urgent duties except correspondence, and with the satisfaction of performing a not unimportant service without any feeling of labor, but merely by kindly and friendly intercourse. My orderly, "Little Mac," is having the time of his life. If I only had a car for him to drive me around in, as Tom Gowdy did in Texas, he would never want to go home to the Bronx.

Father Hanley was made director of amusements and was kept busy providing entertainment five nights a week from our own and other Divisions for the two large halls conducted by the Y. M. C. A. and the K. of C., a task which he accomplished as he does everything—to complete satisfaction.

One thing that astonished everybody in this New York regiment was the number of illiterates amongst replacements from the Southern States. We had two hundred men who could not sign their names to the pay-roll. A strong movement was started throughout the American Expeditionary Forces after the Armistice to teach such men to read and write, and the simplest problems in arithmetic, as well as to give a better knowledge of English to foreign born soldiers. In our regiment this task was confided to Chaplain Holmes, who went at it with his usual devotion to duty and attention to details, so that Chaplain Nash who was Divisional School Officer told me that the educational work in the 165th was by far the best in the Division.

I had many examples of the need of schooling for certain of the men. Many of our recent replacements had been kept going from place to place and had not received pay in months. Whenever I heard of such cases I advanced them money from our Trustee's Fund. One evening three of our old-timers came to my billet to borrow some money to have a little party, but I had to tell them that my stock of francs was cleaned out. Just then a fine big simple fellow from the Tennessee mountains came in to return the money I had loaned him. "How much do you owe me?" I asked. "Thirty-seven francs. "All right, hand it over to these fellows here." "Well, I reckon I'd rather pay you." After a certain amount of joking about it, it dawned upon my slow intelligence that the poor fellow was embarrassed by not being able to count money, so I took him into another room and tried to teach him how much change he should have out of a fifty franc note.

The efforts of our generous friends in New York in supplying funds were much appreciated by the whole regiment. We had been in line for months and the men were seldom paid. Even when pay-day came those who were absent in hospital, or those who had been absent when the pay-roll was signed, got nothing. The funds were left absolutely at my disposal, and I knew from the calibre of our Trustees that it was their wish that they should be disbursed in a generous spirit. Many of our bright sergeants were started off to Officer's School without a sou in their pockets. I believed that our New York backers would like to have the best men of our regiment able to hold up their heads in any crowd, so I saw that every one of them had fifty or a hundred francs in his pocket before starting. When I could be sure of addresses, I sent money to men in hospitals and in casual camps. While the regiment was in line money was no use to anybody, as there was absolutely nothing to buy, not even an egg or a glass of wine, but here in Germany, with shops and eating houses open, my cash was a real boon, and I did not hesitate to disburse it.

Just after the armistice, with the prospect that leaves might at last be granted, I sent to our trustees a bold request for $20,000.00, to guarantee the men a real holiday. When the permissions for leaves came, I found that in most cases this money was not needed, as the long deferred pay gave most of the men sufficient money of their own. So I devoted a generous amount of it to help finance the company dinners which were gotten up on a metropolitan scale in the hotels of Remagen. These were joyous affairs— feasts of song and story-telling and speech-making. Colonel Donovan and I made it a practice to attend them all, and he got in many a strong word on spirit and discipline which had better results in that environment than could have been produced on a more formal occasion. Father Hanley was always a favorite at these gatherings as he handed out the latest rumors (which he himself had manufactured), discoursed on the superiority of Cleveland over New York, and of the 3rd Battalion over any other bunch of fighting men in the whole universe. It was a part of my share in the function to speak on the good men in the Company that had paid the great price; and it is a tribute to the loyalty and steadfastness of human nature to see how the merry-makers would pause in their enjoyment to pay the tribute of a sigh or a tear to the memory of their companions of the battlefield who were absent from their triumph.

Our winter on the Rhine was our happiest period in the whole war. First and foremost the regiment was all together in one place; and companionship is by far the biggest element of satisfaction in a soldier's life. The men had good warm billets and most of them had beds to sleep on. The food was substantial and plentiful, though, for that matter, I think we were at all times the best fed army that ever went to war. There were periods of starvation in battles, but the main difficulty was even then in getting it from the kitchen to the men in line.

The men had enough work to do to keep them in good healthy condition and to prevent them from becoming discontented; but all in all, it was an easy life. All of the old-timers got a chance to go off on leave, most of them choosing Paris, the Riviera, or Ireland. Short excursions to Coblenz by rail or river were given to everybody.

Our band had a prominent part in adding to the pleasures of life. Bandmaster Ed. Zitzman had returned from school, and he with the Drum Major John Mullin and Sergeants Jim Lynch and Paddy Stokes made frequent demands on me for funds to purchase music and extra instruments. In France I had bought sixteen *clairons* or trumpets for the Company buglers to play with the Band. Here on the Rhine I bought other instruments, including orchestral ones, so we were well supplied for field or chamber music. Lieutenant Slayter took charge of the Band in matters of discipline and march time, with excellent results.

One of the greatest of our successes during this period was the 165th Minstrels, organized by Major Lawrence, always active in everything for the good of the men. After having scored a distinct hit at home and throughout the Division, they went on a tour through the Army of Occupation, and were booked to go back through France if we had remained longer abroad. The performers were: *Interlocutor,* William K. McGrath; *End Men,* Harry Mallen, Thomas McCardle, Harold Carmody, Edward Finley, and Charles Woods; *Soubrettes,* Robert Harrison, James O'Keefe, James F. O'Brien, William O'Neill, James Mack, Melvin King, and John McLaughlin; *Chorus:* Charles Weinz, Edward Smith, John Brawley, John Ryan, John Zimmerman, John Mullins, Thomas O'Kelly, Eugene Eagan, Walter Hennessey, Peter Rogers, William Yanss, Clinton Rice, Thomas Donohue, Chester Taylor, Sylvester Taylor, James Kelly, Charles Larson, with T. Higginbotham as strong man and Milton Steckels as contortionist.

The health of the command has been excellent, although since we have come into civilized parts we have developed a certain amount of pneumonia which we escaped while living in the hardships of the Argonne. Since leaving Baccarat I know of only two of our men who have died from other than battle causes; Private Myers of the Machine Gun Company was drowned in the Marne in August and John E. Weaver of Company L died during the same month of illness. In Germany we lost Corporal Patrick McCarthy, Company E, died of pneumonia October 20th, W. J. Silvey of Company D, James Kalonishiskie and Robert Clato of M, James C. Vails of H, Corporal Joseph M. Seagriff, James O'Halloran, Charles Nebel and Terrence McNally of Supply Company, Emery Thrash and George Sanford of L, Carl Demarco of F, and one of the best of our Sergeants, John B. Kerrigan of Headquarters Company.

Our only grievances were the difficulties of getting back our old officers and men, and the stoppage of promotions for officers after the Armistice. Every day my mail had a number of letters from soldiers all over France asking me to get them back to the Regiment; and work on this line constituted my greatest occupation. Many of the men took the matter in their own hands and worked their way across France, dodging M. P.'s, stealing rides on trucks and trains, begging meals from kindly cooks and nice old French ladies, and finally, if their luck held out, getting back amongst their own. Others were returned by a more legitimate route, until, by the time we left the Rhine we had nearly fourteen hundred men who belonged to the original command.

A large number of our officers had been recommended, some of them over and over again, for promotion, and had not received it on account of wounds which kept them in hospitals when the promotion might have come through. And now they were barred from receiving the rank which they had earned on the battlefield, the vacancies being filled by replacements. Some of these replacement officers made themselves a warm place in the heart of the regiment especially Major James Watson, who joined us in Luxembourg and was put in command of the 3rd Battalion; and also an old friend of ours from the 12th New York, Major Jay Zorn, who was with us for a short time.

Finally this legitimate grievance was settled in the most ample and satisfactory fashion. Lieutenant Colonel Donovan was made Colonel, and placed in command of the regiment, Colonel Howland going to take charge of a leave area in France. Major Anderson was made Lieutenant Colonel, and Bootz, Meaney and Merle-Smith Majors. There were also a number of promotions to the rank of Captain both in the line companies and in the Sanitary Detachment. There were two other men that we all felt should have gotten their majority, but when the original recommendations were made they were both suffering from wounds in hospitals with no seeming prospects of ever getting back to the regiment. These two were Captain John P. Hurley and Captain Richard J. Ryan, who also, to everybody's great delight, rejoined us on this river (which we call *the Ryan river*) though still in a doubtful state of health.

Many of these promotions came after Donovan's accession to the command and through his energetic efforts. He also made use of every possible means through official and private channels, to get back every officer and man of the Old Regiment that was able to come. First and foremost amongst these was Lieutenant Colonel Timothy J. Moynahan, who left us in Baccarat as a Major and had won his Lieutenant Colonelcy as well as a D. S. C. and a Croix de Guerre with the 37th Division. Jack Mangan, now Major Mangan, came back from 2nd Army Headquarters. We had an abundance of majors though we had lost one of them—Major Tom Reilley, who had been sent home much against his will for a promotion which he never received, just after the fighting was over.

We also got back a lot of happy lieutenants who had gone to officers Candidate Schools, and had been commissioned in other Divisions, the happiest of the lot, I think, being Leo Larney, a fine athlete and a fine man. We had often recommended men for promotion in the regiment but had been successful in very few cases. Sergeant Thomas McCarthy was commissioned after the Ourcq; and later on Sergeants Patrick Neary and John J. Larkin were sent back to us from school as sergeants because the war started too soon after they left Ireland. When facilities for becoming citizens were extended to men in their case, they received their commissions in the regiment, and both did remarkable work in the Argonne. Sergeant Frank Johnston of Company E was for a long time an officer without knowing it, as his commission had been sent to his home address.

Colonel Donovan also inaugurated a series of little entertainments and dinners, inviting the leading officers of other regiments in the Division to partake of our Metropolitan Hibernian hospitality. Everybody in the Division likes Donovan, and they were as much delighted as we when he finally got command of the Regiment that he had so often led in action. One of our greatest friends is Colonel John Johnson of the Engineers, a manly forthright two-fisted South Carolinian; we delight also in verbal encounter with Colonel Henry Reilly of the 149 Field Artillery, a man of wide experience, unlimited mental resources, and agile wit. The other three infantry colonels Hough, Screws and Tinley have been with the Division from the beginning and our interchange of visits with them will be always one of the pleasantest recollections of the campaign.

We celebrated St. Patrick's Day on the Rhine in the best approved manner with religion, games and feasting. My altar was set up in a field beside the river. The theme for my discourse was the debt that the world owes to the sons of Saint Patrick for their fight for civil and religious liberty at home and abroad, with the prayer that that debt might now be squared by the bestowal of liberty on the Island from whence we sprung.

The day before Saint Patrick's Day the whole Division was reviewed by the Commander-in-Chief, General Pershing, at Remagen. It was a note-worthy military ceremony in an appropriate setting, by the banks of that river of historic associations. When he came to our regiment the eyes of General Pershing were taken by the silver furls which covered the staff of our flag from the silk of the colors to the lowest tip. In fact, that staff is now in excess of the regulation length, as we had to add an extra foot to it to get on the nine furls that record our battles in this war. "What Regiment is this?" he asked. "The 165th Infantry, Sir." "What Regiment was it?" "The 69th New York, Sir." "The 69th New York. I understand now."

This visit was the final hint that our stay was not to be long. The whole Division got together to organize the

Rainbow Division Veterans which we did at an enthusiastic and encouragingly contentious meeting at Neuenahr.

When the orders finally came for our return to America I received them with a joy that was tinged with regret that the associations of the past two years were to be broken up. They had been years full of life and activity, and take them all in all, years of happiness. There never was a moment when I wanted to be any place other than I was. There were times of great tragedy, of seeing people killed and of burying my dearest friends, but all that was part of the tragedy of our generation. It would not have been any less if I were not present, and it was some consolation to be where I could render some little comfort to the men who had to go through them and to the relatives of those who paid the big price.

The sense of congenial companionship more than makes up for the hardships incidental to a campaign. What I am going to miss most is the friendships I have formed. In a very special degree I am going to miss Donovan. Nearly every evening we take our walk together along the river road that parallels the Rhine. It is the very spot which Byron selected for description in Childe Harold. The Rhine turns sharply to the right to make its way through the gorge of the Siebengebirge. "The castled crag of Drachenfels" looks down upon the peaceful cloistered isle of Nonnenwerth, upon pleasant villages and vineyard terraces and beautiful villas which, with the majestic river, make the scene one of the most beautiful in the world.

The companionship makes it all the more attractive. This young Buffalo lawyer who was suddenly called into the business of war, and has made a name for himself throughout the American Expeditionary Forces for outstanding courage and keen military judgment, is a remarkable man. As a boy he reveled in Thomas Francis Meagher's "Speech on the Sword," and his dream of life was to command an Irish brigade in the service of the Republic. His dream came true, for the 69th in this war was larger than the

Irish Brigade ever was. But it did not come true by mere dreaming. He is always physically fit, always alert, ready to do without food, sleep, rest, in the most matter of fact way, thinking of nothing but the work in hand. He has mind and manners and varied experience of life and resoluteness of purpose. He has kept himself clean and sane and whole for whatever adventure life might bring him, and he has come through this surpassing adventure with honor and fame. I like him for his alert mind and just views and ready wit, for his generous enthusiasms and his whole engaging personality. The richest gain I have gotten out of the war is the friendship of William J. Donovan.

That is the way I talk about him to myself. When we are together we always find something to fight about. One unfailing subject of discussion is which of us is the greater hero. That sounds rather conceited, and all the more so when I say that each of us sticks up strongly for himself. Those infernal youngsters of ours have been telling stories about both of us, most of which, at least those that concern myself, attest the loyalty of my friends better than their veracity. There is only one way to take it—as a joke. If either of us gets a clipping in which his name is mentioned he brandishes it before company under the nose of the other challenging him to produce some proof of being as great a hero. The other day Captain Ryan gave Donovan an editorial about him from a paper in Watertown, N. Y. It was immediately brought to mess, and Donovan thought he had scored a triumph, but I countered with a quotation from a letter which said that my picture, jewelled with electric lights, had a place of honor in the window of a saloon on 14th Street. Donovan surrendered.

I got a letter from Tom Reilley, who is back in New York, and disgusted with life because he is no longer with us; and he gave me some choice ammunition. "Father Duffy," he said, "You are certainly a wonderful man. Your press agents are working overtime. Recently you have been called the 'Miracle Man,' thus depriving George

Stallings of the title. In the newspaper league you have Bill Donovan beat by 9,306 columns. I wish you would tell me, How do you wade through a stream of machine gun bullets? And that little stunt of yours of letting high explosive shells bounce off your chest—you could make your fortune in a circus doing that for the rest of your life."

It is all very amusing now, but it is going to be extremely embarrassing when we get back amongst civilians where people take these things too seriously. They kept me too long as a professor of metaphysics to fit me for the proper enjoyment of popularity. Donovan says that after his final duties to the regiment are finished he is going to run away from it all and go off with his wife on a trip to Japan.

On April the second we boarded our trains for Brest—the first leg on the way home. We had a happy trip across France in the most comfortably arranged troop trains that Europe ever saw; remained three or four days at Brest, and sailed for Hoboken, the regiment being split up on two ships. Our headquarters and the first six companies were on the *Harrisburg,* formerly the *City of Paris* in the American Line. Jim Collintine used to sail on it and is very enthusiastic in his praises. It is funny to hear him telling a seasick bunch "Ain't it a grand boat! A lovely boat! Sure you wouldn't know you were aboard her. And she's the woise ould thing. She's been over this thrip so often that if niver a man put a hand to her wheel she'd pick her own way out and niver stop or veer till she turned her nose into the dock, like an ould horse findin' its way to the manger."

After the men had found their sea-legs we had a happy trip. We spent Easter Sunday aboard, celebrating it in holy fashion.

It was a happy throng that stood on the decks of the *Harrisburg* on the morning of April 21st, gazing at the southern shores of Long Island, and then the Statue of Liberty, and the massive towering structures that announce to incoming voyagers the energy and daring of the

Western Republic. Then down the bay came the welcoming flotilla bearing relatives, friends and benefactors.

The number of our welcomers and the ampleness of their enthusiasm were the first indications we had of the overwhelming welcome which was to be ours during the following two weeks. I do not intend to speak here at any length, of these events, as the gentlemen of the press have described them better than I could ever hope to do. The freedom of the city was conferred upon Colonel Donovan and his staff by Mayor Hylan and the Board of Alderman; and a dinner was given to the officers by the Mayor's Committee headed by the genial Commissioner Rodman Wanamaker. Our own Board of Trustees, the most generous and efficient lot of backers that any fighting outfit ever had since war began, gave the whole regiment a dinner at the Hotel Commodore which set a new record in the history of repasts. Our brethren of the 69th New York Guard also gave a dinner to the officers of the 165th. And Colonel Donovan and I enjoyed the hospitality of the Press Assocation and the Lamb's Club. Another big baseball game, through the good will of the owners of the Giants, added fresh funds to the money at my disposal for needy families. My own fellow townsmen in the Bronx prepared a public reception, for which every last detail was arranged except the weather; but I was prouder than ever of them when they put the thing through in good soldier fashion, regardless of the meanest day of wind and rain that New York ever saw in the month of May.

There was nothing that imagination could conceive or energy perform that our Board of Trustees was not willing to do for us. Dan Brady, who has neglected his business for the past two years to look after the 69th, and all the rest of them, devoted themselves entirely to furthering our well-being and our glory. The only thing I have against Dan is that he makes me work as hard as himself, and bosses me around continually. At one of the dinners I said that if Dan Brady had taken up the same kind of a job that I had, he would be a bishop by now; but if he were my Bishop I'd be a Baptist or a Presbyterian; in some Church anyway, that doesn't have Bishops.

The part of our reception which I enjoyed most of all was the parade up Fifth Avenue. The whole regiment shared in it, including the extra battalion, seven hundred strong, of men who had been invalided home, and others of our wounded who had a place of honor on the grand-stand. Archbishop Hayes, who had blessed us as we left the Armory, Mayor Hylan, men prominent in State and City, in Army and Navy affairs, united to pay their tribute of praise to the old regiment. And thousands and thousands of people on the stands cheered and cheered and cheered, so that for five miles the men walked through a din of applause, till the band playing the American and Irish airs could scarce be heard.

It was a deserved tribute to a body of citizen soldiers who had played such a manful part in battle for the service of the Republic. The appreciation that the country pays to its war heroes is for the best interest of the State. I am not a militarist, nor keen for military glory. But as long as liberties must be defended, and oppression or aggression put down, there must always be honor paid to that spirit in men which makes them willing to die for a righteous cause. Next after reason and justice, it is the highest quality in citizens of a state.

Our fathers in this republic, in their poverty and lowliness, founded many institutions, ecclesiastical, financial, charitable, which have grown stronger with the years. One of these institutions was a military organization, which they passed on to us with the flag of the fifty silver furls. To these we have added nine more in the latest war of our country. As it was borne up the Avenue flanked by that other banner whose stars of gold commemmorated the six hundred and fifty dead heroes of the regiment, and sur-rounded by three thousand veterans, I felt that in the breasts of generous and devoted youths that gazed upon them there arose a determination that if, in their generation, the Republic ever needed defenders, they too would face the perils of battle in their country's cause.

Men pass away, but institutions survive. In time we shall all go to join our comrades who gave up their lives in France. But in our own generation, when the call came, we accepted the flag of our fathers; we have added to it new glory and renown—and we pass it on.

HISTORICAL APPENDIX BY JOYCE KILMER

I

Fifth Avenue held a memorable crowd on the afternoon of the ninth of March, 1917. There were old women there in whose eyes was the eager light that only the thought of a son can cause to glow; there were proud old men—some of them with battered blue garrison-caps, and badges that told of service in the War between the States—there were wives, mothers, children—all waiting, in jubilant and affectionate expectation, the sound of a band playing "Garryowen" and the sight of a flag fluttering from a pole so covered with battle-furls as to glisten in the sunlight like a bar of silver.

The Sixty-ninth Regiment was back from the border. Escorted by its old friend, the Seventh New York, the Regiment marched nearly eight hundred strong, down the Avenue and east to the Armory. The crowd—or a large part of it—followed, and soon families separated for months were reunited. When the Sixty-ninth was mustered out of service that March day, after months of arduous service on the Mexican Border, it numbered 783 men. Almost immediately it lost some three hundred officers and men. This was in accordance with War Department orders and the National Defense Act of June 3rd, 1916, which provided that men with dependant relatives should be discharged from the service. Men were lost also because of the system, now discontinued, by which a soldier in the National Guard was furloughed to the reserve after three years of active service.

So in the early Spring of 1917, with participation in the European War a certainty, the Sixty-ninth Regiment found itself far below war strength, having lost a great number of men whom experience and training had made ideal soldiers. At once a recruiting campaign was instituted, but a recruiting campaign of a special kind. The Sixty-ninth has never found it at all difficult to fill its ranks—when it was under Southern fire in the Sixties it was brought up to war strength nine times. But the purpose in view now was to bring into the regiment men who would, in every purpose and way—physically, mentally and morally—keep up its ancient and honorable standards. It was easy enough to enlist hundreds of strong men who could be developed into good soldiers. But this was not the object of the recruiting of the Spring of 1917. It was desired to enlist strong, intelligent, decent-living men, men whose sturdy Americanism was strengthened and vivified by their Celtic blood, men who would be worthy successors of those unforgotten patriots who at Bloody Ford and on Marye's Heights earned the title of "The Fighting Irish."

The Regiment set its own standards in selecting recruits. In weight, for example, one hundred and twenty-eight pounds was established as the minimum. And if some honest man with broad shoulders and a knockout in each fist was unable to read ACXUROKY on a card hung thirty feet away—why, the examining physicians were instructed not to be overly meticulous in their work. But if the candidate, having every physical perfection, seemed to be the kind of man who would be out of harmony with the things for which the Sixty-ninth stands and has always stood, then the rigorous application of some of the qualifying tests invariably resulted in his rejection.

When, on April 6th, 1917, President Wilson declared that a state of war existed between the United States and Germany, his words found the Sixty-ninth Regiment ready, its ranks filled to war strength with soldiers of whom the men who fought at Gettysburg and Chancellorsville would not be ashamed. There was new intensity in the nightly drills; there was new fervor in the resolve of every man, veteran of the Border and recruit alike, to make the Regiment as nearly perfect a fighting unit as possible.

The 6th of April is a date which no American soldier will forget. And almost equally memorable is the 15th day of July of the same year—the day on which the National Guard was called into Federal Service. The Sixty-ninth regiment, 2002 strong, scarcely felt the heat of that torrid midsummer, so intent were all the men on preparing themselves for the great adventure, and so passionately eager were they for the call to service overseas.

On the 5th of August the Regiment, still retaining the numerical designation which is permanently engraved upon the tablets of our nation's history, was drafted into the Regular Army of the United States. This was a step nearer to the firing line—made, accordingly, with enthusiasm. And on the 25th day of August came the electrifying news that the Sixtyninth Regiment had been selected as the first New York National Guard organization to be sent to the war in vanguard of the American Expeditionary Force.

The circumstances in which the announcement was made to the regiment were striking. It was a boiling Saturday afternoon and officers and men were exhausted from the exercises of the morning—a Divisional inspection in Central Park. The regiment marched through the dusty streets and ascended the steps into the Armory to learn that they were not to be immediately dismissed, but were to stay on the drill floor or in the Company rooms. Lieutenant Colonel Latham R. Reed had gone to Governor's Island to attend an important conference, and officers and men were ordered to await his return. Everyone hopefully awaited the arrival of splendid tidings, and the weariness seemed to pass away.

When Lieutenant Colonel Reed returned, he called a meeting of his staff and the Battalion and Company Commanders, and told them such details as were then obtainable of the great honor which had come to the regiment they loved. There were present Major William J. Donovan, Major William B. Stacom, Major Timothy J. Moynahan, Captain George McAdie, Captain Thomas T. Reilley, Captain William Kennelly, Captain James A. McKenna, Jr., Captain Alexander E. Anderson, Captain Michael A. Kelly, Captain James J. Archer, Captain James G. Finn, Captain Van S. Merle-Smith Captain John P. Hurley, and Captain William T. Doyle. They heard the good news with undisguised delight and at once proceeded to prepare for the necessary intensive training.

But as great as was their delight, it was clouded with one regret. And that regret was felt also by every enlisted man. They all knew that the Regiment had been the first selected to go abroad not because of what it had done in the Civil War, nor because it was representative of what was best in the citizenship of our nation's greatest city. It had been selected, after a long and searching examination of the military resources of the country, because its record in the most recent important test—the Mexican Border Campaign—showed it to be the best trained and equipped fighting unit that America possessed. And the man who had done more than all others to bring the Regiment to this point, the man who during the long strenuous months on the Border had moulded it after his own ideal pattern of soldierly efficiency—that man was absent from the conference at which was announced the momentous news. There was not an officer in the conference room, there was not an enlisted man on the drill floor that day, who did not think of Colonel William N. Haskell—of the joy with which he would lead his beloved Regiment into the Great War, of the joy with which that Regiment would follow him across the ocean and over the parapet and through the German lines to the Kaiser's palace. There was not an officer or man who did not recall his last words when he was ordered to another duty "I want to lead the 69th Regiment into a fight."

Colonel Haskell was absent from this historic conference. He had been lent, not given to the Regiment, and now the Government claimed his valuable services to solve some of the problems of the new National Army. But he was present in spirit—in the thoughts of everyone in the building and in the fitness he had given to the Regiment's personnel.

Soon after the announcement that the Sixty-ninth Regiment was to be one of the very first into battle it was learned that the Regiment was to be brought up to a strength of 3500, according to the scheme which the French military experts had developed from their hard-bought experience with the conditions of modern warfare. It would have been a task gratifying to the whole Regiment, including Colonel Charles Hine, who now was placed in command, to build up the Regiment to this size by means of the recruiting methods which already had proved so successful. But it had been decided by higher authorities that the Regiment's numbers should be augmented by additions from other New York National Guard organizations. Accordingly, one day in August, 1917,

there arrived at the armory the first of the new increments—
332 men from the 7th New York Infantry.

The ties that bind the 7th and the 69th are ancient and
strong. The friendship between the two organizations has
often been strikingly manifested. It was much in evidence
when the New York National Guard was stationed on the
Border. But it has never been displayed more convincingly
than on the day that the men from the 7th joined the 69th.
Escorted to the doors of the armory by the rest of the 7th, led
by Colonel Willard C. Fisk, the men found the entire 69th
Regiment assembled to welcome them. They were made at
home; they found it no difficult task to orient themselves to
their new surroundings. Without any disloyalty to the venerable regiment they had left, they accepted as their own the
traditions and standards of the 69th and became not a distinct
group added to the Regiment but a vital part of it.

On the 20th of August the 69th Regiment, now 2,500 strong,
again marched through New York, and again an enormous
crowd witnessed and followed the march. But this crowd,
unlike that of the 9th of March previous, was not composed of
people rejoicing over a long-sought reunion. The same men,
women and children who had been present on the 9th of
March to welcome the soldiers returning from the Rio Grande
were present and they were as proud as, or prouder than before. But faces that had been happy were fearful now and
the gestures were of farewell. Wives and mothers looked
at the bright ranks with smiling anguish. The 69th was
marching to the ferry to cross the East River and entrain for
Camp Albert L. Mills, near Mineola, New York. It was the
first move toward the front, to win new battle-rings for the
pole that saw Cold Harbor and Bloody Ford.

There were many new and strange experiences in store
for the officers and men during the period of intensive training on Hempstead Plains. A carefully planned schedule provided for drill and instruction enough to fill nearly every minute of the day. Much of the work was repetition for those of
the men who had seen service on the Border, but they entered
into it in a way that showed they thoroughly appreciated its
value. There was also training in those phases of offensive
and defensive warfare which have been developed since Aug-

ust, 1914. This work came in for an especially large share of attention. It was no longer a mere drill; it was active preparation for the use of what is, in spite of trench-mortar, cannon, bomb and machine, the most effective weapon of modern warfare. The Regiment was instructed in the use of the bayonet by reserve officers who had acquired their knowledge from men with actual experience at the front. Cold steel propelled by Irishmen was said to be what the Germans chiefly feared and every effort was made to make sure that the 69th should not, through lack of practice, be less skillful with the bayonet than were the Dublin Fusileers and the Connaught Rangers. Visitors to the camp who were so fortunate as to be present at the bayonet drill were greatly impressed by the dexterity which the soldiers had gained in a few weeks, and by the intense realism which pervaded the exercise.

And now the Regiment gained, from day to day, the increments necessary to bring it up to the prescribed war strength of 3500. The men from the 7th had already been assimilated as privates and non-commissioned officers; they had become an integral part of the 69th (for only on paper was the name 165th in use). The 23rd, 14th, 71st and 12th now sent their delegations.

In most cases, the selection of the men in the various armories was made with perfect fairness, the prescribed number of sergeants, corporals and privates being arbitrarily taken from the ranks. But in certain companies it was soon evident that the officers had yielded to the natural temptation to endeavor to retain in their commands their best trained non-coms. Here was, for instance, a corporal to be taken from Blank Company of the Dash Regiment. By strict adherence to the letter of the law, Corporal Smith, a soldier of stainless record, with three month's Border service to his credit, should be the man to entrain for Camp Mills. But here was Private Jones, a recent recruit, not especially happy in the Dash Regiment and probably not likely to be homesick for it if sent away. Why not let him sew a couple of stripes on the sleeves of his new blouse, and go on his way rejoicing.

This is the way some Company Commanders reasoned. And as a result, the 69th Regiment found that among its new members were some Sergeants and Corporals whose military knowledge included little more than the manual of arms, and privates who were physically, morally, and mentally unfit for the service. It was not to be expected that these men would be received with overwhelming enthusiasm.

Many of the soldeirs received from other regiments—most of them in fact, were valuable additions to the 69th and at once proved their usefulness by merging with the rest of the outfit and working for the soldierly perfection of the whole body. Of the others—well, some of them were reformed by thorough disciplinary action, and others were allowed to drift back into civilian life by means of liberal use of dependency and surgeon's certificate of disability.

So many soldiers were lost of those acquired from other regiments that although the time for sailing was almost at hand it was considered advisable to institute another recruiting campaign. There was no difficulty in gaining the desired number of recruits; the prospect of immediate service in France with the most famous regiment in America brought to the Armory doors three times as many candidates as could be accepted.

Now the wives and mothers who thronged the dusty Company streets on Saturday and Sunday afternoons began to show stronger anxiety, to look with new intensity into the eyes of their soldiers as they bade them farewell and returned to the city. For the time for sailing was at hand—no one knew just when or just where the Regiment was going, but all felt it was a question only of days or hours.

Twice secret orders to sail were received at Regimental Headquarters, and twice these orders were hastily countermanded. The suspense began to tell on officers and men, to tell even more, perhaps on those to whom they had again and again to say good bye. At last, on the night of October 25th, Major Donovan led the first battalion through the dark camp and down the silent lanes to the long train that was to take them to Montreal.

And now there were no crowds, there was no music. It was a journey more momentous, greater in historical importance, than the Regiment's triumphant return from the Border, than its flower and flag decked setting forth for Camp Mills. But it was not, like those memorable events, a time for music and pomp. The feeling of the officers and men was one of stern delight, of that strange religious exhaltation with which men of Celtic race and faith go into battle, whether the arena be Vinegar Hill, Fontenoy, or Rouge Boquet. As the trainful of happy warriors steamed through the first leagues of the journey to the Front, Father Duffy, the Regiment's beloved Chaplain, passed from car to car hearing confessions and giving absolution. Rosaries—the last dear gift of mothers and sweethearts—were taken out and by squads, platoons and companies the soldiers told their beads. There was little sleep on the 69th special for Montreal that night—officers and men were too excited, too exalted for that. They had entered at last on the adventure of their lives.

General O'Ryan had said that a soldier is a man who always wants to be elsewhere than where he is. This is not true of soldiers of the race to which General O'Ryan's name indicates that he belongs. They want to be elsewhere—only when they are in some peaceful place. If the Regiment had been restless before, the second and third Battalions were doubly so after they had seen four companies of their comrades go away.

But they had not long to wait. On the night of October 29th, the *America* (formerly the *Amerika* of the Hamburg-American line) pulled out of New York Harbor. There was no khaki on her decks; the only figures to be seen were sailors and deck-hands. But as soon as the vessel was out of range of spying Teutonic eyes, soldiers poured out of every hatchway. And as they thronged the deck-space available and looked their last for a long time at the lights along the fast receding shore, they showed a contentment, a mirth that amazed the crew, long accustomed to transporting troops.

"What's the matter with you fellows?" asked one sailor. "Ain't you sorry to be leaving your homes? Didn't you ever hear there was such things as submarines?" He had helped carry over all sort of soldiers, he said, Regulars, Marines and Guardsmen, but he had never before seen passengers so seemingly indifferent to the grief of leavetaking and the perils of the wartime sea. He couldn't understand it.

He might have been able to understand it if he had read Chesteron's "Ballad of the White Horse." For in that wise poem is an explanation of the psychology of the 69th New

York, an explanation of the singular phenomenon of soldiers leaving their dear ones and setting out over menacing seas to desperate battle in a strange land as merrily as if they were planning merely an evening at Coney Island. Chesterton wrote:

> "For the great Gaels of Ireland
>   Are the men that God made mad
> For all their wars are merry
>   And all their songs are sad."

II

The First Battalion's voyage to France was more interesting than that of the main body of the regiment or of Companies L and M, who followed them in a few days. Sailing from Montreal on the *Tunisian* at 8 on the morning of October 27th, they landed at Liverpool, England, on November 10. There they entrained for Southhampton, reaching that city late in the night. In the night of the 11th they crossed the English Channel to Havre, and after a few hours' rest they were packed into open box-cars for their cold journey across France. They detrained at Sauvoy on November 15.

The voyage of the good ship *America* was made over a sea so glassy-smooth that sea-sickness was an impossibility. The boat-drills, the rules against smoking or showing lights on deck at night and the constant watch for submarines (a work which was put wholly in the hands of the 69th Regiment, and executed by them with unflagging devotion) served to remind the men that, peaceful as the blue water looked, they were actually in the war already.

The discomforts of a crowded ship could not daunt the spirits of the men of the 69th. The dark holes far below the water-level in which they were tightly packed rang with song and laughter every night until taps sounded. There were concerts on deck and in the mess-room every night, except when the ship's course was through the danger zone and silence was enforced. If there is left in the Atlantic Ocean a mermaid who cannot now sing "Over There," "Goodbye Broadway, Hello France," "Mother Machree." and "New York Town," it is not the fault of the 69th New York.

And yet mirth was not the sole occupation of these soldiers, exhilarated as they were by the prospects of battle. During the day, one could find little groups gathered on hatchways and in corners, studying, from little manuals they had bought, such subjects as the new bayonet work and grenade throwing. The talk of the men was very seldom of the homes and friends they had left behind, it was nearly always of the prospect of battle. They talked of what front they might be expected to hold, with what troops they might be trained, and, above all, of how soon they were to go into action. They discussed such methods and instruments of modern warfare as they knew with the keen interest of those who are soldiers by their own choice.

Those who do not know the 69th Regiment would have been puzzled by the spectacle presented by the main deck amidships every afternoon and evening. There could be seen a line of soldiers, as long as the mess-line, waiting their turn to go to confession to the Regimental Chaplain, Father Francis P. Duffy. And every morning—not on Sundays alone—there was a crowd at the same spot, where, on an altar resting on two nail kegs, Father Duffy said Mass.

The voyage passed without any sight of hostile sea or aircraft, and after two weeks the *America* came to anchor in the beautiful harbor of Brest. That is, it seemed a beautiful harbor at first, with its long white quay and its miles of dark green shore picked out with venerable gray stone buildings. But as day succeeded day with nothing for the soldiers to do but tramp the decks and yearn for the feel of sod under their hobnails, the view began to lose some of its beauty. There were two weeks on the open sea—these soon passed. But the week in Brest Harbor, in tantalizing sight of land, separated by only half a mile of green evil-smelling stagnation from shops and cafés and homes—that was cruel and unusual punishment.

When, after six days a detail for the hard work of loading freight cars was formed, every man in the regiment volunteered—and this sort of a detail usually is eagerly avoided. The volunteers who were accepted had little to reward them except the pleasure of being upon comparatively dry land. They were given no chance to taste the delights of the seaside city. When their task of unloading and loading baggage was finished, they and the rest of their shipmates learned what "Hommes 36-40, Chevaux 8" meant. From 40 to 50 men entered the waiting box-cars, with hard tack and canned corn-beef (Corn Willie) to feed them, and their own blankets to protect them from the hardness of the floors and the cold blasts that swept in at the open sides.

Three days and three nights of such travelling as no soldier of the 69th can ever forget, and they were at the village of Sauvoy, in the Department of Meuse. From this point a hike of some two hours brought them to the tiny village of Naives-en-Blois. Here was to be the new home of Regimental Head-quarters, Headquarters Company, Supply Company and Company B. The other companies (including those of the First Battalion, which had arrived in the district on the fifteenth of the month) were quartered in the nearby villages of Sauvoy, Bovée, Vacon, Broussey and Villeroi.

The Regiment was put not in barracks, but in billets. Now billets, to those of the men who had done guard duty in upper New York State during the previous Spring, meant comfortable bedrooms, buckwheat cakes with syrup for breakfast, and the society of good natured farming people. But billeting in the European sense of the term, meant something different, as they soon found out. It meant that certain householders, in return for the payment of a few sous per man per twenty-four hours, were obliged to allow soldiers to sleep in their stables, barns or other outhouses. They were not obliged to furnish any food, light or heat. They were not obliged even to mend the roofs or walls of the shelters. Straw for filling bedsacks was furnished to the soldiers, and they were fairly launched on their first winter in France.

It was a winter of unprecedented severity. A freezing wind blew through the great holes in the tumble-down sheds where the men slept, covering them, night after night, with snow. They learned many soldierly things. How to make blouse and overcoat supplement the thin army blankets, for instance. How to keep shoes from freezing in the night by sleeping on them. How to dress and undress in the dark—for lamps were unknown and candles forbidden.

These things the soldiers taught themselves, or were taught

by circumstances during their stay in Naives-en-Blois and en-virons. Their work consisted of close order drill, guard duty, and the thorough and much needed policing of the ancient village street.

Now, Naives was near the front—so near that the guns could clearly be heard when the wind blew in the right direction. This was cheering for the men, but as there were indications of a strengthening of the German lines at this point, with a possible view to an offensive, it was necessary to use the district for troops whose training had been completed; and, according to the new European standards, that of the 69th had not yet begun. So it was necessary for the Regiment—indeed, for the whole 42nd Division, which then had its headquarters in the nearby city of Vaucouleurs—to give place to seasoned French troops. So the men made their packs, the wagons were loaded, and the Regiment changed station from the 4th to the 5th area.

After two days of hiking (very easy hiking it seemed, in the light of later experiences) the Regiment arrived, on December 13, in the historic town of Grand. Here, centuries before, the conquering Romans had encamped, one hundred thousand strong. The ruins of the mighty ampitheatre that they built still stands, and the tower of the great church was once part of a fort. It was Caesar himself who planned the broad roads on which our Regiment drilled, and Caesar's soldiers who made them. In this venerable church Father Duffy said midnight Mass on Christmas, and all the town came to see these strange, gentle, brave, mirthful, pious American soldiers, who, coming from a new land to fight for France, practiced France's ancient faith with such devotion. The Regimental colors were in the chancel, flanked by the tricolor. The 69th band was present, and some French soldier-violinists. A choir of French women sang hymns in their own language, the American soldiers sang a few in English, and French and American joined in the universal Latin of "Venite, Adoremus Dominum." It was a memorable Midnight Mass—likely to be rembered longer even than that which Father Duffy had said on the Mexican Border just a year previous, which troops for fifty miles around had crossed the prairies to attend.

Now it was considered advisable for the Division to proceed to the 6th area. This meant a hike of some four days and nights. Accordingly, at 8 on the morning of December 26th, the Regiment passed through the main street of Grand and out over the ancient Roman road.

This hike has become so famous—or so infamous—because of the undeniable sufferings of those who took part in it that it needs no detailed description here. It must by any impartial historian be admitted that during it the men of the 69th Regiment were insufficiently fed and shod, that they endured great and unnecessary pains and privations. It must also be admitted that they bore these trials with a cheerfulness which amazed the French civilians through whose villages they passed, accustomed as were these people to soldiers of almost every human race. They would crush their bleeding feet into their frozen, broken-soled hobnails of a black morning, and breakfastless start out, with a song on their lips, to climb the foothills of the Vosges Mountains through the heart of a blizzard. At noon (shifting their feet about to keep the blood moving) they would (if it was one of the lucky days) have a slice of bread or two pieces of hardtack for noon mess. At night they would have a sleep instead of supper. But they were never dispirited; they were never too cold, too hungry or too weary to sing or to teach the innocent French villagers strange bits of New York slang.

No man in the 69th Regiment "fell out" during that terrible hike. But many fell down. That is, no one, because of heartbreaking weariness, or faintness or lameness went to the roadside and waited for the ambulance to pick him up. Those who finished the journey in ambulances or trucks did so because they had fallen senseless in the deep snow, unable to speak or move. And wherever the Regiment passed there were bloody tracks in the white roadway.

"That hike made Napoleon's retreat from Moscow look like a Fifth Avenue parade," said one of the medical officers serving during this period. And many an observer compared the Regiment to Washington's foot-sore soldiers at Valley Forge. It was only the indomitable spirit of the Irish American fighting man that kept the Regiment afoot through those four tragic days.

The Regiment that arrived in Longeau on the afternoon of

December 29th looked different from the Regiment that had left Grand four days before. To judge them by their gait and their faces, the men had aged twenty years. But their hearts were unchanged. As they stood in the deep snow, the ice-crusted packs still on their bruised shoulders, they had a laughing word for every pretty face at a Longeau window. The weary bandsmen started a defiant air, and the Regiment joined in with a roar. The song was "The Good Old Summertime."

III

Longeau, which with the surrounding villages constituted the Regiment's new home, is a small farming town in the Haute Marne District. Unlike those of Naives, its houses are strongly built and in excellent preservation, and the billets in which (awaiting the completion of barracks) the troops were stationed were dry, warm and comfortable. As soon as possible, the Regiment moved into the new barracks built in the outskirts of Longeau and nearby villages, and was thus more nearly consolidated than it had previously been since its arrival in France.

In Longeau, the 69th Regiment was destined to receive much more practical training for the trenches than it had received in Camp Mills, Naives or Grand. These last two towns had really been merely stopping places, Longeau was a training camp. The most important event of the stay in Longeau was the advent of Colonel John W. Barker. Colonel Hine was withdrawn from his post with the regiment early in January, in order that he might take part in the transportation work for which he was especially fitted. He was succeeded on January 12th by Colonel John W. Barker, National Army. Colonel Barker was an up-state New Yorker, who graduated from West Point in the class of '09. He had served in the Regular Infantry ever since in Cuba, the Philippines and on the Mexican Border. He saw considerable active service against the Indians, after taking part in almost the last of the Indian fight at Leach Creek, Minnesota.

Four years ago, he was recommended by his arm of the service to represent the Infantry for one year's duty with a French Infantry Regiment. He was in France on this duty when the great war broke out, and remained as a member of our military organization until the arrival of the American Expeditionary Forces. Then he joined the staff of the Commander in Chief as General Staff Officer, 5th Section. He served General Headquarters in this capacity until personally selected by the Commander in Chief to command the 165th Infantry.

Now the regiment began to take the form of a modern fighting organization. It was Colonel Barker's task to bring it into conformation with the new Tables of Organization, and to this task the best energies of himself and his staff were immediately devoted.

The specialized platoons (pioneers, trench mortar, one pound cannon) were now organized and intensively trained. Competent enlisted men from these platoons were sent to the schools newly established by General Headquarters and given the advantage of instruction by officers who had gained their knowledge of the subjects in actual warfare conditions. Hand grenades were supplied, and every man taught their effective use. Steel helmets now replaced the historic felt campaign hats. To every man were issued two gas masks, one French gas mask and one English box respirator. By means of constant drill in the rapid adjustment of these masks, under the direction of an officer who had specialized in the subject, the men acquired a proficiency in their use which saved many a life in the Lunéville and Baccarat Sectors and during the weeks of desperate fighting on the banks of the Suippes and the Marne.

It was during the stay in Longeau that the 69th Regiment organized its Intelligence Section, the first in the 42nd Division. Under the direction of the Regimental Intelligence Officer, Lieutenant Basil B. Elmer, U. S. R., there was organized and trained a group of scouts, observers, map-makers and snipers so expert in detecting and hindering the movements of the enemy that they were several times, in the course of the action that came later, asked to attach themselves permanently to the Headquarters of the 42nd Division, in order that they might serve as instructors to the other regimental intelligence sections.

There were several changes in the personnel of the Regiment's administrative staff. Lieutenant Colonel Reed had been selected for Staff College, and the Regiment never got him back. Captain William Doyle, who had served as Regimental Adjutant in Camp Mills, had been relieved while the regiment was in Naives-en-Blois, and his place taken by Captain Alexander E. Anderson, long in command of Company E. Now Captain Anderson was relieved as Adjutant and placed in command of Headquarters Company. Its former commander, Captain Walter E. Powers, for several years Adjutant of the Regiment, went to the Headquarters of the 42nd Division, leaving an enviable record for absolute efficiency in company and regimental administration. His abilities were soon recognized by his commission as Major and appointment as Divisional Adjutant. Captain Doyle was attached to Brigade Headquarters. Captain Anderson's work was taken over by Lieutenant William F. McKenna, who was appointed Acting Adjutant, an office which he had filled during part of the Border campaign.

The training of officers and men never flagged while the Regiment was stationed in Longeau. Battalion and company commanders, Lieutenants and enlisted men were sent for brief periods to the special schools instituted by General Headquarters for their benefit, and on their return imparted to others the knowledge they had gained. There were lectures and quizzes every evening in the barracks, supplementary to the instruction received every morning and afternoon in the drill field and on the range. A number of American officers who had seen service at the front were now attached to the Regiment, and their first hand information gave new actuality to the daily work.

The training of the Regiment for the action in which they were soon to take part received new and strong impetus during the month of February by the arrival in camp of the 32nd Battalion of Chasseurs. These famous French soldiers, who had been in violent action ever since 1914, proved to be the most useful instructors for the men of the 69th. On the range and during the long hours of grenade throwing and open and trench warfare practice, their instruction, example and companionship was a constant incentive to the American soldiers. And it was a proud day for the 69th Regiment when its soldiers perceived that in rifle markmanship and in grenade throwing they had succeeded in proving their superiority to their veteran instructors.

From February 7th to February 13th the Regiment took part in manoeuvres in which it was opposed by the 166th Infantry. These manoeuvres took place in the hilly country around Longeau and had as their ultimate objective the seizure and holding of the town of Brennes. This difficult strategic task was eventually accomplished.

Now the desire of the men for immediate participation in the action, the lure of which had drawn them across the ocean, was so strong as to amount to an obsession. It was evident to any competent observer that the whole Division was ready to render valuable service, as thoroughly trained as any unit in the American contingent. This was evidently the opinion of those who directed the movement of American troops, for on February 16th, 17th and 18th the Regiment marched to Langres, under orders to entrain for the city of Lunéville, in the Department of Meurthe-et-Moselle, for training with French troops in the line—that is, for actual duty in the trenches.

Lunéville was the largest town in which the Regiment had been stationed since its arrival in France. Some of the companies were put in billets, and some in the Stanislas Barracks, a magnificent stone building in the center of the town. Regimental Headquarters was established in the Stanislas Palace, a building which had previously housed the Administrative staffs of some of the French regiments who since 1914 had done brilliant work in retarding the German advance.

Now the Regiment was placed under the tactical orders of the General commanding the 164th Division of the French Army, the Division then occupying what was known as the Lunéville Sector. On February 21st, the 1st and 2nd Battalions, Headquarters Company and Machine Gun Company paraded in the central square of Lunéville and were reviewed by Major General Bassilière, then commander of the 17th French Army Corps. A few days later, the Regiment was made happy by learning that orders to go to the front had been received. On February 27th and 28th respectively, Companies D and B marched to their posts in the front line trenches, relieving companies of the 15th Group of Chasseurs of the French Army.

And now came a chapter in the history of the 69th Regiment which blotted out from the minds of officers and men all the hard work of the Camp Mills training period, all the privations and discomforts of the ocean trip and the journey across blizzard-beleagured France. The 69th was actually in the fighting—it was called "a period of training in the trenches," but it was no time of sham-battles and manoeuvres. It was, in fact, an initiation into battle, by way of what was (up to the time of the 42nd Division's entry into it) a quiet sector.

A "quiet sector" is one in which the German and French lines are separated from each other by a considerable distance —sometimes as much as five kilometers—in which there is no immediate objective for which the troops on either side are striving, in which, finally, shots are seldom fired, the opposing forces being content merely to hold their trenches almost undisturbed. These are also termed "rest sectors," and the task of holding them is given either to troops wearied by participation in great battles or to troops fresh from the drill field and lacking in experience in actual warfare.

Nothing could have been more idyllic than the Rouge-Bouquet-Chaussailles Subsector of the Lunéville Sector when Company D marched to its strong point before dawn on the morning of February 27th. The subsector is heavily wooded and almost clear of underbrush. As the company marched up the hill through groves of birch, pine, spruce, and fir, and saw to right and left little summer houses, benches, tables and dug-out entrances elaborately decorated with rustic woodwork they were rather shocked by the idyllic beauty of what they saw. Not for service in such a recreation park had they crossed the seas. Where were the bursting shells, where was the liquid fire, where were the bayonets of the charging Boches? This series of outposts joined by little ditches seemed at first too much like Central Park to satisfy the battle-hungry soldiers of the 69th.

The impression of absolute peacefulness was further emphasized in the course of a thorough reconnaissance of the subsector made on the morning of the 27th by the Regimental Intelligence Section. They stepped across a ditch and learned that they had passed the front line trenches—had gone "over the top." They wandered about what seemed to be à deserted pasture and learned that they were in No Man's Land.

But this tranquillity was not long to endure. The "Fighting Irish" lived up to their reputation—they "started something" at once. Rifles were cracking merrily before Company D's men had been at their posts for half an hour. And by dusk on the evening of the 27th, Corporal Arthur Trayer and Private John Lyons of Company D had earned the distinction of being the first soldiers of the Regiment to be wounded. A high explosive shell burst on striking the roof of a shack in which they were resting, and the fragments wounded them —not seriously, but enough to warrant sending them to a hospital for a few weeks and later awarding them the coveted wound chevrons.

By the night of the 27th the Chaussaille-Rouge Bouquet Subsector had lost much of its reputation for quietness. The Germans may not have known as yet that Americans were in the trenches opposite them, but they knew at any rate that some new and aggressive unit had taken over the line, and they felt in duty bound to show that they were not in the trenches entirely for a rest cure. So the fight was on.

Regimental Headquarters took over the Regimental Post of Command at Arbre Haut on March 3rd. Company A occupied Strong Point Rouge Bouquet from March 1st to March 7th, Company E from March 7th to 13th, Company L from March 13th to March 21st. Company B occupied Strong Point Chaussailles from March 1st to March 6th, Company H from March 6th to March 12th, Company K from March 12th to March 22nd. Company D occupied Strong Point Sorbiers from March 1st to March 5th, Company F from March 5th to March 11th, Company I from March 11th to March 17th, Company M from March 17th to March 22nd.

There were many minor casualties during the early part of this period, but nothing of a really tragic nature occurred until March 7th. Then came a calamity which would have broken the morale of any regiment less high-spirited than this, so sudden was it and so lamentable.

On that unforgettable Wednesday, all was quiet as if there were no war until exactly 3.20 in the afternoon. Then the enemy started a barrage of minnewerfer shells. Interspersed with 77s they fell steadily and thick for about an hour. One shell fell directly on the roof of a dug-out in Rocroi—an old dug-out, built by the French four years before. In it were 21 men and one officer—1st Lieutenant John A. Norman of Company E. All were buried in the broken earth and beams, and some were at once killed. Two men were sitting on the edge of the upper bunk in one of the rooms—a falling beam crushed the head of one and left the other uninjured.

At once a working party was organized and began to dig the soldiers from their living grave. There was bombardment after bombardment, but the men kept at work, and eventually they dug out two men alive and five dead. There were living men down in that pit—their voices could be heard, and they were struggling toward the light. Lieutenant Norman could be heard encouraging them and guiding the efforts of their bruised and weary hands and feet. Several times they were at the surface and willing hands were out-stretched to draw them to safety—when well-aimed shells plunged them down again into that place of death. At last, after almost super-human efforts on the part of men from Company E and from the pioneer platoon of Headquarters Company, after deeds of heroism, brilliant but unavailing, the work was dis-continued. The bodies of fourteen men and one officer still lay in that ruined dug-out—it was unwise, in view of the constant bombardment of it, to risk the lives of more men in digging for them. So a tablet was engraved and erected above the mound, the last rites of the church were celebrated by Father Duffy, and the place where the men had fought and died be-came their grave.

After March 7th, no one called the Rouge Bouquet-Chaus-sailles Sector a rest park, no one complained that it was too peaceful to make them know they were at war. Not only the front line sector but the reserve position at Grand Taille and the road leading from the Battalion Post of Command at Rouge Bouquet to Regimental Headquarters at Arbre Haut were bombarded every day. But the Regiment held the line with undiminished zeal, and gave the enemy an experience novel in this sector in the shape of a *Coup de Main* on the night of March 20th. Of this adventure, the first of many of the kind in which the regiment was to take part, a brief, accurate account is to be found in the citation of its leader, 1st Lieutenant Henry A. Bootz, (later Captain of Company C), by the Seventh French Army Corps.

His citation reads: "In the course of a raid, led a combat group into the enemy's lines, going beyond the objective assigned, and recommenced the same operation eight hours later, giving his men an example of the most audacious bravery. Returned to our lines carrying one of his men severely wounded."

It is a matter of no military importance but of deep interest to everyone who sympathizes with the 69th Regiment and knows its history and traditions, that when the raiding party marched up past Regimental Headquarters on their way to the trenches, there fluttered from the bayonet of one of the men a flag—a green flag marked in gold with the harp that has for centuries been Ireland's emblem—the harp without the crown—and inscribed "Erin Go Bragh!" This flag had been given to Sergeant Evers of the Band and by a stranger— an old woman who burst through the great crowd that lined the streets when the Regiment marched from the armory to the dock on their journey to Camp Mills and, crying and laughing at the same time, thrust it into his hands. The flag went "over the top" twice that night, and for memory's sake the name "Rouge Bouquet" was embroidered on it. Later, the embroidered names became so numerous that the design of the flag almost disappeared. Who the woman was who gave the Regiment this appropriate tribute is unknown. Perhaps it was Kathleen in Houlihan herself.

It was natural that this brilliant and utterly unexpected *Coup de Main* should have the effect of irritating our country's enemy. It did so, and the result was a dose of "Schrecklichkeit" which at first threatened to prove more serious than the fatal bombardment of the dug-out in Rouge Bouquet. It came on the days of the raid—March 20th and March 21st. The French soldiers had been inclined to make light of the 69th Regiment's elaborate precautions against gas-attacks, of the constant wearing of the French gas-mask and the English box-respirator at the alert position (the respirator bound across the soldier's chest ready for immediate use) when in the trenches. The Germans, they said, could not send cloud or projector gas through Rocroi Woods, and their last gas shell attack had been made three years before. Why take such precautions against an improbable danger?

But the French officers and men saw the wisdom of the Regiment's precautionary measures after March 20th and 21st. For on these dates occurred a gas-attack of magnitude unprecedented in this sector, in which the French casualties far outnumbered those of the Americans. The gas sent over in shells that burst along the road from Arbre Haut to the Battalion Post of Command and along the trenches and outposts from Chaussailles to Rouge Bouquet were filled with mustard-gas, which blinded the men and bit into their flesh, and poisoned all blankets, clothing and food that was within the range of its baneful fumes. There were four hundred casualties in the Regiment on those two nightmare-like days— four hundred men, that is, who were taken, blind and suffering, from the fateful forest to the hospital in Lunéville and thence to Vittel and other larger centers for expert medical treatment. Most of these men were from Company K, others from Company M and Headquarters Company. But only two men were immediately killed by the gas, and of the four hundred who went to the hospital only three died—of broncho-pneumonia resulting from the action of the gas on their lungs. To their careful training in the use of the gas mask, the men owed the preservation of their lives in an attack which was intended to destroy all of the battalion then in the line.

A volume could be filled with a record of the heroism displayed by the officers and men of the 69th Regiment during these two days and nights of violent bombardment. The French authorities overwhelmed the Regiment with congratulations and awards. And surely the Croix de Guerre never shone upon breasts more worthy of it than those of First Lieutenant George F. Patton, of the Sanitary Detachment, who, standing in the center of a storm of mustard-gas, coolly removed his mask in order to give a wounded soldier the benefit of his medical attention, or that of First Lieutenant

Thomas Martin of Company K, who, when every other officer of his company had been taken away to the hospital, took command of the unit and held the sector through forty-eight hours of almost incessant bombardments. The French Division commander bestowed the Croix de Guerre on Col. Barker, with the following citation:

"Commands a regiment noticeable for its discipline and fine conduct under fire. Has given his troops an example of constant activity and has distinguished himself especially on the 20th of March by going forward under a violent barrage fire to assure himself of the situation and of the state of morale of one of his detachments starting on a raid into the enemy's lines."

APPENDIX

NEW FURLS ON REGIMENTAL STAFF

LUNEVILLE SECTOR, February 21 to March 23, 1918.

BACCARAT SECTOR, April 1 to June 21, 1918.

ESPERANCE-SOUAIN SECTOR, July 4 to July 14, 1918.
CHAMPAGNE-MARNE DEFENSIVE, July 15 to July 18, 1918
AISNE-MARNE OFFENSIVE, July 25 to August 3, 1918

ST. MIHIEL Offensive, September 12 to September 16, 1918.

ESSEY and PANNES Sector. Woevre, September 17 to September 30, 1918.
ARGONNE-MEUSE OFFENSIVE, October 13 to October 31, 1918
ARGONNE-MEUSE OFFENSIVE LAST PHASE, November 5, to November 9, 1918.

LOSSES IN ACTION

Killed: 644 Wounded: 2,857. Total: 3,501.

Kilometers gained: 55.

Headquarters: 83 different places.

Number of days in contact with the enemy: 180.

355

LIST OF DECORATIONS *

DISTINGUISHED SERVICE CROSS WITH PALM

Colonel
 William J. Donovan

DISTINGUISHED SERVICE CROSS

Lieut.-Colonels
 Timothy J. Moynahan
 Charles A. Dravo
Majors
 James A. McKenna (Deceased)
 Michael A. Kelly
 Thomas T. Reilley
 Van S. Merle-Smith
Captains
 Richard J. Ryan
 Louis A. Stout
First Lieutenants
 James B. McIntyre
 William M. Spencer
 John J. Williams
Second Lieutenants
 Oliver Ames   (Deceased)
 James S. D. Burns   (Deceased)
 John J. Burke
 Andrew Ellett
Chaplains
 Francis P. Duffy
 James M. Hanley
 George R. Carpentier
Sergeants
 Co. C, Joseph W. Burns
 Co. A, John J. Dennelly
 Co. D, Joseph J. Lynch
 Co. C, Thomas P. O'Hagan
 Co. D, John J. Gribbon
 Co. B, Spiros Thomas
 Co. H, Bernard Finnerty
         (Deceased)
 Co. H, Eugene J. Sweeney
 Co. A, Thomas J. Sweeney
 Co. I, Michael A. Donaldson
 Co. C, Thomas O'Kelly
 Co. Hq., Thomas E. Fitzsimmons

Co. K, John J. McLoughlin
Co. M, John McLoughlin
Co. M, G. Frank Gardella
         (Deceased)
Co. M G, John F. Flint
Co. H, Martin J. Higgins
Co. San, Victor L. Eichorn
Co. M G, Peter Gillespie
Co. K, Edward J. Rooney
Co. I, Edward T. Shanahan
Co. K, Herbert A. McKenna
Co. D, Richard W. O'Neill
Co. C, Michael Ruane
Co. H, Dudley Winthrop
Co. A, Martin Gill
Co. A, Matthew Kane
Co. C, Archibald F. Reilly
Co. C, Harry C. Horgan
Co. H, Patrick Travers
Co. C, William McCarthy
Co. K, Peter J. Crotty
         (Deceased)
Co. H, William O'Neill
         (Deceased)
Co. C, Michael Cooney
Co. L, Michael Fitzpatrick
Co. D, Michael J. McAuliffe
Corporals
 Co. C, Thomas F. O'Connor
         (Deceased)
 Co. M G, William J. Murphy
 Co. C, Frederick Craven
 Co. D, William P. White
 Co. E, Frederick Gluck
         (Deceased)
 Co. K, Victor Van Yorx
 Co. M, James E. Winestock
 Co. C, John Hammond
 Co. B, Matthew J. Brennan
Wagoner Supply Co.
 Albert Richford
Privates
 Co. K, William J. Bergen
         (Deceased)
 Co. G, Edmund Riordan
         (Deceased)

* After the Champagne fight, by request of the French military authorities, a number of officers and men were recommended for decoration, including Major Anderson for the Legion of Honor. The lists were lost while going through the French Army channels, but it is still hoped that the honors will be granted.

Co. G, John McGeary
   (Deceased)
Co. M, Robert Riggsby
Co. D, Edward G. Coxe
   (Deceased)
Co. K, Burr Finkle
Co. H, Patrick Reynolds
   (Deceased)
Co. C, John Teevan

DISTINGUISHED SERVICE MEDAL
Chaplain
   Francis P. Duffy

LEGION OF HONOR
Brigadier General
   Frank R. McCoy
Colonel
   William J. Donovan
Lieutenant Colonel
   Timothy J. Moynahan
Major
   Michael A. Kelly
First Lieutenant
   William Maloney

MEDAILLE MILITAIRE
Sergeant
   Co. I, Michael A. Donaldson
Corporals
   Co. A, Matthew A. Kane
   Co. K, Burr Finkle
Private
   Co. M, Robert Riggsby

CROCE DI GUERRA (ITALIAN)
Colonel
   William J. Donovan
Sergeant
   Co. C, Michael Ruane

CROIX DE GUERRE
Brigadier Generals
   Frank R. McCoy
   John W. Barker
Colonel
   William J. Donovan
Lieutenant Colonels
   Charles A. Dravo
   Timothy J. Moynahan
      (Two Citations)

Majors
   Henry A. Bootz
   Michael A. Kelly
Captains
   Henry K. Cassidy
   Oscar L. Buck
   Kenneth Ogle
   Charles D. Baker
      (Deceased)
   Beverly H. Becker
First Lieutenants
   John Norman
      (Deceased)
   Thomas C. P. Martin
   George F. Patton
Second Lieutenants
   Arthur S. Booth
   W. Arthur Cunningham
   Henry W. Davis
      (Deceased)
   Raymond H. Newton
Sergeants
   Co. A, William J. Moore
   Co. A, Daniel O'Connell
   Co. A, Spencer G. Rossell
   Co. B, Spiros Thomas
   Co. C, Eugene A. McNiff
   Co. Hq., Abram Blaustein
   Co. D, Thomas M. O'Malley
   Co. E, Carl Kahn
   Co. E, William E. Bailey
   Co. G, James D. Coffey
   Co. G, James Murray
   Co. C, Thomas P. O'Hagan
   Co. K, Leo A. Bonnard
   Co. D, Joseph J. Lynch
   Co. A, John F. Scully
   Co. G, Martin Shalley
   Co. H, Jerome F. O'Neill
   Co. H, Bruno Gunther
   Co. A, Joseph G. Pettit
   Co. A, Frank A. Fisher
   Co. B, Christian Biorndall
   Co. B, William P. Judge
   Co. D, Thomas H. Brown
   Co. E, Alfred S. Helmer
   Co. F, Theodore H. Hagen
   Co. H, John P. Furey
   Co. D, John Cahill
   Co. A, Michael Morley
   Co. B, Daniel J. Finnegan
   Co. C, James Barry
   Co. C, Michael Cooney
   Co. D, Dennis O'Connor
   Co. D, Patrick Grogan

Co. C, Herman H. Hillig
Co. A, Thomas Sweeney
Co. C, Michael Ruane
Co. D, John J. Gribbon
Co. I, Michael A. Donaldson
Co. A, Matthew A. Kane
Co. Hq., Joyce Kilmer
    (Deceased)
Corporals
Co. F, John Finnegan
    (Deceased)
Co. L, Lawrence G. Spencer
    (Deceased)
Co. D, Marlow H. Plant
Co. C, Bernard Barry
    (Deceased)
Co. A, George A. McCarthy
Co. B, Vincent J. Eckas
Co. Hq., Charles S. Jones

Co. B, Frank Brandreth
Co. C, John J. Brawley
Co. D, Harry H. DeVoe
Co. E, James Quigley
Co. A, Bernard McOwen
    (Deceased)
Co. A, Matthew A. Rice
    (Two Citations)
Co. K, Burr Finkle
Cook
Co. M, Robert Riggsby
Private
John Teevan

ORDER OF ST. LEPOLD
(BELGIUM)

Second Lieutnant
Thomas J. Devine

HEADQUARTERS, 165TH INFANTRY

(Old 69th N. Y.)

REMAGEN, Germany, March 28, 1919.

GENERAL ORDER.
No. 12

To the Officers and the Men of the 165th Infantry, 42nd Division.

The following extracts from orders and letters commendatory of the 42nd Division and the 165th Infantry issued by our own Army and that of our illustrious Ally the French, indicate a deep appreciation of your worth as soldiers and pay a high tribute to your valorous conduct on the Fields of Battle.

WILLIAM J. DONOVAN
JOHN P. HURLEY,
Capt. Adj., 165th Infantry.

*   *   *

March 21, 1918.

The Lieut. Colonel Commanding the 13th Group of Chasseurs reports that in the course of the double *coup de main* executed in the night of the 20-21 March, the conduct of the American detachment of the 165th Regiment has been particularly worthy of commendation, and that Officers and Soldiers have given proof of an enthusiastic bravery.

The General Commanding the 164th Division wishes to make known to all this appreciation, which justifies amply the confidence that we all have in our allies, a confidence doubled by the friendship and by the affectionate sympathy that the common life in the Sector has spontaneously brought into being.

General GAUCHER, Commanding the 164th Division.

*   *   *

April 1, 1918.

From: Commanding General, First Army Corps.

To: Commanding General, 42d Division, A. E. F.

Subject: Commendations.

1. The Chief of the French Military Mission has forwarded to the Commander-in-Chief, A. E. F., copies of citations and proposals concerning three officers and eight enlisted men of the 165th Infantry.

2. The Commander-in-Chief charges me with the conveyance to these officers and soldiers his particular appreciation of their splendid conduct, which has won for them these citations from the French Army.

3. To the appreciation thus conferred by the Commander-in-Chief, the Corps Commander adds his own and desires that the foregoing be made known in a suitable manner to the officers and soldiers cited.

By direction,

Malin Craig,
Chief of Staff.

May 21, 1918.

The First Company, under Captain Edart, penetrated the German line on the night of May 19-20, 1918, and the following night it drove back with vigor the Germans who came out against us from their lines, thus maintaining our superiority in morale.

. In the course of these operations the American Volunteers (from Second Battalion, 165th Infantry), who were attached to the Edart Company displayed the utmost dash and coolness, as well as a splendid comradeship in battle.

I have the honor to ask for them in recompense the authorization to cite them in my Regimental Order.

Colonel Jungbluth, Cdt. 67th R. I.

*   *   *

6th ARMY CORPS H. Q.   June 15, 1918.

At the moment when the 42nd U. S. Infantry Division is leaving the Lorraine front, the Commanding General of the 6th Army Corps desires to do homage to the fine military qualities which it has continuously exhibited, and to the services which it has rendered in the Baccarat sector.

The offensive ardor, the sense for the utilization and the organization of terrain, the spirit of method, the discipline shown by all its officers and men, the inspiration animating them, prove that at the first call, they can henceforth take a glorious place in the new line of battle.

The Commanding General of the 6th Army Corps expresses his deepest gratitude to the 42nd Division for its precious collaboration; he particularly thanks the distinguished Commander of this Division, General Menoher, the Officers under his orders and his Staff so brilliantly directed by Colonel MacArthur.

It is with a sincere regret that the entire 6th Army Corps sees the 42nd Division depart. But the bonds of affectionate comradeship which have been formed here will not be broken; for us, in faithful memory, are united the living and the dead of the Rainbow Division, those who are leaving for hard combats and those who, after having nobly sacrificed their lives on this Eastern Border, now rest there, guarded over piously by France.

These sentiments of warm esteem will be still more deeply affirmed, during the impending struggles where the fate of Free Peoples is to be decided.

May our units, side by side, contribute valiantly to the triumph of Justice and Right:

GENERAL DUPORT.

June 18, 1918.

To: Colonel McCoy,
        Commanding 165th Inf. Rgt.

My Dear Colonel McCoy:

I greatly appreciate the kind thought you had in sending me your order No. 10 relating the numerous citations that have been granted to the 165th.

The old New York regiment has a great past of glory. I am sure it will be famous on the battlefields of France as it has been in America.

I also want to thank you for the kind farewell you gave Captain Mercier. I know this Officer feels sad in leaving your regiment. He will keep a precious recollection of the six months he spent with his gallant Irish comrades.

With the expression of my personal appreciation of your kindness and my best compliments,

I am,

Sincerely yours,

J. CORBABON,

Major, Liaisón Officer,

42nd Division.

*   *   *

4th ARMY H. Q.   July 16, 1918.

SOLDIERS OF THE 4TH ARMY

During the day of July 15th, you broke the effort of fifteen German divisions, supported by ten others.

They were expected according to their orders to reach the Marne in the evening: You stopped their advance clearly at the point where we desired to engage in and win the battle.

You have the right to be proud, heroic infantrymen and machine gunners of the advance posts who met the attack and broke it up, aviators who flew over it, battalions and batteries which broke it, staffs which so minutely prepared the battlefield.

It is a hard blow for the enemy. It is a grand day for FRANCE.

I count on you that it may always be the same every time he dares to attack you; and with all my heart of a soldier, I thank you.

GOURAUD.

21ST ARMY CORPS,   July 17, 1918.
170TH DIVISION,

General BERNARD, Commanding *par interim* the 170th Division.

To the Commanding General of the 42nd U. S. Inf. Division.

The Commanding General of the 170th Infantry Division desires to express to the Commanding General of the 42nd U. S. Infantry Division his keen admiration for the courage and bravery of which the American Battalions of the 83rd Brigade have given proof in the course of the hard fighting of the 15th and 16th of July, 1918, as also for the effectiveness of the artillery fire of the 42nd U. S. Infantry Division.

In these two days the troops of the United States by their tenacity, largely aided their French comrades in breaking the repeated assaults of the 7th Reserve Division, the 1st Infantry Division and the Dismounted Cavalry Guard Division of the Germans: these latter two divisions are among the best of Germany.

According to the order captured on the German officers made prisoner, their Staff wished to take Chalon-sur-Marne on the evening of July 16th, but it had reconed without the valor of the American and French combatants, who told them with machine gun, rifle and cannon shots that they would not pass.

The Commanding General of the 170th Infantry Division is therefore particularly proud to observe that in mingling their blood gloriously on the Battlefield of Champagne, the Americans and the French of today are continuing the magnificent traditions established a century and a half ago by Washington and Lafayette; it is with this sentiment that he salutes the Noble Flag of the United States in thinking of the final Victory.

BERNARD.

*   *   *

21ST ARMY CORPS   Hq., July 19, 1918.

GENERAL ORDER

At the moment when the 42nd American Division is on the point of leaving the 21st Army Corps, I desire to express my keen satisfaction and my sincere thanks for the service which it has rendered under all conditions.

By its valor, ardor and spirit, it has very particularly distinguished itself on July 15th and 16th in the course of the great battle where the 4th Army broke the German offensive on the CHAMPAGNE front.

I am proud to have had it under my orders during this period; my prayers accompany it in the great struggle engaged in for the Liberty of the World.

GENERAL NAULIN,
Commanding the 21st Army Corps.

6TH ARMY   P. C., July 26, 1918.

NOTE.

The PRESIDENT OF THE REPUBLIC, in the course of a visit to the 6th Army, expressed his satisfaction over the results obtained, as well as for the qualities of valor and perseverance manifested by all units of the Army.

The Commanding General of the 6th Army, is happy to transmit to the troops of his Army the felicitations of the PRESIDENT OF THE REPUBLIC.

Signed: GENERAL DEGOUTTE.

*   *   *

July 28, 1918.

From: Commanding General, 1st Army Corps, Am. E. F.

To: Commanding General, 42nd Division, Am. E. F.

Subject, Congratulations:

1. The return of the 42nd Division to the 1st Army Corps was a matter of self-congratulation for the Corps Commander, not only because of previous relations with the Division, but also because of the crisis which existed at the time of its arrival.

2. The standard of efficient performance of duty which is demanded by the Commander-in-Chief, American E. F., is a high one, involving as it does on an occasion such as the present complete self-sacrifice on the part of the entire personnel, and a willingness to accept cheerfully every demand even to the limit of endurance of the individual for the sake of the Cause for which we are in France.

3. The taking over of the front of the 1st Army Corps under the conditions of relief and advance, together with the attendant difficulties incident to widening the front, was in itself no small undertaking, and there is added to this your advance in the face of the enemy to a depth of five or more kilometers, all under cover of darkness, to the objective laid down by higher authority to be attained, which objective you were holding, regardless of the efforts of the enemy to dislodge you. The Corps Commander is pleased to inform you that the 42nd Division has fully measured up to the high standard above referred to, and he reiterates his self-congratulation that you and your organization are again a part of the 1st Army Corps., Am. E. F.

(Signed) H. LIGGETT,

Major General, U. S. A.

6TH ARMY   P. C. August 9, 1918.

GENERAL ORDER.

Before the great offensive of the .18th of July, the American troops forming part of the 6th French Army distinguished themselves in capturing from the enemy the Bois de la Brigade De Marine and the village of VAUX, in stopping his offensive on the MARNE and at FOSSOY.

Since then, they have taken the most glorious part in a second battle of the MARNE, rivaling in order and in valiance the French troops. They have, in twenty days of incessant combat, liberated numerous French villages and realized across a difficult country an advance of forty kilometers, which has carried them beyond the VESLES.

Their glorious marches are marked by names which will illustrate in the future, the military history of the United States:

TORCY, BELLEAU, Plateau d'ENREPILLY, EPIEDS, Le CHARMEL, l'OURCQ, SERINGES-et-NESLES, SERGY, La VESLE and FISMES.

The new divisions who were under fire for the first time showed themselves worthy of the old war-like traditions of the Regular Army. They have had the same ardent desire to fight the Boche, the same discipline by which an order given by the Chief is always executed, whatever be the difficulties to overcome and the sacrifices to undergo.

The magnificent results obtained are due to the energy and skill of the Chiefs, to the bravery of the soldiers.

I am proud to have commanded such troops.

The General Commanding the 6th Army,
DeGoutte.

*   *   *

Headquarters, 42nd Division,

AMERICAN EXPEDITIONARY FORCES, FRANCE,

August 13, 1918.

TO THE OFFICERS AND MEN OF THE 42ND DIVISION:

A year has elapsed since the formation of your organization. It is, therefore, fitting to consider what you have accomplished as a combat division and what you should prepare to accomplish in the Future.

Your first elements entered the trenches in Lorraine on February 21st. You served on that front for 110 days. You were the first American division to hold a divisional sector and when you left the sector June 21st, you had served continuously as a division in the trenches for a longer time than any other American division. Although you entered the sector without experience in actual warfare, you so conducted yourselves as to win the respect and affection of the French veterans with whom you fought. Under gas and bombardment, in raids, in patrols, in the heat of hand-to-hand combat, and in the long, dull hours of trench routine so trying to a soldier's spirit, you bore yourselves in a manner worthy of the traditions of our country.

You were withdrawn from Lorraine and moved immediately to the Champagne front, where, during the critical days from July 14th to July 18th, you had the honor of being the only American division to fight in General Gouraud's Army, which so gloriously obeyed his order: "We will stand or die," and by its iron defense crushed the German assaults and made possible the offensive of July 18th to the west of Reims.

From Champagne you were called to take part in exploiting the success north of the Marne. Fresh from the battle front before Chalons, you were thrown against the picked troops of Germany. For eight consecutive days, you attacked skillfully prepared positions. You captured great stores of arms and munitions. You forced the crossings of the Ourcq. You took Hill 212, Sergy, Meurcy Farm and Seringes by assault. You drove the enemy, including an Imperial Guard Division, before you for a depth of fifteen kilometers. When your infantry was relieved, it was in full pursuit of the retreating Germans, and your artillery continued to progress and support another American division in the advance to the Vesle.

For your services in Lorraine, your division was formally commended in General Orders by the French Army Corps under which you served. For your services in Champagne, your assembled officers received the personal thanks and commendation of General Gouraud himself. For your service on the Ourcq, your division was officially complimented in a letter from the Commanding General, 1st Army Corps, of July 28th, 1918.

To your success, all ranks and all services have contributed, and I desire to express to every man in the command my appreciation of his devoted and courageous effort.

However, our position places a burden of responsibility upon us which we must strive to bear steadily forward without faltering. To our comrades who have fallen, we owe the sacred obligation of maintaining the reputation which they died to establish. The influence of our performance on our Allies and on our enemies can not be over estimated, for we were one of the first divisions sent from our country to France to show the world that Americans can fight.

Hard battles and long campaigns lie before us. Only by ceaseless vigilance and tireless preparation can we fit ourselves for them. I urge you, therefore, to approach the future with confidence, but above all, with firm determination that so far as it is in your power you will spare no effort, whether in training or in combat, to maintain the record of our division and the honor of our country.

CHARLES T. MENOHER,
Major General, U. S. Army.

Headquarters 42nd Division.

SUMMARY OF INTELLIGENCE.

October, 1918.

On October 18, 1917, one year ago today, the Headquarters and certain of the elements of the 42nd Division sailed for France. . . .

The Division is now engaged in the most difficult task to which it has yet been set: The piercing at its apex of the "Kriemhilde Stellung," upon the defense of which position the German line from METZ to CHAMPAGNE depends.

During its service in France, Division Headquarters has had its Post of Command at 23 different points in towns, woods and dugouts. The Division has captured prisoners from 23 enemy divisions, including three Guard and one Austro-Hungarian divisions.

CHARLES T. MENOHER,

Major General, U. S. Army

*　　　*　　　*

HEADQUARTERS 42d DIVISION.

American Expeditionary Forces. France.

November 11th, 1918.

To the Officers and Men of the 42nd Division:

On the 13th of August I addressed you a letter summarizing the record of your achievements in Lorraine, before Chalons and on the Ourcq. On the occasion of my leaving the Division I wish to recall to you your services since that time and to express to you my appreciation of the unfailing spirit of courage and cheerfulness with which you have met and overcome the difficult tasks which have confronted you.

After leaving the region of Chateau Thierry you had scarcely been assembled in your new area when you were ordered to advance by hard night marches to participate in the attack of the St. Mihiel Salient. In this first great operation of the American Army you were instructed to attack in the center of the Fourth Army Corps and to deliver the main blow in the direction of the heights overlooking the Madine River. In the battle that followed you took every objective in accordance with the plan of the Army Commander. You advanced fourteen kilometers in twenty-eight hours. You pushed forward advance elements five kilometers further, or nineteen kilometers beyond your original starting point. You took more than one thousand prisoners from nine enemy divisions. You captured seven villages and forty-two square kilometers of territory. You seized large supplies of food, clothing, ammunition, guns and engineering material.

Worn though you were by ceaseless campaigning since February, you then moved to the Verdun region to participate in the great blow which your country's armies have struck west of the Meuse. You took Hill

283, La Tuilerie Farm and the Cote de Chatillon and broke squarely across the powerful Kriemhilde Stellung, clearing the way for the advance beyond St. Georges and Landres-et-St. Georges. Marching and fighting day and night you thrust through the advancing lines of the forward troops of the First Army. You drove the enemy across the Meuse. You captured the heights dominating the River before Sedan and reached in the enemy lines the farthest points attained by any American troops.

Since September 12th you have taken over twelve hundred prisoners; you have freed twenty-five French villages; you have recovered over one hundred and fifty square kilometers of French territory and you have captured great supplies of enemy munitions and material.

Whatever may come in the future, the men of this Division will have the proud consciousness that they have thus far fought wherever the American flag has flown most gloriously in this war. In the determining battle before Chalons, in the bloody drive from Chateau Thierry to the Vesle, in the blotting out of the St. Mihiel Salient, and in the advance to Sedan you have played a splendid and a leading part.

I know that you will give the same unfailing support to whoever may succeed me as your Commander, and that you will continue to bear forward without faltering the colors of the Rainbow Division. I leave you with deep and affectionate regret, and I thank you again for your loyalty to me and your services to your country. You have struck a vital blow in the greatest war in history. You have proved to the world in no mean measure that our country can defend its own.

CHARLES T. MENOHER,

Major General, U. S. Army.

*   *   *

AMERICAN EXPEDITIONARY FORCES,

Office of the Commander-in-Chief.

France, March 22, 1919.

Major General Clement A. F. Flagler,
    Commanding 42nd Division,
        American E. F.,
            Ahrweiler, Germany.

My Dear General Flagler:
    It afforded me great satisfaction to inspect the 42nd Division at Remagen on March 16th, during my trip through the Third Army, and to extend at that time to the officers and men my appreciation of their splendid record while in France.

The share which the 42nd Division has had in the success of our Armies should arouse pride in its achievements among all ranks. Arriving as it did on November 1, 1917, it was one of the first of our combat divisions to participate in active operations. After a period of training which lasted through the middle of February, 1918, it entered the Luneville sector in Lorraine, and shortly afterwards took up a position in that part of the line near Baccarat. In July it magnificently showed its fighting ability in the Champagne-Marne defensive, at which time units from the 42nd Division aided the French in completely repulsing the German attack. Following this, on July 25th, the Division relieved the 28th in the Aisne-Marne offensive, and in the course of their action there captured La Croix Rouge Farme, Sergy, and established themselves on the northern side of the Ourcq In the St. Mihiel offensive the division made a rapid advance of 19 kilometers, capturing seven villages. Later, during the Meuse-Argonne battle, it was twice put in the line, first under the 5th Corps and second under the 1st Corps, at which later time it drove back the enemy until it arrived opposite Sedan on November 7th.

Since the signing of the armistice, the 42nd Division has had the honor of being one of those composing the Army of Occupation, and I have only words of praise for their splendid conduct and demeanor during this time. I want each man to realize the part he has played in bringing glory to American arms and to understand both my pride and the pride of their fellows throughout the American Expeditionary Forces in their record. My good wishes accompany your command on its return to the United States, and my interest will remain with its members in their future careers.

Sincerely yours,

(Signed) JOHN J. PERSHING.

OFFICERS WHO SERVED IN THE 165TH INFANTRY

Colonels
Barker, John W.
(Promoted to Brigadier General)
Donovan, William J.

Promoted from Major)
Hine, Charles D.
Howland, Charles R.
McCoy, Frank R.
(Promoted to Brigadier General)
Mitchell, Harry D.
(Promoted from Lieut.-Colonel)
Lieut.-Colonels
Anderson, Alexander E.

(Promoted from Captain)

Dravo, Charles A.
Moynahan, Timothy J.
(Promoted from Major)
Reed, Latham R.
Majors
Bootz, Henry A.
(Promoted from 1st Lieut.)
Doyle, William T.
(Promoted from Captain)

Guggenheim, Robert M.
(Promoted from 1st Lieut.)
Kelly, Michael A.
(Promoted from Captain)
Lawrence, George J.
McAdie, George
(Promoted from Captain)
McKenna, James A *
(Promoted from Captain)
Mangan, John J.
(Promoted from Captain)
Meaney, Martin H.
(Promoted from Captain)
Merle-Smith, Van S.
(Promoted from Captain)
Powers, Walter E.
(Promoted from Captain)
Reilley, Thomas T.
(Promoted from Captain)
Stacom, William B.
Kennelly, William
(Promoted from Captain)
Watson, James
Zorn, Jay

* Deceased

Captains

Archer, James
(Promoted from 1st Lieut.)
Allen, Richard J.
(Promoted from 2nd Lieut.)
Baker, Chas. D.*
(Promoted from 1st Lieut.)
Becker, Beverly H.
(Promoted from 1st Lieut.)
Behrends, Jerome B.
(Promoted from 1st Lieut.)
Billings, Forest E.
(Promoted from 1st Lieut.)
Burns, Coleman
(Promoted from 1st Lieut.)
Buck, Oscar L.
(Promoted from 1st Lieut.)
Cavanaugh, William P.
(Promoted from 1st Lieut.)
Cooke, William C.
(Promoted from 2nd Lieut.)
Cassidy, Henry K.
(Promoted from 2nd Lieut.)
Conners, John F.
(Promoted from 1st Lieut.)
Connelly, Edmond J.
(Promoted from 2nd Lieut.)
Clifford, John J.
(Promoted from 2nd Lieut.)
Cooper, Jackson S.
Dudley, Gerry B.
DeLacour, R. B.
(Promoted from 1st Lieut.)
Elmer, Basil B.
(Promoted from 1st Lieut.)
Finn, James G.
Foley, James L.
(Promoted from 1st Lieut.)
Given, William B.
(Promoted from 1st Lieut.)
Green, John A.
(Promoted from 1st Lieut.)
Graham, Walter R.
Hurley, John P.
Hudson, William E.
Houghton, James T.
(Promoted from 1st Lieut.)
Grose, Howard
(Promoted from 1st Lieut.)
Josselyn, Ralph R.
Kinney, Thomas A.
(Promoted from 1st Lieut.)
Landrigan, Alfred W.
(Promoted from 1st Lieut.)

Lyttle, John D.
(Promoted from 1st Lieut.)
Lawrence, Austin L.
(Promoted from 1st Lieut.)
O'Brien, Joseph F.
(Promoted from 1st Lieut.)
McKenna, William F.
(Promoted from 1st Lieut.)
McNamara, Francis J.
(Promoted from 2nd Lieut.)
McDermott, Thomas B.
(Promoted from 2nd Lieut.)
Mangan, James M.
(Promoted from 2nd Lieut.)
Martin, Arthur H.
(Promoted from 1st Lieut.)
Marsh, Frank
(Promoted from 1st Lieut.)
Smith, Samuel A.
(Promoted from 1st Lieut.)
Seibert, Kenneth C.
Stout, Louis A.
(Promoted from 1st Lieut.)
Riggs, Francis P.
Ryan, Richard J.
Ogle, Kenneth
(Promoted from 1st Lieut.)
Prout, John T.
(Promoted from 1st Lieut.)
Gillespie, Francis H.
Walsh, Michael J.*
(Promoted from 1st Lieut.)
Rowley, John F.
(Promoted from 2nd Lieut.)

First Lieutenants

Allen, Harold L.
Arnold, Howard W.*
Bell, Ernest L.
Board, Walter
Benz, George A.
Byrne, Bernard E.
Baldwin, William W.*
Boag, Joseph J.
Burns, William J.
Burke, John J.
Brownstone, Michael
Betty, Harold J.
Carroll, Joseph V.
Carson, Allen G.
Cowett, Max P.
Collier, James
Crandall, H. W.

----

* Deceased

Crawford, Henry E.
Doris, Roscoe
Damico, Joseph G.
Dowling, Patrick J.*
Everett, Eugene F.
Force, Russell
Fechheimer, John H.
Friedlander, William M.
Furbershaw, Arthur W.
Goodell, Guy F.
Guignon, Emile S.
Hanley, James M.
Howe, Paul D.
Henry, John T.
Heller, Abraham I.
Horak, Frank
Hutchinson, Warren B.
Heinel, John P.
Hurt, Paul A.
Holmes, Merril J.
Irving, Lawrence
Johnson, Clarence E.
Knowles, Ralph S.
King, George I.
Kirkland, John
Kilcourse, John J.
Ketcham, Ralph C.
Kane, Bothwell B.*
Keveny, John
Korst, Donald F.
Kelly, Henry E.
Kirschner, William J.
Lawrence, Andrew W.
Leslie, J. Langdon
Light, Wesley W.
Leaper, Robert B.
Levine, A. A.
McNamara, Joseph D.
McIntyre, James B.
McCartney, A. R.
McCormick, Charles A.
McCormick, Edward J.
McKeon, Andrew J.
Martin, Thomas C. P.
Martin, Reune
Norman, John *
O'Donohue, Joseph J.
Orgle, Samuel Z.
O'Sullivan, John F.
Otto, George F.
Patton, William H.
Pierce, Charles H.
Platt, Sherman T.
Poore, John G.
Perry, Donald A.

Powers, Robert E.
Robertson, Allen D.
Stevens, Floyd L.
Stone, Thomas F.
Spencer, William M.
Sims, Anthony J.
Springer, Franklin H.
Seidelmann, Joseph H.
Smith, Francis
Smith, Herman H.*
Surber, Paul
Stokes, Horace W.
Schwinn, John M.
Terry, Alvah L.
Tarr, Marshall A.
Trotter, L. S.
Williams, Harry V.
Williams, Allen R.
Williams, John J.
Wheeler, William D.
Warren, George H.
Young, Thomas H.*

Second Lieutenants

Ames, Oliver *
Ahern, David H.
Alexander, John M.
Arenholz, William J.
Beach, Clayton W.*
Bocard, Fred J.
Burns, Zenas T.
Burns, James S. D.*
Burns, Edwin J.
Boone, Philip T.
Bunnell, A. L.
Bonner, Robert
Brocard, Frank
Brosnan, John J.
Bracken, Benjamin
Burke, John H.
Cunningham, Arthur W.
Carten, James E.
Carleton, Howard C.
Callahan, Andrew J.
Crane, William D.
Collier, James
Crimmins, Clarence
Crandall, Harold M.
Carter, Franklin W.
Daly, Edwin A.*
Daly, Ewing P.
Devine, Thomas J.
Davis, Henry W.*

*Deceased

DeAguerro, Miguel E.
Ellett, Andrew L.*
Elliott, Don
Finn, William
Flynn, Daniel K.
Field, Eugene B.
Graham, William H.
Greff, Lester M.
Goodwin, Schuyler
Hutchinson, Roderick
Hawes, Lincoln
Hervey, Frank
Henry, J. F.
Huelser, Charles A.
Johnston, Frank
Johnson, Cortland
Johnson, Clarence E.
Jewell, William A.*
Jackson, Thomas J.
Kotz, George I.
Kelly, William T.
Koenig, Paul S.
Katch, Joseph J.
Laughlin, James C.
Levenberg, Lawrence F.
Lacy, Philip S.
Larkin, John J.
Lawson, Alexander
Larney, Leo
Lenoir, Frank
Levy, Morris R.
Lisiezki, Stanley K.
Lanette, Kenneth
McKnight, John
McMullin, James C.
McNulty, William
McMullin, Frank
Metcalfe, George T.
Metcalfe, Earl K.
McCarthy, Thomas J.
Meyer, John L.
Mixon, Robert
Morthurst, Aloysius F.
Mela, Alvin S.
Monohan, John J.
Monohan, Humphery J.
Murphy, Frank M.
Neary, Patrick
Newton, Raymond
Norris, Elton R.
O'Connor, William L.*
Orr John P.*

Parker, Charles
Peace, Walter
Philbin, Ewing
Reynolds, Arthur W.
Richardson, D. M.
Rupe, Forest D.
Rowe, Lester G.
Shultes, Clarence L.
Searles, William
Sasser, Frank M.
Scheffler, Edward S.
Swift, Samuel S.
Sherrell, William J.
Stott, Gerald R.*
Slayter, Russell B.
Samuels, Charles G.
Sears, Stephen C.
Smith, McRae
Smoot, Walter E.
Shanley, Bernard
Sharp, James W.
Stovern, Gotfred
Sleep, Leroy
Strang, Albert L.
Sasnett, Lucien
Sipma, Edward
Self, Frank M.
Sebert, G. A.
Sasser, F.
Sense, W. J.
Sipp, Paul
Silliman, Harper
Schert, Gustavious A.
Temple, Francis C.
Tucker, Milton H.
Todd, Fred L.
Tuttle, Malcolm W.
Underhill, Charles A.
Urban, Paul J.
Vance, Vernon
Vandiver, Basil A.
Van Alstine, Frank
Veach, Columbus H.
Williams, Henry C.
Winans, Chester B.
Weller, Reginald
Warner, Hunt
Watkins, George F.*
Worsley, Thomas H.
Wallace, Williamson N.
Wilkerson, Marcus E.

* Deceased

ROSTER OF SERGEANTS *

*Abbreviations: KIA (Killed in action or died of wounds); A.C.S. (sent to Army Candidates' school); Com. (commissioned).

Sergeants—Co. A.

John J. O'Leary, 1st Sgt.—KIA
James J. Hughes, Sgt. Major, 83rd Brig.
Joseph S. Higginson
Martin V. Cook—Com.
Charles Lanzner—KIA.
Charles Schmidt
Daniel O'Connell—Com.
John F. O'Sullivan—Com.
Michael J. Walsh
Stephen L. Purtell
Timothy J. Monohan, Sgt. Major
Frank H. Squire
Thomas J. Sweeney, 1st Sgt.
William G. Moore—Com.
C. Donald Matthews—A.C.S.
Bernard J. White—Sgt. Major
Spencer Rossell—A.C.S.
Charles A. Underhill—Com.
John F. Scully
Patrick Ames—KIA.
Hugh J. McPadden
John H. Dennelly
Clancy VanArsdale
Lester Hanley—KIA.
Frank J. Fisher
William M. Walsh—KIA.
Patrick J. Doolan—KIA.
John A. McDonald—KIA.
Edward J. Mooney
Clyde G. Evans
James J. Duff—KIA.
William F. Ogilvie
Frederick R. Stenson—KIA
George V. Armstrong
Harold J. Henderson
Michael Morley
Joseph C. Pettit
William Mehl
Albert Kiley, Co. Clk.
Harry Blaustein
Edward P. Wylie

Sergeants, Co. B.

John O'Neill, 1st Sgt—A.C.S., KIA.
Michael C. Horgan
James Taylor
James Brogan—KIA.
Ole J. Olsen
Harry Ashworth
John A. Donovan
Speros Thomas
John A. Sullivan
Alexander Whalen
Francis J. Lynch
Henry J. Kiernan—KIA.
William G. Braniff
Patrick Kelly
Edward J. Kelly
Preston D. Travis
Joseph Gilgar
James J. Cullinan
Thomas F. Brady
William Thornton
William S. Gilbert
Vincent P. Mulholland, 1st Sgt.—A.C.S.
James Donnelly—KIA.
John J. Mahoney—KIA.
Joseph D. Graham
James E. Coyne
Lawrence Steppello
James Langan
Matthew J. Brennan
Martin Naughton
Frederick Coyne, Co. Clk.
Herbert P. McClymont
Alfredo Menicocci
John A. Donovan
Frank A. Frederick—A.C.S.
James Gilhooley
Edward Kraemer—KIA.
William F. Mallin, Bn. Sgt.-Major, A.C.S.
Hugh E. Stengel
John A. Sullivan
Joseph Gilgar

Sergeants, Co. C.

William Hatton, 1st Sgt., Sgt.-Major, H. Q., 42nd Div.
R. S. Powell, 1st Sgt.—A.C.S.
Eugene B. Halpin, 1st Sgt., U. S. A. as instructor
Thomas P. O'Hagan, 1st Sgt.
John D. Crittenden—A.C.S.
Thomas Halpin—A.C.S.
James J. Grace
Edward J. O'Connell
James F. Nelson

James Barry
Joseph W. Burns
James T. Burns
Denis Cahill
J. H. Casey
Edward P. Clowe—KIA.
Frank W. Colyer
Walter S. Coon
Nathaniel B. Crittenden
Frank L. Curtis
Daniel J. Davern
John P. Duffy
Frank L. Drivdahl
Daniel S. Garvey—KIA.
Herman Hillig
Harry E. Horgan—KIA.
Edward J. Kearin—KIA.
Peter Keller
John W. Knight
John E. McAuliffe
Eugene A. McNiff
Hugo E. Noack
Thomas O'Kelly
George E. Richter
Bernard Ryan—KIA.
Matthew Synott—Com.
Louis J. Torrey—KIA.
Arthur C. Totten
John F. Vermaelen—KIA.
Anthony Gallagher
Joseph Hennessey
Michael Cooney
Louis C. Dedecker
Frederick R. Garrison
Thomas P. McPherson
Joseph Peisel
Archilbald F. Reilly
Michael Ruane

Sergeants, Co. D.

Thomas H. Sullivan, 1st. Sgt—Com.
Thomas W. Brown
Colton C. Bingham, U. S. A., as Instructor
John Cahill
Martin E. Carroll
Stephen J. Crotty
Thomas J. Curtin, 1st Sgt.—KIA.
John Curtin, Color Sgt.
John Daly
Harold J. Dibblee—Com.
Edward J. Geaney, 1st Sgt.—A.C.S.
John J. Gribbon—A.C.S.

Patrick Grogan
Joseph W. Halper, Co. Clk.
Patrick J. Heaney
John F. Ingram—KIA.
Stanley W. Jones
Thomas F. Keyes
George H. Krick
Joseph J. Lynch
Denis McAuliffe
Patrick J. McDonough
Edward A. McIntee
Martin McMahon
John McNamara—KIA.
John P. Mohr
John F. Moran
George R. Morton
Lester J. Moriarty
Hubert V. Murray, 1st Sgt.—A.C.S.
Denis Murphy
Denis O'Brien
Denis O'Connor
Daniel B. J. O'Connell, Reg. Sgt.-Major
Thomas M. O'Malley
Richard W. O'Neill
Daniel J. O'Neill
William J. Maloney—Com.
Edward B. Smith
Arthur C. Strang—Com.
Joseph P. Tracy
James S. Whitty
Joseph L. Sheehan, 1st Sgt.
James O'Brien
Herbert DeWilde
Dalton Smith
Edgar T. Farrell
Michael J. McAuliffe
Martin J. Hurst
Robert K. Niddrie

Sergeants, Co. E.

William L. Bailey, 1st Sgt.—U. S. A., as Instructor
Thomas A. Carney—Com.
Charles F. Finnerty—Com.
William Lippincott—Com.
William T. Kelly—Com.
Andrew Callahan—Com.
Frank Johnston, 1st. Sgt.—Com.
William Maloney
Archibald Skeats
Douglas McKenzie
Frank E. Donnelly, 1st Sgt.—A.C.S.

Bernard J. Kelly
Hugh McKiernan
John F. Riordan
John A. Wilde
William J. Foley
James Moran
Daniel Donohue
Harold J. Carmody
Michael Lynch—KIA.
Lester Lenhart—KIA.
William A. Halligan—Co. Clk.
Leon Hodges
John Schluter—A.C.S.
Alban A. Delaney—A.C.S.
James Hyland
Carl Kahn
Edward P. Scanlon, Reg. Sup. Sgt.
Edward J. Vahey
Alexander Smeltzer
John Burke
Michael Darcy
Arthur J. Lefrancois
James McCready
Augustus Morgan
Thomas J. Reidy
Thomas Gaffney
Alfred S. Helmer
George S. Malloy
Edward J. Rickert
John J. Horan, Co. Clk.

Sergeants, Co. F.

Joseph V. Blake, 1st Sgt.—A.C.S.
Timothy J. McCrohan, 1st Sgt.—A.C.S.
James J. McGuinn
Philip Gargan
John J. Keane—Com.
William F. Hanifin—Com.
Herbert L. Doyle—Com.
Joseph A. Wynne
Michael J Bowler, Bri. Sgt. Major—A.C.S.
Edward A Ginna
Charles B. Echeverria—KIA.
Joseph H. Trueman—A.C.S.
Eugene Cunningham—A.C.S.
Philip T. Boone—Com.
Raymond A. Long
William E. Boone
John P. Mahon—Com.
Thomas Leddy—A.C.S.
Thomas J. Erb—KIA.
Charles E. Denon—KIA.
Michael Douglas—A.C.S.

Patrick J. Wynne
Malcolm F. Joy
William Boland
James J. McCormack
John R. Butler
Theodore H. Hagen
Lawrence J. Whalen—KIA.
Cornelius Behan
James W. Brennan, 1st Sgt.
James J. Bevan
Leo J. McLaughlin
John J. Gill
Louis D. Edwards
William Graceley
Albert E. Curtis
Maurice Fine
Harold E. Dahl, Co. Clk.
Timothy Keane

Sergeants, Co. G.

John H. Burke, 1st. Sgt.—Com.
John Meaney, 1st Sgt.—U. S. A. as Instructor
Charles B. Grundy, 1st. Sgt.—A.C.S.
Frank W. Bull, 1st Sgt.—Com.
Alfred H. Taylor, 1st Sgt.
John McNamara, 1st Sgt.
Charles J. Meagher, 1st Sgt.
Charles Sulzberger—Com.
Joseph McCourt
John W. Farrell
William Farrell
Patrick Donohue
Leroy T. Wells—Com.
William Durk
James P. Robinson—KIA.
Denis Downing—KIA.
Thomas Slevin
John J. Conroy
James Murray—Col. Sgt.
James D. Coffey
Edward McNamara
Thomas T. Williamson
Martin Shalley
Denis O'Connor
Denis Corcoran
Thomas W. Ferguson—A.C.S.
Martin Murphy
Ralph Holmes
Michael Hogan
Denis Roe
Carl G. Kemp—A.C.S.
Kenneth B. Morford
Irving Framan

Roy L. Bull
John W. Brogan
Frank Malloy
Patrick Regan
Hugh Lee
John J. McMahon
Howard B. Gregory, Sgt.-Major,
  42nd Div.
John Ryan, Co. Clk.
Franklyn Dorman, Co. Clk.
Maurice Dwyer
James J. Elliott
James Regan
Patrick Keane

Sergeants, Co. H.

Joseph E. Nash, 1st Sgt.—Com.
Bernard Finnerty—KIA.
Patrick F. Craig—Com.
Robert V. Frye—Com.
James J. Hamilton—KIA.
Joseph Mattiello
Patrick Neary—Com.
Daniel J. O'Neill, 1st Sgt.—KIA.
Jerome F. O'Neill, 1st. Sgt.—A.C.S.
George G. Ashe—Com.
Daniel L. Dayton—Com.
Reginald Mitchell—Com.
John F. Tully—A.C.S.
John F. O'Connor, 1st. Sgt.
Frank S. Condit
James A. Dooley
Miles V. Dowling
John P. Furey
Charles J. Gavin
Bruno Gunther
Martin J. Higgins
James Hogan
John Lynch
Andrew Murray
William J. Murray, Co. Clk.
James F. O'Brien
William O'Neill, 1st Sgt.—KIA.
William Smythe
James Todd
Patrick Travers
Michael Treacey
Dudley M. Winthrop
Frank A. Mader
John J. Ryan
William J. Fleming
Patrick J. Dwyer
John J. Walker
Joseph O'Rourke—KIA.
Eugene J. Sweeney

Sergeants, Co. I.

Henry K. Adikes
William T. Beyer—Batt. Sgt.-
  Major
Charles A. Connolly—KIA.
Charles R. Cooper
Patrick Collins—KIA.
Martin Durkin
William G. Dynan
Otto Fritz
Patrick Flynn
Charles J. Ford—KIA.
Alfred F. Georgi—Co. Clk.
Charles H. Garrett
Michael J. Jordan—A.C.S.
William Harrison—KIA.
James J. Hennessey—A.C.S.
Edward P. Joyce—Batt. Sgt.-
  Major, A.C.S.
John F. Joyce—Com.
William Lyle
William F. Lyons
Leo Larney—Com.
William McLaughlin—KIA.
Richard McLaughlin
John C. McDermott
Hugh McFadden
Patrick T. McMeniman, 1st Sgt—
  U. S. A., as Instructor
Frank McMorrow, 1st Sgt.
Frank Mulligan
Harold J. Murphy
Wilfred Fee
Joseph F. Neil
Thomas P. O'Brien
James Quilty
William Reutlinger
Patrick Rogan
John J. Sheehan
Edward Shanahan, 1st Sgt.
Charles B. Stone—KIA
James Sullivan
George Strenk
James Warnock

Sergeants, Co. K.

Timothy J. Sullivan, 1st Sgt.—
  A.C.S.
Francis Meade—A.C.S.
James J. Mullen
Claude Da Costa—A.C.S.
John H. Embree—KIA.
Frank Doughney—KIA.
John L. Ross—KIA.

John Gavaghan—KIA.
Peter J. Crotty—KIA.
Bernard J. McElroy—KIA
John J. McLoughlin
William B. Montross
John J. Gibbons
James J. Sullivan
Herbert F. McKenna—A.C.S.
Patrick Boland
Bernard Leavy
Joseph M. Farrell—Com.
Leo G. Bonnard—A.C.S.
Wilfred T. Van Yorx—A.C.S.
Herbert J. Kelly—A.C.S.
Harold A. Benham
John T. Vogel
George F. Meyer
George C. Sicklick
Edward K. Rooney
James F. Kelly
Patrick J. Ryan
Max Puttlitz
Michael Costello, Co. Clk.
Francis Caraher
William P. McKessy
John Naughton
Cornelius Rooney
Philip Hellriegel
Oliver Atkinson
Robert L. Crawford
James J. Dalton
James W. Daly
Thomas M. Gleason
Augustus F. Hughes

Sergeants, Co. L.

Eugene F. Gannon, 1st Sgt.—U.
S. A., as Instructor
John J. Ahearn
Joseph Beliveau
Christian F. Bezold
Richard Blood
Thomas F. Collins—Com., KIA.
Raymond Convey—KIA.
John J. Donoghue—A.C.S., KIA.
Frank J. Duffy, Sgt.-Major, 42nd
Div.
Thomas E. Dunn
Michael Fitzpatrick
Lewis M. French
Joseph A. Grace
Thomas A. Heffernan, 1st Sgt.—
A.C.S.
George S. Kerr—KIA.
Thomas Kiernan—A.C.S.

Nicholas A. Landzert—KIA.
John J. Larkin—Com.
Patrick McCarthy
Eugene McCue, 1st Sgt.
Harry McDermott
Hugh McGriskin
John B. McHugh
Arthur McKenny
Thomas McLoughlin
William E. Malinka—A.C.S.
John J. Mulvey
John E. Mullen
James J. Murphy
William J. Murphy
George V. Murphy
John J. Murphy
Daniel O'Brien
Thomas P. O'Donovan—KIA
Charles Peacox
David Redmond—A.C.S.
Valentine Roesel
William Sheahan, Col. Sgt.—KIA.
Charles Siedler—A.C.S.
Walter F. Watson
Fred G. Wittlinger, 1st Sgt.
Bernard Woods
John Southworth
Patrick McCarthy
Leo Mullin

Sergeants, Co. M.

John J. Kenny, 1st Sgt.—A.C.S.
Joseph E. Jerue—A.C.S.
Ambrose Sutcliff
Francis Eustace, 1st Sgt.
Denis McCarthy
Richard J. McCarthy—A.C.S.
Peter Cooney—KIA.
Sydney A. DaCosta—A.C.S.
David G. Morrison—Com.
Charles Pfeiffer—Com.
Howard D. Emerson, 1st Sgt.—
A.C.S.
James McGarvey, 1st Sgt.—Com.
Frank J. Rogers—Com.
William J. Francis—KIA.
Patrick B. Hayes
Herman H. VonGlahn—Com.
Henry S. Fisher—A.C.S.
James J. Hughes—A.C.S.
Harry Messemer
Frank May
John Barrow
James M. Major
Patrick J. Clark

Joseph A. Moran
'Fernand C. Thomas
Edward F. Flanagan
Francis X. McNamara
John J. McLoughlin
Thomas Courtney
John O'Connor
John B. Manson
John J. Feeley
James F. Shanahan
Eddie I. Stevens—Co. Clk.
Denis Donovan
Daniel Flynn

Sergeants, Supply Co.

Joseph F. Flannery, Reg. Supply Sgt.
Edward P. Scanlon, Reg. Supply Sgt.
John J. Kennedy, Reg. Supply Sgt.
Joseph Comiskey, 1st Sgt.
Roland Ferdinando, 1st Sgt.
James W. Henry
Charles Feick
James J. Heffernan
William Nicholson
James Murphy
Walter Bishop
Robert Goss
Thomas S. Lacey—Com.
William G. Fagan
Harry Mallen
Charles Larson
James McMahon
William J. Drennan—A.C.S.
Robert Stanton—Co. Clk.
Edward L. Callahan
Bernard Lowe
Arthur B. Nulty

Frank Nelson—Co. Clk.

Sergeants, Headquarters Co.
Donald P. Adair
William J. Arenholz—Com.
Pendleton Beall—A.C.S.
Abram Blaustein—Com.
Leonard J. Beck
Robert A. Blackford
John F. Boyle
Herbert E. Clarke
Robert L. Clarke
Stewart S. Clinton
Gustav Cosgrove
Richard J. Cray

Fred W. Cudmore
Ronald O. Dietz
Robert Donnelly
Francis Driscoll, U. S. A., as Instructor
Lemist Esler, U. S. A., as Instructor
William Evers—Band
Alfred H. Fawkner—Com.
William E. Fernie
Thomas E. Fitzsimmons
Lawrence J. Flynn—Band
Jerome Goldstein
Leonard P. Grant—Com.
Constantine J. Harvey
Gerald L. Harvey
George D. Heilman
Diedrich Heins
Edward J. Hussey—KIA.
Arthur C. Jaeger
John V. Kerrigan
Joyce Kilmer—KIA.
Russell Klages
George D. Kramer
Robert N. Lee
Charles Leister
James Lynch—Band
Thomas E. Lynch
Thomas J. McCarthy, 1st Sgt.—Com.
Samuel G. McConaughy
Leonard Monzert—A.C.S.
Thomas Mullady
John J. Mullins, Sgt. Bugler
William P. Murray—Band
Frank Miller—Band
Erwin L. Meisel
William P. Neacy—A.C.S.
James O'Brien
Francis A. O'Connell, Col. Sgt.—Com.
Denis O'Shea, 1st Sgt.—Com.
Medary A. Prentiss—Com.
Theodore C. Ranscht
Michael Rendini
Leslie B. Reynolds
Kenneth G. Russell—Com.
John J. Ryan, 1st Sgt.
Walter T. Ryan
William F. Shannon
William J. Sieger
James V. Smith
Ambrose M. Steinert, Reg. Sgt.-Major
Patrick Stokes—Band

Albert L. Strang, Batt. Sgt.-Major
—Com.
Miles Sweeney—Band
Thomas J. Taylor
Walter F. Thompson—Co. Clk.
Robert Taggart
Harrison J. Uhl, Col. Sgt.—Com.
George W. Utermehle
Emmett S. Watson
Roy A. West
Marcus E. Wilkinson—Com.
Charles F. Willermin
Frederick T. Young
Howard R. Young
Henry E. Zitzmann—Band Leader
Edward H. Jeffries—Com.

Sergeants, Machine-Gun Co.

A. Andrews
Gerald Beekman
Harry P. Bruhn—KIA.
Thomas J. Berkley—Com.
J. T. Brooks—KIA.
Anthony J. Daly
Thomas J. Devine—Com.
Thomas F. Doherty
William A. Drake—KIA.
Victor M. Denis
Maurice Dunn
E. O. Ericksson—Com.
Paul R. Fay
John H. Flint
Frank Gardella—KIA.
J. J. Hagerty—Com.

Peter Gillespie
C. F. Hunt
J. R. Keller
L. Kerrigan
Ralph C. Ketchum—Com.
John Kilgannon
James E. Ledwith
Allen J. McBride—Com.
John J. McBride, 1st Sgt.
Harry J. McKelvey—Co. Clk.
John T. Malvey
T. J. Meredith
K. F. Morey
John Mulstein
Maurice M. O'Keefe
William Patterson
Sidney F. Ryan
William A. Sheppard, U. S. A., as
Instructor
John J. Spillane
Joseph McCourt, 1st Sgt.
Frank Stevens

Sergeants, San. Det.

Warren W. Lokker, Sgt. 1st Class
William Helgers, Sgt. 1st Class
Victor L. Eichorn
Arthur Firman
William F. Hayes
William J. Maher
Daniel McConlogue
William K. McGrath
Thomas V. Boland—Co. Clk.

IRISH NAMES

Since returning home I have read with great interest the unique historical study of Mr. Michael J. O'Brien on the part played by the Irish in the early history of the Colonies and particularly in the Revolutionary War, founded on an exhaustive examination of Irish names inscribed in army rosters and other records of the period. In order to avoid the suspicion of over-playing his hand, Mr. O'Brien had to confine himself to names like his own, which undeniably indicate Irish birth or descent. He must have passed over many names which are common in every group of Irish throughout the world.

If we take only the names which have become prominent in the recent endeavors to establish the independence of Ireland—De Valera and Marcoviecz do not sound particularly Irish (even the militant lady's maiden name of Gore-Booth does not much improve the matter) ; and while Kelly, Ryan, Dunn and Duffy are to the manner born, there was a time when Walsh, Pearse, and Plunkett were foreign names, Norman or Danish; and Kent, McNeil and Griffiths might very well be respectively English, Scotch or Welsh.

In the Regiment we had some good men of Scottish descent, but we had a number who volunteered for the Regiment drawn by Irish race feeling, bearing the names of Johnston, Cowie, Wilson, Bailey, Armstrong, Saunders, Campbell, Thompson, Chambers, Gordon, Ross, Scott, Watson, Stewart, Christy, Finlay, Grimson, Hamilton, Barr, Graham, Gillespie, Black, Walker, Catterson, Robinson, Holmes, Grant, Dunbar, Fraser, Kirk, Patterson, Gould, Wylie, Robinson, Roberts, Donaldson, Ferguson, McMillan, McDonald, McGregor, McPherson, Ogilvie, Craig, Cameron, McAndrews, McLean, McKay, MacIntosh, not forgetting our Lieutenant Colonel Alexander Anderson.

We had three or four score Jews in the Regiment that went abroad but there was a Coen, a Leavy and a Jacobs who were Irish.

Other regimental names that do not sound Irish to the ears of the uninitiate but are familiar in every Irish group are Clifford, Duane, Clark, Freeman, Winters, Phillips, Williams, Cunningham, Curtis, Johnson, Gough, Harrison, Grace, Jones, Loftus, Medler, Matthews, Morrison, Newman, King, Crawford, Biggar, Bambrick, Ring, Rice, Blythe, Gray, Judge, Morgan, Caulfield, Gilbert, Gilgar, Campion, Booth, Humphreys, Cook, Hill, Parks, Hunt, Garland, Gill, Warren, Reed, Hurst, Jenkins, Rogers, Grimes, Summers, Smith, Green, Brown, White, Martin, Mason, Lowe, Roe, Wade, Woods, Goodman, Fleming, French, English, Holland, Thornton, Wall, Travis, Travers, Morgan, Fletcher, Clinton, Richards, Jennings, Lynn, Taylor, Reynolds, Grundy, Stanley, Turner, Edwards, Dean, Meade, Conville, Ward, Clayton, Eustace, Lavelle, Clyne, Battle, Nelson, Wynne, Coppinger, Morton, Oakes, Fullam, Lynott, Lynar, Lysaght, Long, Fennell, Tuers, Birmingham, Hetherington, Temple, Whitty, Granville, Howard, Bealin, Stanley, Vaughan, Adams, Nash, Coneys, Mylott, Brickley, Mitchell, Diamond, De Witt, Hopkins, Quigg, Igo, Taylor, Ferris, Ledwith, Forrestal, Lever, Hoey, Fox, Russell, Sutcliffe, Hillery, Fisher, Kent, Boyce, Bevan, Rothwell, Adkins, Courtney, Mannix, Orr, Harris, Farnan, Hackett, Hopkins, Gaynor, Gunn, Broe, Bush, Goss, Wilde, Cox, Seagriff, Marshall, Davis, Bergen, Singleton, Rankin, Webb, Small. Not all of the possessors of these names in the Regiment were bearers of the Irish racial tradition, but the great majority of them were.

Sometimes the English sounding name was imported directly from Ireland, and the man's nationality was never in doubt after one heard him speak, as in the case of Mansfield, Bugler, Maddock, Elwood, and others. Sometimes all doubt was removed by the Christian name, as in the cases of Patrick Ames, Patrick Stokes, Patrick Thynne, Patrick Porteous, Patrick Carlisle, Patrick Benson, Patrick Travers, Patrick Fawcett, Patrick Gorham, Patrick Masterson, or Michael Goodman, Michael Douglas, Michael Bowler, Michael Gettings, Denis Richardson, Bernard Clinton, Robert Emmett Mitchell, Bernard Granville, Francis X. Goodwin, John J. Booth.

The future historian who writes of the part played by the Irish element in this war will have a good deal of trouble collecting his data, partly on account of the tendency to bestow on children what our grandparents would call "fancy" names, and partly through the intermarriage of women with Irish names to men whose names indicate a different racial descent. Especially when the religion is the same, the children are very definitely Irish in race feeling. All of the following had the Irish kind of religion, and most of them claim to be of Irish descent; George Lawrence, James Archer, Wilton Wharton, Colton Bingham, Sherwood Orr, Melvin King, Earl Withrow, Lester Lenhart, Archibald Skeats, Dudley Winthrop, Warren Dearborn, Hurlburt McCallum, Harold Yockers, Dallas Springer, Joyce Kilmer, Clifford Wiltshire, Pelham Hall, Elmore Becker, Everett Guion, Lester Snyder; while others in the same category bore names such as Dayton, Lovett, Lappin, Trayer, Shepherd, Harndon, Harnwell, Ashworth, Bradbury, Everett, Adikes, Keyes, Boone, Bibby, Beverly, Aspery, Cornell, Morthurst, Battersby, Dawson, Chamberlain, Cousens, Hasting, Blackburne, Griswold, Bagley, Forman, Myers, Nye, Firman, Weaver, Irons, Garrett, Kyle, Forms, Kear, Alnwick, Boomer, Dobbins, Ogden, Dresser, Frear, Bennett, Cooper,. Gracely, Schofield, Fredericks, Walters, Voorhis, Chatterton, Kolodgy, Law, Vail, Field, Throop, Menrose, Hawk, Waddell, Drake, Flint, Elworth, Maryold, Knott, Hagger, Espy, Cuffe, Peel, Stiles, Willett, Leaper, Gauthier and Denair.

A number of volunteers were drawn to the old Irish Regiment by the bonds of a common faith. And in the course of two years spent amongst them it was an easier matter while performing my office as Chaplain to get a line on their personal beliefs than on their racial descent. We had for example Guignon, Bonnard, Pierre, Viens, and Pepin; Mendes, Echeverria, Rodriguez and Garcia; Gardella, Brangaccio, Georgi, Lorelli, Guida, Menicocci, Tricarico, Depietro and Speranza; Romanuk, Ragninny, Hovance, Sypoula, Puttlitz and Ivanowski, with plenty of names like Arenholz, Schmidt, Stumpf, Dietrich, Weick, Schmedlein, Schluter, Leudesdorf and Kahn. Some with names sounding just like these last ones were Irish on the distaff side, such as Almendinger, Winestock, Schwartz, Ettinger, Schroppel, Mehl, Rohrig, Peisel, Hans, Landzert, Clauberg, Ritz, Steinert, Messmer, Zimmerman, Finger, Richter, Herold, Schick, Buechner, Sauer, Beyer, Haerting, Meyer, Roesel, Willermin, Miller, Dryer, Hugo, Wilker, Fisher, Staber, Augustine, Dierenger, Morschhauser, Ritter, Haspel, Becker, and Grauer.

Two small groups of "Irish" struck my fancy—one with Scandinavian names like Drivdahl, Malmquist, and Larsen; and a few of the Vans; Van Pelt, Vanderdonck, Van Wye and Van Benschoten.

One way of estimating the character of the regiment would be to examine the lists of the dead, to find what names preponderate in them. In those lists we find *seven* men named Kelly; *five* McCarthy; *four* O'Neill, O'Brien, and Brennan; *three* Baker, Brown, Campbell, Cook, Cronin, Daly, Kane, Lynch, McDonald, McKeon, McLoughlin, Martin, Murphy, O'Connor, O'Rourke, Scanlan, Smith, Sullivan and Wynne; *two* Adkins, Allen, Ames, Boyle, Byrnes, Collins, Coneys, Connelly, Conway, Curtin, Dolan, Dunnigan, Donovan, Dougherty, Farrell, Fitzpatrick, Ford, Gavin, Geary, Gordon, Gray, Gunnell, Hamilton, Hart, Higgins, Johnson, Lane, Leonard McMillan, McKay, McKenna, McSherry, Mahoney, Minogue, Mitchell, Morrissey, Naughton, Peterson, Philips, Quinn, Reilly, Riordon, Robinson, Rooney, Ryan, Scott, Slattery, Thomson, Williams and Walsh.

OFFICERS OF THE NEW YORK CHAPTER RAINBOW. DIVISION VETERANS

President, William J. Donovan.
1st Vice Pres., George J. Lawrence,
2nd Vice Pres., T. W. Ferguson,
3rd Vice Pres , John Farrell,
Secretary, Daniel B. J. O'Connell,
Treasurer, Timothy J. Moynahan,
Financial Secretary, John McNamara,
Historian, Francis P. Duffy,
Chaplain, James M. Hanley.

BOARD OF TRUSTEES OF THE 165TH INFANTRY

Morgan J. O'Brien, Chairman, (former Presiding Justice of the appellate division.)

Daniel M. Brady, Vice Chairman, (President of Brady Brass Co.)
John Whelan, Treasurer, (former Corporation Counsel)
Joseph P. Grace, (President W. R. Grace & Co.)
Victor J. Dowling, (Supreme Court Justice)
John D. Ryan, (Chairman Anaconda Copper Co.)]
James A. Farrell, (President U. S. Steel Corp.)
Thomas E. Murray, (1st V.P. New York Edison Co.)
James A. McKenna, (Public Accountant)
George McDonald, (Contractor)
Major Thomas T Reilley, (165th Inf.)
Nicholas F. Brady, (Chairman Brooklyn Rapid Tr. Co.)

Clarence H. Mackay. (Pres. Postal Telegraph Co.)
John J. O'Keefe, (H. L. Horton & Co.)
Louis D. Conley, (former Col. old 69th)
Bryan L. Kennelly, (Real Estate Operator)

WOMEN'S AUXILIARY TO 165TH INFANTRY

U. S. A. Inc.

President	Mrs. George R. Leslie
Vice-Pres.	Miss Catherine A. Archer
Rec. Sec.	Miss Elizabeth M. Hughes
Cor. Sec.	Miss Louise Reilley
Fin. Sec.	Miss Margaret Casey
Treas.	Miss Nora A. Thynne
Trustees	Mrs. Theresa Hughes
	Mrs. William J. Grady
	Miss May A. O'Neill
	Miss Mary Duffy
	Mrs. V. Merle-Smith

THE ENTRY INTO BELGIUM

HEADQUARTERS AT REMAGEN
GROUP OF RECIPIENTS OF D. S. C.

BOOK JUNGLE

Bringing Classics to Life

www.bookjungle.com *email: sales@bookjungle.com fax: 630-214-0564 mail: Book Jungle PO Box 2226 Champaign, IL 61825*

The Two Babylons
Alexander Hislop
QTY

You may be surprised to learn that many traditions of Roman Catholicism in fact don't come from Christ's teachings but from an ancient Babylonian "Mystery" religion that was centered on Nimrod, his wife Semiramis, and a child Tammuz. This book shows how this ancient religion transformed itself as it incorporated Christ into its teachings....

Religion/History   Pages:358

ISBN: *1-59462-010-5*   MSRP *$22.95*

The Power Of Concentration
Theron Q. Dumont

It is of the utmost value to learn how to concentrate. To make the greatest success of anything you must be able to concentrate your entire thought upon the idea you are working on. The person that is able to concentrate utilizes all constructive thoughts and shuts out all destructive ones...

Self Help/Inspirational   Pages:196

ISBN: *1-59462-141-1*   MSRP *$14.95*

Rightly Dividing The Word
Clarence Larkin

The "Fundamental Doctrines" of the Christian Faith are clearly outlined in numerous books on Theology, but they are not available to the average reader and were mainly written for students. The Author has made it the work of his ministry to preach the "Fundamental Doctrines." To this end he has aimed to express them in the simplest and clearest manner...

Religion   Pages:352

ISBN: *1-59462-334-1*   MSRP *$23.45*

The Law of Psychic Phenomena
Thomson Jay Hudson

"I do not expect this book to stand upon its literary merits; for if it is unsound in principle, felicity of diction cannot save it, and if sound, homeliness of expression cannot destroy it. My primary object in offering it to the public is to assist in bringing Psychology within the domain of the exact sciences. That this has never been accomplished..."

New Age   Pages:420

ISBN: *1-59462-124-1*   MSRP *$29.95*

Beautiful Joe
Marshall Saunders

When Marshall visited the Moore family in 1892, she discovered Joe, a dog they had nursed back to health from his previous abusive home to live a happy life. So moved was she, that she wrote this classic masterpiece which won accolades and was recognized as a heartwarming symbol for humane animal treatment...

Fiction   Pages:256

ISBN: *1-59462-261-2*   MSRP *$18.45*

The Codes Of Hammurabi And
Moses - W. W. Davies

The discovery of the Hammurabi Code is one of the greatest achievements of archaeology, and is of paramount interest, not only to the student of the Bible, but also to all those interested in ancient history...

Religion   Pages:132

ISBN: *1-59462-338-4*   MSRP *$12.95*

The Thirty-Six Dramatic Situations
Georges Polti

An incredibly useful guide for aspiring authors and playwrights. This volume categorizes every dramatic situation which could occur in a story and describes them in a list of 36 situations. A great aid to help inspire or formalize the creative writing process...

Self Help/Reference   Pages:204

ISBN: *1-59462-134-9*   MSRP *$15.95*

The Go-Getter
Kyne B. Peter
QTY

The Go Getter is the story of William Peck.He was a war veteran and amputee who will not be refused what he wants. Peck not only fights to find employment but continually proves himself more than competent at the many difficult test that are throw his way in the course of his early days with the Ricks Lumber Company...

Business/Self Help/Inspirational   Pages:68

ISBN: *1-59462-186-1*   MSRP *$8.95*

Self Mastery
Emile Coue

Emile Coue came up with novel way to improve the lives of people. He was a pharmacist by trade and often saw ailing people. This lead him to develop autosuggestion, a form of self-hypnosis. At the time his theories weren't popular but over the years evidence is mounting that he was indeed right all along...

New Age/Self Help   Pages:98

ISBN: *1-59462-189-6*   MSRP *$7.95*

The Awful Disclosures Of
Maria Monk

"I cannot banish the scenes and characters of this book from my memory. To me it can never appear like an amusing fable, or lose its interest and importance. The story is one which is continually before me, and must return fresh to my mind with painful emotions as long as I live..."

Religion   Pages:232

ISBN: *1-59462-160-8*   MSRP *$17.95*

As a Man Thinketh
James Allen

"This little volume (the result of meditation and experience) is not intended as an exhaustive treatise on the much-written-upon subject of the power of thought. It is suggestive rather than explanatory, its object being to stimulate men and women to the discovery and perception of the truth that by virtue of the thoughts which they choose and encourage..."

Inspirational/Self Help   Pages:80

ISBN: *1-59462-231-0*   MSRP *$9.45*

The Enchanted April
Elizabeth Von Arnim

It began in a woman's club in London on a February afternoon, an uncomfortable club, and a miserable afternoon when Mrs. Wilkins, who had come down from Hampstead to shop and had lunched at her club, took up The Times from the table in the smoking-room...

Fiction   Pages:368

ISBN: *1-59462-150-0*   MSRP *$23.45*

Holland - The History Of Netherlands
Thomas Colley Grattan

Thomas Grattan was a prestigious writer from Dublin who served as British Consul to the US. Among his works is an authoritative look at the history of Holland. A colorful and interesting look at history...

History/Politics   Pages:408

ISBN: *1-59462-137-3*   MSRP *$26.95*

A Concise Dictionary of Middle English
A. L. Mayhew
Walter W. Skeat

The present work is intended to meet, in some measure, the requirements of those who wish to make some study of Middle-English, and who find a difficulty in obtaining such assistance as will enable them to find out the meanings and etymologies of the words most essential to their purpose...

Reference/History   Pages:332

ISBN: *1-59462-119-5*   MSRP *$29.95*

www.bookjungle.com *email: sales@bookjungle.com fax: 630-214-0564 mail: Book Jungle PO Box 2226 Champaign, IL 61825*

The Witch-Cult in Western Europe
Margaret Murray
The mass of existing material on this subject is so great that I have not attempted to make a survey of the whole of European "Witchcraft" but have confined myself to an intensive study of the cult in Great Britain. In order, however, to obtain a clearer understanding of the ritual and beliefs I have had recourse to French and Flemish sources...

Occult   Pages:308
ISBN: *1-59462-126-8*   MSRP *$22.45*

QTY

The Science Of Psychic Healing
Yogi Ramacharaka
This book is not a book of theories it deals with facts. Its author regards the best of theories as but working hypotheses to be used only until better ones present themselves. The "fact" is the principal thing the essential thing to uncover which the tool, theory, is used...

New Age/Health   Pages:180
ISBN: *1-59462-140-3*   MSRP *$13.95*

Bible Myths
Thomas Doane
In pursuing the study of the Bible Myths, facts pertaining thereto, in a condensed form, seemed to be greatly needed, and nowhere to be found. Widely scattered through hundreds of ancient and modern volumes, most of the contents of this book may indeed be found; but any previous attempt to trace exclusively the myths and legends...

Religion/History   Pages:644
ISBN: *1-59462-163-2*   MSRP *$38.95*

Tertium Organum
P. D. Ouspensky
A truly mind expanding writing that combines science with mysticism with unprecedented elegance. He presents the world we live in as a multi dimensional world and time as a motion through this world. But this isn't a cold and purely analytical explanation but a masterful presentation filled with similes and analogies...

New Age   Pages:356
ISBN: *1-59462-205-1*   MSRP *$23.95*

Advance Course in Yogi Philosophy
Yogi Ramacharaka
"The twelve lessons forming this volume were originally issued in the shape of monthly lessons, known as "The Advanced Course in Yogi Philosophy and Oriental Occultism" during a period of twelve months beginning with October, 1904, and ending September, 1905."

Philosophy/Inspirational/Self Help   Pages:340
ISBN: *1-59462-229-9*   MSRP *$22.95*

Ambassador Morgenthau's Story
Henry Morgenthau
"By this time the American people have probably become convinced that the Germans deliberately planned the conquest of the world. Yet they hesitate to convict on circumstantial evidence and for this reason all eye witnesses to this, the greatest crime in modern history, should volunteer their testimony..."

History   Pages:472
ISBN: *1-59462-244-2*   MSRP *$29.95*

The Aquarian Gospel of Jesus the Christ
Levi Dowling
A retelling of Jesus' story which tells us what happened during the twenty year gap left by the Bible's New Testament. It tells of his travels to the far-east where he studied with the masters and fought against the rigid caste system. This book has enjoyed a resurgence in modern America and provides spiritual insight with charm. Its influences can be seen throughout the Age of Aquarius.

Religion   Pages:264
ISBN: *1-59462-321-X*   MSRP *$18.95*

Philosophy Of Natural Therapeutics
Henry Lindlahr
We invite the earnest cooperation in this great work of all those who have awakened to the necessity for more rational living and for radical reform in healing methods...

QTY

Health/Philosophy/Self Help   Pages:552
ISBN: *1-59462-132-2*   MSRP *$34.95*

A Message to Garcia
Elbert Hubbard
This literary trifle, A Message to Garcia, was written one evening after supper, in a single hour. It was on the Twenty-second of February, Eighteen Hundred Ninety-nine, Washington's Birthday, and we were just going to press with the March Philistine...

New Age/Fiction   Pages:92
ISBN: *1-59462-144-6*   MSRP *$9.95*

The Book of Jasher
Alcuinus Flaccus Albinus
The Book of Jasher is an historical religious volume that many consider as a missing holy book from the Old Testament. Particularly studied by the Church of Later Day Saints and historians, it covers the history of the world from creation until the period of Judges in Israel. It's authenticity is bolstered due to a reference to the Book of Jasher in the Bible in Joshua 10:13

Religion/History   Pages:276
ISBN: *1-59462-197-7*   MSRP *$18.95*

The Titan
Theodore Dreiser
"When Frank Algernon Cowperwood emerged from the Eastern District Penitentiary, in Philadelphia he realized that the old life he had lived in that city since boyhood was ended. His youth was gone, and with it had been lost the great business prospects of his earlier manhood. He must begin again..."

Fiction   Pages:564
ISBN: *1-59462-220-5*   MSRP *$33.95*

Biblical Essays
J. B. Lightfoot
About one-third of the present volume has already seen the light. The opening essay "On the Internal Evidence for the Authenticity and Genuineness of St John's Gospel" was published in the "Expositor" in the early months of 1890, and has been reprinted since...

Religion/History   Pages:480
ISBN: *1-59462-238-8*   MSRP *$30.95*

The Settlement Cook Book
Simon Kander
A legacy from the civil war, this book is a classic "American charity cookbook," which was used for fundraisers starting in Milwaukee. While it has transformed over the years, this printing provides great recipes from American history. Over two million copies have been sold. This volume contains a rich collection of recipes from noted chefs and hostesses of the turn of the century...

How-to   Pages:472
ISBN: *1-59462-256-6*   MSRP *$29.95*

My Life and Work
Henry Ford
Henry Ford revolutionized the world with his implementation of mass production for the Model T automobile. Gain valuable business insight into his life and work with his own auto-biography... "We have only started on our development of our country we have not as yet, with all our talk of wonderful progress, done more than scratch the surface. The progress has been wonderful enough but..."

Biographies/History/Business   Pages:300
ISBN: *1-59462-198-5*   MSRP *$21.95*

www.bookjungle.com *email: sales@bookjungle.com fax: 630-214-0564 mail: Book Jungle PO Box 2226 Champaign, IL 61825*

QTY

The Rosicrucian Cosmo-Conception Mystic Christianity by *Max Heindel* ISBN: *1-59462-188-8* **$38.95**
The Rosicrucian Cosmo-conception is not dogmatic, neither does it appeal to any other authority than the reason of the student. It is: not controversial, but is: sent forth in the, hope that it may help to clear... New Age Religion Pages 646

Abandonment To Divine Providence by *Jean-Pierre de Caussade* ISBN: *1-59462-228-0* **$25.95**
"The Rev. Jean Pierre de Caussade was one of the most remarkable spiritual writers of the Society of Jesus in France in the 18th Century. His death took place at Toulouse in 1751. His works have gone through many editions and have been republished... Inspirational Religion Pages 400

Mental Chemistry by *Charles Haanel* ISBN: *1-59462-192-6* **$23.95**
Mental Chemistry allows the change of material conditions by combining and appropriately utilizing the power of the mind. Much like applied chemistry creates something new and unique out of careful combinations of chemicals the mastery of mental chemistry... New Age Pages 354

The Letters of Robert Browning and Elizabeth Barret Barrett 1845-1846 vol II ISBN: *1-59462-193-4* **$35.95**
by *Robert Browning and Elizabeth Barrett*
  Biographies Pages 596

Gleanings In Genesis (volume I) by *Arthur W. Pink* ISBN: *1-59462-130-6* **$27.45**
Appropriately has Genesis been termed "the seed plot of the Bible" for in it we have, in germ form, almost all of the great doctrines which are afterwards fully developed in the books of Scripture which follow... Religion Inspirational Pages 420

The Master Key by *L. W. de Laurence* ISBN: *1-59462-001-6* **$30.95**
In no branch of human knowledge has there been a more lively increase of the spirit of research during the past few years than in the study of Psychology, Concentration and Mental Discipline. The requests for authentic lessons in Thought Control, Mental Discipline and... New Age Business Pages 422

The Lesser Key Of Solomon Goetia by *L. W. de Laurence* ISBN: *1-59462-092-X* **$9.95**
This translation of the first book of the "Lemegton" which is now for the first time made accessible to students of Talismanic Magic was done, after careful collation and edition, from numerous Ancient Manuscripts in Hebrew, Latin, and French... New Age Occult Pages 92

Rubaiyat Of Omar Khayyam by *Edward Fitzgerald* ISBN: *1-59462-332-5* **$13.95**
Edward Fitzgerald, whom the world has already learned, in spite of his own efforts to remain within the shadow of anonymity, to look upon as one of the rarest poets of the century, was born at Bredfield, in Suffolk, on the 31st of March, 1809. He was the third son of John Purcell... Music Pages 172

Ancient Law by *Henry Maine* ISBN: *1-59462-128-4* **$29.95**
The chief object of the following pages is to indicate some of the earliest ideas of mankind, as they are reflected in Ancient Law, and to point out the relation of those ideas to modern thought. Religion History Pages 452

Far-Away Stories by *William J. Locke* ISBN: *1-59462-129-2* **$19.45**
"Good wine needs no bush,' but a collection of mixed vintages does. And this book is just such a collection. Some of the stories I do not want to remain buried for ever in the museum files of dead magazine-numbers an author's not unpardonable vanity..." Fiction Pages 272

Life of David Crockett by *David Crockett* ISBN: *1-59462-250-7* **$27.45**
"Colonel David Crockett was one of the most remarkable men of the times in which he lived. Born in humble life, but gifted with a strong will, an indomitable courage, and unremitting perseverance... Biographies New Age Pages 424

Lip-Reading by *Edward Nitchie* ISBN: *1-59462-206-X* **$25.95**
Edward B. Nitchie, founder of the New York School for the Hard of Hearing, now the Nitchie School of Lip-Reading, Inc, wrote "LIP-READING Principles and Practice". The development and perfecting of this meritorious work on lip-reading was an undertaking... How-to Pages 400

A Handbook of Suggestive Therapeutics, Applied Hypnotism, Psychic Science ISBN: *1-59462-214-0* **$24.95**
by *Henry Munro*
  Health New Age Health Self-help Pages 376

A Doll's House: and Two Other Plays by *Henrik Ibsen* ISBN: *1-59462-112-8* **$19.95**
Henrik Ibsen created this classic when in revolutionary 1848 Rome. Introducing some striking concepts in playwriting for the realist genre, this play has been studied the world over. Fiction Classics Plays 308

The Light of Asia by *sir Edwin Arnold* ISBN: *1-59462-204-3* **$13.95**
In this poetic masterpiece, Edwin Arnold describes the life and teachings of Buddha. The man who was to become known as Buddha to the world was born as Prince Gautama of India but he rejected the worldly riches and abandoned the reigns of power when... Religion History Biographies Pages 170

The Complete Works of Guy de Maupassant by *Guy de Maupassant* ISBN: *1-59462-157-8* **$16.95**
"For days and days, nights and nights, I had dreamed of that first kiss which was to consecrate our engagement, and I knew not on what spot I should put my lips..." Fiction Classics Pages 240

The Art of Cross-Examination by *Francis L. Wellman* ISBN: *1-59462-309-0* **$26.95**
Written by a renowned trial lawyer, Wellman imparts his experience and uses case studies to explain how to use psychology to extract desired information through questioning. How-to Science Reference Pages 408

Answered or Unanswered? by *Louisa Vaughan* ISBN: *1-59462-248-5* **$10.95**
Miracles of Faith in China Religion Pages 112

The Edinburgh Lectures on Mental Science (1909) by *Thomas* ISBN: *1-59462-008-3* **$11.95**
This book contains the substance of a course of lectures recently given by the writer in the Queen Street Hall, Edinburgh. Its purpose is to indicate the Natural Principles governing the relation between Mental Action and Material Conditions... New Age Psychology Pages 148

Ayesha by *H. Rider Haggard* ISBN: *1-59462-301-5* **$24.95**
Verily and indeed it is the unexpected that happens! Probably if there was one person upon the earth from whom the Editor of this, and of a certain previous history, did not expect to hear again... Classics Pages 380

Ayala's Angel by *Anthony Trollope* ISBN: *1-59462-352-X* **$29.95**
The two girls were both pretty, but Lucy who was twenty-one who supposed to be simple and comparatively unattractive, whereas Ayala was credited, as her Bombwhat romantic name might show, with poetic charm and a taste for romance. Ayala when her father died was nineteen... Fiction Pages 484

The American Commonwealth by *James Bryce* ISBN: *1-59462-286-8* **$34.45**
An interpretation of American democratic political theory. It examines political mechanics and society from the perspective of Scotsman James Bryce Politics Pages 572

Stories of the Pilgrims by *Margaret P. Pumphrey* ISBN: *1-59462-116-0* **$17.95**
This book explores pilgrims religious oppression in England as well as their escape to Holland and eventual crossing to America on the Mayflower, and their early days in New England... History Pages 268

www.bookjungle.com email: *sales@bookjungle.com* fax: *630-214-0564* mail: *Book Jungle PO Box 2226 Champaign, IL 61825*

QTY

The Fasting Cure *by **Sinclair Upton***　　　　　　ISBN: *1-59462-222-1*　**$13.95**
In the Cosmopolitan Magazine for May, 1910, and in the Contemporary Review (London) for April, 1910, I published an article dealing with my experiences in fasting. I have written a great many magazine articles, but never one which attracted so much attention... New Age/Self Help Health Pages 164

Hebrew Astrology *by **Sepharial***　　　　　　　ISBN: *1-59462-308-2*　**$13.45**
In these days of advanced thinking it is a matter of common observation that we have left many of the old landmarks behind and that we are now pressing forward to greater heights and to a wider horizon than that which represented the mind-content of our progenitors... Astrology Pages 144

Thought Vibration or The Law of Attraction in the Thought World　　　ISBN: *1-59462-127-6*　**$12.95**
*by **William Walker Atkinson***　　　　　　　　　　　*Psychology/Religion Pages 144*

Optimism *by **Helen Keller***　　　　　　　　　ISBN: *1-59462-108-X*　**$15.95**
Helen Keller was blind, deaf, and mute since 19 months old, yet famously learned how to overcome these handicaps, communicate with the world, and spread her lectures promoting optimism. An inspiring read for everyone... Biographies/Inspirational Pages 84

Sara Crewe *by **Frances Burnett***　　　　　　　ISBN: *1-59462-360-0*　**$9.45**
In the first place, Miss Minchin lived in London. Her home was a large, dull, tall one, in a large, dull square, where all the houses were alike, and all the sparrows were alike, and where all the door-knockers made the same heavy sound... Childrens Classic Pages 88

The Autobiography of Benjamin Franklin *by **Benjamin Franklin***　　ISBN: *1-59462-135-7*　**$24.95**
The Autobiography of Benjamin Franklin has probably been more extensively read than any other American historical work, and no other book of its kind has had such ups and downs of fortune. Franklin lived for many years in England, where he was agent... Biographies/History Pages 332

Name	
Email	
Telephone	
Address	
City, State ZIP	

☐ **Credit Card**　　　　☐ **Check / Money Order**

Credit Card Number	
Expiration Date	
Signature	

Please Mail to:　Book Jungle
　　　　　　　　　PO Box 2226
　　　　　　　　　Champaign, IL 61825
　or Fax to:　　　630-214-0564

ORDERING INFORMATION

web: *www.bookjungle.com*
email: *sales@bookjungle.com*
fax: *630-214-0564*
mail: *Book Jungle PO Box 2226 Champaign, IL 61825*
or PayPal *to sales@bookjungle.com*

Please contact us for bulk discounts

DIRECT-ORDER TERMS

**20% Discount if You Order
Two or More Books**
Free Domestic Shipping!
Accepted: Master Card, Visa,
Discover, American Express

Printed in the United States
127357LV00006B/137-138/A

9 781594 628665